to Rom
I hope [illegible]
useful -
Enjoy!
[signature]

The Dignity of
Working Men

The Dignity of Working Men

MORALITY AND

THE BOUNDARIES

OF RACE, CLASS,

AND IMMIGRATION

Michèle Lamont

RUSSELL SAGE FOUNDATION
New York, New York
HARVARD UNIVERSITY PRESS
Cambridge, Massachusetts
London, England
2000

Printed in the United States of America

Library of Congress Cataloging-in-Publication Data

Lamont, Michèle, 1957–
The dignity of working men : morality and the boundaries of race, class,
and immigration / Michèle Lamont.
p. cm.
Includes bibliographical references and index.
ISBN 0-674-00306-3 (alk. paper)
1. Blue collar workers–United States.   2. Blue collar workers–France.   3. Men–
Employment–United States.   4. Men–Employment–France.   5. Working class–
United States. 6. Working class–France.   7. Work ethic–United States.   8. Work
ethic–France.   I. Title.

HD8072.5.L36 2000
305.5′62–dc21
00-031087

A ma belle fille Gabrielle

Acknowledgments

THE WRITING of acknowledgments marks the true end of a project. It provides an occasion to repress the difficulties, to remember the moments of ecstasy, and to express appreciation for the good deeds that made it all possible.

First, I want to thank the 150 men who were interviewed for this book. They were trusting enough to tell me how they see things, and I hope that my analysis does not betray them. Their remarkable openness helped me to understand the conditions underlying their views. Many also showed great humanity, which I found very inspiring. Without people like these men, qualitative sociology would simply not exist and I would be deprived of one of the pleasures of my life. For all this, thanks!

This research began in 1992 with small grants from Princeton University, namely from the Committee for Research in the Social Sciences and the Humanities, the Center for Excellence in French Studies, and the Center for International Studies of the Woodrow Wilson School. These grants sowed the seeds that resulted in a generous grant from the National Science Foundation, which covered the research expenses of this project. A fellowship from the German Marshall Funds of the United States freed me to conduct interviews. During this period, I benefited from the hospitality of the Schomburg Center for the Study of Black Culture at the New York Public Library, the Institute for French Studies of New York University, and the Centre de sociologie politique et morale at the Ecole des hautes études en science sociales in Paris.

Most of the book was written when I was on leave with the support of fellowships from the Russell Sage Foundation and the John Simon Guggenheim Memorial Foundation. I spent the fall of 1996 at the Russell Sage Foundation, where, like many generations of scholars, I found ideal working conditions and a stimulating environment. I thank Eric Wanner, president of the Foundation, for his support and intellectual engagement. Alan Brinkley, John Logan, Paul Gottenberg, and Tom Csordas were particularly treasured colleagues. My lunch conversations at RSF contributed considerably to my transition from the field of cultural sociology to those of poverty, immigration, and race. Cheryl Seleski, Nancy Casey, and Madge Spitaleri facilitated my life in a thousand ways and added good humor and womanly warmth and solidarity during a special time in my life.

The Guggenheim Fellowship enabled me to spend productive time at the School for Social Sciences at the Institute for Advanced Studies in Princeton. There, Clifford Geertz and Michael Walzer provided considerable "big book" inspiration. Sarah and Albert Hirschman, Webb Kean, Jocelyn Létourneau, Mohamed Naciri, Dorothée Schneider, and, above all, Riva Kastoryano were very valued friends and intellectual companions. Joan Scott generously made it possible for me to extend my stay at a time when I needed peace and quiet to write.

At Princeton University, colleagues in my department and elsewhere contributed to this book by engaging or reading my work or by making my life more pleasant. Among sociologists, Thomas Espenshade, Patricia Fernandez-Kelly, Alejandro Portes, Howard Taylor, Bruce Western, Robert Wuthnow, and Viviana Zelizer contributed in various ways. As chair of my department, Paul DiMaggio helped create the conditions that made it possible to finish the book in a timely fashion. Colleagues in other departments also contributed substantively, particularly Abdellah Hammoudi, Jennifer Hochschild, Stan Katz, Tali Mendelberg, Dale Miller, Nell Painter, Daniel Rodgers, Carl Schorske, and Ezra Suleiman. Virginie Guiraudon, Karin Knorr-Cetina, Hans-Peter Mueller, Gérard Noiriel, Kyung Park, Andrew Pickering, and John Skrentny also stimulated my thinking during the time they spent in Princeton.

Colleagues who have read the full manuscript (in a number of cases, at the request of university presses) include Elijah Anderson, Randall Collins, Frank Dobbin, Frank Furstenberg, Wendy Griswold, Eva Illouz, Riva Kastoryano, Ira Katznelson, Howard Kimeldorf, Annette Lareau, Kathy Newman, Marty Schain, Ann Swidler, and Robert

Wuthnow. Outside Princeton, those who have commented on sections bearing on their area of expertise include Herrick Chapman, Adrian Favell, Miriam Feldblum, Gary Gerstle, Virginie Guiraudon, Gérard Noiriel, Emmanuelle Saada, Hilary Silver, and Howard Winant. I thank them all for their time and wise advice. Other people who have contributed in small and big ways by their friendship and knowledge, or by helping me solve practical problems, include Jeffrey Alexander, Sophie Body-Gendrot, Luc Boltanski, Diana Crane, Alain Desrosières, Nancy DiTomaso, Joe Feagin, Cynthia Fuchs Epstein, Kathleen Gerson, Muge Gocek, Claude Grignon, David Halle, Randy Hodson, James Jasper, Jane Mansbridge, Sarah Rosenfeld, Magali Surfatti-Larson, Michael Schudson, Richard Sennett, Yasemin Soysal, Laurent Thévenot, and Mary Waters.

The success of this project depended on a number of research assistants in various phases of the research. Among those who helped I want to thank in particular the very able Sarah Caban, Alexandra Kalev, and Virag Molnar, who provided considerable help and enthusiasm in the last two years of the project. Other Princeton students who have worked on the project include Bethany Bryson, Kieran Healy, Jason Kaufman, Michael Moody, Ann Morning, John Schmalzbauer, Maureen Waller, and Daniel Weber. In Paris, I benefited greatly from the assistance of Cyril Lemieux.

Aspects of my argument were presented to a number of audiences over the years in conferences and at colloquia at Alborg University, Cornell University, CUNY–Graduate Center, Duke University, the Ecole des hautes études en sciences sociales, the European University Institute, the Fondation nationale de science politique, Harvard University, Hebrew University, Howard University, the Institute for Advanced Study, the Institut International de Paris–La Defense, McGill University, the National Conference of Norwegian Sociology, the New School for Social Research, New York University, Northwestern University, the Russell Sage Foundation, Rutgers University, the Schomburg Center, Tel Aviv University, Temple University, Université de Montréal, Université de Paris IV–Nanterre, the University of California at Santa Barbara, the University of California at Davis, the University of California at San Diego, the University of Chicago, the University of Illinois at Urbana-Champaign, the University of Michigan, the University of Pennsylvania, the University of Virginia, and Washington University—St. Louis. The stimulation provided by these many experiences sustained my interest in the project, and I thank the colleagues who extended these invitations.

Harvard University Press and the Russell Sage Foundation did excellent work in producing the book. I extend warm thanks to my editors, Michael Aronson and David Haproff. At Princeton University, I benefited from the secretarial and administrative assistance of Donna DeFrancisco and Cindy Gibson, and it is with pleasure that I acknowledge their contribution to my work.

This book came into this world at the same time as my angel daughter, Gabrielle. Like her, this book is a labor of love. I dedicate it to her for this reason, and in celebration of the first two years of her life. I wish to thank my family, and in particular my parents and my sister, Natalie, who offered their continuous love and support, which remain priceless. On the home front, Vilma and Karla Lopez made everything possible, and they have my deep gratitude. As always, Frank Dobbin is a terrific partner. For your deep kindness and intelligence, thanks.

Contents

The Dignity of
Working Men

Introduction: Making Sense of Their Worlds

I don't like people that live for the moment. I am not a big person about saving money, but I'm always looking for the future. I try to base my decisions today on how they'll affect me tomorrow, not just on what I want to do today. If I want I can go out tonight and get totally drunk, I'm going to say, well, I have to work tomorrow . . . Sometimes, I wish I could be more carefree. And then I say no, I like the way I am . . . I like people who are responsible. So many people, you walk up and say something and they say, "I don't care." I like people who are close to family, close to friends. I guess you look at yourself and say I wish people could be like me, like that. People who have the same values as me. (White printer, Rahway, New Jersey)

No matter who you are at Exxon, you're making pretty good money, so it's not like you've got a disadvantaged person. Their kids are going to good schools. They're eating, they're taking vacations because of Exxon. You don't see the division or whatever, so Exxon kind of eliminated that because of the salary structure . . . With black people, you talk sports, you talk school, you're all in the same boat. It isn't "What's it like to have a new car?" You know, you talk to the guy, and you went on vacation, and he went on vacation. (White foreman, Rahway, New Jersey)

There is a difference between the corporate and the working class. Corporate is only concerned with the dollar. The working class is concerned with doing the job right, the feel, and getting the job done. That's the satisfaction I get. (White train conductor, Elizabeth, New Jersey)

I've got the mind of a poor person. If I become rich, I'm going to carry the same mind I got now. I'm still going to be caring . . . And the people that don't have it, I would never turn my back on them, never . . . People's hearts should come first. [Don't] put money before people, or use people to get money. (Black recycling plant worker, Hillside, New Jersey)

THE QUESTIONS

THIS BOOK is about the world inhabited by working class people—the world as they understand it. I talked with a large number of blue-collar workers and lower white-collar workers who have stable employment and are high school graduates, but not college graduates, which means that they face severe barriers in access to jobs and other social benefits.[1] Many believe that this group, which represents roughly 40 percent of the American population, is the backbone of American society.[2] Its members exercise an especially strong influence on social and political change since the group includes the bulk of American swing voters.[3] Hence, it is crucial that we listen to their voices, especially at a time when the upper middle class is becoming more isolated socially and geographically from other groups.[4] This isolation may foster social myopia, making it increasingly difficult for the college-educated, academics, and policy makers to see how distinctive their particular understandings of the world are. It is in part to correct this myopia and to amplify the muted voices of the working class that I have written this book.

I am most interested in steadily employed white and black working class men, whom I will also call the "lower middle class" following the workers' own usage. I explored through interviews their sense of identity, worth, and status. As their living standards are in long-term and uninterrupted decline,[5] notwithstanding the recent period of economic prosperity,[6] the ideal of social success may appear increasingly unreachable to them.[7] It is in this context that I explore how they construct a sense of self-worth and how they perceive social hierarchy by interpreting differences between themselves and others.

Morality is generally at the center of these workers' worlds. They find their self-worth in their ability to discipline themselves and conduct responsible yet caring lives to ensure order for themselves and others. These moral standards function as an alternative to economic definitions of success and offer them a way to maintain dignity and to make sense of their lives in a land where the American dream is ever more out of reach. Workers use these standards to define who they are and, just as important, who they are not. Hence, they draw the line that delimits an imagined community of "people like me" who share the same sacred values and with whom they are ready to share resources.[8] These communities may overlap with, or cut across, class and racial lines.

The central object of the first part of this book is to analyze the mental maps of American working men, to identify which social categories they perceive as violating moral norms, and to explore why they see them as such. More broadly, I examine how workers construct similarities and differences between themselves and other groups—how they perform what I call boundary work.[9]

White American workers extend to professionals and managers the moral standards they use to evaluate people in general. They often draw boundaries against this group, judging professionals and managers to lack personal integrity and sincerity and to have poor interpersonal relationships. By doing so, the workers dissociate socioeconomic status from moral worth and thereby locate themselves above the upper middle class according to a standard to which they attach overarching importance. Hence, they contradict the classical view that American workers are deprived of dignity because they are unable to live the American dream.[10] These workers draw even stronger boundaries against blacks and the poor on the basis of a universal morality organized around the "disciplined self," particularly their work ethic and sense of responsibility—this time, equating socioeconomic status with moral worth. Finally, these men are also largely indifferent toward, and in many cases, tolerant of, immigrants, as if this group was overall less salient in their lives or, in a few cases, understood to share the values that the workers praise most.

Although they often lead their lives side by side, white and black workers perform different types of boundary work and their cultural worlds overlap only partly: if white workers most value a disciplined self, black workers most value a "caring self." While many whites see blacks as lazy and contrast their own work ethic with that of black

3

workers, blacks see whites as domineering and contrast them with their own solidarity and warmth. Each group perceives the other as lacking with respect to the specific universal moral rules each embodies and privileges most. Disciplined and caring selves are the moral grounds on which racist beliefs get their legitimacy.

Compared to whites, blacks are also more accepting of the poor, offering structural, rather than individual, explanations of poverty. They are more critical of the exploitative character of the upper half, although they also buy more wholeheartedly into the American dream. More specifically, they attach great legitimacy to money but are also very critical of many middle class values. Hence, for black and white workers alike, moral boundaries on the one hand, and class and racial boundaries on the other, often work together to provide them with a space in which to affirm their worth and preserve their dignity, a space for expressing their own identity and competence.[11] Nevertheless, cultural divergence between whites and blacks persists at a time when social contacts between the two groups remain limited[12] and when the socioeconomic gap that divides them increases.[13]

This book identifies inductively the most salient principles of classification and identification that operate behind workers' evaluations of worth and perceptions of social hierarchies. Whereas recent writings on identity often describe abstractly how the self is defined in opposition to an "other," I explore how workers concretely define "us" and "them" and draw the lines between the worthy and the less worthy. In open-ended interviews, I asked workers to describe their friends and foes, role models and heroes, and the kinds of people they like and dislike.[14] I also asked whom they feel similar to and different from, and superior and inferior to. I compared the criteria of evaluation behind their responses[15] to create a template of their mental maps—the grammar of evaluation they use.[16] In doing so, I tap the order through which they hierarchize (or differentiate themselves from) others when, for example, they declare that money is not a good indicator of a person's value.[17]

The inductive method used in this study has power because it lets us see into the theories that people use to make sense of their lives, into the taken-for-granted categories they mobilize when interpreting and organizing the differences that surround them, without predefining specific dimensions of identity as particularly salient. It allows us to re-

construct the internal coherence of their worldviews and understand
how, for instance, workers come to adopt racist positions given the cultural and material worlds they inhabit. This method generates a comparative sociology of boundaries and ordinary models of definition of
community[18] that documents patterns of inclusion/exclusion based on
morality, race, class, and citizenship across groups.[19] The systematic
study of boundaries distinguishes our approach to working class culture
from other influential studies of this group.[20] It complements state and
institution-centered approaches to national identity that focus less on
how social groups define who is "in" and "out" than on the role of institutions in shaping—sometimes mechanistically—these definitions.[21]
We will see that workers' definitions of who is "part of us" often overlap little with those implied by the state, and that the political/legal
has much less explicit salience in the worldview of the non-college-educated majority than is generally assumed. In the conclusion, we will
see that this research contradicts recent postmodern writings on the self
and on the declining importance of class, as well as traditional views on
class consciousness. Moreover, it brings a needed corrective to studies
of working class resistance by viewing it as the by-product of workers'
attempts to protect their dignity and get respect. Finally, it demonstrates the analytical benefits of studying racism and class boundaries in
the context of people's broader worldview, as opposed to approaching
them as isolated attitudes.

❖ ❖

I would feel superior to people who have no education, who
don't know how to behave, who don't respect anything, people
who are egotistic. I would feel superior to them because I have
had an education, I know how to carry myself . . . This means respecting people, your neighbor, the traffic lights . . . everything
that is normal for me. (French bellman, Nanterre)[22]

We have to be honest. The problem is that North African immigrants don't have the same education, the same values as we do.
We have a general Christian education. Most of the French do
not believe in God but we all have a Christian education that

regulates our relationships. But in the Muslim world, the Koran does not have the same values at all. They send children to get killed in the minefields of Iraq. But in France, if you kill children, it is really a major drama. (French railway technician, Clichy)

The familial feeling, you don't have this. I say "you" in general because I am Arab and you are Catholic or Protestant. For us Muslim Arabs, we keep our parents with us, and you send them to the nursing home. You send them to the nursing home to go to the movie theater or somewhere else. (Tunisian screw cutter, Bobigny)

In the second part of the book, we look at the American working men through comparative lenses and discover that nothing is inevitable in how American workers draw racial and class boundaries. I focus on French workers and show that in interviews they also define their worth and dignity through morality but often give it different meanings than American workers do. The true "others" for them are not blacks or the poor but North African immigrants who are perceived as culturally incompatible with French values. In contrast to white American workers, French workers embrace the poor—as well as black citizens—in the name of solidarity. However, their stress on solidarity draws on different cultural resources than that of the African Americans—for example, the republican, socialist, and Catholic traditions as opposed to such American influences as the black churches and the civil rights movement. Compared with their American counterparts, these French workers use a language of class struggle to draw stronger boundaries against the upper half, whom they associate with exploitation and dehumanization. The two groups adopt alternative definitions of success that allow them to locate themselves above, or next to, "people above" and preserve self-worth and dignity although they cannot live up to traditional norms of success. Hence, both the French and American models of cultural membership involve definitions of an "us" and "them,"[23] but these definitions are structured differently, as the same process of boundary work singles out different moral offenders,[24] drawing on somewhat different moral standards.

Whereas traditional explanations for national cultural differences have been psychological in nature, with a focus on national character,[25] I explain differences in boundary ideology by the cultural resources that people have access to and the structural conditions in which they are placed. These push them toward using some cultural resources rather than others.[26] This "cultural-materialist" causal framework focuses on the structured context in which people live, which is shaped by the relative availability of cultural resources (narratives made available by national historical and religious traditions and various sectors of cultural production and diffusion—intellectuals, the educational system, the church, the mass media)[27] and by structural conditions (the market position of workers, their networks, and the level of criminality in the communities in which they live). The general features of the society also have an impact—for instance, the level of social and geographic mobility and the size of the welfare state. Available cultural resources make it more likely that specific patterns of boundaries will resonate with individual experience in one national context than in the other or in one racial group or class than in another.[28] I show that groups that find themselves in relatively similar structural positions can draw very different lines precisely because their environment and/or subculture exposed them to different sets of cultural tools.

The goal of the comparative study is not to condemn one society as more racist or intolerant than the other but to show that exclusion takes different forms.[29] French and American societies are a particularly felicitous comparative couple because they have equally universalistic pretensions. The values promoted by the French and American revolutions—equality, freedom, democracy, human rights, and so forth—have been presented to the world by politicians, ideologues, and intellectuals as the key values of modernity and the embodiment of reason and civilization. In fact, at different times both France and the United States have been defined as having a special destiny as redeemer-nations of the world, which gave their citizens a privileged status. For instance, the paradigmatic French historian Jules Michelet described France as a "universal fatherland" incarnating "the moral ideals of the world" and the interest of humanity, with a role to "help every nation be born to liberty."[30] On this side of the Atlantic, a 1996 national survey reveals that nine out of ten respondents agreed that we should teach our children that America from its beginning "has had a destiny to set an example for other nations."[31]

Despite such self-appointed missions, these societies have produced high levels of racial violence and hatred. Indeed, although the world guardian of democracy and freedom, the United States has been exceptionally slow to grant its main minority group, blacks, the full privileges of social citizenship, especially when compared with other advanced industrial societies.[32] On the French side, the picture is equally grim: with a long, difficult, and partly repressed colonial past in the background, a full 28 percent of the French voters have, since 1983, voted at least once for the openly racist and anti-Semitic National Front.[33] This paradoxical French and American combination of universalistic claims and established patterns of exclusion makes the comparative study of boundary patterns specific to these societies particularly enticing. Moreover, in recent years, French republican politicians and intellectuals have repeatedly reaffirmed that their society is devoid of racism, especially when compared with the United States. They have offered as supporting evidence the high intermarriage rates between races,[34] the "success story" of Asian immigrants, and the early political incorporation of blacks. In the face of the rise in popularity of the National Front, it is urgent to determine whether this holds water, especially when issues of national identity have moved to the forefront of France's social agenda due to the growing cultural influence of the United States, the problems associated with increased Muslim immigration, and the threat that globalization and the European Economic Union pose to France's economic sovereignty.[35]

The comparison between American and French workers is also enticing because the two groups have reacted very differently to the economic pressures they have experienced over the last decades. During the Great Depression, American responses to the worsening of conditions were often collective. After the Reagan years and the centrist Clinton era, solidarity occupies a fairly marginal place in the worldview of American workers. In comparison, French workers continue to draw on a language of class solidarity to justify their continuous support of the poor, and their response to recent attacks on the welfare state has been largely collective. For instance, in the nineties, they engaged in massive strikes while American workers barely reacted to the downsizing of the welfare state.[36] This is a significant and intriguing difference, given that in both countries union membership is at a low point.[37] Analyzing how workers define cultural membership and draw the boundaries of their community will help us make sense of these different responses.

Analyzing how workers define worth and cultural membership is particularly pressing today in our era of neoliberalism. We know that national welfare systems reveal implicit rules about conceptions of merit and social citizenship that vary across societies.[38] Yet conceptions of moral communities and cultural membership that underlie policy choices remain underexamined.[39] Using the tools of cultural sociology, I attempt to get at moral communities by focusing on the schemas of evaluation used by ordinary citizens. National social policies are more likely to be adopted if they resonate with conceptions of the boundaries of the community that citizens uphold.[40] Moreover, boundary ideologies also have a powerful impact on the agendas of political parties and the electoral strategies they use. Hence, we must study these conceptions if we are to make sense of some of the most important social and political changes that we are facing today, at a time when community boundaries appear to be narrowing and when principles of solidarity seem to apply to an increasingly small number of "people like us."[41]

I have described the main stories told by this book, the threads that bring it all together: workers assess the world in moral terms, and this results in different patterns of social boundaries in France and the United States. However, there are also two subplots lurking in the background. The first one has to do with cultural differences between these American and French working men and their upper middle class counterparts, whom I studied in a book published in 1992.[42] Throughout, I consider whether workers share the culture of the upper middle class by comparing the criteria of evaluation used by members of these groups. I find that while middle and working class worlds largely overlap, workers also have a distinct moral code focusing on personal integrity and the quality of interpersonal relationships. This comparison sheds new light on the worlds inhabited by the two groups located in the advantaged and disadvantaged ends of the increasingly crucial "college-degree" divide. Second, I analyze how workers assess the issue of the relative worth of races in the context of their discussions of worth in general. I compare the antiracism of the majority and minority groups (blacks in the United States and North Africans in France) and show that minorities develop antiracist rhetorics far more complex than those of their white counterparts. This subplot speaks to how workers think about universalism (or bridging boundaries) in the context of constructing intergroup differences that are central to their own identity. It also adds a new dimension to our understanding of racism by considering how the two groups perceive one another and establish the notion of racial equality and inequality.

The People

The American men I talked to include plumbers, electricians, truck drivers, letter carriers, plant workers, painters, bank clerks, and other blue- and white-collar workers—French workers will be discussed in Chapter 4. What do these workers have in common? Certainly not their standards of living. Their median family income is $49,000,[43] and many make much more or much less than this.[44] Because of its diversity, this group is best defined negatively, in opposition to the poor and to professionals and managers who have completed college.[45] This latter group makes up approximately 20 percent of the American population and is monopolizing an ever-increasing portion of the resources that American society offers.[46] In contrast, members of the lower middle class without college degrees see their share of the pie diminishing, although they make up a large portion of the population. In 1993, 44 percent of Americans who responded to the General Social Survey identified themselves as working class.[47]

In interviews workers often remarked on their limited market power or life chances due to the absence of a college degree.[48] A shared experience of "struggling" is at the center of workers' collective identity and symbolic community: it is what appears to unify them.[49] They said that they had to fight tooth and nail to get where they are, largely because they did not go to college. This struggle is present even among those who have reached a high level of income: they do so by working overtime, holding two jobs, or by having a spouse in the labor force. That these men do participate in a symbolic community is evidenced by the fact that, as we will see, they often take workers as a universe of reference when assessing their lives and that of others.[50] They also use workers to differentiate themselves from other "sorts of people" and to define what is important for them.[51] Finally, they define themselves by labels such as "lower middle class," "middle class proletarian," "working man," "blue-collar worker," or simply "worker," which point to similarities in their social position.

Workers' collective identity is reinforced by the fact that (1) the mass media often represent them as a cultural unit, providing workers with "models for" thinking about who they are and "models of" who they are,[52] and (2) many have been in the working class for at least one generation and are part of large working class networks through their families, their communities, and their work.[53] Most have lived their whole life in working class suburbs.[54] They are often immersed in tight networks of sociability, in part because their extended family often resides within a few miles (the children appear to spend considerable time visiting their cousins). Moreover, workers themselves say they have strong roots in these working class communities, as a number of them serve as Little League coaches, volunteer firefighters, or in some capacity in the neighborhood school, church, or American Legion post. These are not postmodern men who recreate themselves anew every morning: their lives are lived within clearly defined parameters, within networks they know inside out and which they define as remarkably (and often too) stable. Their daily experience, the people they meet, confirms their view that there are "people like us."

In the United States the comparison between white and black workers imposes itself: not only has the black/white divide been historically central to American society; the black lower middle class remains largely understudied[55] despite its numerical importance.[56] I compare African Americans in the United States with North African immigrants in France because these two groups are the prime victims of racism in these countries.[57] They also occupy similar positions in the American and French economies: the two groups are concentrated in low-skill, low-pay jobs.[58] Both have limited occupational mobility and a rate of unemployment higher than that of all other ethnic groups.[59]

The men I talked to live in the suburbs of Paris and New York. These research sites were chosen because they were comparable and easily accessible. While I am careful about making generalizations concerning national trends based on regional data, throughout the book I use survey data to explore the extent to which the men I interviewed resemble larger national groups.

THE RESEARCH

The interviews that provide information on the mental maps of American and French workers were conducted in the suburbs of Paris and New York in 1992 and 1993. These complement interviews I conducted with college-educated professionals and managers in these same suburbs in the late eighties. After randomly selecting names of potential respondents, individuals were contacted by telephone to screen them for eligibility. Those who agreed to be interviewed met with me at a time and place of their choosing for approximately two hours. While the United States interviews were mostly conducted in diners and homes located in working class towns along Interstate 95 south of the working class city of Newark, New Jersey (in places such as Elizabeth, Rahway, and Linden), the upper middle class interviews conducted in the eighties took place in the living rooms of large and expensive houses located in exclusive communities such as Summit, New Jersey, and Rockville Center Village on Long Island. Similarly, while interviews with French upper middle class men were conducted in Versailles and other bourgeois suburbs of Paris, French working class men were mostly interviewed in cafés and homes located in the towns that surround Paris—such as Clichy, Bobigny, and Nanterre.

Altogether, I conducted 150 interviews with lower middle class men. I talked to 30 blue-collar workers in each of the four groups: white and black American workers, French white workers, and North African immigrant workers. I supplemented these with 15 interviews with lower white-collar workers in the "majority" group in both the United States and France.[60] Although I use quotations from all groups in providing evidence, quantitative comparisons between "majority" and "minority" groups are based on blue-collar populations only.

The working class interviews are complemented by the previous upper middle class study. In this earlier work, I conducted 160 interviews with professionals, managers, and entrepreneurs, and 80 of them resided in the suburbs of Paris and New York. The appendixes of this book provide further information on the research procedures, the characteristics of the interviewees, the contexts in which they live, and the samples. They also address the character and limitations of the interviews.[61]

In the earlier project, I focused on white upper middle class men because I was interested in the group wielding most power in the workplace—white American men still make up the large majority of managers and professionals.[62] The logic of comparative research involves keeping constant the socio-demographic characteristics of the populations under study in order to illuminate variations in the way they construct the world, along dimensions privileged by the research. Hence, here again, I will focus on men only, although female labor force participation is increasing and transforming the character of the American working class.[63] However, I discuss the gendered aspects of the workers' discourse, that is, whether historically dominant conceptions of masculinity permeate how they assess worth.[64] Finally, I focus on intergroup differences and do not put much emphasis on the considerable internal heterogeneity of groups (for instance, across generations, between white- and blue-collar workers,[65] or in definitions of morality among white workers).[66]

The argument is developed in several steps, each of which is elaborated in a chapter that describes and accounts for a specific aspect of the lines that workers draw—pertaining to the boundaries drawn toward blacks, immigrants, the upper middle class, and the poor. The first three substantive chapters concern American workers while the last three are comparative.

PART I

American Workers

1

The World in Moral Order

BEN MACINTYRE is a white working man.[1] Of medium height, he is very strong and weighs over 300 pounds. The day I met him he had on a clean brown cotton work shirt and matching pants and his hair was very short. He wears thick glasses and an earring. He is extremely talkative. I interviewed him in his single-family home in Roselle Park, New Jersey. The fireplace in the living room/dining room is adorned with a large beer mug collection. There are also beer signs on the walls and plastic flowers on the coffee table. Ben is a volunteer firefighter, and this is reflected in the decor—an area rug has the imprint of a fireman's hat. His wife brings us coffee with amaretto-flavored creamer. A homemaker, she is heavyset and wears a lounging suit.

Ben is in his mid-thirties and works as an electrician. He used to work in construction but he took a pay cut to accept employment at a hospital because he liked the better benefits package, the steady job, and the "controlled" environment ("before the hospital, I would go to work Monday morning and I wouldn't thaw out until Sunday night"). His real passion is being a firefighter: the camaraderie is "phenomenal," and he loves fire science. He is now a fire prevention specialist and is working toward becoming a fire subcode official. He just sent his folder, an inch thick with certificates, to Thomas Edison Community College for accreditation. He is very safety-conscious and is proud to be able to save lives and property. He is a firm believer in the Lord, and when it's his time to go, he will go—that's how he accounts for his not being afraid to enter burning buildings. As a firefighter, he is able to do things that "99 percent of the other people in this world can't or won't do." For this reason, he views himself as part of an elite. In fact, he thinks he can do anything but give birth.

Crucial to Ben is keeping his integrity and being able to look at himself in the mirror in the morning. He believes he is not being promoted at work because he does not like to kiss ass. Also, he is very direct and some think he has a big mouth. He is not motivated by money and does not feel inferior to wealthy people with power. He believes that "people are equal . . . What makes you better than me or me better than you? Just because you may have a degree or maybe because I can go through a burning building or because I coach Little League or you teach? Everyone has different values for what they want to do." He adds: "There's nobody in this world better than me. You may have more money than me, more smarts than me, nicer clothes, better house, but that doesn't make you any better than me. As far as I'm concerned, Bill Clinton is not better than me . . . I don't mean to sound egotistical, but I feel very good about myself. I have a lot to offer." Ben sees himself as "a hell of a guy" because he would help anybody, white or black, if they don't screw him. He is successful because "I am me . . . I'm very well known in this town. I can go down the street, everybody's like 'Hey Ben! How you doing today?'"

Ben says that he is not prejudiced because if he enters an apartment building on fire "I won't stop and ring doorbells and say: 'Are you black? Are you white? Are you Puerto Rican?' . . . I take people for face value and as far as I'm concerned, anybody can be my friend . . . I'll help anybody." He knows blacks very well because he grew up with them in Newark where he belonged to gangs and got into trouble. His family came to Roselle Park when he was a teenager to remove him from "the elements." Now, Roselle Park is deteriorating: "We have a lot of apartment houses, so we have a lot of transients . . . The minority level is 22 percent . . . They've had to remove phone booths from town because too many kids were using them for drug deals." He thinks we live in a cruel world, because "nobody stops and pulls over anymore . . . *I'm* even wary. I won't pull over if I got my wife and kid anymore because there are so many wackos out there running around . . . People don't care anymore, they just don't care. And you gotta care. We're on this boat and everybody's got to row at the same time. It makes it go a lot smoother." He coaches football in his neighborhood because "I remember where I came from and I'm trying to help these kids. I try to keep them active and busy."

Ben describes his best friend as caring and responsible and "a lot like me. He'd help somebody out, he's got high standards for his kids and his family, very protective . . . He takes pride in his work." He likes "people who have good heads on their shoulders, who can use their brain, have common sense, skip the b.s., and don't jerk me around . . . I don't like people who play these two-faced games." He also has no use for liars, rapists, drug dealers, people who have no pride in their work, and people who abuse their wives and kids. He wishes that "they would use the death penalty a lot more." In fact, he would "volunteer time to go down to the county jail every Sunday: 'You like to beat up kids? Well guess what? Now you're going to go a few rounds with me.' You would not have to pay me." He would like to be more influential to be able to stop murders and car-jackings. His goal in life is to "bring up my child right. Bring him up with a good set of values. Take care of my wife. Keep plugging along and eventually become a subcode official and keep saving lives."

❖ ❖

Ben MacIntyre describes what preoccupies most of the American workers I talked with. Keeping the world in order—in moral order, that is—is at the top of their agenda. Making sure that their family is secure in a threatening world is an unending task, and one that is increasingly difficult to carry out because the environment they live in is perceived as unstable, and buffer zones (spatial and, sometimes, psychological) are disappearing. Indeed, moral norms of interpersonal relations create a more predictable world by reducing environmental uncertainty.[2]

As Ben exemplifies, morality plays an extremely prominent role in workers' descriptions of who they are and, more important, who they are not. It helps workers to maintain a sense of self-worth, to affirm their dignity independently of their relatively low social status, and to locate themselves above others. When questioned on the traits they like and dislike most in others, the majority of American workers, blacks and whites alike, spontaneously mention moral traits: they like "people who care," "who are clean," "not disruptive," and "stand-up kind of people"; they dislike "irresponsible people who live for the moment," "people who get into fights," "people who forget where they come from," and "wormy kinds of people."[3] Similarly, when asked to rank positive and negative traits, whites and blacks emphasize moral qualities: the four qualities they value most are "honesty" (77 percent), "being responsible" (72 percent), "having integrity" (52 percent), and "being hardworking" (52 percent). Three of the four negative traits they dislike most are "dishonesty" (87 percent), "being irresponsible" (58 percent), and "being lazy" (44 percent).[4] Finally, morality is central to the meaning they attach to success, although it is not much more valued than socioeconomic success. When asked to define success, 49 percent of white and 43 percent of black blue-collar workers use moral references of one type or another (e.g., "being a good father and a faithful husband"). In contrast, 38 percent in each group stress socioeconomic achievement (e.g., "doing well").[5] These figures—as well as those pertaining to qualities valued in friends—are comparable to figures obtained from national surveys.[6]

My goal is less to provide a systematic quantitative comparison across groups—although I do this at times—than to describe white and black working class culture by focusing on the criteria of evaluation salient across groups.[7] I find that in these working class worlds, key factors are (1) being hardworking and responsible as a means of ensuring a predictable environment for oneself and others; (2) providing for and protecting the family; (3) being straightforward and having personal integrity; and (4) respecting religion or other traditional forms of morality. I aim here to analyze how these dimensions of morality are understood by white and black workers, and by white workers as compared to white professionals and managers. The table on page 21 provides a road map of the most salient dimensions to be discussed here. Again, Chapter 4 will take on these issues for French workers.

The most important racial difference is found in the emphasis that black and white workers put on individualist and collectivist dimensions of morality: while black workers value responsibility and hard work, they put more stress on solidarity and generosity—what I call "the caring self." In contrast, whites put more of a premium on "the disciplined self." This is clearly reflected in the terms they use to describe how they separate "people like us" and the undesirables. This disci-

Dimensions of morality most salient to white and black workers and to professionals and managers

WHITE WORKERS	BLACK WORKERS	PROFESSIONALS AND MANAGERS
Hardworking ++	Hardworking +	Hardworking
Responsible	Responsible	−
Providing +	Providing +	Providing
−	−	Self-actualization
Protecting	Protecting +	−
Personal integrity	Personal integrity	−
−	−	Flexibility/team orientation
Straightforwardness/ sincerity	Straightforwardness/ sincerity (esp. in the context of racism)	−
−	−	Conflict avoidance
−	Religious participation +	−
Traditional morality + (anti drugs and crime)	Traditional morality ++ (anti drugs and crime)	Traditional morality
−	Collective solidarity	−
−	Generosity	−
Interpersonal altruism	−	−

+ = frequent
++ = very frequent

plined self goes beyond the standard references to individualism that are frequent in the literature on American cultural orientations: white workers also stress traits of responsibility, protecting the family, and straightforwardness, which are not part of a classical model of individualism that centers on self-reliance and the work ethic.[8] While being concerned with the same challenges as whites, blacks also place a premium on collective solidarity, in part because of their experience of fighting together against racial segregation and discrimination. The black church also sustains a rhetoric of solidarity that is absent among white workers. The decline of unions and of progressive religious institutions leaves whites without important sources of discourse promoting collective solidarity, and this leads them toward a more individualistic conception of altruism. Hence, white and black working class cultures differ from one another, although the structural conditions of existence of the two groups resemble one another in many ways.

As for class differences, a quantitative analysis of the significance of moral, socioeconomic, and cultural criteria in the boundaries that white workers and white professionals and managers draw suggests that workers put more emphasis on moral criteria than their upper middle class counterparts.[9] They also put less emphasis on socioeconomic criteria than professionals and managers. The main difference in their boundaries is not so much that workers stress moral criteria more than professionals and managers do;[10] instead, they are more exclusively concerned with them.[11] Also, upper middle class men emphasize some dimensions of morality, such as self-actualization and conflict avoidance, that are of little interest to workers. In contrast, workers place more value on straightforwardness and personal integrity than do the upper middle class.

"DISCIPLINED SELVES": SURVIVAL, WORK ETHIC, AND RESPONSIBILITY

Tony Sansone is a slightly overweight 30-year-old who grew up in a traditional Italian neighborhood in Brooklyn. He owns a two-family house and spends much of his free time maintaining it, doing the plumbing and the electrical work. He has never been married and he works in a refrigerated dairy warehouse, where he loads and unloads trucks. He dreams of driving tractor trailers and is most happy when, every few weeks, he is sent to Long Island to deliver one thousand pounds of sour cream: "Once I leave in the morning, it's my responsibility. If I want to listen to the radio and drive with the windows open and it's freezing out, it does not matter . . . It's just me and my truck, and I go do my work." He thinks he has a good job because it is well paid and unionized. Also, his bosses are fair, he gets along with them, and he is always ready to do overtime to "pay the bills and keep the car insured." Like his friend Frank, he has long hair and wears dungarees, t-shirts, boots, and a black leather belt with a key chain hanging on the right side. He defines his goals in life as "making it through. It's real tough out there and there's a lot of people looking for work. I'm lucky I'm working . . . every day, and just have some place to get up every morning and go to and come home after a day of work. My own bed and my own house." He defines his worth through his work: "I have friends that I grew up with and they all work in video stores. Their thought of the day is 'I had to work eight hours and only five people came in today to buy tapes.' It's like 'Gee, you must have worked hard doing that.' They're sitting there all day reading the paper and watching TV; that's what you do in a video store . . . Meanwhile I'm out there driving trucks and dealing with people in traffic when it's snowing. When it's the middle of summer, there'll be heat in the truck and no air-conditioning and it's 100 degrees out, the sun's beating down. I'm out there working and they're complaining about 'I was in the bakery today and we had to make six batches of cookies.' Everybody works and you do what you got to do." He says that he is successful because "I mean I made it to 30 . . . I've always fed myself, I buy my own clothes and pay my mortgage and car insurance . . . I've been doing it pretty much since I was 19. I've worked ever since."

❖ ❖

The collective identity of the men I talked to is articulated around their struggle to "make it through" and keep the world together in the face of economic uncertainty, physical dangers, and the general unpredictability of life. For a mechanic who has two children, "[being] a survivor means a lot. It means that you can maintain [yourself] . . . Overcome some of the bad things that can happen in life . . . You'll make it, you'll make it through. It's the way you lead your life." These men have "disciplined selves" of the type valued by Tony Sansone: they don't let go, they don't give up, and it's largely through work and responsibility that they assert control over uncertainty. They wake up every morning, go out there in the cold, and do what they have to do to "keep it going." When asked to describe a hero, some point to their fathers, praising their perseverance at work and capacity to keep it all together in the face of adversity.[12]

Working and Facing Responsibilities

Writing about changes in the meaning of work at the threshold of industrialization, the American historian Daniel Rodgers points out that "[e]ven for those who chafed at labor, the appeal to the moral centrality of work was too useful to resist. Pitched in the abstract, it turned necessity into pride and servitude into honor."[13] Similarly, for these men, work signals a form of moral purity and is often mobilized to draw boundaries between decent people and the others. A strong work ethic is often construed as a matter of honor and an essential source of personal worth. For instance, when asked what kinds of people he likes, Danny Easton, an audio technician who repairs electronic equipment for a manufacturer on Long Island, points to "folks that work hard and give a day's work for a day's wages," echoing a storage worker who appreciates people who "whatever they have, they had to kick and scream to get, and actually worked for it. They are honest people."[14]

In this drawing of boundaries, workers willingly oppose their "disciplined selves" to the more carefree dispositions of those they dislike. Coworkers who are not hardworking are a frequent object of scorn. Take Jack Getty, a stage technician employed by a major Broadway theater in Manhattan. He hates having to interact with "people who whine and complain . . . people that are chronically late and people that go out and have a couple of drinks at lunch and come back a little lit up . . . I am cursed with a strong ethic. Other people just aren't." Similarly, Billy Taylor, a foreman who supervises an assembly line at a cosmetics company in Rahway, New Jersey, says, "I feel superior to dregs, slugs. People that just won't do anything. People that just automatically give up . . . I don't want to be around this person." People who, in the words of one civil servant, are "just trying to have a good time" and "are milking the system to the fullest" are deeply resented and time and again described in hostile terms.

Whereas lazy parasites are absolutely despised, people who are able to hold more than one job are objects of admiration. Take Tim Williams, who lives in Hempstead, Long Island, and has always been a biker. He now works as a laborer in the construction business and feels he is very lucky to be steadily employed. He says, "Because life is so rough, if you're working hard, I give you a lot of credit. It's not an easy deal to do. I met a waiter, he had three jobs . . . I respect a person like that. He's doing what he has to do, whereas he could bail out and say 'To hell with it, I'll give up the family and just go somewhere.'"

Being hardworking is also often associated with other positive traits such as being responsible and caring for others, as if it were part of a package that characterizes "good people." This is expressed by Ben

MacIntyre, our electrician who links these traits when explaining why he is appalled by "people who take no pride in their work, people who don't care about anybody." Ben stresses the importance of responsibility in various realms of life, from work to family life and community life, and frequently uses this standard to distinguish between "people like us" and others, because he views it as essential to the well-ordered world he is striving to maintain. This need for order is also expressed by Danny Campbell, a Jersey City plumbing inspector who believes that "that's what's wrong with society today . . . If you can't own up to what you have done, what good are you to anybody else!" Whether or not these workers live by their commitment to work and responsibility, these themes are very central to the self-presentation they offered in the context of our interview.[15]

Unlike workers, professionals and managers do not mention responsibility in their descriptions of the people they dislike, as if they take responsibility for granted among their peers. They are more likely to point to people who "are mediocre and don't develop their minds" (in the words of a labor arbitrator), "who don't know how to reason" (custom broker), "who don't achieve what they are capable of" (earth science teacher), and who are "not as successful" as they might be (hospital controller). On the other hand, workers resemble professionals in the importance they attach to self-reliance and long-term planning as elements of responsible behavior, especially in the realm of money. For instance, a civil servant says he is successful because "I have worked for everything I've got. Nothing was given to me. I did it all myself." Workers also admire proper management of one's impulses, time, and budget. Focusing on planning and budgeting, John Bridges, a warehouse worker, considers one of his coworkers irresponsible. He "would eat off the lunch truck and he had no money. That's $50 a week. You see me, I make my lunch everyday: a beautiful big roast-tomato sandwich, piece of fruit cake, you know, a soda. He can't send his wife to the store and buy some cold cuts to make some lunch, but he cries poverty! I have no respect for you. Simple mathematics. Tell your wife to go out and get a job instead of sitting home and reading love magazines and watching soap operas."

Similarly, an electrician praises the long-term financial management of his friend: "He's a real nitpick and real organized. They bank a lot and do everything right. They buy gas with cash. They don't have credit card bills and stuff like that. They never seem to have any kind of bills or anything like that."

Why do workers place such emphasis to being hardworking and responsible? The importance of work resonates with central themes of Protestantism and of the liberal and republican contract on which American civic religion is built: self-sufficiency and industriousness are widely understood to be the main sources of individual and community welfare.[16] Hard work is the basis for a producer democracy in which the demands of citizenship, economic contributions, and social utility go hand in hand.[17] In this edifice, American individualism is largely defined by the principle of self-reliance and its role in providing self-respect and self-rule.[18] Other cultural repertoires contribute to the centrality of work and responsibility as well, such as cultural constructs concerning masculinity: being hardworking is a mode of expressing manliness, especially if it involves productive or physical activities. Thus, Tony Sansone insists that he does not bake cookies but drives a truck.[19]

The very conditions in which these men work reinforce the importance they attach to being hardworking: their labor is often painful and time-consuming, yet underpaid, physically demanding, or psychologically challenging because repetitive. Being able to stick to it demands emotional energy and moral fortitude.[20] Workers know this from their own experience and, again, often express admiration for others who can show persistence. Work becomes an occasion to display competence and a source of pride. Furthermore, the mastering of work, and work speed in particular, is one of the means unskilled workers have to gain a sense of autonomy and control in the workplace; work is also the only means workers have to achieve upward mobility measured by material acquisitions. Dennis Young, a firefighter in his thirties, explains that he works two jobs to pay his mortgage in Bayonne and to build a house along the New Jersey shore:

> Work is more important to me right now than having any kind of social life . . . I work in the firehouse until 8:00 in the morning and then I work at the construction site until 6:00 . . . Me and my wife's social life is very lacking . . . I do it now because I'm

young now and able to do it. So you can get, like, financially secure by the times you can't do this no more . . . The husband
should take care of the family but, realistically, it's hard. Hard to
support a wife.

Finally, the condition of the economy and the downsizing of the
welfare state also sustain this emphasis on work: the living standards of
workers have been steadily declining since the seventies,[21] and they
often complained that they have to work more hours to make the same
amount of money as before. Industrial restructuring and the growing
influence of human resources consultants are leading toward leaner
workplaces everywhere, which has affected the climate of workplaces.
Those who keep their jobs often face increasing levels of economic insecurity.[22] The growth in the number of homeless people and of the
working poor in the eighties, combined with the downsizing of welfare
benefits, are additional incentives for workers to do all they can to keep
economic insecurity at bay.[23] Thus, workers are acutely aware that
"hanging in there" depends above all on their capacity to work. Although the late nineties have been prosperous economically, as of 1998
workers have benefited little from this economic upswing,[24] which may
suggest that they continue to be preoccupied with issues of security although a language of economic optimism is now predominant nationwide.

These workers value responsibility for some of the same reasons they
value being hardworking. But they also value responsibility because
they are highly dependent on the actions of others. They point out that
the physical conditions in which they work and live and their limited
financial resources make it difficult for them to buffer themselves from
the actions of neighbors, coworkers, kin, and friends. They have no private space at work and live in neighborhoods where houses are set very
close to one another. Compared with their professional and managerial
counterparts, they can less readily escape crime, drugs, and undesirable
people by moving to high-income suburbs. They have to pay daily for
their lack of resources, and the costs are aggravations, headaches, and
the obligation of channeling time into solving a myriad of problems.
Vincent Marchesi, an electronics technician who lives in Roselle Park,
puts it this way: "A person's irresponsibleness can cause a lot of prob-

lems for myself. It can cause me to be more responsible than I have to be. Like I mean, if you leave my car unlocked in a shitty area . . . Now it's gonna cost me x amount of dollars and I've got to spend two hours downtown somewhere." Again, in explaining the importance of responsibility, these workers are expressing their yearning for predictability as well as the frustrations resulting from their dependency on others. Chapter 4 will show that similar trends are present among French workers whose life conditions are not unlike those of their American counterparts.

The Disciplined Selves of African Americans

Work also provides black workers a common basis of identity, wherein they define themselves as "decent people" fighting together against the deterioration of the environment. In my interviews, black workers repeatedly praise people who don't give up, get up early in the morning, and do what they have to do to put bread on the table.[25] They also talk at length about the role played by work in their lives. They say they work extremely hard and know many people who work equally hard. Their position at the bottom of the American labor market often forces them to work extra hours or two jobs to make ends meet. Their investment in work is also revealed in surveys: compared with the black middle class, black workers are more likely to believe that "unless minorities shape up and realize they can't get a free ride," they cannot expect much in the way of gains in race relations.[26] Hence, black workers, like white workers, value the disciplined self.

My interviews also suggest that blacks place less emphasis on being hardworking and responsible than whites do. Indeed, when asked to choose from a list a quality or trait they dislike, 40 percent of blacks chose irresponsibility, compared to 70 percent of their white counterparts. Also, 40 percent chose hardworking as one of the qualities they like most, compared to 59 percent of their white counterparts. Moreover, while none of the African Americans put work at the center of their definition of success, a fifth of the whites did.[27] This does not mean that blacks define worth less through morality than whites do: as we will see, they simply put *most* emphasis on other dimensions of morality (the caring self). In other words, their definition of morality overlaps with, but also differs from, that of whites. However, as

Chapter 2 will show, blacks are not about to yield to the notion that they are less moral than white people.

Providing for and Protecting the Family

A tall, overweight, and bald white man, Jim Jennings works as a foreman at a tin factory in northern New Jersey. He lives in the same house as his in-laws and has raised his family on the second floor of a single-family home located in a neighborhood where residences are separated by narrow driveways. He extols the virtues of having a close family and of structuring one's life around it: "My wife's side of the family has always been very close. Whenever me and my wife were gonna do anything, we'd go and pick up my nieces and nephews and take them with us. I even went out and bought a station wagon so I could put all the kids in it. It was great. This has always been headquarters because my father-in-law loves to have a tight-knit family. To this day my brothers-in-law still come."

He considers it very important to fulfill his role of provider. "Family is very important in my life. You need to work to support your family. So, I don't worry about a job. I mean, I don't care what I have to do, I'll go out and do it to support my family." He explains that "my wife was always there for [the kids], which I thought was right. I mean you have some of these people that don't care about their kids. People have kids now, they're 5, 6, 7 months old and the mother works and the father works . . . I'm old-fashioned that way, where I feel my mother was home, my wife's mother was home and I feel that a mother should be home to raise her child in most circumstances. I know things are rough. I didn't have; I'm not a wealthy man. I had it rough but you have to make ends meet the way you can . . . I got a pool in the backyard to keep my kids, where they could have their friends come over here and go swimming in the pool and stuff like that. Now, even after high school and everything, my son's friends still come over here. They call me Pop and they call my wife Mom." Jim Jennings is proud of the control he still exercises over his two grown sons, who are police officers: "It's not that I'm a Gestapo guy, but my kids still have the respect of us even though they're of age to do whatever the hell they want . . . [I tell them] if you're not doing nothing, get your butt home so we don't have to worry about you . . . We just have a close-knit family, lucky me." He describes his relationship with his wife in emotional terms: "I started going with my wife when we were 14 years old. It is a binding true love."

❖ ❖

In 1969, John Goldthorpe, David Lockwood, and their colleagues published what was to become a classic study of the British working class, *The Affluent Worker in the Class Structure.* They offered a critique of the "proletarian embourgeoisement" thesis and proposed that British post-war workers are less allied with the bourgeoisie in their class interests (as traditional Marxists had argued) than engaged in instrumental behavior: they are selling their work to the highest bidder while turning all their emotional commitments toward family life. In contrast to the traditional worker, they are seeking satisfaction outside the workplace while deserting the political realm and accepting the inherent meaninglessness of their work. Consumption is becoming a privileged sphere in which one finds self-satisfaction.[28]

The white and black men I interviewed resemble these British affluent workers in their overriding commitment to private life, which takes the particular form of "providing for and protecting the family." As documented by previous research, blue-collar workers put family above work and find greater satisfaction in family than do upper middle class men.[29] Family is the realm of life in which these workers can be in charge and gain status for doing so. It is also a realm of life that gives them intrinsic satisfaction and validation—which is crucial when work is not rewarding and offers limited opportunities.[30]

Providing

For workers, being the provider means at a minimum being able to keep necessity at bay, put food on the table, and maintain "a roof over [our] heads." It can also mean providing such luxuries as a trip to Disneyland or an above-ground pool. However, for some, "taking care of the family" has paradoxically meant putting family above work and money: they have learned to do "without" in order to allow their wives to stay home and take care of the kids. In a few cases, they have given up time-consuming but well-paying jobs to have a greater presence in their children's lives. This is the case for Jimmy Brown, a truck driver who delivers liquor on the Jersey shore—he used to be a car salesman. He says: "There isn't a doubt in my mind that I could be making more money, but it's not as important as [my family]. It just isn't." Hence, for these working class men, a key indicator of moral character is how committed one is to one's family and what one is ready to sacrifice to this goal. Many equate a high quality of family life with "being able to keep the wife at home."

Upper middle class people are also very concerned with providing, although they are less likely than workers to view the fulfillment of their family's emotional and financial needs as incompatible. In their worlds, paramount are saving for their children's college education and creating the conditions for their self-actualization and growth by exposing them to a wide range of experiences. Self-actualization, "be all you can be," occupies a key position in the upper middle class culture as a whole.[31] In contrast, self-actualization is rarely mentioned in the discourse that workers hold on child-rearing values or on what is important in their own lives.[32] These men tend to give rather concise responses to questions concerning the hopes they have for their children. That their children do well in school and stay out of trouble are what most fathers wish for. This supports well-established findings on class differences in child-rearing values.[33]

Protecting in a Threatening Environment

The importance that workers put on protecting their families is illustrated by their repeated use of the term "very protective" to describe qualities they appreciate in their friends—this term was never used by the upper middle class men I interviewed. When asked why he likes his best friend, Jim Jennings says, "He's a family man. His family comes first to him as well . . . He's a lot like me. He's got high standards for his kids and his family, very protective." Many workers feel that they should do all they can to ensure the safety of their family. For instance, Gary Finn, an assembly line worker employed by the GM plant in Linden, says that nothing would stop him when it comes to protecting his family: "If my wife or my kids are going to go out in the street and somebody's going to try to do them harm, you gonna wish you never came into this state. You'd be safer in jail. I'm gonna be in the courtroom and I'm going to hope you get out on bail because I'm gonna be outside waiting for you . . . because you're touching my family."

Similarly mixing "providing" and "protecting," Vincent Marchesi, the electronics technician who lives in Roselle Park, says, "I will do anything to make sure my family stays secure. Physically, emotionally, financially . . . If there's something they need of you, you do it, regardless of the sacrifices you have to make to do it. You do it, no questions asked. That's it."

Many of the men I talked to perceive their environment as threatening.[34] They make frequent mention of an epidemic of car hijacking that was hitting northern New Jersey at the time. Joe Lasco, an Elizabeth police officer who hopes to retire soon, explains that "people don't realize it's a war, an undeclared war and innocent people are going to get killed; it's a shame." He cannot believe that murders are committed for no other reason than "he was just in my face." Evening television reports and newspaper articles featuring crime and violence have an important role in generating these feelings, although crime rates have been steadily declining since 1990.[35] During the course of our interviews, workers described how being the direct victim of crime, being personally acquainted with victims, witnessing crimes, and following community gossip provide daily confirmation of the gravity of the situation. For Harry Donaway, a tool and dye maker, "you wouldn't believe what is going on, even in better towns than this town. Money doesn't buy you safety." Even the Herculean Ben MacIntyre contrasts the safer neighborhoods in which he grew up with the situation that now prevails in Roselle Park, where the outdoors has become a dangerous zone: "If my son wants to go down to the playground, he has to check in with us every 45 minutes or so. My wife is ten minutes late and I start panicking . . . There is a lot of sick individuals running around . . . Roselle Park is not Newark, but I can see it deteriorating very rapidly."

The importance of "protecting" in these men's world is underscored by the fact that they stress the importance of being street-smart, a vital form of intelligence defined as the ability to survive in one's environment by knowing how to navigate around its perils and how to negotiate shady characters whose sole purpose in life is to exploit and defraud the innocent.[36] They believe in the importance of "not trusting anyone," and one or two even scolded me for conducting interviews in the living rooms of strangers.[37] The salience of "protecting" is also symbolized by the physical appearance of the neighborhoods where they live, and particularly by iron bars that adorn many windows and by large attack dogs tied inside tiny backyards. Workers are convinced that they *need* to protect their families. In contrast, protecting is less salient for professionals: for this group, contact with violence comes more exclusively through the ten o'clock news.

The Specific Challenges of Blacks

Even more than for whites, providing is not taken for granted by black workers, given the greater instability of their position in the labor market.[38] Blacks also point to their fathers as role models and to illustrate the importance of providing for the family. A technician explains that his father "held down two full-time jobs for sixteen years . . . This is how they were raised; back in this era, you went to work to support your family. Whatever you had to do, you did it." For some men, given their inferior market situation, "to do anything to give a sense of security for my family" meant crossing the boundaries of legality—this did not come up in interviews with white workers. Tyrone Smith, a 53-year-old chemical plant operative and father of four, explains that in the past he ran numbers, begged, borrowed, and stole to support his children: "The things that we'd do sometimes to make ends meet, not even thinking about the consequences . . . I could have been locked up, you know."

Black workers also appear to be more concerned than whites with the dangers of their environment and the importance of protecting their family. In fact, protecting is as important, and more of a challenge, for them because of higher levels of criminality in the black population, which affects their perceptions of threat.[39] This is reflected in a national survey that shows that while 36 percent of blacks say that they are very concerned for their personal safety when they go out alone at night in their neighborhood, only 11 percent of whites shared this attitude.[40] This concern for protecting one's family and for the dangers present in the environment is exemplified by Craig Patterson, an assistant cable splicer with young children who lives close to Newark. He says, "I am so petrified by baby sitters . . . Kids being harassed and sexually molested everywhere . . . That's why I'm trying to bust my butt now." He wants to move to quiet suburbs: "It's like twenty minutes from here, and it's like a whole other world . . . And things happen there too, but it's not as frequent." Speaking of the dangers that exist in the New York area, he says, "It just hurts me so much to have to think about all this stuff. You have to think about surviving and you think about your kids and your wife, because things happen . . . God probably says 'Please stop calling Me!' because I'm always like 'Please just get me through it all.'"

Gender Roles, Protecting, Masculinity, and Nationalism

The importance of "protecting" for white and black workers also has to be considered in the context of gender roles and the meaning given to manliness by the two groups.

Among the interviewees who are married or live with someone,[41] only 16 percent have a partner who is a homemaker. Nevertheless, many keep alive the notion that men should be the principal providers. This generally means that, although most spouses are de-facto coproviders, men are viewed as having prime responsibility for providing.[42] However, the importance of providing appears to be less tied to traditional gender roles for blacks than for whites.[43] Compared with their white counterparts, blacks are more likely to believe that wives should also work. This is not surprising given that during most of this century, the labor force participation of black women was twice that of white women.[44]

In the United States, the breadwinner model of manhood came to be broadly diffused only in the mid-nineteenth century, and until the 1960s it was "unattainable for all but the upper and upper-middle classes and an elite minority of the working class."[45] Although there remain important class differences in the extent to which this model still prevails,[46] it continues to be a pervasive means for men to assert control over the environment. Because providing cannot be taken for granted—budgets are tight, bills accumulate, emergencies happen—workers value it as an achievement, and they take consistency in being able to provide for the family to be proof of moral fortitude and masculinity.[47]

Protecting evokes images of willpower, honor, courage, discipline, and physical strength that have historically been directly linked to "normative masculinity."[48] Workers easily extend this imperative to the country at large, defending nationalist ideologies and the importance of fighting to preserve American international dominance through a show of physical strength if needed. Being an American is one of the high-status signals that workers have access to; this identity has resonated historically with glorious and elitist images of "freedom fighters" and "chosen people,"[49] along with the manifest destiny of bringing American values to other regions of the world.[50] For this reason, workers might be particularly proud of their manly protective mission and their national status. This is suggested by Gary Finn, the GM assembly line worker:

> I know that we are the most powerful country in the world and have been for a long time. Not just with the Bay of Pigs with Kennedy but like with Russia, all their lives have been trying to come up with our standards. Same thing for the French. Whatever we do, they will come after. So we really had no military or economic fear. Other countries have learned enough from us to stand on their own. Especially Japan, but they are not our equal. We yell about Japanese cars, Japanese parts, they bought Rockefeller Center, but they are not equal! We have to remember *America makes the law!*

Or in the words of Alan Hayward, a train conductor, "I'm proud of this country. I've been to other countries to see the way they live, dictatorship, warlords, monarchies, and things like that and I don't like it a bit."

Being ready to defend freedom, liberty, and all that the United States represents might be a way to defend a particular notion of oneself as courageous, strong, and as "making the law." As pointed out by sociologist Joane Nagel, "terms like honor, patriotism, cowardice, bravery, and duty are hard to distinguish as either nationalistic or masculine since they seem so thoroughly tied both to the nation and to manhood."[51] Hence, workers are busy keeping moral order not only in their home and neighborhood but also in the world at large. Notably, these themes never emerged in the interviews I conducted with managers and professionals. I now turn to the other means by which order is achieved.

STRAIGHTFORWARDNESS AND PERSONAL INTEGRITY

Sociologist Rosabeth Kanter argues that in large organizations in which professionals and managers often work, it is important to know how to signal trust because such organizations generate much uncertainty: they require constant interaction with large networks of people who have only superficial familiarity with one another.[52] Hence, having the appropriate operating style, or presentation of self, is important for professional success. For American professionals and managers, the legitimate personality type rewarded by large organizations presents the following traits: conflict avoidance, team orientation, flexibility, and being humble and not self-assuming.[53] These personality traits are not of primary importance for the white and black workers I talked with. For them, trust and predictability are not attained via conflict avoidance, team orientation, and flexibility but by being straightforward. When asked what kind of people he likes, Ben MacIntyre points to "people who can skip the b.s., and don't jerk me around. If you have a problem with me, come talk to me. If you have a way you want something done, come talk to me. I don't like people who play these two-faced games." Similarly, a maintenance worker says he likes "a person that's straight up, you know, what I call the term, 'shooting from the hip.' You have to take what they say, and if you're wrong, then you're wrong and I'll tell you you're wrong, but if you're right, then I'm man enough to admit that you're right." In a more prosaic way, another worker says he likes an open person who can tell you "you know, you ought to brush your teeth a little more often, or you know, you've got a hair sticking out of your nose. Simple things like that." Several workers resemble Dick Turner, a security system installer, in describing Ross Perot as someone they truly admire, precisely because he is direct and straightforward. This trait may be more important to workers in New

York than to those residing in the South or the Midwest where gentility may be more valued.[54]

The importance that workers attach to being straightforward is reflected in the dislike this letter carrier expresses for phonies who "put on a facade, put over an unreal profile of themselves . . . They ain't what they want to be and they try to put all this impression and usually you can see through it. They don't think too much of you because they don't think you're intelligent enough to see through it." Like the Italian lower middle class men studied by Jonathan Rieder, workers oppose their "straight talk" and toughness to middle class gentility.[55] However, their dislike for the latter is shared by some professionals who use the label "phonies" (along with low-moral types and social climbers) to designate groups they do not like.[56]

Workers also value personal integrity, that is, standing up for one's principles even in the face of adversity. This trait is not always compatible with the conflict avoidance, flexibility, and team orientation praised by professionals and managers.[57] Unlike professionals, they put sincerity above flexibility, perhaps as a form of working class resistance. Personal integrity often requires manly courage, showing that you are not, in electronics technician Vincent Marchesi's words, "a total wuss and a wimp," but it also brings rewards in the form of dignity. As explained by Steve Dupont, a postal worker, who likes telling his boss what he thinks, "This has gotten me in trouble but as I always say to [my foreman], 'I can always find another job, I can't always recoup my pride and my own dignity.' In that sense I find that [speaking up] makes me stronger." Similarly, Joe Lasco, the Elizabeth police officer, explains with pride that many of his coworkers admired his integrity when he stood up to defend his partner, who was accused of killing someone: "It made me feel so good. It made my day. It made my month. My partner is that way too, he's not afraid to speak up." He describes himself as "a stand-up person, a thick or thin type of person . . . You're your own person . . . Don't go with the crowd."

Among blacks too, a strong emphasis is placed on personal integrity, on standing up for oneself, especially in the face of racism.[58] For them, upward mobility, the idea of becoming a foreman, is not construed as desirable if it means having to put up with white abuse.[59] In general, they particularly appreciate straightforwardness on the part of whites when it comes to racism and race relations. Tyrone Smith, the 53-year-old chemical plant operative, stresses this when he says, "If you're honest and tell me 'I don't like you because you are black or white or what have you,' I could deal with that better than somebody being racist in a backward way . . . At least, I would know where a man or a woman is coming from. That's where the honesty comes in. I've gotten along with people that are racists." Lou Johnson, a maintenance worker originally from Florida, discusses the advantages of southern racism along the same lines. He prefers it because it is more straightforward. "They'll say, 'I don't like you, you don't like me.' We can say that, we can work together, shop together, and go our separate ways and that's it and you live over there and I live over here, which is no problem for me." Hence, being straightforward alleviates tension with whites, even when they are self-professed racists. Some view avoiding conflict as a way of "acting white" and reject it as antithetical to their code of honor.

SALVATION FROM POLLUTION:
RELIGION AND TRADITIONAL MORALITY

Alan Hayward drives commuter trains in Queens, but he has chosen to live in the quiet working class town of Rahway, New Jersey. A white man, he is tall and handsome and is a self-confessed former womanizer. As he describes it, "when I broke up my third engagement before I met my wife, I went dog nuts. I went with fifty or sixty women in a six-month period. I was out every night and I didn't care . . . I must have seen the movie *American Gigolo* with Richard Gere maybe 15 or 20 times . . . I know I hurt a lot of people, but some men get a lot of women and some men can't get any. It's just the way things are. That's all." This life is now behind him as he "went back to the way I was brought up." He married a Catholic woman who grew up in the Middle East, had three daughters, and has found God. His present goal is to raise his children by teaching them to "believe in God, and you know, all the rights and wrongs, no grays. I don't believe in gray. Truth, honesty, responsibility, that's what I believe in . . . Believe in God and believe in parents. Must have two parents in the family. I don't believe in divorce." He thinks the world is "going to hell" and is a strong believer in capital punishment. He has been robbed at gunpoint twice in the New York subway and has had his jaw broken by drug addicts. He says, "without religion, there's nothing. Without religion or some sort of background, we would have anarchy, total breakdown. We have to put religion in children. I'm Catholic and proud to be Catholic. Honesty and morals. I'm really worried about the country, [especially] the groups that are trying to break our morality. For instance, in New York now, they are trying that Rainbow coalition and the Rainbow curriculum, but I don't believe in lesbianism and gayism. It's against God and it's against man . . . Don't do things that are not meant to be." Now that he is very religious, he feels that at work "there is a certain aura when I walk in. They really listen to what I say, you know. They listen. I try not to say any of my beliefs or anything, but they listen. I like that, but I don't want them to take every word and if I tell them a fib or a lie, they'd believe it, you know. I want them to take me as I am and try to experience what I've experienced."

❖   ❖

Social analysts from Alexis de Tocqueville to Seymour Martin Lipset have emphasized the link between traditional morality and religious participation and affiliation.[60] This connection persists. Nowadays, church attendance is a strong predictor of how much importance people attach to God, marriage, and children, and traditional sexual mores are often seen as key markers of religious affiliation.[61] Hence, we should explore how religious and nonreligious interviewees understand the relationship between religiosity and worth, as well as the importance they attach to the respect of traditional morality.

Religion and Keeping Dangers at Bay

Among all the American working class men I talked to, only 25 percent can be described as very religious,[62] and the vast majority do not define themselves as particularly religious. When asked to choose qualities that are important to them, only 18 percent picked "religious." For this minority of very religious men, religion plays an important role in clarifying rules and enforcing protection against the crumbling environment in which they live. Indeed, Alan Hayward clearly views religion as providing tools for the reproduction of the social order, for fighting pollution (alcohol, drugs, sex, and "gayism"), and for cultivating a disciplined self. Similarly, Dick Woolworth, a mailman who used to drink too much, explains that becoming a Christian has played a crucial role in helping him to leave liquor behind and come back to his family.

These particular men view religion as a source of status. Like Hayward, Jimmy Brown, the truck driver who delivers liquor on the Jersey shore, thinks that his coworkers value his opinion because he is religious: "It's the way they talk to you, or that they talk to you at all sometimes. Or that they ask questions. I get a lot of that down at work . . . Like 'This last guy who just got fired, do you think they should have fired the guy? What do you think about the AIDS crisis? You go to church, what do you think about this? . . . Why are they so pro-life?' I tell them 'I'm not a spokesman of the Catholic Church, but I'll tell you why I think they think that,' but that doesn't make me feel the be-all-and-end-all. That kind of stuff."

Religion also offers an alternative to social status and is often defined in opposition to it. When I asked Dick Woolworth, the mailman, if he is more successful than his brother, who serves in the House of Representatives of an eastern state, he responds, "I'm very successful now because I know Jesus Christ . . . But I don't put success on a monetary level. That's not important to me. If I see an old person, I'd rather take care of them. I have everything I need." Another Christian postal worker who used to work on Wall Street, Randy Sinclair, similarly explains, "Before I was a Christian, I lived for myself, that's basically the whole tenor. When I became Christian, it changed my whole perspective on life because my whole purpose became to live for Christ, to be faithful to the word of God, and basically, wealth and fame and success and other things [became] not important." Finally, Jimmy Brown, the truck driver, uses his rejection of drugs and prostitution to establish his own moral value, which allows him to stand above his station in life:

> You are more than what your job is, no matter what you do . . . I think that some people think that because you're the boss or you're well connected, you're smarter. But you have to be more than just what you do. If I was your typical truck driver, I'd have stayed that night in the parking lot [to share a prostitute with his coworkers]. I'd drink with them and I'd be stealing like a lot of

them . . . I don't think it matters what our job is, you have to do what you feel is right.

Among the other white interviewees who are not particularly religious, a relatively large portion are Catholics from Irish or Italian descent. Their grandparents and great-grandparents were part of the great immigration to the New World that brought newcomers to New York City at the beginning of the twentieth century.[63] They lived in the type of working class ethnic enclaves that have attracted the attention of a number of sociologists, where cleavages pertaining to religious identity (Protestant vs. Catholic), country of origin (northern vs. southern Europeans), and skill level (high vs. low) overlapped to create fault lines within the working class population that hindered the development of the labor movement.[64] They define themselves as sons of immigrants *and* as Americans, and they engage occasionally in acts of symbolic ethnicity, participating in specific events, such as the St. Patrick's Day parade, without any feeling of obligation.[65] However, their status as "white ethnics" does not seem to be particularly salient to them. Neither is religion (in the context of the interview), although they may believe in life after death and send their children to parochial school to ensure that they receive a "decent" education.[66]

Religion and Boundary-Policing in the Black Community

Slightly more African-American than white interviewees described themselves as very religious. While 85 percent of African Americans say that they like religious organizations, among whites only 60 percent said so. Also, while only a third of African Americans never or rarely participate in religious activities, it is the case for roughly 47 percent of whites.

That the church is the key organizational force in the African-American community is well established. Several black-controlled independent denominations (known as "the black church") were founded after the Free African Society of 1787 and still account for more than 80 percent of all black Christians.[67] Their leadership is exercised not only in the spiritual realm but in the social realm as well, as they bring together collective resources to fight for economic and social justice.[68] Hence, the black church has been at the origin of the creation of a wide range of new institutions, including schools, banks, insurance companies, low-income housing, and so forth. Partly as a consequence of this, church involvement and religiosity have always played important roles in delimiting moral and "respectable" African Americans from others,[69] and this is clear from the interviews. In fact, black workers more readily use religion as a proxy of moral character than do white workers.[70] John Robinson, a union representative who works in a GM plant in Rahway, expresses this succinctly when he says "religious people is people that got a heart, that care for people, regardless of what color you is, they care for what's going on around them . . . Religious people is people that believe in the family, don't believe in bad things . . . If you're not a religion person, you believe in anything, good things and bad things." Similarly, Abe Lind, a plumber on Long Island, chooses his friends on the basis of whether they "believe in God, to a large extent, [because] that's who they answer to, and they treat people fairly."

Being able to use clear signals to distinguish between good and bad people is crucial in a dangerous world where one cannot know whom to trust, as pointed out by John Lamb, a recycling technician from Georgia who moved to the North a few years ago. He describes his friends in the following terms: "We basically have the same background . . . Baptists have a lot of respect for people, believe in just doing the right thing . . . They are 'family-going people,' people you can trust . . . That's not like the average person you meet in the street that you gotta second-guess."

African Americans who are religious establish a strong boundary between their neighborhood environment and their religious community: the former is viewed as dangerous and as offering many temptations (drugs, for instance). Also, the reciprocal use of social capital (networks and resources) among church members requires strong boundaries between insiders and outsiders in order to avoid depletion.[71]

More than whites, blacks also seem to point to the role of religion in helping them to avoid pitfalls and resist temptation. They cite the Bible and refer to the presence of Satan around them, at a time when references to sin are declining in American society.[72] For Tyrone Smith, the chemical plant operative, father of four, and stable middle-aged man who lives in East Orange, "Satan taunts all of us. What will happen in life that will bring me down, I don't know. But I can't let that kind of influence, I can't be around that kind of influence."[73]

When discussing child-rearing, time and again black workers point to the role of religion as a tool for success and a guarantee against the dangers of the environment. Leon Davis, a letter carrier, describes the values he has tried to impart to his children as

> just regular Christian values because they grew up being regular church members and things like that. You know I think I just trying to teach them to be, I guess what we would call a "good American." Good citizens, you know, and just clean, upright, morally, spiritually, and physically. And they did! Their friends are not street-type of people. All their friends are like white-collar-type guys, you know, and that kind of things. So they don't associate with the bad element either.

Even black interviewees who are not very religious associate success with religion, as does Howard Hamilton, who grew up in Harlem and saw most of his friends die as a result of drugs or crime. After a string of bad jobs, he now works as a security supervisor, and of his "social progress" he says, "I needed a college education, and I needed to go in the right direction in the first place. Then I felt that in order for me to get there I would need the religion aspect of the situation in my life. So both of them worked together."

Traditional Morality and Moral Pragmatism

I now turn to workers who support traditional morality without being very religious, and deal first with class differences. High school graduates generally uphold more rigid moral norms than college graduates: they are less supportive of freedom of choice and self-expression, especially in the area of sexual morality, divorce, and abortion.[74] They also give more support to "cultural fundamentalism," the cluster of values that motivate moral reform activists who support "adherence to traditional mores, respect of family and religious authority, asceticism, and control of impulse."[75] Their child-rearing values can also be described as more rigid.[76] Against this backdrop, I compare the workers and professionals I interviewed in terms of their attachment to traditional morality.

43

As in the case of religion, workers use traditional morality to put themselves a notch above others (as we will see in Chapter 4, in this respect they contrast with French workers). Much like the maintaining of personal integrity, holding oneself to high moral standards is a way to acquire or affirm one's dignity. Hence, Rudy Evans, an animal food and medicines deliveryman, says that he is very proud that he is trusted to transport drugs for his work: "To me, that's like putting a medal on my shirt. Anybody else would go in there and clean the place out. I just walk in, do my stuff, and go. That's the biggest compliment you can pay me when you give me trust like that." Dishonesty is viewed as a stigma because it "lowers the person." Henry Link, a bank supply salesman, says, "There are many opportunities to cheat or steal. [But you have to stop and say] 'Hey, wait a minute! That's not what I want to do.' I think that's the difference between people I appreciate and don't appreciate."

Liars, "shysters," and con men are particularly despised because they take advantage of people and create environmental uncertainty.[77] Many believe that honesty should be valued in and of itself because it tells you your worth as a person. In this, workers resemble professionals and managers, who express a dislike for "low-moral types."[78] However, they also draw much stronger boundaries against immoral people than do upper middle class men. They use traditional morality, like religion, to keep pollution at arm's length, including drugs, alcohol, promiscuity, and gambling.

Many workers mention that they feel superior to drug addicts. Alcohol abuse is not viewed as much of a problem, in part because alcohol consumption is part of normal male socializing for many, while only two workers volunteered that they take illegal drugs.[79] The pattern followed by Johnny Page, a printer, is a typical one. He confesses, "I'm a heavier drinker than most people. If I get out of work at noon, I go out for a couple beers before I go home . . . I'm friends with the bartender there, we just talk and say hello and everything, but the people who hang out there I would never want to socialize with them . . . they are bikers." Drinking is not a major "polluting" activity, except for those who lose control.[80]

Criminality is also particularly despised, again perhaps because it is common in these men's neighborhoods. Vincent Marchesi, the electronics technician who lives in Roselle Park, where vandalism is frequent, expresses his deep hatred for thieves who, he alleges, come from nearby Newark: "I hate people who break into cars for no reason, just to see . . . [or] for 50 cents sitting on the front seat. Car thieves. I hate mischievous dirtbags. Or the type of person who walks down the street and runs a key along a row of cars down the block. For what? That's a dirtbag, that's the kind of people I hate." His frustration at having to fight constantly to protect his property is palpable.

Similarly, workers often evoked the importance of respecting the law.[81] They also use moral arguments to draw strong boundaries against people who are violent and abusive. For instance, when describing the types of people he dislikes, a store manager points to "people who are abusing their kids, abusing their wife verbally, in public places." A policeman also says that he dislikes "anybody who has hit a woman without good reason, an abuser of kids, animals, anybody that's abusive, obnoxious."[82] These categories were never mentioned by professionals and managers nor was respect for the law.[83] This difference is a clear indication of the extent to which workers perceive their surroundings as threatening and in need of moral order.[84]

A number of workers share the moral pragmatism found among professionals and managers, adopting a flexible moral code with a weak core that is highly adaptable to situations.[85] For instance, Billy Taylor, a foreman in a cosmetics plant, understands dishonesty in relative terms when he says that he taught his children that "it's not worth it to steal or lie unless you are sure that there is a million waiting when you get out because you're going to pay a price . . . That kind of logic comes from my grandfather, through my father, through me. I was very strong on that with the children and they all seem to have gotten it. I don't have any bank robbers or drug addicts, which in this society is saying something right off the bat." He mentions in passing that he has slept with a number of women he supervises, and he is proud of his sexual prowess, suggesting that he willingly subordinates moral principles to circumstances. For others, this pragmatism takes the form of workplace pilfering, which is viewed not as stealing but as a legitimate job benefit to be taken advantage of within understood limits.[86]

Blacks and Traditional Morality

Partly as a result of the harshness of the environment in which they live, African Americans appear to be more vehement defenders of traditional morality than whites and to draw even stronger boundaries against pollut-

ing elements, just as some of them hold tenaciously to traditional definitions of sin. When asked to describe the qualities he likes in his companions, Jimmy Light, an upwardly mobile phone technician, says "she's
quiet, not drinking, not a party-goer, somewhat religious, that's basically
it." Similarly, Joe Taylor, a fumigator in his mid-fifties, says of his girlfriend, who is in her thirties, "She don't drink. She don't smoke. She don't
dance in bars or clubs, nothing like that. She will work." By criticizing
moral laxity in the context of the interview, respondents may be attempting to counterbalance the racist association between blackness and over-
sexualized behavior, and offer guarantees of their own morality.[87]

Blacks' condemnations of criminals are particularly strong. A few
condemn black criminals for bringing down the entire race. Others resent that the criminal behavior of some blacks reinforces negative racial
stereotypes. For instance, Bill Washington, a UPS mail sorter, explains
that "I shouldn't be condemned for the black guy they're showing on
the news who murdered a white lady. Don't condemn me because he
did that. He did that as an individual, as a person. So too often, the
whole society is condemned for the picture that is painted on the news,
on the TV and it's not fair."

Finally, black southerners often draw strong boundaries against black
northerners, whom they largely perceive to be less moral.[88] Jim Bloom,
a machinist, explains that "people that are born in South Carolina are a
lot different than the people up north. You respect each other's lives.
Down there you would never hear somebody sass an older person . . .
The North is no place to raise our children." Others concur. For John
Lamb, the recycling plant worker from Georgia, northerners "don't
have a heart, they do anything . . . They don't have respect for people,
for life, for basically anything. It's just like a rat race and whatever happens, happens." Thirteen out of 30 black interviewees were born in the
South, primarily in the Carolinas and Georgia.

CARING SELVES: BLACK CONCEPTIONS
OF SOLIDARITY AND ALTRUISM

At the beginning of this chapter, we explored the place given by white
and black workers to the disciplined self, and their reactions to slackers
and parasites. While respect for this disciplined self is largely shared by

African Americans, they also place greater emphasis on the collective dimensions of morality, solidarity and generosity—what I call the "caring self." When asked to choose from a list a quality that they value, more than a third of blacks, as compared to only a fifth of whites, chose "shows solidarity." The same proportions of blacks and whites chose "generous" as one of the qualities they value highly.

The emphasis that black workers place on solidarity is expressed in their greater reluctance to describe themselves as feeling superior or inferior to others. More than twice as many blacks than whites say that they never feel superior to people. This was illustrated by the following statement made by Tom Green, a hospital orderly: "you are no better than nobody and nobody is better than you." Several justify this reluctance by wishing that "people [would] realize that we have one creator, and not many creators, and . . . there are many different colors of birds, and trees, and fishes, and everything that crosses this globe."[89]

In my interviews, black workers frequently defined their financial goals in altruistic terms, in terms of being able to "try to help a lot of people, create jobs for them, and keep them working" (in the words of a recycling specialist) or being able to "help people if I could. If you don't share it you lose it . . . because God will not bless you if you don't put it to good use" (the view of a chemical plant operative). A medical supply salesman explains that "I would like to be able to have enough in my house that if somebody else comes to my house and needs help, I can be able to help them . . . I don't have to take a trip every summer."

When discussing the types of people they do not like, several black workers point to people who took advantage of their generosity. They criticize individuals who do not reciprocate when expected and who break the implicit social contract that unifies people, thereby violating the honor of those who help.[90] Concretely, this means borrowing money and not returning it, taking advantage of friends' generosity, free-loading, or even manipulating friends to get certain benefits from a relationship. For instance, when asked to describe the types of people he does not like, Jerry Flowers, a machinist, mentions "people that sponge, that try to use you or con you . . . People that be your friend and tell you anything in the world as long as you have money." For his part, John Robinson, a black union representative who works in a large automobile plant, says that he dislikes people who are "looking for something for nothing." This widespread dislike for people who "use" others is expressed succinctly by Lou Johnson, a maintenance worker who says "There's a thing you just don't do. You don't take a person's kindness for weakness or play him for a fool . . . 'cause they're giving from here, you know, they feeling sorry for you and giving it from here [pointing to his heart]." This dislike for users might suggest the diffusion to the lower middle class of cultural models more frequent among ghetto dwellers where exploitative individualism has been found to be a norm, given conditions of general scarcity of resources.[91]

The social science literature widely supports these findings concerning the centrality of solidarity and generosity for African Americans, which also manifests itself concretely in the way black workers discuss their friendships. Like white workers, they often define happiness in terms of being able to relate and to have good, warm relationships with friends and family. However, some evidence suggests that the ability to establish deep intimate connections has been found to be more characteristic of working class blacks than other groups.[92] The literature also includes countless narratives that describe black people as having strong senses of interpersonal connection and shared memories that translate into strong communities.[93] The black church is often described as an extended family network involving interdependence and mutual responsibilities.

In recent years social scientists have described African Americans as an "imagined community" of sorts because blacks have strong connections with one another independently of interpersonal connections.[94] This is confirmed by social psychologists, who find that middle class African Americans feel warmer toward other blacks than toward other middle class people.[95] This strong collective identity continues to nourish the notion that one belongs to a community of interest, that "what is good for my race is good for me."[96] In this "nation within a nation," individuals have strong feelings of communality based on their shared historical experience and the continued impact of their common racial identity on their fate and life chances.[97]

Indeed, a number of black workers put solidarity toward the black race above solidarity toward the human race. For instance, Jimmy Light, the phone technician, defines the whole black race as his kin. He says he would like to have enough money to help people: "They don't have to be our relatives, just be black and need it." Using the kinship metaphor, Tyrone Smith, the chemical plant operative, also states that his goal in life is "helping my brothers as much as I can."[98] The promotion of solidarity among blacks means not only helping "the brothers" but also fighting daily for social justice. As a phone technician states, "I've always been for the underdog because of my upbringing—when you're discriminated against." Concretely, this requires standing up against people who make racial slurs at the workplace and "getting on the case" of those who "feel through the thing of being slaves and things like that, they're supposed to be superior to you." The historical figure of the "race man" evoked by St. Clair Drake and Horace Cayton in *Black Metropolis* embodies this necessity of standing up.[99] When asked to name their hero, several black workers mentioned Martin Luther King, expressing their commitment to the peaceful fight for social justice.

Racial solidarity is part of racial identity and is associated with a general claim for moral status. As recently suggested by J. Phillip Thompson, this solidarity is valued in and of itself as a source of self-worth by people who might otherwise be considered negatively by the larger society.[100] It is a crucial component of the lasting social scripts that blacks use to make sense of their culture in contrast to that of whites. And indeed, a few white workers point to it to distinguish whites from blacks. For a white laborer, blacks "taught themselves and learned that blood is thicker than water so they tend to group with each other very quickly. If there is a black and white union worker fighting over something, automatically the blacks will stand together where the whites don't tend to. The blacks call each other blood, they stand together." Ideologies such as Afrocentrism and black nationalism constitute coherent cultural worldviews that explicitly contribute to promoting collective racial identity, stressing collective over individual strategies of resistance to white domination. However, they still have limited popularity.[101] The presence of an influential discourse on racial solidarity suggests that, in the mind of these black working class men at least, there still exists a black subculture that encompasses all social classes, disconfirming the thesis that, as compared to class, race is losing its significance as a basis for differentiation and inequality.[102]

Generosity and solidarity are also highly valued by the white workers I talked to. However, the meaning they give to these traits is more individualistic than that given by blacks. Few white workers elaborate a collective notion of solidarity the way black workers do.[103] The examples of altruism they give generally involve a one-to-one relationship and often have to do with helping someone solve practical or technical problems—for example, giving a hand to someone who has car trouble or helping a neighbor fix his gutters. None attached importance to social action and working for social justice or mentioned the importance of coming to the help of the needy in the name of Christian values.[104] Although these white workers are less involved in volunteering activities than middle class people,[105] community involvement through volunteer fire-fighting groups or Little League coaching is central to the lives of several of them.

How can we explain these racial differences in emphasis on collective and individualistic dimensions of solidarity? One cannot understand the importance put on solidarity by black workers outside their daily experience with racism and their aspiration to equality and respect. The mainstream black religious tradition has historically made available to blacks a ready-made discourse about the need for collective solidarity as a means to transcend hardship.[106] It has also supported this collectivist tradition by framing freedom as communal in nature, and by stressing that it can only be realized for the race as a whole, given that racists evaluate blacks not as individuals but as representatives of their race.[107] Other institutions, such as political organizations, have reproduced these collective frames of morality in the context of antisegregation and antidiscrimination struggles and have reinforced the influence of the black church.[108] Furthermore, black popular culture has had a powerful influence in reaffirming the strength of the African-American imagined community.

For white workers, a more collectivist discourse would primarily be made available through labor unions and progressive churches, which have had little influence in recent years.[109] These institutions have been unable to counteract the discourse of individualism that has become omnipresent in the media and political debates since the Reagan years. In Chapter 3, we will see that some workers explicitly and proudly trace the origin of this discourse to the Republican Party. Perhaps in parallel to a "de-ethnicization" of white workers, the Catholic Church in particular has been less effective in diffusing a rhetoric of solidarity. These changes were accentuated by the centrist turn of the Democratic Party under Bill Clinton, as it has moved away from a solidaristic discourse to adopt an individualistic take on work and responsibility that was historically associated with the Republican Party.[110] Had I conducted the interviews in the mid-seventies, white workers would probably have promoted group solidarity to a greater extent.

Black workers point to another factor that might help us understand the importance of collectivist morality for them. We will see that they are prompt to condemn upwardly mobile African Americans who forget to give back to the community and help their brothers. "Bounded solidarity" may be a necessity for black Americans as their marginality in American society pushes them to turn to each other to find help rather than to enter in the market to satisfy their needs.[111] In interviews, they point out that having access to resourceful networks is particularly crucial in the context of scarcity and economic insecurity, which was particularly marked in the early nineties. The widely perceived decline of the black community may have incited them to affirm the importance of standing together, investing in local business, showing racial solidarity, and moving toward the realization of collective projects.

THE POLICING OF MORAL BOUNDARIES

Morality is the structuring principle in the worldviews of American workers, black and white. Through it, they define who they are and, perhaps more important, who they are not. It is also important in maintaining a sense of self-worth and dignity. In particular, hard work, personal integrity, and traditional morality allow workers to put themselves above others and help them compensate for their low socioeconomic status.

Our cultural-materialist explanatory framework suggests that the structural conditions in which workers live, and the cultural repertoires they are exposed to, account for the dimensions of morality that workers value most. They value hard work because it is their exclusive source of welfare and means for upward mobility. Their neighborhood and workplace leave them little buffering space from others. By working hard and being responsible, they hope to be able to maintain order in an environment that they perceive to be increasingly threatened by economic restructuring, criminality, and social decay. Ensuring the protection of their families and providing for their security are their foremost concerns. Traditional morality and, for some, religion provide tools for keeping pollution at bay. The centrality of work for these men is also reinforced by cultural repertoires concerning the meaning of masculinity and by repertoires provided by Protestantism and by American republican culture that make citizenship conditional on self-sufficiency and production.

We saw that whites and blacks are not alike in the dimensions of morality they privilege. For blacks more than whites, protecting their families and guarding themselves against polluting elements and criminality through religion and traditional morality are key, perhaps because the boundary between the working class and the underclass/underworld is more tenuous for them than for their white counterparts. Also, they more often live in areas of high crime and unemployment, which may lead them to draw stronger moral boundaries as a means of keeping disorganization and danger at bay. Second, and more important, black workers emphasize collective dimensions of morality, putting the "caring self" above the "disciplined self": they are particularly concerned with solidarity, egalitarianism, generosity, close interpersonal connections, fictive kinship, and the defense of the black imagined community.[112] In contrast, white workers have a more individualist understanding of altruism and are less exposed to cultural repertoires (such as the black church) that can sustain solidaristic notions. Hence, the class cultures of black and white workers are somewhat different because they are fabricated from different cultural materials, and are exposed to harsher structural conditions. In Part II, we will see that, like blacks, French workers also value solidarity, in part due to the influence of the Socialist and Communist parties, which have played important roles in keeping collectivism alive.

Note that my interviews support the view that while there are persisting cultural differences between whites and blacks, black and white workers live in largely overlapping worlds. They support surveys that have found important differences in black and white beliefs concerning, for instance, governmental conspiracies against blacks,[113] reactions to the O. J. Simpson trial, estimates of the size of the black and white communities in the United States, and the impact of race on interpretations of reality and politics.[114] My analysis enriches our understanding by illuminating the content of racial differences, such as those pertaining to solidarity, and the role given to traditional morality.[115] These findings clearly contradict the portrayal by some media and politicians of African Americans as morally lax.[116]

Finally, morality is a more important criterion of worth for workers than for professionals and managers, who stress socioeconomic status instead. Chapter 3 will show that this is reflected in the boundaries that workers draw against the upper middle class.[117] Both groups are influenced by cultural repertoires central to the American civic religion, the religious tradition, and liberal republicanism: they value the work ethic and traditional morality. However, workers are more concerned than professionals with keeping the world in moral order (with protecting and providing in particular) because of the environment in which they live, which is more dangerous and less predictable and economically stable.[118] Professionals and managers are concerned less with reducing insecurity in the environment at large than with interactions with their peers—hence their emphasis on conflict avoidance and team orientation and their comparative indifference to personal integrity and straightforwardness.[119] Their discussions of family responsibility revolve less around protecting and providing for basic needs than around facilitating the self-actualization of children and providing for a college education.

Together these comparisons suggest that working class and upper middle class conceptions of morality remain distinct. As in the case of racial differences, class differences cannot be easily measured because they take place within distinct schemes of reference. However, quantitative research on attitudinal change points to a convergence over the last 20 years between the college-educated and those with no more than a high school degree.[120] This adds weight to the increasingly popular view that class cultures are less differentiated than they used to be,[121] due to a number of interacting factors such as processes of individualization of lifestyle.[122] The fact that many workers are concerned with long-term planning is an illustration of such declining differences.

In the next two chapters, I turn to an examination of the ways in which moral boundaries are used by white and black workers to draw class and racial boundaries in the contemporary United States. We will see that these are often drawn in a single stroke, using the very same moral signals that workers use to evaluate everyone to judge members of specific groups: work ethic and responsibility are privileged in drawing boundaries against blacks and the poor, while personal integrity is privileged in the drawing of boundaries against the upper middle class. The use of these moral signals contributes to making both types of boundaries seem natural, universal, and legitimate. Herein lies the key to symbolic exclusion as it most often presents itself among contemporary American workers.

2

Euphemized Racism:
Moral qua Racial Boundaries

WE MET Tony Sansone in the last chapter. He is single, owns a two-family house, dreams of driving a tractor trailer, and thinks he is successful because he had made it to 30 and has always fed himself. He has long hair, makes a point of only wearing dungarees, and describes himself as a "renegade." He works in a refrigerated dairy warehouse, where he loads and unloads trucks, and he sometimes delivers sour cream on Long Island. At work, he is the only white guy and hates the situation. He sees many differences between himself and his coworkers:

> The music, the neighborhoods we're from, the clothes. The way we dress for work. They come in with two different color shoes and baseball hats. I just wear regular clothes like today: blue pants, blue shirt, white sweatshirt . . . We all have to work together, so you pretty much put up with what's there. If you have an argument, you're still going to have to see the guy the next day for eight hours and for eight hours the next, so you let a lot of stuff slide . . . It's just the way they grew up. They have their own little sublanguage, with the hat, with the baseball hat on backwards. Just stuff like that. There's nobody in my neighborhood really like that!

Tony is upset that the warehouse radio is tuned in to the rap music station favored by his coworkers: "It really gets crazy all day long. It really is annoying. The radio station plays the same ten songs over and over all day long." He thinks that whites and blacks live in different worlds ("blacks don't know about new Paul Newman movies; many of them voted for Mayor Dinkins here in New York"). Tony also resents the fact that his black coworkers are not submitted to the same discipline that he is:

> Black people, they think that just because they're black, they're special and should be treated differently, which is bull. Because now they get special treatment and because I'm white, I don't get it. Like at work, there's three of them so they get away with more . . . I get yelled at if I use the public phone, but meanwhile the phone rings because all their friends have the phone number, all their relatives have it, their girlfriends call, their friends call . . . But if I got to call my insurance company because I gotta call them, I have to ask permission. If they get yelled at, they complain that it's unfair and racist. They've done it already on the job. So it's watched, what goes on and who says what. You have to watch what you say and when you say it.

His dislike for blacks crystallizes around what he perceives to be major differences in work ethic and ambition:

> They're happy they've got a job where they make a couple of bucks and they can go out and drink or do whatever they want to do. Like the guys I work with. They're happy working in the warehouse and to them they'll do it the rest of their lives. I don't even want to drive the trucks. Hopefully, like in 10 or 15 years, I won't have to work. Hopefully, my family town house will make more money . . . Maybe I'll get my own truck. They don't want to move up . . . Like when 5 P.M. comes, everybody punches out and goes home and I'm saying "what else do you need done?"

Tony's own identity as a hardworking guy makes him particularly sensitive to what he perceives to be the inadequacies of his black coworkers. He draws racial and moral boundaries simultaneously by pointing to blacks' moral failings.

How Morality Defines Racism

The white professionals and managers I talked to in my previous study very rarely mentioned race when they were asked to compare themselves to others and to talk about their likes and dislikes. They were more likely to mention people like themselves, that is, white middle class people who are highly educated. Their feelings of superiority and inferiority were often organized around income and around their children's educational and occupational success. By contrast, workers read such questions as pertaining directly to race, although I did not mention race in questioning them on these issues. For example, when a fire-fighter, who is also an Army veteran, was asked what kind of people he feels superior to, he answered: "I'm not in the position where I work to feel superior to anybody. As far as race goes in our fire department, there is one guy who is considered an American Indian that is considered a minority. The other one is one black fellow but he don't work with us . . . In the service the blacks stay together and the whites stay together . . . In this town, black veterans have their own legion."

This chapter will show that moral and racial boundaries are intertwined, and that white workers repeatedly and spontaneously referred to blacks when drawing moral boundaries. This pattern also generally holds when black workers discuss whites, although their racial boundaries are much weaker: while some are quite critical of whites, many offer a wide range of arguments supporting the view that races are equal. Both groups, however, rarely mentioned immigrants and other racial groups as significant others in the context of the interview. If workers have negative feelings toward immigrants, these feelings are not strongly held.

Both groups define their collective identity in opposition to one another, in an "us" versus "them" relational logic. While this relational dynamic is a well-documented feature of racism,[1] our analysis puts flesh on it by documenting inductively the building blocks of boundaries: we will see that a number of whites criticize blacks for not stressing the disciplined self they value and believe themselves to embody. In turn, blacks emphasize the caring self they privilege when evaluating whites whom they describe as domineering and egotistical. By doing so, each group places itself above the other and defines its collective identity.[2] They also express a "feeling of belonging together," to use Max Weber's expression.[3] This self-identification complements and affects predominant representations of races.

It makes a difference that workers, whites and blacks alike, use moral criteria to evaluate the other racial group: these criteria are purportedly universalistic—that is, apply to the whole of humanity and transcend individual groups or ascribed characteristics.[4] They are an extension of the criteria workers use to evaluate everyone, as we saw in the previous chapter. Thus, their racist feelings appear justified in their eyes instead of reflective of their own personal biases.[5]

To get at the boundary ideologies of whites and blacks, I asked workers to describe "my type of folks" and "the type I don't like much."[6] In analyzing the interviews, I systematically traced the relative salience of different themes in the full repertoire of arguments and types of evidence used to demonstrate that racial groups are above one another or equal[7]—what I call their rhetoric of racism and antiracism.[8] My research contributes several novel findings. First, I document which norms whites perceive blacks as violating instead of predefining these norms, as does the survey work on this question (the symbolic racism literature in particular). Second, I provide evidence about the antiracism of ordinary white Americans, a topic unexplored to date.[9] I find that the most popular form of antiracism in academia, multiculturalism, is absent from the worldview of these workers. Third, unlike recent analyses of racist discourse,[10] I characterize simultaneously racist and antiracist discourse across populations and thus illuminate new aspects of racial boundary work (e.g., specific types of evidence, such as earning capacity, are used to demonstrate both racial equality and inequality). Fourth, I address another crucial, yet largely neglected, topic: how contemporary ordinary blacks construe whites and understand the differences between blacks and whites.[11] We will see that blacks employ a much broader set of arguments to demonstrate equality between the two races, perhaps in response to their everyday experience of racism. For instance, only blacks find support for equality in our common origin as children of God, our common physiology, and in a shared American citizenship. While a third of the black interviewees used arguments that are primarily antiracist, among whites only 20 percent of white-collar workers and 13 percent of blue-collar workers did so. Also, among white Americans, 60 percent of the white-collar workers and 63 percent of the blue-collar workers provided arguments that were primarily racist, the rest being indifferent. As for African Americans, a little more than a third indicated that they believe blacks to be superior to whites or that whites have significant flaws, and a third did not discuss these issues.[12]

I will refer to a number of factors to explain the prevalence of moral arguments in the drawing of racial boundaries and to explain differences in the arguments used by white and black workers. I focus less on psychological factors than on how institutions such as churches, political parties, and the media shape the cultural repertoires to which blacks and whites have access. I also focus on how workers' life conditions, such as economic insecurity and the frequency of interracial encounters, lead them to draw on specific aspects of these repertoires rather than others.[13] I argue that the difficulties experienced by white workers in providing for their families and "keeping on" make them more likely to buy into the depiction of blacks by some media and politicians as violating the norms of American individualism.[14]

This chapter first examines the moral standards white workers use to evaluate blacks, which are in line with the moral worlds depicted in the previous chapter. I show that their work ethic and the defense of traditional morality are the main criteria white workers use to place themselves above blacks. In contrast, white antiracism is primarily grounded in earning capacity and in the notion that human nature is universal, that is, that there are "good and bad people in all races." The second part of the chapter turns to blacks' perceptions of whites. Blacks point to their earning capacity, buying power, and competence (i.e., the "disciplined self") to establish racial similarity. Drawing on more collective conceptions of morality, they describe whites as domineering. In addition, they use nonmoral evidence of racial equality, such as basic human needs, lineage, physiological similarities, and citizenship.

In the third part of this chapter, I turn to white and black workers' attitudes toward immigrants, toward whom most workers are indifferent. Some workers perceive the most salient immigrant group, Hispanics, as demonstrating a work ethic and family values. Others argue that Hispanics' lack of desire to assimilate brings down the country. However, the racial boundaries they draw are much stronger than those they draw toward immigrants. This will receive further attention in the second part of the book, when French workers' attitudes toward blacks and immigrants will be compared.

WHITES ON BLACKS

The "Nigger" and "The Kind That Work Like You and Me": Work Ethic and Responsibility

Many white Americans describe blacks as lazy and irresponsible. Surveys suggest that whites' perceptions of black moral failures center first and foremost on work ethic, self-reliance, and socioeconomic status.[15] When the 1990 General Social Survey asked white respondents to place blacks as a group on a seven-point scale with "lazy" at one end and "hardworking" at the other, 44 percent placed blacks on the lazy side of the scale and only 17 percent chose the hardworking side. When asked whether blacks prefer to live off welfare or be self-supporting, 55 percent of white respondents placed them on the "welfare" side of the scale as opposed to 11 percent who placed them on the "self-supporting" side. Finally, 60 percent agreed with the proposition that "blacks have worse jobs, income, and housing than whites because most blacks just don't have the motivation or will-power to pull themselves up out of poverty," while 33 percent disagreed.[16] Many of the white workers I interviewed associated blacks with welfare, dependency, and affirmation action, just as they think of their own identity as organized around responsibility and hard work.[17]

Vincent Marchesi was introduced in the previous chapter. A white electronics technician who lives in Roselle Park, he would do absolutely anything to keep his family secure. He hates irresponsible people who "leave their car unlocked in a shitty area" and who violate private property "just for the fun of it." He lives in the neighborhood where he grew up, in a tight-knit Italian family. His industrious father immigrated to New York in his youth to become a successful construction contractor. Like him, Vincent is a workhorse. He considers himself "top gun" at his job and makes a very decent living. His comments on blacks suggest that he associates them with laziness and welfare and with claims to receiving special treatment at work, through programs such as affirmative action. He says:

> Blacks have a tendency to . . . try to get off doing less, the least possible . . . to keep the job, where whites will put in that extra oomph. I know this is a generality and it does not go for all, it goes for a portion. It's this whole unemployment and welfare gig. A lot of the blacks on welfare have no desire to get off it. Why should they? It's free money. I can't stand to see *my hard-earned money* [said with emphasis] going to pay for someone who wants to sit on his ass all day long and get free money.

That the fruits of his own efforts are appropriated by people who do not have his courage is unbearable to Vincent, and his self-identity as hardworking is tied to his depiction of blacks as being the opposite of himself. Jim Jennings, the tin factory foreman, echoes these feelings when he associates blacks with laziness and welfare. He thinks that if there is a problem today, "it's mostly among the blacks, where you see them sitting on a street corner . . . Make them earn their money instead of just sitting around drinking their beer, or wine, or whatever, or just collecting [voice raising] *off us poor guys that gotta work.*"

Other white workers complain that blacks do not want to take responsibility for their situations and that they claim special privileges because of their past exploitation. For Vincent, "you hear it on TV all the time: [blacks say] 'we don't have to do this because we were slaves 400 years ago. You owe it to us.' I don't owe you shit, period! I had nothing to do with that and I'm not going to pay for it." A printer states, "I hate people using the excuse that we were oppressed because we were black. Let's face it [the Los Angeles rioters] who were out to start to make trouble, they were dressed better than me. They weren't that oppressed. I hate that part of the differences in races, to use that as an excuse, to have a chip on their shoulder." Similarly, Tony Sansone resented that his black coworkers get preferential treatment—in his view, they can receive phone calls from their girlfriends while he himself cannot call his insurance company, even though his black coworkers are less dedicated to their work than he. Speaking of blacks in general, he

wishes they would fight more to survive on their own, just as he himself does against all odds. For these white workers, their perceptions of
African Americans take their meaning against the backdrop of their
own incessant efforts to struggle for survival. In their view, this situation is unbearable because "not giving up" is so central to their own
senses of self. They underscore a concrete link between the perceived
dependency of blacks, their laziness, and the taxes that are taken from
their own paychecks.

Whites also cite special privileges associated with affirmative action,
perhaps the most contentious policy issue around which the American
racial drama is played. Whites view it as particularly unfair because they
believe they can count only on themselves to get ahead in life. This is
essential to their class identity as they believe that it differentiates them
from the middle class: they rarely get a break and no one is trying to
pass on advantages to them.[18] They are angry that they have to work
harder than blacks to be promoted while they also go through great
pain to remain self-reliant. Tim Williams, the construction worker on
Long Island, captures this tension: "It just bitters me that even at work,
the [minority] coalition comes in and I have to give up my job because
I'm not black. That's ridiculous. I mean I'm out there, I've got a wife
and kid. The money is green, it doesn't care whose hands it's in." Similarly, a heating system specialist who takes great pride in his expert
knowledge and work ethic complains about the laziness of black people
who are hired to satisfy quota requirements for federal government
contracts. He believes that "they make you prejudiced by using their
skin. The blacks that 'made' their job [had an internal promotion] are
good. The new ones, the guys come in late, nothing happens. The
supervisors couldn't even say 'boo' to these guys, so they sat on their
butt all day long."

Even workers who do not view themselves as racist express concern
about affirmative action because it makes white people bitter: "All that
it does is if someone is white and they lose their job to a black person
only because that person is black, the white person now has a great
amount of animosity, his family is going to be bitter, his friends are
going to be bitter, he's going to tell everybody . . . So where one person
gets a job, maybe 25 people have said, 'Oh! They've done it again, we're
losing out to the blacks.'" In fact, a 1990 survey by the National Opin-

ion Research Center reveals that only 7 percent of white respondents believe that they have personally experienced reverse discrimination, while only 16 percent said they know someone who has. Also, fewer than 25 percent claim that they have witnessed reverse discrimination in their workplace. Nevertheless, over 70 percent of whites believe they are likely to be hurt by affirmation action for blacks.[19]

The central role of work performance in the racial attitudes of whites is also supported by the claims of whites who argue for the equality of the races. They say that they have real respect for blacks who know their job and pull their weight. For instance, Joe Lasco, the Elizabeth police officer, expresses this in criticizing white southerners he knows who think that every black is a "nigger": "I tell them no. There is two different kinds. The kind that work like you and me and then you have your 'nigger.'" Men like Joe believe they apply the same criteria of evaluation to all, criteria grounded in the universalistic principles of hard work by which they judge themselves and by which others give them status. These universal criteria lead some of these men to feel justified in evaluating blacks negatively and to perceive themselves as moral people who are not racists, but realistic.

Blacks as Collective Violators of Traditional Morality

A remarkably large number of Americans believe that blacks and whites live in different worlds,[20] that we are witnessing a unique crisis in black America, and that the destruction of the black family is to blame for it because "morals don't get taught." This theme is echoed by a number of moralist books published over the last few years that lament the moral crisis of society, of the black family, and "of our times,"[21] and by academic books that depict the United States as split by a deep moral divide.[22] Similarly, the workers I talked to come to the defense of traditional morality while drawing racial boundaries.

Talk of family values by politicians and other public figures offers workers important points of reference, and indeed these workers often discuss "family values," a theme central to media discourse at the time I conducted the interviews.[23] In the eyes of Stan Morley, a pipe fitter, "I could have ended up stealing cars and stuff too if I wanted. I was brought up better than that . . . I think [blacks] have less family values. If you don't have a family, how can you have family values?" To a civil servant, "it has to go back to the way they was raised as a kid. They had to be taught by somebody with certain morals involved. Today the kids, the blacks, they don't even have respect for their parents today and it's getting bad . . . The kids today take everything for granted." Similarly, Larry Relles, a policeman who works outside of Newark, in Paterson, says that among blacks, "there's no sense of family . . . I come across kids that have no conception of reality, no respect for life, no respect for property, no respect for themselves." Alan Hayward, the born-again train conductor, says of black people, "their morals aren't being taught. You know it should be instilled in your children from the beginning. Because of one-parent families. Because of the broken families." He adds that his place of work has been trying to hire black engineers, but the ones hired "gamble, they are not married, they're more or less hanging out. It's strange, you know. Everyone's going home to their families while these two . . . Believe me, I went through phases too. I liked the black nude women, stuff like that. But they have no leader. They have no leader to lead them out of any problems."

The views of these workers resemble those of the nineteenth-century white workers studied by historian David Roediger: they equated being disciplined with whiteness and viewed blacks as embodying a "preindustrial, erotic, careless style of life the white worker hated and longed for."[24] According to Roediger, this caricature of blacks provided white workers with a way to cope "with the fear of dependency on wage labor and the necessities of capitalist work discipline." Similarly, the workers I interviewed wage a symbolic fight to keep racial groups separate from one another, partly in response to their insecurity concerning their own social status. Although an invisible or taken-for-granted category, whiteness continues to stand for what these workers cherish and value.

White workers also readily associate blacks with violence. For instance, Larry Relles, the policeman who works in the Newark area, explains that he is prejudiced against blacks because "it's pretty much from bad experiences through work and as a kid. Blacks were always the perpetrators of crime . . . through experience you become prejudiced. To say I'm not would be a lie." Black tenants destroyed an apartment he owns. He confesses that "I was ready to give up on the black race as far as being tenants . . . I'm trying to be liberal and keep an open mind.

Technically by law whoever answers the ad, you got to rent to them. But I was going to sell the house before I rent to blacks again." He has now reached a point where he is ready to move to the country to create a buffer between himself and "the environment." In his view, "It's getting real hard nowadays, living so close to Newark, it's real hard to like black people. Anytime I see a black person, I'm like 'Am I going to get robbed?' That's just the way you got to feel."

Murray DiPrete, a receiving clerk, also associates blacks with crime, pointing to the experience he has gathered in the neighborhood where he lives. "I try not to be prejudiced, but it seems that I have a real hatred for these car thieves. I live in a very high crime area and it's predominantly black. When I can afford it, I'll leave . . . I'm sick and tired of seeing these skuzzy individuals. So I have my animosities and I have my prejudices." Along these lines, when asked by the 1990 General Social Survey to locate blacks on a seven-point "violence" scale, 50 percent of white respondents agreed at least somewhat with the statement "Almost all blacks are prone to violence" while only 15 percent agreed at least somewhat with the statement "Almost all blacks are not prone to violence."[25] Other surveys also show that blacks are perceived as being more aggressive and more likely to engage in crime than whites.[26]

Finally, white workers believe that blacks often violate the moral norm of personal integrity, which was emphasized in their discussions of the types of people they appreciate most. One man I talked to, John Bridges, a warehouse worker, questions the integrity of blacks, providing evidence from his own experience growing up with blacks:

> They have no integrity. I'm not even saying some, I'm saying most. They shift with the moon . . . The ones in this area specifically. The ones that I've grown up with, who come from the socioeconomic background that I'm accustomed to, I do not like and I do not trust . . . I've come to a point in my life where I have sit through a lot of the bullshit. I've been wrestling with it a lot too because I also feel compassion for a lot of "those people" as I call them . . . I've noticed bleeding hearts are often people who have never lived with them . . . In my life, I've lived 36 years in a racially mixed community. I'd like to spend my next 35 in a less racially mixed place. I think that's my prerogative.

If white workers are so anxious about black violation of moral boundaries, it is in part because, as shown in Chapter 1, they feel that their world is threatened on various fronts simultaneously. Studies have often linked racism to the dominant group's perceptions of economic threat.[27] These threats affect not only workers' economic and social position, as is generally suggested, but also their general sense of social order. Workers often condemn the moral failings of blacks in the same breath that they lament the downfall of American society. This is best expressed by train conductor Alan Hayward, who brings together concerns about social decline, family values, law and order, and protecting the family:

> They're going down hill. We think racism is being caused by a lot of people [whose] parents don't teach them the right way—or they don't have parents. Or just one parent. We see it and hear it. When I go to work, I travel into New York to Queens by train. What I see lately, I don't like. Very evil-looking faces. I think Mayor Dinkins has not done a great job as mayor . . . He is pandering too much . . . I'm against special interest groups like the ACLU. Like I see black and white, they see gray. I don't see gray. You're either black or white, that's it! Right or wrong. If you commit murder, I think you should be put to death, I'm sorry! . . . I am worried about my daughter, my wife, when they go outside right now because something will happen when I'm not there.

White workers frame their own racism in patriotic terms when they argue that blacks threaten what is good about American society. They are particularly upset by this because being an American is one of the few high-status characteristics they claim. Accordingly, research shows that "patriotism among whites [is] associated with classical racism, whereas patriotism among minorities is associated with opposite attitudes, suggesting that very different aspects of American society are tapped into by nationalists in the two groups."[28] For white workers in New Jersey, the economic decline of Newark in the seventies and eighties and the simultaneous growth in the black population confirm the connection between blacks and social decline. Harry Donaway, the tool and dye maker who grew up in Newark, notes: "I'll put it to you this way. I grew up in an all-white town . . . They ruined my town . . . White people moved out. I can deal with a black person. But you give me the kinds of things they're doing today! I have no feelings for those people at all. I have no feelings for a lot of the people that ruined *our* Newark."

Whites perceive blacks as taking over spatially as well as demographically. As Alan Hayward points out, "the blacks right now, one in six of the kids being born are black. It used to be one in thirty in 1968 or something like that, just to give you a comparison. Now it's one in six. The whites got to learn to stick together more." Similarly, Larry Relles, the white policeman, says, "The stores in my town for the most part are 90 percent blacks or better, being there's no more stores left in Newark. I know what it's like to be the reverse where I'm the minority. I go in there and the way the people act and behave in there, I can't take it. They're rude. Would never yield to let you go, you always have to force your way."

My white respondents explain racial differences by a mix of natural, historical, psychological, and cultural arguments. Several suggest that laziness is part of the "nature" of blacks or comes from a culture that is so deeply ingrained and rooted in history that it is not easily changed and is passed on from one generation to the next in an almost unalterable manner.

A few workers offer genetic explanations of perceived racial differences in intelligence. For instance, a warehouse worker believes that "you can't make [blacks] learn" and that "white people pick it up much faster." Another warehouse worker believes that blacks have less practical intelligence than whites—a dimension of intelligence particularly valued by workers. In his view this is evidenced by Michael Jackson's failings: he makes millions and is unable to save. Survey data suggest that these workers are not exceptional. Indeed, when the 1990 General Social Survey asked white respondents to place blacks as a group on a seven-point scale with "unintelligent" at one end and "intelligent" at the other, 28 percent placed blacks on the unintelligent side of the scale and only 20 percent chose the "intelligent" side.[29] Nevertheless, the use of genetic arguments about racial differences has declined since World War II, as symbolic racism based on cultural differences gained in popularity.[30] However, the lasting cultural influence of eugenics is suggested by the popularity of *The Bell Curve,* by Richard Herrnstein and Charles Murray, which sold 400,000 copies in a few months after it was published in October 1994. The book has been interpreted as an attempt to give a genetic basis to attacks against the welfare poor by providing evidence of their lower performance on standardized tests.[31] Chapter 5 will reveal that French workers do not provide genetic explanations of racial inequality.

To summarize: for white workers moral and racial boundaries are inseparable from one another. Whether they focus on differences in the areas of work ethic, responsibility, family values, or traditional morality, interviewees move seamlessly from morality to race, extending their moral distinctions to broad racial categories. They view these moral boundaries as legitimate because they are based on the same universal criteria of evaluation that are at the center of their larger worldviews. They are thus able to make racist arguments and still feel that they are fundamentally good, fair people. They also avoid feelings of responsibility toward the disadvantaged while defining themselves as whites—that is, disciplined and moral. By doing so, they contribute to the formation of racial inequality.

White Antiracism: Market Arguments and the Universality of Human Nature (Purple or Green)

There are, to be sure, white workers who express antiracist positions. They privilege two types of arguments to demonstrate that whites and blacks are equal, and these have to do with earning ability and human nature.

In the American workplace, where an ideology of meritocracy prevails and where ascribed characteristics are in principle irrelevant in the assessment of employees' performances, money is often used, paradoxically, as a basis for equalization.[32] Just as racists use work ethic and self-reliance to criticize blacks, nonracists argue that earning capacity makes people equal, market mechanisms being the ultimate arbitrator of the value of people. Most tellingly, as we saw in the introductory chapter, Michael Brandon, a petroleum company foreman, explains that "No matter who you are at Exxon, you're making pretty good money, so it's not like you've got a disadvantaged person. Their kids are going to good schools. They're eating, they're taking vacations because of Exxon. You don't see the division or whatever, so Exxon kind of eliminated that because of the salary structure . . . With black people, you talk sports, you talk school, you're all in the same boat. It isn't 'What's it like to have a new car?' You know, you talk to the guy, and you went on vacation, and he went on vacation."

Michael presumes a community of citizens in which membership and dignity are based on work, earning capacity, and consumption.[33] In fact, the legitimacy of earning capacity as a criterion of evaluation is one of the few assumptions shared by American racists and nonracists. Michael echoes the productivist/republican tradition central to the American workers' movement from its inception, and according to which individuals legitimized gaining social and political membership by being self-reliant and productive.[34] A number of antiracist (and racist) workers take market performance to be a legitimate and efficient arbitrator of worth, in contrast to the socio-democratic European (and French) model in which the market produces inequalities that must be remedied by the state.[35] Having high-status occupations can make blacks equal to whites, but otherwise, at least in the eyes of John Bridges the warehouse worker, there is no such equality. He explains that "most of the black people I get along with either come from parents who are professionals or families where there were both parents. [They are] more stable. Not the street niggers. They're different. They live more off the land." This claim about racial equality, a form of antiracism, is classist as it correlates people's worth with their class position.

White workers often offer as additional evidence of the equality of races the universality of human nature across races. While racists treat the black individuals they know well—their coworkers or neighbors—as exceptions, stating that "you might not like the race but you like the person,"[36] nonracists argue that good and bad people are found in all races. In the words of Billy Taylor, the foreman in a cosmetics company, "I could have a problem with you as a black but I could have the same problem if you were white, or green, or yellow, or whatever. People are people. There's good cops, there's bad cops. There's good whites, there's bad whites . . . I haven't noticed any major cultural differences."

Similarly, for Murray DiPrete, the receiving clerk who admits to having "my prejudices," "there are blacks and there are niggers. There are whites and there is white trash. There are wonderful Spanish people and there are Spics . . . If you are a skuzzball, then I want nothing to do with you no matter where you come from . . . I like nice people, period." A truck driver also stresses the importance of treating people case by case: "If you treat me nice and you and I get along, great. If you treat me bad, then I try to decide on my own how people are and how I'm going to deal with people, and it does not matter if you are black or white, or pink, or purple, or yellow, or green. If you're a miserable SOB, you're just a miserable SOB, no matter what color you are."

These men posit that human nature is universal and that one should not generalize about blacks or any other races since there are so many differences among people.[37] A mechanic goes further by universalizing this principle beyond race to talk about the importance of treating everyone equally, even in the context of class differences:

> It comes down to: whatever color you are, treat everybody fairly and don't be prejudiced. I don't want the blacks to be prejudiced against me [thinking] I'm the same as every other white person. I think I'm willing to give them a chance and the same thing as white people. Just because they don't own a house, they live in an apartment, they're driving a bombed-up car, and their kids are dressed sloppy, I'm not gonna just assume that they're white trash and I'm gonna treat them fairly. If I did work for them, I'd do just as good a job as I could and I'd give them a price as fairly as I could until I see them doing something that's gonna hurt me or somebody else.

This mechanic is exceptional in his belief that we should ignore ascribed characteristics and accord equality to all. He also rejects the notion that we should only be fair to "our own kind." The infrequency of this universalist argument among workers is particularly striking in light of the prominence of egalitarianism in American political culture, starting with the first lines of the Declaration of Independence. In Chapter 4, we will see that French workers' attitudes toward blacks are very different: there, antiracism is articulated around arguments pertaining specifically to human solidarity and to the equal dignity of human beings, and market performance arguments are absent.

Note that only one American respondent, a clerical worker, promotes the principle of multiculturalism by celebrating the importance of "exposing our children to a diversity of people so that when they hear slurs, they can ward off these preconceptions [better] than others who don't have experience with people from different backgrounds." Cultural relativism, multiculturalism, or the celebration of racial differences, which are widely viewed in academic circles as effective antidotes to racism,[38] are absent from the worldviews of the workers with whom I spoke.[39] Perhaps antiracist academic discourse should focus more on the theme of the universality of human nature, as it might resonate better with the worldview of ordinary people than more intellectual arguments having to do with multiculturalism and cultural relativism. The latter arguments (also called "race recognizance" in the literature)[40] might appeal more to college graduates, who tend to be more tolerant and to appreciate a wider range of cultural tastes and practices than high school graduates.[41]

Morality, Racial Boundaries, and the Broader Context

Theories of racism that emerged in the last 20 years have generally been concerned with new forms of racism that are moral in character, and that are contrasted with the old-fashioned racism prevalent under Jim Crow segregation that was more explicit and often stressed the biological inferiority of blacks. Most notably, social scientists have proposed the terms "symbolic racism,"[42] "subtle racism,"[43] "aversive racism,"[44] and "modern racism"[45] to point out that racism now takes the following form: white Americans value individualism, self-reliance, a work ethic, obedience, and discipline, and they believe that blacks violate these values. Thus, they say that their racism is motivated not by a dislike of blacks but by a concern for key American values.[46] While these contributions all focus on the importance of whites' beliefs concerning the moral qua cultural failings of blacks, they generally posit such beliefs or predefine a few of them as particularly important.[47] My interviews complement this influential work by documenting inductively whites' perceptions of the differences between themselves and the "racial other." They also illuminate meaningful patterns by the absence of arguments that are telling of what whites take for granted. For instance, it is notable that whites do not stigmatize blacks for not being straightforward. Thus, by using as a point of departure the general moral worldviews of workers, rather than racism itself, we can get at the very framework through which they think about racial differences instead of predefining the issue for them with questions that speak to racism as we understand it.[48]

That white workers struggle to keep the world in moral order in the face of adversity and uncertainty explains why they would be particularly concerned with those whom they perceive as upsetting this order. That they come to single out blacks as the main source of disturbance, and that they generalize specific observations to encompass the group as a whole, has to do with a number of cultural and structural factors.

At the cultural level, guided by survey responses documenting what political platform would appeal to workers, the Republican Party has had a profound impact in influencing how this group thinks about racial differences. This party's position toward blacks resembles that of Democrat George Wallace, who combined an antigovernment position with a rejection of racial desegregation policies to win white working class votes in the sixties.[49] The ascendancy of the Republican Party in the eighties and the move of the Democratic Party to the right in the nineties meant that justifying social policies in the name of solidarity among all human beings, as promoted by progressive forces, became increasingly difficult.[50] This same Republican ascendancy has emphasized family values to attack both welfare programs and race-targeted policies. Public figures, such as political commentator Rush Limbaugh, increase the availability of a racialized moral language through the mass media.[51] This language often treats blacks as a useful explanation for all that is wrong with American society.

Some of the main characteristics of the antiracism of the workers can also be accounted for by cultural factors, such as the growing legitimacy of egalitarian strands of thought in American culture over the last 30 years. Support for egalitarianism, defined as equality in the opportunity to compete, is alive and well in American society. Indeed, 98 percent of whites responding to a national survey agreed with the statement "everyone in America should have equal opportunities to get ahead."[52] Also, 97 percent believe that blacks should have a chance equal to that of whites to get any kind of job.[53] This support for egalitarianism makes it increasingly difficult for individuals to promote old-fashioned racism that affirms biological inequality between races or to assert racial discrimination in the name of blatantly bigoted beliefs. That market performance is used as evidence of racial equality is also not surprising, given the centrality of market ideology in American society.

At the structural level, economic recession, such as that in the early 1990s, the time of the interviews, fosters among workers a sense of economic insecurity, lack of opportunity, and racial threat, especially in the context of personal and national downward mobility. The increase in black teenage pregnancy also supports the view that, demographically, blacks are "taking over" and pushing the country downhill. These structural factors, along with the relative availability of specific cultural repertoires discussed above, have combined to perpetuate to some extent the lasting impact of slavery and Jim Crow segregation on the way white Americans understand and evaluate black Americans. This structural and cultural account of the construction of blackness by white workers centers on their environment and as such eschews elements of psychological reductionism found in some influential studies of the construction of blackness.[54]

I mentioned at the beginning of the chapter that blacks play little role in the mental maps of professionals and managers. This is in part because blacks are even less present in upper middle class neighborhoods and workplaces than they are in those of white workers.[55] The low salience of blacks to professionals may also be accounted for by the fact that the latter have learned to conceal racist attitudes. This hypothesis is supported by research showing that (1) compared to the non-college-educated, the college-educated express subtle, as opposed to blatant, racism, and hence are less likely to make explicitly racist statements[56] (and, indeed, high school graduates are repeatedly found to express more prejudiced attitudes than the college-educated);[57] and (2) opposition to race-targeted policies is weakest among the college-educated and strongest among the self-identified working class.[58]

BLACKS ON WHITES

How do blacks think about whites? This has rarely been studied. White and black folks have "stomach equality," I was told by a black textile-industry worker. They have similar needs but also similar dreams: "a decent paying job, a few credit cards, a car that's decent and a nice place to live. I think people in a certain age, a certain income bracket, their thinking is just about equal or the same." "Inner peace is the same for all," a chemical plant operator told me, by which he means "good education for the kids, an environment that you could come to and have nice things and not have them destroyed or vandalized, or threatened in any way, and have a lawn to cut." For a black supervisor who works in a book bindery, "black, white, green, blue, whatever, we all want to be happy, we all want to be loved. We all want to be comfortable. I think it is a human thing."

These men share with the white nonracists a belief in the universality of human nature. However, they also have to confront the fact that the principles of "stomach equality" or "common human nature" do not translate into equal treatment. They turn to arguments having to do with market performance (as producers and consumers) to ground equality, making worth conditional on individual achievement and class. They also mobilize criteria of evaluation related to the "disciplined self" valued by whites, suggesting the pervasiveness of the criteria whites take to be universal. However, exemplifying the tension between assimilation and separation that has historically divided the black community, black workers also offer a critical perspective on whites by describing them as domineering and antithetical to the caring qualities blacks value. In doing so, some rebut the notion of racial inequality not by showing that races are equal but by showing that blacks are superior to whites.

"Money Makes You Equal": Earnings, Consumption, and Competence as Bases of Cultural Membership

John Lamb is a black worker employed by a recycling plant in Paterson. A native of Georgia, he thinks that northerners are uncaring and hopes to return to the South soon, perhaps to find a wife ("a high quality person"). He built a house in Georgia, and on his last trip there he found it defaced with "KKK" graffiti on the front door and the porch. Barely 31, he "pulls in $60,000 a year" thanks to "lots of overtime." He remains very close to his family and the tight-knit community where he grew up, but he also likes to "do his own thing." He "like[s] religious people, people that believe in respecting people and treating people right," and is attracted to black homeowners.

John has often had to deal with racial discrimination at work and has given much thought to racial equality. In his theory of how the world works, money is what gives everyone voice, including blacks. He says: "Money separates people . . . It gives you power in the world, it gives you an ability to do anything you want in the world . . . That's the way the world's set up. Regardless of what you hear on this or that, money means everything." John also believes that money is the key to respect and, implicitly, to equality and social membership (i.e., to being construed as "belonging"): "If you ain't got no money, you got no respect at all. You can be the smartest, prettiest woman, man, or whatever, on earth, but that don't get you nowhere. You got to have some money to back you up. Money gets you places. Money gets you to get to meet anybody you want to meet, get involved in anything that's going on. Money's basically everything, without a doubt."

For John, competence is the other key to access to mainstream society and to social membership:

> Basically it comes down to, once you prove yourself that you're just as good as [your white coworkers] . . . that you can do anything they do just as well as them, and you carry yourself with that weight, then people respect you, they kinda back away from you. I'm kind of quiet, I just go there, I don't miss a day on the job, I do what I gotta do, and I'm one of the best throughout the whole plant at what I do.

Competence is a particularly legitimate piece of evidence of equality in a blue-collar world where coworkers are often direct witnesses of each other's expertise on the job and where physical proximity leaves little room for hiding mistakes. Accordingly, skilled workers often express pride in their know-how and respect for those who do their work properly.

Tyrone Smith, a chemical plant worker, shares John's perspective, though he extends it to cultural membership and stresses consumption over production. He says:

> I'm accepted [at work] and I work with really white people. I think when you get into the money scheme, it doesn't really mat-

ter [what color you are], because then the money makes it equal
. . . I'm overcoming [the limits put on me because of my race]
because I am achieving the same thing [as my coworkers]
money-wise. If I was poor and on welfare, they would just call
me another nigger on the street. I may not be as equal as them,
but they know it's not too much below. If they buy a house, I
could buy a house too.

It is this reasoning about money that leads Tyrone to say that class is
a greater divider than race in American society: "I don't see Caucasians
as having different values than blacks. I see people in different places in
life, different classes having different values. The upper blacks and
upper whites are all the same. The poor whites and the poor blacks,
they are all the same. It's more class. It is basically more of what your
background is."

Others follow Tyrone in stressing consumption as a criterion for cultural membership, equating money with "belonging."[59] Abe Lind, a 32-
year-old plumber who lives on Long Island, offers evidence of his place
in mainstream society by describing his childhood as follows: "I never
lived in an apartment, I always had my own room. I never thought that
I was lacking anything that was provided by a white man, that my father was inadequate in any way . . . I always got a new bike. We had
Christmas, I mean. I received allowances. They had new shoes, I had
new shoes. I never had that problem."

These workers put less emphasis on production than consumption as
evidence of equality. Under slavery and Jim Crow, the ability to work
did not give African Americans cultural, let alone civic, membership.
They indeed produced but could not consume. Today, work gives access to consumption, that is, to external signals that one is "in" (a bike,
new shoes, and, later, a car, a house). Working and consuming are individual strategies for coping with racism, in that they signal that one
"belongs."[60] However, these strategies of equalization perpetuate particularism, in the sense that they are unevenly spread across groups, even
though they are in principle available to all.[61]

When using market performance as a criterion to establish equality,
workers follow in the footsteps of black leaders who have promoted

similar strategies to "uplift the race," sometimes to assert their own elite status and sometimes to signify collective aspiration to citizenship and humanity.[62] Indeed, both Booker T. Washington and W. E. B. Du Bois advocated work as a means to establish the worth of blacks. The historian of black liberation ideology George Fredrickson also notes that "to counter [the claim that black people are morally and intellectually inferior] . . . the case had to be made for the natural equality of all human beings, and specifically black or African achievements and capabilities had to be demonstrated."[63] This universalistic strategy of claiming equal status can be opposed to a particularistic one that consists of reversing the racial hierarchy "that would place formerly subordinate groups in a position of dominance over their erstwhile superior."[64] It is to this latter strategy that I now turn.

The Moral Failings of White People and the Superiority of Black People

John Lamb and Abe Lind have much to say about the moral flaws of white people. John describes the other workers in the recycling plant, who are predominantly white, as sneaky. He says:

> They try to basically figure, get into your personality, [see] what you think about certain things, and why. Ninety-nine percent of the white people constantly ask you . . . How you spend your money, what you do with your money, what kind of girlfriend you deal with. Do you deal with Hispanic women? Do you deal with white women? . . . A black person couldn't care less . . . I guess it's competitive. I guess [whites] probably [want to know]: Do black men think their womens is the choice of the female over black race or Hispanic race? Or their politician is the choice over a black politician?

John thinks that white people always try to trick you, that they are rarely favorably disposed. Abe Lind, the Long Island plumber, has an even more negative perspective. He works for a white boss in a totally white environment. Although he wants to "be absorbed in the American dream," he says,

White people . . . probably 95 percent of the time they're going to . . . screw me over, and probably 35 percent of the time I think that blacks are going to do that. So when I meet a white person, I'm scared they're going to do something really sneaky and nasty . . . Screw you over, trying to set you up, being nosy, trying to get you fired from your job, trying to trick you to go to certain places and do something wrong, . . . frame you, everything you think that a person can do that's no good . . . Sell you things that are no good, get you hooked on drugs, alcohol. Yeah, I believe in that. A matter of fact I think black people do think about white people that way, yeah. Honestly, I think 95 percent do believe that.

John thinks that whites are inherently domineering. Blacks, he says, "didn't create the bomb, we didn't play with gunpowder, we didn't do this . . . The interest of white America was always to build and be better and be competitive, and in doing that, that's more reading and sitting and studying and being more manipulative, and more deceiving, and more, you know, whereas we weren't."

The domineering tendencies of whites are also emphasized by Leon Davis, a letter carrier concerned with white cultural imperialism. He explains:

I see [whites] as being, or as wanting to be, the dominant force in everything. I see them as being intolerant of other lifestyles and other thoughts from other people—what other people think. Especially American whites . . . They think everybody, I mean other people from other countries or other races, should bend and do things their way. If your clothes are not like theirs, you're funny. If you can't speak English, you're inferior . . . [Americans] want to impose their philosophy or thoughts on other people.

Similar examples abound. For instance, a phone installer told me that whites have a "superior attitude. They think they are above you, you know." A bindery worker concurs: whites "try to be more domineering. Some of them have a more superior attitude if you allow them to get away with it."

In describing moral differences between whites and blacks, black workers often point to whites' individualistic worldviews and their lack of caring. A truck driver contrasts the domineering tendencies of whites with the playfulness of blacks when he says that "white people are always looking for a way to beat you . . . [Blacks] enjoy having a good time, hanging out in the park, playing sports, stuff like that." For a worker in a medical firm, blacks are also more laid-back: "We have more fun because we weren't pressured into studying. That's not a big priority for blacks." Blacks are also more caring and intimate, especially when compared to whites. This is explained by Craig Patterson, who works as a cable splicer for a New York City utility:

> Blacks have a strong sense of family, a strong sense of togetherness. White people they don't take as much time with their families as we do . . . They let their kids be much more on their own. Whites, their kids will go maybe to school away from home and might come home one weekend a year . . . And then when they're there, the parents are always going somewhere and they have a baby-sitter, then they have a nanny. That's to me, that's a big difference in a lot of the black families compared to the white families. I mean, I don't know if it makes the kid eventually better. But it's just, as far as the closeness and stuff, it's different.

Jerry Flowers, a machinist who works in Elizabeth, New Jersey, captures the situation succinctly: "Black people are sensitive toward human needs because we are concerned humans, whereas the white people that I have met in my life seem detached from the human thing."

Some black workers indirectly point to the disciplined selves of whites, which they define in opposition to the worldview of blacks. Tony Clark, who works for a medical supply company on Long Island, contrasts how whites and blacks experience spirituality. For blacks, what is important is to believe in God, to believe in hope, believe in Heaven and Hell. To believe that if you live a good life, and you are a good person, generally, good will come from it. When I relate to a white person, they seem to have a more structured aspect of it . . . They say you can't go [to church in blue jeans and sneakers] because that wouldn't be polite. That's not right . . . They live in boxes. Some have more corners cut off. There are things they can't relate to.

Whites' overly disciplined self is defined in opposition to "black soul," which is manifested in the black religious experience and has been defined as natural "primal spiritual energy and joy available only to members of the exclusive racial confraternity."[65] A worker in a car factory finds in the spiritual realm additional evidence of the moral superiority of blacks over whites: "White people, they go to church too, but their worship, mostly, is different than blacks. I don't think they get the same feeling, the same results. We go to church and we feel the Holy Ghost."

In sum, blacks describe whites as nosy, competitive, disciplined ("reading and sitting," "studying"), domineering, sneaky, manipulative, deceiving, and intolerant, but they describe blacks as more accepting, caring, tolerant, straightforward, egalitarian, and fun-loving.[66] They define the identities of the two groups relationally, and they value most those aspects of the self that they perceive whites as valuing less. This resonates with a key finding in social psychology concerning the dynamics between in-group and out-group: one of the mechanisms by which members of stigmatized groups protect their self-esteem from negative feedback is by "selectively devaluing, or regarding as less important for their self-definition, those performance dimensions on which they or their group fare poorly and selectively valuing those dimensions on which they or their group excel."[67]

Hence, the white individualist, domineering, and disciplined self is opposed to the caring black self. These black perspectives on whites are not surprising given African Americans' experience of slavery, segregation, discrimination, and racism, which do not sustain a "kinder, gentler" view of whites. This portrayal of whites echoes more general themes central to black nationalist groups, including the Black Power movement. As pointed out by historian William Van Deburg, the portrayal of "whitey" in Black Power writings was not flattering: "A people who pretended to be the crown of creation actually were the scum of the earth . . . It was said that from earliest times, whites had exhibited a vast array of unflattering traits."[68] Recent surveys show that "one in four blacks agree that more than half [of whites] 'personally share the attitudes of groups like the Ku Klux Klan toward blacks.'"[69] This is echoed in results from a 1994 national survey that shows that 79 percent of blacks agreed with the claim that whites "believe they are superior and can boss other people around" while only 15 percent of blacks disagreed.[70] However, when a 1992 Gallup poll asked black respondents whether "on the whole . . . white people . . . want to keep blacks down," only 20 percent believed so, and 36 percent believed that whites simply don't care one way or the other.[71]

There is another arena in which blacks find evidence of their moral superiority: in the resilience that comes from experiencing hardship. A maintenance worker says, "We have had to fight, that fighting edge is inside of you. [If] a black person loses all his money, the IRS takes all the money, he falls right back down and he'll have to live with that. He's been there, he knows that place. Where the white guy, he might commit suicide and kill himself because he don't have that much money left."[72] Dealing with hardship also teaches blacks to appreciate what they have. This is something that is lacking among white children, in the eyes of a truck driver who coaches Little League: "When you deal with black kids, you dealing with attitude kids. They gotta sort of fight. In reality they gotta fight for everything they get . . . Most of them don't live at home, they live with grandma. They don't have nothing and when they find someone that's really nice to them, they really appreciate it more than white kids. No matter how much you give to a white kid, that ain't enough for him. Especially if he's from the suburbs."

Finally, several African Americans ground their belief in the superiority of blacks in genetic, as opposed to moral, resilience. John Lamb, the recycling specialist, explains that blacks could survive slavery by their superior genetic endowments and through God's protection:

> I guess one way to describe and bring [what I think] out to you is, if blacks wouldn't be the superior race, I don't think we'd be living now . . . If there wasn't a God, black people shouldn't exist

in this country. Throughout slavery, the way the black women was raped, the way black people was hung and killed by animals and dogs, and stuff like that . . . The white race, they tried to destroy the Jewish race. They destroyed the Indians, they don't exist anymore, very rarely do you see some. The black race was under the same situation, but it was worse for the black race than for them races. And you look at the population of the black race now . . . Somebody above had to look out for them. The black race is the only race you can marry with a thousand nationalities, have a kid, that kid is going to come out black, you know when you mix that blood. There's a lot of different things that make me wonder why is the black race superior.

Black constructions of whites are correctly described in the historical literature as part of a process of resistance to the domination of whites.[73] However, I view them above all as an expression of blacks' sense of common identity and the standards (the "caring self") they invest in, independently of the unintended consequences of this process for resistance. These men "feel" a racial difference, and this feeling comes out of their understanding of their everyday experience and the repertoires to which they have access—such as those provided by the black nationalist movements—as much as from the need to preserve their dignity and integrity. My interviews shed light on how contemporary black resistance is framed by spelling out some of the underexplored categories through which black collective identity is defined in opposition to that of whites.[74]

How can we account for differences in the boundaries drawn by whites toward blacks and blacks toward whites that have been described so far? Social psychologists have identified fundamental psychological processes suggesting that the combination of moral and racial boundaries just described is universal: they argue that there is a universal tendency for members of all groups, including racial groups, to have in-group biases and to be discriminatory toward out-groups. There is also a tendency to attribute behavior to enduring dispositions, such as attitudes and personality traits (often moral traits), instead of to situation and to associate high-status social identity with worthiness.[75] This may explain why white workers rarely use structural explanations to account for racial differences (but not why blacks do use such explanations): white workers seldom refer to the socioeconomic situation of blacks or to their lasting experience of discrimination and white domination to explain their plight. They interpret the alleged economic "failure" of blacks as a consequence of moral failure. They use much the same explanation to account for poverty generally, as we will see in the next chapter.[76] The existence of such universal psychological mechanisms, however, does not account for the specific moral themes that I have documented for whites and blacks. Neither does it account for their greater salience for a racial out-group than for an immigrant out-group (as discussed in the next section) or for their greater salience in the United States than in France (as we will see in Chapter 5). To account for these patterns, we have to refer to structural and cultural conditions that have characterized American (and French) society over the last decades.

The institutions that played an important role in diffusing black collectivist conceptions of morality (discussed in Chapter 1) have an impact here—for instance, the black church. The civil rights movement has also given blacks a collective experience of a kind that whites rarely share. Hence, the notions of solidarity and egalitarianism resonate with their shared past. Finally, the less collectivist aspects of their understanding of racial equality can also be linked to their group experience. For instance, that they use consumption (as opposed to production) as a proof of equality has to be related to the historical meaning of production for them as dislocated from citizenship.

What Brings Us Together: Children of God, Family of Man, Physiology, and Citizenship

To rebut the notion of racial inequality, blacks mobilize other pieces of evidence than those used by whites. Unlike most of the evidence analyzed so far, these are not articulated around the notions of the "disciplined self" and the "caring self" or around the notion that blacks are superior to whites. It is useful to examine these pieces of evidence because they suggest that blacks use a wider range of antiracist arguments than whites. We will see that blacks rebut racism by adopting universalistic strategies: they provide evidence having to do with whites' and blacks' shared status as children of God, common physiology, and common status as Americans. However, some also appear to take for granted the predominance of a culture of particularism when they affirm that protecting your own kind is a universal human tendency.

Reflecting on the importance of divine intervention in black narratives of emancipation, W. E. B. Du Bois pointed out that historically the church played an important role in affirming equality and providing blacks with tools for spiritual empowerment.[77] The biblical notion that "God created men equal" was also alluded to by Martin Luther King, and it rests on a notion of basic humanity for all, with love as a basis for similarity.[78] Accordingly, blacks use religion to demonstrate that we all share something fundamental.[79] For instance, Abe Lind, the plumber, points to the diversity of God's creation to demonstrate that the races are equal. He wishes that "people would realize that we have one creator, and not many creators, and as there are many different colors of birds, and trees, and fishes, and everything that cross this globe [there are different types of people]."[80] Similarly, a black Jehovah's Witness draws on biblical themes: "Where has a man come from but the dust of the earth? If we look at the dust of the earth, we're all of color."

Black workers that I talked to do not ground racial equality in the view that as human beings we are equal before God—that divine grace is in all of us.[81] Moreover, like whites, blacks do not suggest that racial inequality results from God's will, although this view remained popular during a good part of the twentieth century.[82] Nevertheless, religious arguments are appealing to blacks in part because they offer a useful counterpoint to racist evolutionary accounts, according to which blacks are lower on the scale of human development. For instance, a photo technician combines God's creation ("we all come from Adam and Eve"), physiological evidence ("we all come out one way"), and a lineage account that stresses common descent ("family of man")[83] to refute both evolutionism and Afrocentrist views. Pointing to our common physiology adds "incontestable"—empirically grounded—proof of the wrongheadedness of racism. Other black workers noted that "we all spend nine months in our mother's womb," that we all have the same red blood running in our veins, or that we all have ten fingers. This view was not expressed among whites and goes unmentioned in survey-based studies of antiracism. We will see in Part II that

North Africans share with African Americans the use of such naturalistic pieces of evidence to counteract racism.

African Americans also rebut racism by pointing to diversity in levels of intelligence among whites, as if they presume that they have to refute what they perceive to be the widely held notion of white intellectual superiority. A young painter from New York City, who experienced other regional cultures when he was in the Army for several years, explains his perspective thus: "White people who are from rural areas would be considered less [intelligent] than people from an urban metropolitan area . . . Same people, same color." A phone technician also refers to his personal experience attending school with whites to contest the myth of their superior intelligence. He explains that when he was a kid "we were all led to believe that whites were always smarter . . . When I went to school, I found that there were dumb white people, you understand? There were poor white people . . . there was no differences in their learning ability. It made me proud." A few black workers spontaneously mentioned that they believe whites to be more intelligent than blacks. However, they accounted for this difference not by genetics but by institutional factors influencing the distribution of resources. Such factors were rarely mentioned by whites. As John Lamb explains, whites control "the education system, the school system. It comes down to money, like you said—money, money's power, influence's power."

The last type of evidence used by blacks, but not by whites, to establish equality between the two groups is that of citizenship. Several black workers refer to their common membership in the American nation, the best nation of the world, to demonstrate their social membership and, implicitly, equality between the races. Abe Lind is compelled to justify his nationalism, given the country's history of racism. To do so, he focuses on the historical openness of American society to people of all nations and races:

> I claim allegiance to America because this is the only country I
> know. Our title has been colored, blacks, African Americans
> now. My name's always been Abe. I served in the service, my fa-
> ther served in the service. I guess my forefathers were maybe
> somewhere down the line slaves, but I am not. We moved on . . .

Evolution is going on. I'm a part of America, it's a changing America. We accept more people from other countries than any other country in the world . . . This is my country, I'd fight for it, I'd die for it . . . America is built on opportunity for each and every different type of race that came through this place. It's a young country, it's growing, and we're doing a lot better than a lot of other countries to tell you the truth. You ask me where else in the world I would want to live, I'd tell you nowhere.

By defining himself as American, Abe links his racial identity with his national identity and identifies himself with the positive aspects of his national culture, which include openness to outsiders. In this, he follows eighteenth-century African Americans who grounded their equality in territory instead of lineage.[84] Workers who stress their Americanness in demonstrating equality often have a military background, as does Abe. They define themselves as part of a "we" who comprise the "head honchos" of the world. Some also value the democratic tradition of the country, as does Tom Green, the hospital orderly, who says that he is proud of being American because he can talk about the president, curse him, "yet you are not going to be killed for that."

The Culture of Particularism

While these pieces of counterevidence to the myth of racial inequality are universalistic (in the sense that they point to what is universally common among all human beings—or all Americans), a few black workers also take for granted a culture of particularism: they do so when they explain racism by referring to the view that "preferring and protecting your own kind" is ingrained in human nature. This belief is expressed by a black warehouse worker who says that he thinks he is racist because "I have a tendency to trust my own kind. I relate to them better. If I was in a position to help others, I would probably help my own kind before I would help someone of another race." Some, like John Lamb, explain it by a need to create a pecking order: "Whites influence what district, what state, what county gets the proper money it takes to run the school system. The people you look out for is your own people. I truly believe that. Whites is going to look out for whites for schooling, and whites not going to look out for blacks." A sorter in a mailing company concurs when he says that, for whites, "Pure advantage is that you are white-funded. That's why all the white people have all the money in this country. So the president of a company is white, the CEO is white, so who gets the job? Bam! But that's good! I would never mock that because if the whites [are looking for workers], I'm not going to bring somebody I don't know even if they are qualified. I'll bring people I know, who happen to be black. If you were in the same shoes, you would do the same thing."

Within this culture of particularism, black workers think of racism as a universal and unavoidable phenomenon, and this reinforces a zero-sum approach to group positioning: dominant groups will always maximize their position to the detriment of others, and this will occur whether whites or blacks are "on top." It is as if the discourse of universalism had not deeply penetrated the worlds inhabited by these workers, as if a number of them saw universal claims as merely rhetorical, given their own experience of America.[85] Moreover, unlike professionals, their work is unlikely to require them to maintain a veneer of universalism in making decisions concerning promotion and the distribution of resources, which may contribute to the perception that universalism is mere fantasy.[86] Universal human rights, the American Constitution, cultural relativism, and multiculturalism are not salient in their discourse, as if they were not commonsensical realities and as if they had great cultural distance from these languages. Arguments having to do with our common lineage as children of God, the universality of our physiological needs and characteristics, and a shared American citizenship are more readily used, perhaps because they emerge from everyday experience. These latter themes were not salient among white workers, perhaps because whites do not confront the task of disproving racial inequality in their daily lives and are not forced to (or concerned with) developing a large battery of arguments.

The first two parts of this chapter provided ample evidence of the importance of race as a basis for drawing boundaries for American workers. White and black workers alike use race to differentiate between good and bad people. If they do not use race as a status signal, they are compelled to respond to racism and to demonstrate that people of different races are in fact equal. In contrast, immigrants, a category to which Asians are assimilated, are not very salient in the world-view of black and white workers. It is to this topic that I now turn.

IMMIGRATION

Overall, as with professionals and managers, the workers I talked to were not much concerned with immigrants. A few workers described immigrants as good, hardworking, family-oriented people and as solid community members who take good care of their houses. However, immigrants were not salient in the vast majority of the interviews. To the extent that white workers drew boundaries against this group, these boundaries were weaker than those drawn against blacks, and they mostly targeted Hispanics.[87] The latter's unwillingness to learn English was described as their greatest failing: it brings down the entire country and poses a direct threat to the workers for whom national identity stands as a symbol of pride and as one of the few high-status signals they can claim. Before examining these boundaries in detail, demographic information about immigration in the United States and in the New York area should be considered.

The number of immigrants to the United States has doubled in the last 30 years—the country experienced the largest wave of immigration in the country's history in the 1980s.[88] While in 1960 the foreign-born represented only 4.7 percent of the American population, they represented 8.4 percent of the population in 1990.[89] For their part, second-generation children of immigrants now make up another 10 percent of the population.[90]

Immigration is rapidly changing the face of New Jersey and New York, which are among the six states that have received the largest share of newcomers.[91] Currently, about 35 percent of the New York City population is foreign-born, and many are nonwhites: between 1940 and 1985, the percentage of whites in the population of New York City fell from 94 percent to 49 percent.[92] New Jersey has fewer immigrants than New York: in 1991, only 12.5 percent of its population was foreign-born, and almost half of them had entered between 1980 and 1990.[93] While people of Hispanic origin represented 9.5 percent of the New Jersey population in 1990,[94] they made up only 4 percent of the population of Union County, where most interviewees reside.

In spite of these changes, immigrants generally go unmentioned in the interviews I have conducted with white and black men. This contrasts starkly with the strong racial boundaries I just described. In this lack of concern, respondents resemble the American public as a whole. Survey research shows that while Americans have negative feelings toward immigrants, these feelings are not strongly held.[95] Also, attitudes toward immigrant policies are inconsistent, lack intensity, are not well organized, and are ineffectively articulated.[96] Immigration ranks lower than "don't know" in surveys when respondents are asked about the "most important problems" facing the nation today: "don't know" in fact is chosen five times as frequently as "immigrants."[97] Moreover, while many Americans are concerned with the growing number of immigrants, opinion polls report that controlling immigration ranks well below controlling taxes, crime, and health costs in public priorities.[98] We will see that this relative indifference toward immigrants contrasts sharply with the situation in France. The comparatively low salience of immigrants in the United States is possible in part because in this country, as in other English-speaking settler societies, immigration "policy is normally created within a tightly contained subsystem largely out of public view and with comparatively little broad debate."[99]

To the extent that workers referred to immigrants in interviews, they often described them in positive terms. For instance, speaking of his neighbors who are increasingly "a mixture of Portuguese and Cuban, right down the line," Dick Turner, the security system installer, says, "they are very nice, they are clean. They are family-oriented and I suspect that's part of the reason why the neighborhood has stayed like it has over the years." Dick's description of "good immigrants" echoes that upheld by American politicians as documented in a study of congressional hearings: for them, the ideal citizen is above all someone who pays his taxes, is family-oriented, and has a strong work ethic.[100] Positive views of immigrants are also reflected in some national surveys: in the early eighties, only 20 percent of Americans did not perceive immigrants as "basically good, honest people," and 18 percent did not consider them as hardworking[101]—with higher figures for illegal workers. This may suggest that although Americans generally oppose opening the door of their country to new waves of immigrants, those who attempt to achieve the American dream can be made part of "us."[102] Even within immigrant communities, important symbolic distinctions are made between national groups, separating those who conform most to the American dream from others.[103] While white European immigrants are more easily made "part of us" than others, the labeling of Asians as a "model minority" suggests that incorporation depends more on perceived cultural orientation than on skin color, except for black immigrants who are often assimilated, symbolically and de facto, with African Americans.[104]

The positive attitudes of white workers toward immigrants resonate with the role given to immigration in the formation of the country. While restrictionist and nativist movements have played an important role in the history of this country,[105] predominant narratives about American national identity are also replete with metaphors pointing to "golden doors," "city on the hill," and "the land of the new beginning," reminding us that immigrants fled to America in search of opportunity and liberty, to find here what their countries could not offer.[106] The United States has been repeatedly described as a "democracy of nationalities" and a "nation of nations,"[107] and 95 percent of respondents in a recent survey agreed that "it is important to teach children that America is the world's great melting pot in which people from different countries are united into one nation."[108] The country's success is often attributed to immigrants who incarnate symbolically "the American spirit." The availability of such repertoires contributes to the fact that the men I interviewed do not draw strong boundaries against immigrants.[109]

To the extent that workers draw boundaries against immigrants, they are less concerned with their moral character than with their lack of desire to assimilate, and as Aristide Zolberg and Long Litt Woon point out, anxieties concerning assimilation revolve around language.[110] Hence, some of the men I interviewed call for respect for the long-established contract between immigrants and the receiving country: the newly arrived should give up a good part of their ethnic identity as they embrace the American dream. This is the position of Jim Jennings, the tin factory foreman, who expresses his anger at what he perceives to be a refusal to learn English by exclaiming, "You're in my country. You come to me, to my business, speak my language. Why do I have to learn your language to communicate with you? My family learned English. It's a new ball game." Dick Woolworth, the letter carrier, echoes this point of view when he says, "I usually just don't have anything to do with [foreigners]. And I dislike the fact that they don't speak [English] . . . If you're going to come to this country, you should at least learn the language and use it every day." These feelings are also present in the wider population: a report prepared for the Ford Foundation on relationships between immigrants and established residents in six American communities found that language was "the great divider" between the two groups.[111] In fact, evidence suggests that immigrants today learn English as rapidly as their predecessors.[112] Nevertheless, during the eighties the number of people speaking a language other than English at home grew by 37 percent, while the number of students who did not speak English very well grew by over 50 percent.[113]

The issue of language is sensitive because it symbolizes the downfall of the American nation. That immigrants are perceived as less willing to abandon their native tongue for English than the ancestors of the men I talked to is taken to be evidence of the destruction of the greatness of America and of its fall to the rank of lesser countries. In the words of Alan Hayward, the train conductor: "I heard today that they are thinking about changing English in some states to Spanish. Like Florida. They want to change the signs and there was a fight going on. See we're losing. We're becoming a Third World nation." In the eyes of Dick Woolworth, while he is proud of being American—"just our whole general background and what we stand for"—he fears that "we've definitely been going downhill as a country."

I spoke with only two white workers whose strong boundaries against immigrants are not drawn around this language issue but around their failure to display the disciplined self. While welfare use among working-age (15 to 64 years) nonrefugee immigrants is lower than that of native-born Americans and decreased during the 1980s,[114] these workers believe that immigrants get more than their fair share of common resources (in education, health, and welfare). This view is expressed by a tool and dye worker who draws a direct connection between his hard work and the cost of welfare. He says of the Central Americans he works with: "Two, maybe three, are honest and sincere workers. The rest are out to beat the system. They're so-called married but they're not. And in the meantime, the wife is collecting unemployment, welfare, the whole bit, while he is still living with his wife. And this is a little trick they do and they all do it. And that upsets me because I'm paying for it. That upsets me. And they'll flaunt you with it. They'll just shove it in your face." Similarly, in the eyes of a civil servant, immigrants "don't respect you. They don't respect people's rights. They don't respect what's yours . . . The more you let them in, the more they come in. The unemployment base gets bigger and the welfare base gets bigger. What happens in the end is that you and I have to pay for it whether you like it or not . . . Whether you're a school teacher, a professor at Princeton University, or whether you work at Kmart, we're all paying."

Surveys show that over the last 20 years, the percentage of the population that expresses negative attitudes toward immigrants has increased.[115] Latin Americans and Caribbeans rank near the bottom and are viewed as less likely to work hard, have strong family values, or do well in school than Asian immigrants.[116] Anti-immigrant attitudes can be explained by perceived threats to national security and/or unemployment,[117] which was high in these last decades.[118] Immigrants frequently replace whites in existing and new low-wage jobs—60 percent of Latinos over 25 years old don't have high school diplomas.[119] They represent a threat to workers in such jobs, although they are disproportionately employed in the informal economy (in sectors such as apparel, construction, toys, electronics, jewelry making, and packaging).[120]

These negative views toward immigrants reflect the continuing availability of cultural repertoires stressing the moral failure of immigrants. In the view of historian David Kennedy, in the United States "on the one hand . . . immigrants were judged to be noble souls . . . whose talents and genius and love of liberty account for the magnificent American character. On the other hand . . . [they] were thought to be degraded, freeloading louts, a blight on the national character and a drain on the economy . . . 'The wretched refuse of your teeming shore' . . . Both [perspectives] explain immigration in terms of the moral character of immigrants."[121] These two forces of acceptance and rejection and their relative strength vary over time and across regions, with immigrants being more positively valued and more integrated politically in the New York area than in California.[122]

To conclude: workers do not define "people like us" in clear opposition to immigrants. In interviews, most were indifferent to them. Other held relatively positive views of this group. A few had more negative views and focused almost exclusively on language issues as opposed to moral character issues. This patterns holds for white and black workers.[123] Research needs to be conducted not only in states with exceptionally large immigrant populations, such as New Jersey and California, but also in "modal" states before firm conclusions can be reached on the question of the place of anti-immigrant boundaries in the United States as a whole. However, the patterns documented here should be found elsewhere because immigrants are likely to be more salient to the workers I talked to than to the average American who lives in a low-immigration state.

THE POLICING OF RACIAL BOUNDARIES

This chapter showed that whites and blacks alike subtly move from drawing moral boundaries to drawing racial boundaries. Whites' moral standards center around a work ethic, responsibility, and the defense of traditional morality ("family values" and anticrime). Hence, the "disciplined self " is absolutely at the center of the rationale that leads white workers to view blacks as moral violators. Similarly, blacks' condemnations of whites have to do with their perceived lack of caring and with their domineering tendencies: whites are too competitive and imperialistic and less human, caring, and spiritual than blacks.[124] They also have less moral fortitude, as illustrated by their inferior ability to handle hardship. This "us" versus "them" dynamic animated by two different conceptions of morality is closely associated with the collective identities of the two groups.

How useful is it to link this racist rhetoric to the moral boundaries that were documented in Chapter 1? It makes us understand better the internal coherence of workers' worldviews and helps us comprehend why racist views can make sense to them, given the cultural and structural contexts in which they live. This, of course, is not to justify racism—negative stereotyping of a racial or ethnic group is never justified. However, we can see why white workers blame blacks for their lack of work ethic and violations of traditional morality: the centrality of these values in their own lives (for reasons described in the previous chapter), the sense of threat to their group position, the fear of being demographically outnumbered, and of losing status as Americans, as well as the cultural repertoires provided by the Republican Party, all contribute to making this possible. Similarly, a number of factors make it possible for some blacks to view whites as domineering and uncaring. These include the factors that led them to emphasize the "caring self" (as described in Chapter 1), their common experience of slavery, segregation, and discrimination, and the continuous supply of Afrocentrist repertoires.

There are also similarities and differences in the rhetoric of antiracism used by white and black workers. White "racists" and "antiracists" as well as blacks use market performance to define worth. A notion of equality based on a common dignity as human beings is conspicuously absent from the interviews.[125] This suggests the growing influence of neoliberalism, which defines cultural membership in terms of middle class status. While white workers ground racial equality exclusively in earning capacity and the universality of human nature, blacks mobilize a much broader range of arguments to show that they are equal to whites because they are more concerned with rebutting racism than whites. Some point to their competence at work and to their own ability to earn money and consume, responding to white racism on its own terms by demonstrating a "disciplined self." Others rebut racism by showing that blacks are superior to whites because they are less domineering and more caring and "sensitive to the human thing." Yet others draw on a wide range of evidence—common lineage, physiological characteristics, or citizenship.

This comparative study of boundaries not only makes visible the unexplored territories of ordinary white and black antiracism: by looking specifically at how workers define similarities and differences, including racial ones, we are able to identify and explain the presence and absence of different arguments that had gone unnoticed to date. For instance, we find that whites and blacks alike use evidence drawn from everyday experience—such as the commonsensical notion that human nature is universal—to rebut the notion of racial inequality. Their rhetoric is in stark contrast with that produced in academia, and popularized by school curricula, which stresses multiculturalism. The latter appeals less to workers than to professionals due to their desire to keep the world in moral order and to distinguish clearly what is permissible and "normal" from what is not.

We are witnessing the ascendancy of the "disciplined self" over the "caring self" and collectivist logics, which shape the dominant representations of whites and blacks. The notion that whites are uncaring and domineering is not widely available in American society the way representations of blacks as lazy and violent are. Whites are in general better able to communicate through the mass media and political discourse their standards of evaluation. Indeed, the portrayal of blacks as lacking in terms of work ethic and respect for traditional morality (including law and order) reappears intermittently in the mass media[126] and in politics (for instance, the Welfare Reform Bill of 1995 identified blacks as morally fallen).[127] The media also make a repeated and selected use of social statistics pointing to blacks' moral failings while underplaying those of whites.[128] Whites are also successful at asserting their own definition of moral legitimacy in the workplace, as suggested by the research of Kirschenman and Neckerman that shows that white employers discriminate against black employees based on preconceptions concerning their work ethic.[129] The ascendancy of these dominant criteria is revealed by surveys showing that a relatively large number of blacks agree that they are unintelligent, prefer welfare, and are hard to get along with.[130] It is also revealed by the fact that many Americans reject affirmative action in the name of individualism and oppose collective rights.[131] Such rights are in line with the collectivist logic of black solidarity. By opposing these rights, whites naturalize the ideal traits that they value most ("the disciplined self") and pressure dominated groups to adopt them.

The asymmetry in the ability of the two groups to disseminate a demonized view of the other is key to understanding the crucial role that culture plays in the reproduction of racial inequality in American society. The definitions of moral worth, on which these demonized views are based, are not only different; they also have very unequal impact on American mainstream culture. They are central to the construction of white and black racial identity and to American racism. They contribute directly to the growing inequality in the resources that whites and nonwhites have access to.[132] As taken-for-granted "cultural structures," they define the frames of human life as thoroughly as material resources.[133]

At the same time, the extent to which whites are ignorant of the complexities of black culture, and vice versa, should not be underestimated. That Craig Patterson, the assistant cable splicer, describes white people as typically having nannies is evidence of this gap, as is the dismay of the medical supply worker, Tony Clark, when he finds that his white colleagues think that he resembles the lanky television personality Arsenio Hall although he himself is fat and short. Though talk of racism is pervasive in American public discourse, it is easy to forget how little contact, overall, blacks and whites have with one another due to segregation in housing and employment. With the increase in the level of education of African Americans, many are now closer to white culture than they were 20 years ago.[134] Yet many still live in communities that are almost exclusively black and enter into contact with white culture primarily through the mass media. The relative isolation of blacks from whites and whites from blacks plays a role in sustaining racial stereotypes and an impoverishment of understanding of the culture of the other in both groups. The spatial distance reinforces a social and cultural distance that remains largely understudied, and this chapter is one step toward filling this gap.

3

Assessing "People Above" and "People Below"

I MET Frank Lucas in a restaurant at the Sheraton Hotel next to Newark Airport. It was early in the morning and we were having coffee. Frank was honored to be interviewed. He had put on a white shirt and a tie because he was to meet clients later in the day. This white 32-year-old sells paper goods to restaurants—place mats, table cloths, and the like—all over New York, New Jersey, and Connecticut. He handles specialized lines, such as customized napkins. He is very proud of his work, which represents a big step up for him. He says he meets more people and "a better class of people" than when he worked in warehouses and factories:

> The grade of the people you met just wasn't appealing to me—they didn't have a direction in life, and they lived from week to week . . . What you eat is what you're made of, or whatever. It's what I was hanging around with that I was being turned into. So getting into this type of field, you know, the people you deal with on an everyday basis is more professional, have a direction and a lifestyle, goals, and they have things that we all like. It's just better, good to hang around with people who are successful rather than not successful.

It is easy to tell that Frank makes the American dream his, hoping to gain as much distance as possible from the milieu of misery from which he came. Moving out of this milieu has required that he change his style of dress and learn to be better-spoken. Not having a college degree has been a big barrier, but he feels that he is now doing well nonetheless. He bought his first book just a month ago at Dalton's: "It was a big day for me! You know, walking in, 'I'm buying a book!' You know I don't read books. My concentration level drifts off and I don't know a whole lot of the meaning of words . . . But I bought a book, *Dianetics* [the Scientology bible], only $5.99, and it has explanations of words and things at the bottom [of the pages] . . . It's about discovering yourself and success and how to cope and free your mind."

To reach his American dream, Frank also invests in vending machines, hoping to make it big. His mother, with whom Frank lives, thinks that being in sales is not a good idea because he is on commission; she'd rather have him receive a steady paycheck. Frank feels very distant from his mother and is resentful that she did not give him direction or encourage him to go to college. He is critical of her because she has a bad mouth ("the hollering and the screaming"), is overweight ("she just constantly eats; even my dog is overweight"), and does nothing with her life ("she is a very bitter, angry person . . . the personality just in itself"). She is now 52 and has worked in the same factory for 33 years. It is about to close.

When I asked Frank what it means for him to be a lower middle class person (the label he gives himself), he says, "it means that I'm this much closer to the next step, so it's just step-by-step quality increments, is what I call it. That's want I want to do, is keep on making strides in life," which he thinks he is doing:

> I went to one of my wholesale distributors yesterday. I was inside and I was who I am, jacket and tie and everything, and I understood that they were interviewing for a warehouse job or whatever. I saw all these guys coming in, that were wearing jeans and sneakers and everything else and I just thought that I used to be in that position. I used to be there and look at who I am now. But still I don't feel superior over that guy, but I felt better about myself when I looked at them because I was there. But I won't say it was superior because I treat everybody with respect. You can't mistreat anybody.

Frank defines himself as middle class and as having middle class values. He defines his newly acquired lower white-collar status in opposition to that of blue-collar workers.

I found a number of blue-collar workers who identify with middle class values. But I found more who, although they dream the American dream, are quite critical of middle class mores. Dennis Young, the white Bayonne firefighter, is one. Dennis works full-time at the fire station and part-time in construction, and he never takes a vacation. He wants to be financially secure and believes that because he is young and strong, he should work toward this goal now. He views the firefighter job as a great one because of the health benefits. He also likes his boss, in part because he is very knowledgeable, and Dennis can ask him questions about how to invest money ("he'll get his accountant on the phone and he'll get you different suggestions. He saves you a lot of running around and mental anguish"). At 33, Dennis is already talking about retirement: if all goes well, he plans to retire from the firehouse in 13 years, at 46.

Like Frank, Dennis is very materialistic and hopes to improve his lot, but he is ambivalent toward middle class people, and he knows them well from having worked as a messenger in a bank on Wall Street. Comparing the firehouse or the construction site with the bank, he says of these workplaces: "It's more friendly, open, not as conservative. In big business, there's a lot of false stuff going on. A lot of people are 'How are you doing?' And then you turn your back and they are like 'He's a jerk.' At least at the job in the firehouse, if you're a jerk, someone is going to tell you you're a jerk. There, there's no one going to say it to you . . . Here, if you don't like a guy, you can tell him what's bothering you about him. And if he doesn't like that, it's like 'Tough then, don't bother me.'" Dennis also says of professionals, "they care more about showing off to other professionals. They have more of a contest with each other. I mean like 'I've got a Jaguar,' drive by to see his friends. As for me, I could not care less what the other guy thinks of me. Because if I feel good about myself, and my wife thinks good about me, and we're all happy, that's what matters to me. My family is what I center myself around. I'm not trying to keep a race with the Joneses, like that."

Dennis says of people who look down on others, "they're trying to hide one of their own things, that they are lacking in. They don't feel comfortable about themselves." He is not a power-hungry person: "I'm happy the way I am just now. I don't have to be in charge with a thousand people to try to make them feel less. Power is, like to me, another insecurity of some sort somewhere in your mind or something." He says of Donald Trump, "power doesn't make the person . . . I know a lot of people that give stuff away, just so they can feel more important, that they're better than you: 'Yeah, you can have some of it,' but then they kick you in the head."

Whether they are critical of the upper half or not, people like Frank and Dennis are generally quite harsh toward people below them. They frequently blame the poor for having the wrong attitudes, that is, for not pulling their weight, not being "forward-looking," and lacking the courage to "stick to it"—one of the traits they most value. In fact, we will see that as much as they often hesitate to equate socioeconomic standing with moral worth when discussing middle class people, whites especially have a unequivocal and opposite view when it comes to the poor.

MORALITY AND CLASS RELATIONS

The first objective of this chapter is to examine how workers like Frank and Dennis evaluate people who are above them in the social structure.[1] They construct the upper half as having a socioeconomic status to aspire to but values that should be rejected.[2] Most workers ground their moral critique of "the upper half" in an alternative set of standards that are independent of social status and that center on straightforwardness and personal integrity. We saw in Chapter 1 that these are less valued by professionals and managers than by workers. By stressing these dimensions of morality, workers dissociate moral worth from socioeconomic status and can locate themselves above or side by side with "people above."[3] While most resemble Frank in their simultaneous acceptance and rejection of the upper half, a quarter of the workers resemble George in their unequivocal embrace of middle class values.

My conclusions challenge previous studies that have argued that the American working class identifies with middle class values,[4] interpret workers' middle class self-identification as a rejection of their working class status,[5] or present workers as passive victims of broader social forces.[6] In contrast to these views, many of the men I talked to find meaning, value, and worth in their own lives, and they achieve this in part by stressing moral criteria of success that are available to all (such as personal integrity and good interpersonal relationships) and by downplaying the status criteria that are the dominant currency of the upper middle class world. Whereas most analysts view the development of alternative codes of honor and the rejection of mainstream norms of success as an explicit goal and act of resistance,[7] I view them as an unintended consequence of the search for respect and alternative spheres of worth.

Do black and white workers differ in their attitude toward the upper half? Black workers appreciate the importance of money more than whites, perhaps because it is a passport that can trump their racial stigma. While fewer blacks draw boundaries against the upper half, those who do so draw stronger boundaries than whites. They extend the moral collectivism they cherish to describe the upper half as egoistic and exploitative, at times confounding the categories "white" and "middle class." As was the case for racial boundaries, they draw class boundaries by emphasizing different aspects of morality than whites.

The second objective of this chapter is to examine the boundaries that workers draw toward "people below." White workers have a less ambivalent attitude toward this group than toward "people above." A small majority clearly constructs the poor in opposition to "people like us." While they often hesitate to equate socioeconomic standing with moral worth when discussing middle class people, most do not hesitate when it comes to the poor and, more broadly, welfare recipients, the homeless, and part-time workers: it is not social position but attitude that counts, I was told, and, most important, not giving up. This is what distinguishes the deserving from the undeserving poor. And just as black workers associate "the middle class" with whiteness, white workers associate "the poor" with blacks.

Black workers also set limits to racial solidarity when they discuss the "no-good niggers," whom they describe as having "no morals, no respect, no plans, no hopes, no outlook." However, blacks are more supportive of public redistribution measures than whites, in line with their collectivist moral orientation. As sociologists have shown, blacks are also more likely than whites to account for poverty by pointing to structural causes beyond individual control. Moreover, their own experience with racism makes them less likely to believe that upward mobility reflects superior moral character. When black workers draw strong boundaries toward the poor, they do so mostly in relation to tactical, pragmatic purposes: they want to prevent a drain of their own resources and guard what they perceive to be the fragile boundary separating stable society from the underclass and the underworld. Hence, as compared to whites, blacks find themselves in the paradoxical position of drawing weaker moral boundaries toward the poor while keeping greater symbolic distance from them, and identifying themselves more strongly with "people above" while being more critical of their mores.

The overall pattern that emerges from the interviews is one whereby the poor, like blacks, are often defined in opposition to "people like us" and "our values," and whereby "people above" are simultaneously in and out, with values to reject but a socioeconomic status to aspire to. As we saw in Chapter 2, these boundaries are complemented by relatively weak boundaries drawn toward the symbolic outsiders, the immigrants. Also, as was the case for the racial boundaries described in the previous chapter, class boundaries are extensions of the moral criteria that workers use to evaluate everyone. By locating these boundaries within the broader moral worldview of workers, I submit that the issue of class consciousness (or that of workers' consciousness of their distinctiveness) is best understood as embedded in the context of a range of categorical comparisons drawn by workers: these boundaries are an application of broad moral principles to a specific subset of relationships (class relationships). Also, by focusing on the multiple forms of class boundaries that workers draw, we obtain a more complex understanding of class consciousness and class identity than if we center our analysis around the traditional categories used to study the topic (such as issues of class "in itself" and class "for itself").

I now turn to the language white workers use to describe "people above." I begin with those who identify themselves with the middle class and later turn to those who adopt a more critical stance.

"People Above"

Whites Evaluating "People Above"

THE IMPORTANCE OF HIGH SOCIAL STATUS. Altogether, some 50 percent of the white blue-collar workers I talked to can be described as "middle class-identified" because they evaluate others largely in terms of financial success, authority, and ambition; we will see, however, that half of these men are also critical of the upper half.[8] As Richard Wrong, a car mechanic puts it, "people are brought up in this society to respect money, power, and good looks . . . Mother Theresa is a role model only to certain categories of people. Not a general role model." These men have little resentment toward those who do well. Tim Williams, the laborer, says that he "can't knock anyone for succeeding . . . I feel very good for them people. I feel sorry for the poor, people busting their butt their entire life and getting nowhere. It's a shame. But I have no hard feeling toward people who are wealthy or doing good." Murray DiPrete, the receiving clerk, also agrees: "I don't believe that people who are wealthy did something unscrupulous or deceiving or deceptive to get their wealth. There's a lot of people out there who are wealthy and I'm sure they have worked darned hard for every cent they have." These attitudes are consistent with surveys that show that large numbers of Americans buy into the central tenets of the American dream, that is, they believe that the current distribution of rewards is fair, that opportunity is available to all, and that people can make it if they work at it.[9]

These white men attribute great legitimacy to wealth-producing activities. While some engage in moneymaking activities beyond their regular jobs to improve their lot, others only dream of buying real estate or getting involved in financial speculation or entrepreneurial risk-taking. Those who most want their piece of the American dream use their evenings and weekends to satisfy their aspirations. Larry Relles, the Paterson policeman, explains that he hopes to make it big by "buying homes and renting them out. I'm a landlord and I get a positive cash flow. I get money I didn't physically go out and work for, which is what I like." He perceives himself as successful because his income gives him freedom, which he largely defines in terms of consumption: "I own three homes. I'll be living in a $300,000 house when it's all said and done. I'm only 34 years old . . . I got a boat, a jet ski, a motorcycle. I can pretty much do what I want to do, which a lot of people can't." Vincent Marchesi, the electronics technician, also associates success with consumption. He says, "If I could figure out a way [to get rich], I would definitely pursue it. I would love to have more money, enough money to say [snaps his fingers] I can get anything I want. I'm materialistic, I'm not going to deny that . . . I would love to have a Porsche or a Ferrari. That would make me extremely happy. It would be a tool for . . . not necessarily a happier, but an easier, life. You can't associate money with happiness. But I'd sure like to give it a try."

Like Vincent, several workers resemble the upper middle class in that they are taken by the comfort and facility created by money and value it as a way to avoid headaches, to have "an easier life," and "keep it together."[10] Linden firefighter John Seamen says that in his next life he would like to come back upper middle class "for the monetary reason . . . being able to join a country club, not having to go to the public golf course. Not having to worry about, you know, scraping up the pennies. Better house, whatever."

Altogether, a third of the white workers I talked to mentioned economic standing as a proof of success. In an interesting twist, several individuals who have relatively low incomes also use financial success to show that they are successful, while redefining appropriate economic standards. For instance, an office clerk says that he is successful because "I can support myself—which is hard to do these days."

White workers put income above education in evaluating peoples' worth: the former is perceived as more within reach than the latter and can help workers to locate themselves above the college-educated. These men also rank formal education below competence and know-how, and even common sense, which are crucial in the establishment of a pecking order among workers. These attributes are also much more important than formal knowledge in providing advantages and respect in the workplace, given that workers are de facto excluded from positions that require a college education.

Just as many white workers claim to have no resentment toward people who do well financially, most have fairly positive views of authority—another positional attribute of "people above." Here again they resemble professionals and managers.[11] They do not associate authority with domination, as blacks do. Instead, they think it results from a necessary division of labor. Leo Norton, a broadcast worker, explains: "I don't think that for me, to show up five days a week and do certain things in turn for them paying me to do this job [means that they are] controlling me. It's a contract that we have . . . It's not because [people] pick up a check every two weeks that you own these people." The exercise of authority is viewed as functional, as a mean to getting things done and accomplishing goals. Like professionals, workers value authority if it is associated with competence—this is in part related to the fact that most of the skilled workers I talked to define their own value largely through their skills and know-how. In interviews, they were merciless when talking about incompetent bosses or coworkers, just as they express high regard for the competent ones. For instance, Murray DiPrete, the receiving clerk, says of his boss: "I definitely recognize Jim as the boss . . . What he says, goes. You can see when you ask him a question, he is thinking about the options, the contingencies that are involved. He thinks before he comes to a conclusion." Murray believes that his boss is above him because he is smarter. He validates the view that people who are promoted are "the best individual, the one who is the best at his job, the one who can express his ideas, who can communicate better . . . So really a lot of it depends on the individual, side-stepping politics." Although many workers view promotions as the result of favoritism, Murray's perspective is far from exceptional.

Finally, a few workers also follow the lead of the upper middle class in stressing ambition. Stan Morley, the pipe fitter, links this trait to the American national character: "Everybody needs to have ambition. You have to want to make better of yourself because that's what America was founded on." Accordingly, many resemble the printer Johnny Page, who feels guilty for not being ambitious enough. He says that "I like to see people show that they can leave a mark, and not just be lax and fall into a rut. I should say that I see me lacking a bit in ambition lately."

Ambition is often equated with intelligence. As one worker told me: "Intelligence probably ranks high among [standards of] distinction. The fact that there are some people out there that could do better and don't try." Similarly, Paul West, an insurance salesman with a high school degree, says that he feels superior to people who are uneducated, stigmatizing them on the basis of an amalgam of standards having to do with education, self-direction, passivity, and poverty:

> You know something more than they do. [It's] people who have
> no control over their lives, who are just a doormat or a dishrag.
> Somebody that just does what everybody tells them to do. Peo-

ple who don't know what's going on in the world . . . They are just victims. I refuse to be a victim of any kind, for anybody. There's no reason why a person should be that way . . . If a person just does nothing to help themselves, I'm very hard on these people. My parents didn't go to school or college and I was the worst student around and if I can do all these things, then certainly anybody else can.

"Making it" is viewed as living proof of one's intelligence, and feelings of inferiority and superiority are shaped by this belief. The relationship between intelligence, success, and education is also described by Vincent Marchesi, who says of professionals: "I feel envious of them, but if they're rich, well, hey! They were smart enough to get rich. I wish I could be it, but I don't necessarily feel inferior to them. Not even intellectually. They may be smarter than me because they had enough smarts to get [the degree]. But that doesn't install the feeling of inferiority in me. But like I said, the engineer that's talking circles around me, for some unknown reason . . . that gives me the inferior feeling."

Other positive traits are associated with middle class status. Middle class people are described as having broader horizons, whereas, according to another electronics technician, working class people "can just sit there with their friends and talk about [sports] all day, and they look at each other as equal because of that . . . They feel good about that because they know what year, who hit what, when, and where." A Long Island auto mechanic describes himself as middle class because he shares "this whole idea of being concerned a little more about other things rather than your immediate self. That for me starts to define middle class."

Some of these workers who identify with the middle class define their feelings of inferiority around the raw power that comes with money and authority. Tim Williams, the laborer, says that he feels inferior to people

with a lot of money, people with power who have control. Like at my job, the CEO. He's a regular guy. He'll talk to you like anybody else. But if he says, "we've got to cut costs, so this has to go," he goes. So he's a very powerful man. He drives a Lincoln. He's a power executive, a very influential person. Who else would I feel inferior to? People I guess with money and power—the ones who have the authority, power over people, not the ones who just think they do, but people who are actually in authority—where if you say the wrong thing to him, it can cost you your job . . . My foreman, if he yells at me, I can yell back at him. But if the CEO told me I'd messed up, I'd say "I'm sorry, I'm sorry."

While in many respects white workers who identify with the middle class resemble their upper middle class counterparts, we will see that they are also quite different from most black workers and from the French workers I talked to.

THE MORAL FLAWS OF "PEOPLE ABOVE." These positive evaluations of the upper half, which tend to conflate social status and worth, tell only part of the story. We saw that 50 percent of white blue-collar workers identify with middle class values, and that half of them are simultaneously critical of these values. We now turn to the remaining 50 percent who draw strong boundaries against the upper half. Altogether, 75 percent of the white blue-collar workers make negative evaluations of the upper half that supersede positive ones.[12]

Workers disentangle worth and social status by emphasizing other criteria of evaluation, such as the quality of interpersonal relationships. These men mobilize the standards of personal integrity to draw moral boundaries toward the upper middle class; in Chapter 1, we indeed saw that these traits are central to workers' definitions of worth. The use of such standards allows them to locate themselves at the top of a hierarchy—or, at least, side by side with others. These standards are democratic ones to the extent that, unlike power, money, and prestige, they are available to all and their distribution is not a zero sum.[13]

Danny Easton, an audio technician who works for the service department of a Japanese electronics manufacturer on Long Island, knows middle class people well. As he describes it, he lost his girlfriend to them because she thought he was going nowhere. She had recently started college and hoped to go on to medical school. Danny has had ample opportunity to see middle class people in action while associating with the college friends of this former girlfriend. He describes them as "very cold, shallow people . . . concentrating a lot on finances and not that much on personal needs." Alan Hayward, the train conductor, concurs with this description when he compares himself to his "corporate" brother: "I feel that I'm more sensitive a person. He's in a business atmosphere, where he has to be tough. He acts sometimes, you know, 'corporate' when he's talking to me, so I get upset . . . He doesn't show any sensitivity to some things that I would like him to show." Alan associates "corporate" with "domination, domination . . . like if a guy is wearing a suit and he has that attitude when he walks in a room, like 'Do this! Do this!'"

Men like Danny and Alan have developed elaborate moral critiques of "people above." They have identified the moral flaws typical of this group, specifically, the poor quality of their interpersonal relationships and their lack of sincerity. Dennis Young, the firefighter, made the same point when he commented on the double-faced attitudes of his former coworkers on Wall Street, stressing that "at least . . . in the firehouse, if you're a jerk, someone is going to tell you you're a jerk."

Stan Morley, the pipe fitter, shares this negative view of the upper half. For him, the "shirt and ties types" engage in "too much politicking": "They are jockeying for jobs and worrying about whether they are making the right moves and stuff. I feel that I don't have to get involved in that. Their hair is turning gray, and they look older than I do. That's the way I would measure [my happiness], where I can come home and enjoy myself where they are sweating out things."

Workers stigmatize middle class people who mark distance toward people "who are not their own kind." Richard Wrong, the car mechanic, voices this view: "Oh! You know what I hate? Two-face. I can't stand that. You're a fake, you're a fake. Why be a fake? . . . Like with this person, they are snobby, and with this person, they are a regular down-to-earth person . . . Well, if you have to become snobby for them to want to be around you, well, then screw this person . . . If you're a snob, stay a snob."

This rejection of snotty people is an expression of class homophily among workers—just as work ethic and responsibility are code words used to draw boundaries against blacks. Larry Relles, the Paterson policeman, slips easily from moral to class language when he says that the type of people he does not like are "people with facades or snotty people. I just like regular people. I don't try to hang out with lawyers and doctors." When asked how he recognizes that someone is real, Larry says that he does so by "the way they dress, the way they talk, the way they treat you." Unreal people are what he calls "Barbie and Ken people. Basically people who are, like, super preppy, and talk a certain way, and only hang out with certain people and have a very narrow view on life." Contrary to those who believe that the college-educated are "broader," Larry perceives himself and his friends as more open and accepting. For Pete Lawrence, a heating system specialist, elitism is also a code word he uses to draw class boundaries based on personal integrity, explaining that these boundaries have less to do with money than manners:

> You don't have much in common with them . . . I don't like to be around people that I'm uncomfortable with, it's as simple as that . . . I don't want to be bothered . . . nothing wrong with the guy, but something don't click, why hang around? . . . I was always taught one thing. When an educated person comes in, he should always speak to the level of the person in the house. [You] don't go in a person's house and look down on people. Otherwise, you haven't got a goddamn bit of common sense in the world.

Another moral flaw of "people above" that affects the quality of their interpersonal relationships is their competitiveness. Dennis Young, the Bayonne firefighter, criticizes "the suits" who drive around in their Jaguars to show off. Richard Wrong, the mechanic, believes that professionals "power-play people. They're better than them, or they're stronger than them . . . I have no time for it at all." This type of competitiveness generates dishonesty among "people above" who do not hesitate to "screw" others to get what they want. In the words of Tim Williams, the laborer, "When you get that almighty dollar, you hate to lose it. So you step on somebody's feet, or somebody's hand, or somebody's head to make sure you stay on top, which is not the greatest thing in the word . . . The lower middle class people, they got nothing to lose by being honest." These workers believe that, like competition, ambition can potentially lead to violating much-valued aspects of traditional morality, such as honesty. Along these lines, a study conducted in 1980 revealed that 40 percent of white men without a high school degree explained that the rich get rich by their dishonesty, compared to 35 percent of those with high school degrees and 5 percent of college graduates.[14]

A third of the white workers I spoke to were critical of ambition. Most argued that it leads people to miss what is truly important in life. For Henry Link, the bank supply salesman, people who are too ambitious "have blinders on. You miss all of life . . . A person that is totally ambitious and driven never sees anything except the spot they are aiming at." Similarly, for Vincent Marchesi, the electronics technician, overly ambitious people are "so self-assured, so self-intense that they don't really care about anyone else . . . It's me, me, me, me, me. I'm not that kind of person at all, and that's probably why I don't like it." The selfishness of the overly ambitious is shocking even to this ultimate materialist who dreams of making it big. Jimmy Brown, the liquor deliveryman, also ponders the moral character of rich people when he describes his cousin thus: "He always had everything he wanted and absolutely despised his parents . . . When his mother died, it didn't bother him a bit. The way he looked at it was 'Great, my bank account is going up and I'm that much closer to the whole thing.' And he looked at his three brothers as if it was like a competition . . . What the heck went wrong there? So you times that by every other rich person, how many of them are like that?"

Workers appreciate one category of wealthy people: those who "worked their way up and remember where they came from." An electrician praises one of his clients because he invited him and his coworkers to a Fourth of July party for which they were getting the house ready. "I think a lot of people forget where they came from . . . If you get somebody who was middle class and worked their way up, I think I like people like that much better." Mentioning his client's invitation, he says:

The guy never batted an eyelash when he said it. The guy knew where he came from, and we were more than welcome . . . That's somebody who I value. The only difference is he had got millions of dollars, and I didn't . . . He was just a regular guy who got lucky and got a lot of money. He remembered how a guy in my position is . . . He remembered that we're just working stiffs trying to make ends meet and pay the bills every month. We knew our job and we did our job . . . You can give people all kinds of money, but it doesn't make him a good person.

This electrician respects his client because he recognizes the value of workers' skills and accords them dignity. He does not deny their humanity on the basis of status differences. He signals all of this by inviting them to a party. For this electrician, the ability to recognize workers' dignity is *the* standard by which the worth and quality of a person is measured, and the client's ability to do this is explained by his working class roots. This resonates with the interviewees' emphasis on dignity, grounded in integrity, work ethic, responsibility, and providing for the family, which was discussed in Chapter 1. It suggests, again, that workers draw class boundaries by using the same standards they mobilize to distinguish people they like from those they don't like in general. It also suggests that we should understand class consciousness, and the general salience of class in workers' identity, in this broader context. Workers assert their conviction that high social status does not necessarily go hand in hand with worth when they emphasize the poverty of the interpersonal relations of the upper half and their lack of straightforwardness, their competitiveness, and their excessive ambition. By subordinating social status to what they perceive to be the "real" value of a person, workers create the possibility of locating themselves at the top of the hierarchy.

Similar conclusions can be drawn from what white workers said about power and money. Far from perceiving power as prestigious, a number of workers resemble Dennis Young, the Bayonne firefighter, in describing the outright exercise of power as a sign of weak character; in fact, a fourth of the blue-collar whites have a negative view of power. Tim Williams, the laborer, says, "Power has no value in life. If you're more powerful than me, what are you going to do? Beat me up? There's always somebody more powerful than you, and it goes up the chain and never stops . . . It's meaningless. You get more results finding out what the person's about, or being nice to the person, or whatever . . . You don't get paid for being powerful, you get paid for intelligence."

Tim Williams opposes power to "treating somebody as a human being," which also echoes workers' emphasis on dignity. Similarly, for a mechanic who lives on Long Island, power denies the dignity of the person. People with power "have no time for anything but themselves. Unless you're someone that can make them powerful, or something that they want as a toy, they would have no use for you . . . What would you use power for? Manipulating people? To make people do something just for the fun of it? Stand on your head for half an hour and I'll give you $100? I think it's degrading to manipulate people just for the sake of manipulating them."

A third of the white workers I talked to downplay socioeconomic status by explicitly dissociating money and wealth from worth, subordinating these attributes to happiness. From observing the upper half, they often conclude that the quest for money is unending and provides little satisfaction. For a postal worker, rich people "are always, like, out to get something, and they feel they haven't gotten to where they want to get. To me they're successful, but to them they're not. They're always looking for something, trying to strive to get there, and it seems that they never get there." Respondents often follow Jim Jennings, the tin factory foreman, in subordinating money to familial bliss. As he puts it: "Money isn't a big thing in my life. I don't have to be a rich man. I have riches. As long as you have the love and a tight family and that my kids grew up good, I don't need a lot of money. For what? To spend it on this, spend it on that. How much money can you spend? . . . I have the respect of people who know me. I'm cared for by a lot of people . . . I have those kinds of things, so I have a sense of self-worth." Self-worth serves as a measuring stick for these men and a more important measuring stick than wealth. The emphasis on self-worth also emerges from a close examination of the alternative definitions of success adopted by workers.

EGALITARIANISM AND ALTERNATIVE DEFINITIONS OF SUCCESS. The literature on alternative definitions of success adopted by workers has centered on the importance they attach to job security and stability as opposed to upward mobility.[15] The range of alternative definitions I find is much wider and, like workers' criticisms of the upper half, they revolve around interpersonal relations and happiness. The electrician Ben MacIntyre, whom we encountered at the beginning of Chapter 1, adopts a definition of success that resembles Jim Jennings's definition in that he puts the respect and love that people have for him above social status. Similarly, Johnny Page, the printer, says that he is successful because "I'm not making anything earth-shaking, but I'm doing a lot better than a lot of other people . . . I see people who just don't care about what they are going to do in the future . . . They don't have much self-esteem, self-respect. [I respect myself] because I don't screw people over . . . I'm the kind of person that somebody can come and talk to."

Other alternative definitions of success have less to do with interpersonal relationships than with raising decent children or enjoying oneself. Richard Wrong, the car mechanic, defines success as "keeping it together" when he explains that, for him, "rich" means "If I can sit here and survive through this whole rush around here . . . and with the kids making out all right, without getting all wired out on dope, or getting in any sort of trouble. Now that's rich! . . . That's surviving!" Others define success in terms of being able to keep their wife at home, to ensure a better quality of life for the whole family. This locates them above two-income middle class families. Yet others, such as Billy Taylor, the cosmetics plant foreman, explicitly contrast traditional definitions of success to the goal of tasting everything that life has to offer:

I'm 47 now. The chances of me finding a better mousetrap are pretty slim. So what I am doing is looking for now instead of the future . . . You realize that the president of a large corporation doesn't have any time . . . So I'm trying to do everything I ever thought I wanted to do . . . I took a scuba diving lesson and now I keep scuba diving. I got on skis once and now I work on the hill. I jumped out of a plane once. I got on a flying trapeze, when you go to the circus, you always wanted to do it. I did it . . . There's a couple things that are still on my list. One is rappelling and the other is bungee-jumping. If I could try those, then, I think I'll have done everything I wanted to do.

Other whites implicitly promote alternative definitions of success by arguing that all human beings are equal, independently of their social status. Ben MacIntyre, the electrician, explained that there is not one measuring scale and that we are equal because we are different. Recall that he puts education on the same plane as the courage of a firefighter or the skills of a baseball coach: "What makes you better than me or me better than you? Just because you may have a degree or maybe because I can go through a burning building or because I coach Little League or you teach? Everyone has different values for what they want to do." Similarly, for a storage worker, "Everybody's born and everybody's gonna die. Nobody's any better or worse than I am. They may be better at certain things, but just because they have money, or they may have gone to school, or because they didn't go to school and they have been working since they were ten years old, or whatever, that's no reason to put me down. Everybody's got a different life." Hence, the evidence workers mobilize to demonstrate class equality is more diversified than the evidence they mobilize to show racial equality. Perhaps class inequality is a topic of greater concern to white workers, just as racial inequality is of greater concern to blacks. The use of these criteria allows them to emerge on top or at least side by side with others.

Note that, when they evaluate others in terms of interpersonal relationships, white workers are not proposing an alternative socialist model of social organization that would distribute rewards more equally. Instead, they suggest that people are fundamentally equal and downplay economic success as a criterion of worth.[16] Their counter-ideology, which revolves around the simple idea that people on top are no better than themselves, contests one of the central tenets of the American dream by questioning a posited link between social position and merit. In this respect, they appear to be less under the spell of the market logic of evaluation than many observers suggest.[17] Their framework of reference is much broader than that of American individualism, on which research focuses—if only because self-reliance is less exclusively at the center of their worldview than is usually implied. Their oppositional ideology also goes beyond the usual models of working class consciousness. In fact, interviews reveal a whole world that is largely unexplored—a wide range of arguments about worth that are not made by professionals and managers. As such, these interviews help us transcend the traditional opposition between structural and individualist explanations of equality by showing that the critical stances adopted by workers are shaped by cultural assumptions that go beyond structural explanations.[18]

One could argue that these alternative definitions of worth are a direct reflection of the life conditions of the workers and the ideologies to which they are exposed: because their market positions do not allow them to aspire to high socioeconomic attainment, they redirect their energies toward the pursuit of other, more attainable, goals, and these are found in the realms of family and interpersonal relationships. Their subordinate position at work pushes them toward valuing behavior that implies respect for the dignity of people in low-status positions. Finally, their work experience may give them a negative view of power relationships, since they are primarily exposed to the "negative effects" of such relationships as opposed to their "positive outcomes" (such as the accumulation of resources). The tension that workers experience between identifying with middle class values and rejecting them is illustrative of the strong power of attraction exercised by the mainstream definitions of success that are diffused by American cultural institutions, ranging from the educational system to the mass media and the entertainment industry. Religious organizations now stand almost alone in diffusing the message that happiness is to be found elsewhere than in the pursuit of the American dream. However, most denominations act to reinforce dominant standards of evaluation instead of to weaken and relativize them. In contrast, we will see that, for French workers, political parties and unions continue to diffuse cultural repertoires that promote the definitions of success not connected to socioeconomic status.

How does the perspective of these workers compare with that of professionals and managers? The upper middle class men I talked to are considerably more likely than the workers to measure people's value by their social position and to describe themselves as feeling inferior to rich, powerful, and successful people. A few say that they value integrity more than success in others, but this stance is much more common among workers.[19] While the child-rearing values of professionals and managers stress teaching achievement orientation,[20] they often view ambition, dynamism, a strong work ethic, and competitiveness as doubly sacred because they signal both moral and socioeconomic worth.[21] Accordingly, surveys show that this group is most likely to think that their society is one of open competition, where mobility is determined by psychological and moral fortitude rather than by background and chance.[22] In my interviews, fewer New York professionals and managers expressed alternative definitions of success, and most measured freedom by consumption, for instance, by being able to buy a house in a good neighborhood or to take off regularly for a weekend of skiing in Vermont.[23]

Our results are bolstered by recent studies of class differences in conceptions of prestige that also show that workers and professionals use different criteria to organize the world that surrounds them. For instance, comparing how electricians and academics categorize occupations, Michèle Ollivier found that the academics spontaneously privilege responsibility and authority as criteria of classification, and that they lump together professional and managerial/white-collar occupations, putting skilled trades and service/lower-skilled occupations in another category. In contrast, electricians liken themselves to professionals on the bases of the usefulness of their work and the educational training it requires, and lump together managerial and white-collar occupations because they perceive them as neither useful nor admired.[24] Other studies find a higher degree of consensus on the relative prestige of occupations among the more privileged social groups, suggesting the greater hegemony of a single set of standards within this group as compared to others.[25] Finally, higher prestige groups are also found to polarize and maximize social differences more than groups at the lower end, and this underscores the importance of alternative criteria for lower status groups.[26] Such findings suggest that we need to rethink the nexus between respect, worth, socioeconomic standing, and social position in the community.[27] At a minimum, we need to examine empirically whether the privileging of economic standards of evaluation found in much of the literature is justified. With this in mind, I now turn to the paradoxical position of black workers.

Blacks Evaluating "People Above"

The attitudes of African-American workers toward the upper half are similar to those of white workers in many respects: like whites, many measure success on the basis of income and ambition. They value money but appear to do so in part because it acts as a racial equalizer by making respect—as well as necessities and luxuries—accessible to blacks. They also attach great importance to social status, as illustrated by Craig Patterson, the assistant cable splicer, who believes that races are equal because there is a black elite. He explains that "to me everyone is born equal . . . You know, there are people who are equal out here: there are black doctors, lawyers, and politicians, the whole bit."

Compared to whites, blacks are more likely to define success in financial terms (half of blue-collar blacks compared to a third of their white counterparts) and to praise ambition (a third of black workers compared to a fourth of whites).[28] In fact, more black workers value standards of evaluation associated with the upper half, such as money. They are also more convinced that their quality of life is inferior to that of middle class people. They often stress middle class attitudes, such as "leadership" and "goal orientation," when describing the qualities they appreciate. Also, more black than white interviewees identify with the middle class—63 percent of the blue-collar blacks compared to 50 percent of their white counterparts.[29] Fewer blacks than whites—20 percent versus 27 percent of the total sample—have contradictory positions: they simultaneously identify with the upper half and draw boundaries against it. Finally, fewer blacks than whites are unambiguously critical of the upper half (30 percent compared to 47 percent).[30]

While fewer blacks draw boundaries against the upper half than whites, those who do so draw stronger boundaries than whites: they draw moral, class, and racial boundaries simultaneously, which whites did not draw when discussing "people above" but did when discussing the poor, as they often conflate the poor and blacks. More specifically, blacks often explicitly treat "white" and "middle class" as synonyms, and they are very vocal in describing "people above" as immoral because too selfish. As compared with whites, they attribute less legitimacy to authority and are more attuned to its exploitative and coercive aspects. They are also less likely than whites to equate high socioeconomic status with moral character because their own experience with racism contradicts the view that individual worth is reflected in a person's success. These patterns provide evidence that African-American culture differs from mainstream white culture. As with white workers, my discussion first turns to workers who identify with the middle class.

"THERE'S NO ADVANTAGE TO BEING ANYTHING BUT ON TOP": THE POWER OF MONEY. We encountered Abe Lind in the last chapter. A young plumber working on Long Island in a company owned by whites, Abe spends much of his time driving around the suburbs to service white middle class homes. When I met him in the bar of a hotel next to a sports complex in Nassau County, Abe explained why he dreams of being middle class:

> I am lower middle class by income. That means I have a lot of improvement to do. There's no advantage to being anything but on top, let me tell you. That's where you want to be, on top. Middle class people have a nice lifestyle because their income is in excess of $40,000 . . . There's no advantage to be working class, a person who works daily to pay bills, no . . . It sucks, all right? If I was middle class, that means I'd have probably more savings away and work less. My goal is to do less work and have more people working for me. If upper class means people having authority to make decisions that affect people's lives, I think there's nothing wrong to be in that position . . . One of my dreams and desires is: I want me this house on the water, about five acres, nice area where I can get my boat in and out. Why do I want this? Because this is what I see everybody else wants. I want me a couple of cars in the driveway, in the garage, and I want it clean. I want the maid coming in, I want the landscapers doing landscaping. All right? I want marble and glass everywhere. I want leather everywhere, I don't want to see nothing cheap, I want my granite sinks, I mean, tiles . . . This is what I want.

While Abe has dreams of prosperity inspired by "Lifestyles of the Rich and the Famous," he finds little redeeming virtue in his own social position. Others who are consumed by daily battles to keep necessity at arm's length share this view. This is the case for Art Mann, the poorest worker I interviewed, who is a maintenance man and a former drug addict. I met him in his near-empty apartment—his brother had been selling the furniture to get money for drugs. Art explained that, if he were to be born again, he would not like to come back at the same income level: "There's too many limitations to the mind, and the soul, and the spirit. Your concentration is too monetarial. You've got to take time out now to really think about where you going to get your next meal. That's a lot of thinking. You're better off reading a book. But if you're hungry, you can't concentrate on your studies, there are too many limitations." Art knows about these limitations because he experiences them in a very concrete manner—he is forced to pay child support for two children and simply cannot make ends meet.

Leon Davis also shares the view that there is no advantage to being anywhere but on top. His position is very different from Art's: a letter carrier, he has been working for the post office for many years and has accumulated some money. He enjoys visiting New York to attend events and go to fine restaurants. He also owns a big white American luxury car. However, in his sixties, he lives in a large housing project where the walls are covered with graffiti and the perimeter is surrounded by barbed wire. He says, "I can't think of any advantage of being lower working class . . . I think statistically, say, you live longer, you're healthier [if you are middle class]. Every advantage that I could think of, that's connected to life, is with a person with formal education . . . I can't think of ever having met a person who wouldn't have rather been a professional. And I don't think I've never met a professional who wanted to be working class. So you hear it from both sides."

These black workers find no romantic appeal to their own positions, and they look at the other side of the fence as an unreachable ideal from which they are excluded by lack of education, lack of resources, and lack of contacts. It is in this context that the American dream has a particularly mythic power for them. A middle class lifestyle looms large on their horizons of hope, and it can be simply defined, following Tyrone Smith the chemical plant operative, as "raising my son in a nice environment and giving him the better things in life. Teach him a nice set of values and morals. Own my home. Hopefully buy another home and own two homes by the time I'm sixty."

In the context of worsening economic conditions in many African-American neighborhoods where drugs are readily available, hanging on to this American dream is particularly important for stable blue-collar workers: they are the ones patrolling the borders of the mainstream black community, upholding the norms, and keeping deviance at bay. They have to work hard at keeping "a monetary focus" because of their liminal positions at the interstices between what they often perceive to be a white middle class world and a largely threatened and/or disenfranchised black world.[31]

It is in this context that workers discuss at great length the importance of money. We saw that black workers take it to be a basis for racial equalization, a universal standard that allows them to be evaluated independently of their ascribed characteristic. They also take it to be the key to social membership. In the words of Tyrone Smith, "There's too much money in America to be poor . . . Money in some circles breeds power and respect, especially in America. I don't want to be strangled or a hostage to anybody for that," adding "you need a job, everybody should work, people that don't work don't have any voice." He echoes John Lamb, the recycling worker, for whom money "[gives you] a voice in the world. It gives you power in the world. It gives you an ability to do anything you want in the world . . . and people listen to you. That's the way the world is set up, where money means everything. Regardless of what you hear on this or that, money means everything."

IN PRAISE OF MIDDLE CLASS ATTITUDES: GOAL ORIENTATION AND LEADERSHIP. Black workers had elaborate theories about how to achieve success, most often emphasizing middle class values such as goal orientation, ambition, and leadership. In line with popular self-improvement literature, they emphasize setting goals for oneself, trying to better oneself, and not losing interest "in terms of advancement and things of that nature," in the words of a security supervisor. For instance, when asked what qualities he looks for in prospective friends, Craig Patterson, the assistant cable splicer, says, "Ambition. Mainly, I look for ambition—people who just constantly want to do things to better their lives and not just settle for less. So many people, I feel, do that. I don't want to go [without a] struggle. I mean it's hard. I never just, never wanted to just be [average]. I never was a follower. I always was a leader."

Art Mann, the maintenance worker and former drug addict, believes strongly in ambition and success: "Life is really a game. The game is to strive to succeed to get better, you know, and to do that, you have to start at the bottom and work your way up. I have done that . . . I know what the bottom is. So now, I'm at the middle part. Once I get from that middle part into another part when I get my break, if I could get a break, then I would know how to [settle] into that part, the rich part, and live comfortably and enjoy it."

Art believes that "there is the American dream, because too many people that made it, made it through the American dream. Maybe they had to cut corners, but they made it. Success is out here. It's just finding it."[32] Art's aspirations contrast starkly with the grimness of his daily battles to keep afloat, and in this he resembles many poor blacks who invest much in the American dream with little chance for success, as if this belief in ambition and endless possibilities was part of what they do to perform their collective identity as Americans.[33] Ambition and determination to reverse fate against all odds take on a sacred value for them, and this is reflected in their descriptions of their heroes. For instance, Bill Washington, the UPS mail sorter, expresses great admiration for a friend who "really wants to be rich": "He is money-hungry. He wants to be rich. Brian wants to be wealthy. He cuts hair in New York City . . . He's got a stockbroker, he's got a commodities broker. He could buy a car for $500, fix it up, and sell it for $1,500 to make a profit. He has done it. He keeps his clippers, you know his hair stuff with him, and brings it home to make extra money at night."

Bill also describes his father as a hero because he "traveled a long rough road but he made it and that's why I admire him. He worked seven days a week to keep the house." Bill himself hopes to attend community college to get an accounting degree, but he has had to postpone his plans and is still working at UPS after many years.

One of the key differences in how black and white workers understand middle class attributes is that black workers place greater emphasis on leadership—a trait that went unmentioned by whites. This is illustrated by a health inspector, one of the few black interviewees who has a positive view of power: "If I had a choice I would definitely be in a leadership capacity, an upper class capacity. And not for prestigious reasons, either, but because of the ability to effect change. I see no reason to strive for mediocrity." Similarly, Tyrone Smith defines self-respect as "being a leader, not compromising yourself for your friends, not doing anything that's detrimental to yourself," while Harvey Stack, who works as a quality inspector in a paper plant, believes that it is important to be a leader just to show what black people are capable of and "set an example for the kids."

Workers discuss the importance of leadership in the context of the urgent need to keep drugs at bay and to patrol the boundary between the mainstream world and the underworld within black neighborhoods. They also emphasize leadership because they believe in "giving to the community," which resonates with the issue of collectivist morality discussed in Chapter 1.

THE MORAL FLAWS OF THE MIDDLE CLASS VERSUS A CARING AND COLLECTIVIST MORALITY. Racial discrimination makes it difficult for black workers to believe in social status as a signal of moral character and that market position is a good indicator of people's ability, since most do not believe that they are playing on an even field. In the words of Leon Davis, the letter carrier, "There are so many advantages in being white; it's just so advantageous to be a member of the dominant group . . . To me, there's no real reason for a white guy to be a failure. There's nothing that's not in his favor." Through racial discrimination, workers encounter structural limitations to their own mobility, which means, in the words of a machinist, that "average black people don't get to the top. It's the excellent ones, whereas the average Caucasian can make it. This is something I have known from day one." Concretely, discrimination takes subtle forms. For instance, Tyrone Smith, one of a handful of black workers employed in a large chemical plant, believes that he is more closely supervised and scrutinized than other workers: "You have to watch your p's and q's because one mistake may not be overlooked as far as somebody else making the same mistake. My absenteeism, my personal leave, and sick time, all that is scrutinized thorough a microscope . . . They let you know that they have enough minorities to keep the government contracts . . . The way I deal with it is really I don't trust anybody there . . . I started out with a major handicap because I'm black." For George Silver, a truck driver, discrimination means that he is constantly underestimated: "They don't think you're smart, O.K.? . . . Give them ideas and they don't do it. When a white guy say the same thing I say, they'll try it . . . They don't ask questions . . . You get no help."[34]

In line with these views, survey data show that African Americans believe in equality of opportunity less than whites.[35] Racial discrimination also encourages black workers to decouple socioeconomic standing from moral worth. Again, they value money so highly because they recognize it as a key that opens doors rather than because they view it as revealing true moral superiority—unlike whites, who are more likely to associate earning power with moral worth. This frame facilitates the development of a critical stance toward the middle class.

The critique that blacks offer of the middle class resembles the one they offer of whites: they emphasize its domineering and exploitative character and its selfishness and lack of concern with giving back to the community. In contrast, white workers are more preoccupied with the middle class's lack of sincerity and personal integrity. Black and white workers alike are critical of the poor quality of interpersonal relationships among middle class people, which we discuss first.

Middle class people have poorer interpersonal relationships than workers, in part because they lack loyalty toward their friends. Jimmy Light, the black phone technician, is the epitome of the materialist worker. A union steward, he is very proud of how much money he makes. He drives a brand-new jeep and is thinking of getting married, now that his fiancée makes good money as a phone operator. Despite his materialism, Jimmy is critical of middle class people, and he describes the differences as follows:

> I think a distinction, from my own experience, between, say, a lower middle class and perhaps an upper middle class is the quality, the depth of the people. To use as an example: the guys on the job, they are more or less down-to-earth, you know, relate on an eye-to-eye level, more so than someone who is an upper middle class, a yuppie, or whatever the case may be. Mostly from what I see, most of their friendships are kind of superficial. While the going is good, we are all peachy keen, but then when something is bad, you get fired from your job or something like that, all of the sudden your friends disappear. But more or less the people I associate with, they are always there . . . These people are in the same class that I am, from the same background, the same kind of upbringing.

Echoing the view that blacks are more caring human beings than whites, Jimmy Light thinks that professionals lack sincerity and generosity. Art Mann, the maintenance worker, makes a similar point when he explains that it is better to be friends with "a poor honest person because I know that in the long run, if I get in a jam and he can help me, he will. Where that guy that has all the money, he'll look back and go 'The hell with him, I ain't got no use for him.'" Abe Lind, the plumber, concurs when he criticizes his successful friends who left the neighborhood. He says that they will regret it because "you find out what's important are friends and time shared, not money and prestige. Most of the friends that are on my level, we have the best of times when we have a picnic or a barbecue, watch football together, or just tell each other how we're screwing up each other's lives. That's life, that's living." Rich people cannot have genuine relationship with others because, as Tom Green, the hospital orderly, points out, "they are miserable because they think you're out to get something for nothing . . . They think you want to beat them out of their money."

This resonates with the view encountered in Chapter 2 that whites (as middle class people) are less communal than blacks. This is why John Lamb, the recycling plant worker, says, "I've got the mind of a poor person. If I become rich, I'm going to carry the same mind I got now. I'm still going to be caring . . . And the people that don't have it, I would never turn my back on them, never . . . People's hearts should come first. [Don't] put money before people, or use people to get money."

John makes clear his view of the middle class when he says that he wants the money, the social position, the easy life, the chance to "give back to the community," but not the values.[36] Thus, he expresses succinctly what I perceive to be the predominant view about the desirability of middle class attributes among the black workers I talked to. However, the standard American dream is not necessarily conducive to the caring and collective orientation of blacks. When Art Armstrong, a newspaper worker, explains that he has his own American dream, he says, "I don't want to climb the ladder that someone says I should climb. I am ambitious, but I am not a person who feels I should step over other people or beat them down to get somewhere . . . Not necessarily 'go get the money,' but if you can, good, and if you get it, put it to good use, don't be selfish."

He and others view the Republican Party as the epitome of this middle class lack of caring. For Art Mann, the maintenance worker, for instance, Republicans "look down on people, just like with Bush's trickle-down economics . . . The rich get the money and then basically sometimes it would come back down to us and we'll help each other. That's the stupidest proposal to come out of his face because all he was doing is make the rich richer. And you know, if you're poor, the hell with you."

It is this lack of concern for others that characterizes professionals, according to Craig Patterson, the assistant cable splicer. He compares his caring style of personal interaction with that of his brother, who works as an academic administrator: "My brother is very business-like and stuff and maybe not cold, but it's different . . . You know like how some people never put their guard down. I guess I let mine down. I'm friendly with everybody. I must have six or seven phone books in my gym bag." Linking middle class arrogance to whiteness, Jimmy Light describes his experience repairing phones in Manhattan: "Sometimes you have some people, the yuppies or whatever it is quote unquote, they think their shit doesn't stink . . . They think they own you . . . Because of their own upbringing or whatever it is, they are more or less shouting out commands: 'You do this and you do that,' all the time. It is second nature . . . Sometimes whites have a tendency to sound worse than they are, from your own perception, your own lifestyle, or your own background."

It has been argued that black American workers have a stronger sense of social injustice and are more militant than their white counterparts in that they more willingly point to exploitation at work.[37] And, indeed, exploitation is a recurrent theme for many of my black respondents, much more so than among whites. They argue that profits come at the expense of workers. For a man who works in the textile industry, "management is trying to squeeze us like a grape and get more, more, more, more," while for a fumigator, "it could take five guys to do a job and [if the bosses] could get away with two, that's more money in [their] pocket. It's as simple as that." Also, for George Silver, the truck driver, "anything they can beat you for, they gonna do it . . . They hate when you go to the doctor . . . They crying poverty but they're always buying the machines and hiring people left and right." Jimmy Light summarizes the situation thus: "Our objective is to make as much money as we can. Their objective is not to let us make much money because they have to hold down costs. It's always 'us' and 'them.'" The theme of exploitation may be more salient among black than white workers in part because they are more frequently exposed to repertoires stressing social justice, due to their higher level of unionization than white workers. We will see that this theme is also central to French workers.

In many cases, this exploitative attitude is also linked to the lack of caring discussed earlier. For Art Armstrong, who is employed by a newspaper as a production worker, his bosses "don't really care about anyone anyway . . . Sometimes they will do things that will remind you 'Well, you're a commodity to us, and if we feel we're not getting anything out of you anymore, or we feel we can get more out of that person, you're out.'" A number of interviewees echoed this sentiment when discussing the impact of corporate downsizing on work relations.

Black workers have a more negative view of power and authority than whites. They do not conceive of them as tools for achieving the common good, as whites sometimes do, but as arbitrary attributes associated with abuse and based on violence. For Tom Green, the hospital orderly, "Because some people get power, they want to be dominating, take advantage, they mistreat people, step on you." For George Silver, the truck driver, "People want power because they want to control people. When you want to control people, it's because you feel inferior. You want to control people to bring people down." Some associate power with the underworld, a connection not made by white workers. For a worker in an x-ray firm, "When I think powerful, I think someone's gonna be corrupted, you're gonna buy someone and if that person doesn't do this as they're supposed to do it, they get killed." Bringing together this underworld theme with the criticisms of power formulated by whites, Larry Wright, the park maintenance worker, asks, "How many powerful people do you know that ain't got shot, got assassinated, or whatever? What's the use of being powerful if you ain't going to be here so long? What's the use of being rich if you can't take it with you? So you should just survive and take care of yourself while you're here . . . Power means nothing to me . . . Power is something I would like to have only if I use it in the right way . . . I'd use it in the way of helping people to do better."

Art Mann, the maintenance worker and former drug addict, reflects on the relationships of dependency that are at the heart of power relationships when he explains why he does not want to owe anything to anyone: "Survival is by getting your own and don't have to ask nobody for nothing. Because once you ask somebody for something, then you owe them something. Never owe nobody nothing. Nobody can never come back to you and say 'Do this for me' and you don't feel like doing it. 'Well, I did this for you,' you know, that type of thing. No . . . And I don't like to ask nobody for nothing, knowing what they'll do. Since they'll give it to me, then they'll have to give me a lecture, and they gonna have to talk about it as soon as I was out, and I don't like that."

Money is more impersonal than power and as such might be easier to deal with in a situation of pervasive racism. Furthermore, money can lead to self-sufficiency and create a buffer between one's family and a dangerous environment, but power is generally experienced in a negative manner, through humiliation and subordination, and is positively valued only as a tool for collective empowerment by blacks, "to help people do better."

Partly influenced by the mass media depiction of society as an overwhelmingly white middle class world, black workers easily move from drawing boundaries against whites to drawing boundaries against the middle class, at times confounding the two categories and using similar rhetorics to describe both as uncaring, exploitative, lonely, and uncommunal groups. This association is crucial in helping black workers make sense of racial discrimination, which they often resent as class discrimination. This connection is expressed by Jimmy Light, the black phone technician, who points again to the role of consumption in granting cultural membership:

> We find that some people are prejudiced against the working class. And these people happen to be white . . . They treat you like shit. It's human nature. People when they have more money, we're back to that again . . . They know that if you're a telephone man or Con Edison, building maintenance, they know that you only make a certain amount of money. And I can fool them. When I wear a certain tie and a suit, I can be the same person,

but they would think I had more money than I have and they would treat me differently.

Jimmy is furious that these middle class whites lack respect for his integrity and dignity and for that of workers more generally. Hence, the class/racial struggle has a distinctively moral character for him, and despite his materialism, he uses measuring sticks that put him above the middle class and white people in general. He rejects and resists those who would assign him a lowly place. This is not part of a culture of poverty or an underclass culture: Jimmy and workers like him share much with mainstream culture. They distinguish themselves from this mainstream culture precisely by stressing black respectability and moral superiority.

In this context, as we saw, black workers elaborate alternative definitions of success that are more collectivist than those of whites. Although some white workers define their success by the fact that they coach Little League, blacks are more likely to provide alternative definitions of success that are collective in orientation and focus on giving back to the community. However, several blacks equate success with simply escaping the dangers of the environment in which they live. A 60-year-old bindery worker considers himself successful "as far as being able to say that I have escaped the ways of the streets . . . When I was a young man, heroin was the thing. I was successful in escaping that era. I was successful in that I was never a street walker or anything of that nature." Similarly, Bill Masters, a photo technician who used to be a drug addict, says, "I've graduated in lots of different things . . . Just to come out of the drug world. I have come a long ways." Finally, because of their experience with racism, blacks may be more inclined to develop alternative American dreams that do not depend on middle class status. In the words of Tony Clark, a medical supply worker, "I believe everybody has an American dream, but everybody's dream is not the same. The basic American dream is not for everybody."

In sum, the definitions of worth that black workers offer are paradoxical. On the one hand, they prize financial success, consumption, goal orientation, and leadership. On the other hand, they are particularly critical of the exploitative dimension of interclass relationships. They do not believe that social achievement correlates with moral character, in part due to their experience with racial discrimination.[38] They are also critical of the selfishness of the upper half and position themselves above "people above," based on the quality of their interpersonal relationships. Their position is more paradoxical than that of whites: they are less ambivalent than whites in their critique of money (perhaps because it is viewed as a key to cultural membership) yet more critical of the exploitative character of the middle class. They point to middle class selfishness, suggesting that their critiques of the middle class draw heavily on collectivist themes discussed in Chapter 1. These patterns lead me to conclude that among black and white workers alike, boundaries are drawn against "people above": middle class people have a position that deserves to be emulated, but their values are not always to be respected. The one exception is ambition, which is admired by most blacks and many whites.

Explaining the Patterns

Why do many workers privilege moral criteria of evaluation over socioeconomic criteria? This practice has been interpreted in the literature as an instance of low-status group resistance to the culture of dominant groups: adopting a distinct view of morality provides workers with a sphere of cultural autonomy.[39] In contrast, I view this resistance as an unintended consequence of the dimensions of morality that workers value most and of their quest for respect as human beings and workers.[40] As suggested in Chapter 1, moral criteria are particularly important for these individuals because they live in dangerous environments where predictability is valued: in these environments, personal buffering zones are scarce and interdependence is high due to limited physical space and resources. The Protestant emphasis on the work ethic, the republican and liberal social contract, and the culture of masculinity are cultural factors that contribute to making morality particularly central to workers. The role of work as a tool for mobility also pushes them toward putting morality above socioeconomic status in their evaluation of people. Moreover, by stressing morality over socioeconomic success, workers affirm their own value and dignity and reject the notion that one's station in life defines one's worth.[41]

How can we account for our main finding concerning racial differences, namely, that African Americans appear to be simultaneously more and less critical of the standards of worth valued by the upper half than whites (i.e., they value middle class criteria of worth while drawing stronger boundaries toward "people above")? I suggested that the experience of racial discrimination leads blacks to dissociate moral from socioeconomic worth more readily than whites. They are more likely to understand money as a tool and a key to membership rather than as an indication of a person's moral value. This is reinforced by the fact that whites identify poverty with blackness. In fact, black workers want money but not the values associated with the rich, which are often tainted by a lack of respect for people. At the same time, the vulnerability of blacks' social position and their experience with social exclusion make money de facto particularly important to them. When asserting the importance of goal orientation and leadership, black interviewees indirectly disprove the racist discourse that depicts blacks as lacking in ambition[42] while affirming the importance of working purposefully toward policing the boundary between mainstream black society and the underworld. By affirming their belief in their American dream, they proclaim their identification with the sacred values of their society and their full membership in it.

Blacks' experience at the bottom of the labor market, their stronger appreciation for the "caring self," and their collective experience with segregation and racism may make them more attentive to the negative aspects of power and to the exploitative nature of authority relationships, and push them toward viewing the (white) middle class as selfish and domineering. The black church, Afrocentric organizations, and other political institutions have played an important role in diffusing the view that people's worth should be assessed independently from their social status: this is a central theme of the racial pride movement, and it is also a powerful way to counteract racist arguments that ground racist belief in the lower socioeconomic performance of blacks. The impact of these cultural institutions may have been reinforced by the historical role of blacks as subordinate service workers: these jobs placed blacks in positions where they could closely observe middle class people, and this experience fed into narratives that white middle class people are domineering, selfish, have poor interpersonal relationships, and lack intimacy in friendships.[43] We now turn to attitudes toward people below to discover that workers draw strong boundaries against this group. Here again, blacks adopt more paradoxical positions than whites.

"People Below"

The classification system workers use to organize their environment gives a lowly place to the poor. White and black men who elaborate alternative definitions of success are much less likely to mobilize alternative measuring sticks to evaluate "people below" than "people above." If they often hesitate to equate socioeconomic standing with moral worth when discussing middle class people, a small majority among white interviewees have a unequivocal and opposite view when it comes to the poor, perhaps because they associate poverty with laziness. In Chapter 1, we saw that many workers define their honor and worth by their work and are contemptuous of people who don't work hard. This translates into the drawing of strong boundaries against "people below." While some white workers like to be "helpful" and feel compassion toward the poor because they have been there or have known people who are poor, many of them are very critical of "people below": this is the case for 50 percent of blue-collar and 66 percent of white-collar workers. Compared to whites, black workers are more accepting of the poor and of the conditions that may explain their plight: only 28 percent of black workers draw strong boundaries against the poor. However, blacks also maintain their distance to protect their own position and keep the world in moral order. In the second part of the book, we will see that, compared with American workers, French workers draw very weak boundaries toward the poor: they take them as "part of us," as part of a community of cocitizens or similarly exploited individuals toward whom society has responsibilities.[44] I begin with whites' views of this category.

Whites Who Are against "Looking for Something for Nothing" Types

More than half of white American workers do not express feelings of solidarity toward the poor. They reject the poor less because of their lack of resources than because of their faulty values; after all, workers also have limited means. Two categories of people are particular objects of scorn for white workers: first, the poor who have the "wrong attitude," those who are not "forward-looking"–the guy who "just doesn't care about life and the future and everything," in the words of a printer; second, people located at the bottom of a Malthusian hierarchy of producers and consumers grounded in economic individualism. The standard here is whether people are able to keep material needs at bay. A postal worker puts it succinctly: "If I felt superior to somebody, it would be toward people whom I feel I'm better off than they are. Like 'Gee, you've got it rough and I haven't had it that bad.'" The specific categories of "people below" toward whom white workers are critical are primarily welfare recipients and the homeless and secondarily part-time workers. I discuss these categories separately because they are treated differently by workers.

WELFARE DEPENDENCY, HOMELESSNESS, AND SELF-SUFFICIENCY. Welfare dependency and homelessness were very salient in public debates at the time I interviewed workers in 1992–1993.[45] Accordingly, white workers often mentioned welfare recipients and the homeless in their discussions of worth, and they stigmatized these groups simultaneously for their socioeconomic and moral failings. As we saw in Chapter 1, for white men dignity is obtained through work and the independence it affords, and living on the public dole defines an important boundary between the worthy and unworthy. To Henry Link, the bank supply salesman, "If you are a half decent person at all, you have to hate yourself for having to accept [welfare] in the first place . . . Anybody who takes advantage isn't worth their salt." For Dennis Young, the Bayonne firefighter, "I dislike people that are looking for something for nothing . . . People who don't work and they sit at home and collect money . . . To me it's people like that who are looking for something for nothing who should be given nothing. There's like homeless people and stuff that I won't give a dollar to."

The issue here is less social position than "your outlook": people should be responsible and respect the implicit social contract to pull their weight[46] and not give up–again, traits central to workers' own self-identity. For Vincent Marchesi, the electronics technician, there are distinct marks of worth distinguishing the deserving from the less deserving: "The fact that I can make do, that I forced myself to make do, that does give me an edge, I guess, if nothing else. I don't feel that in the long run I am a fantastic person compared to these people, but I think they missed the boat somewhere along the line. And I have to give myself a little credit there." Hence, the "disciplined self" that workers mobilize to evaluate people in general is central to their evaluation of the poor.

The normative requirement of self-sufficiency came up time and again in the interviews. The homeless are often described as having "given up." Jack Getty, the stage technician, points to this group not only for having given up, but also for being unable to keep material needs at bay. When asked whom he feels superior to, he says, "It's unfortunate, but I'd have to say the people on the streets, homeless people. People who don't have what I have . . . [I feel superior] because I have the basic necessities, I haven't given up. I feel that a lot of people out there that are destitute have given up. I don't want to run right out there and help them . . . I have trouble feeling empathy, compassion, and sympathy. I don't know whether you're supposed to feel or not."

A bank clerk condemns beggars when he explains, "I can't stand people like that. I've also gotten into a couple of confrontations with people when I was going to get a newspaper. You know, 'you got a dime, you got a nickel.' 'Get out of here, don't bother me.'"

Gary Finn, the GM assembly line worker, has a more nuanced position than many when he distinguishes between the able-bodied who do not deserve help and the needy who do: "You got to do the right thing. You have responsibility to your family, you have responsibility to yourself . . . You can't just go out and rob somebody. You need money, you go out and get a job. Responsibility to society . . . You don't sit in the street and say, 'Guess what? Feed me and take care of me.' You can't become lazy . . . If you're sick or disabled, that's one thing. But for me to say that the United States owes me a living, I think the people are wrong."[47] Because his employer was laying off workers at the time I met Gary, his sensitivity to his obligations as an American took on a very concrete meaning.

The premium that white American workers place on responsibility and self-sufficiency shapes their political allegiance. An electronic technician explains his support for the Republican Party by saying it shares his principles: "Don't give anything for nothing. Incentive . . . Go get a job . . . [We should not] make it so easy to stay on unemployment, on welfare." The insurance salesman explains that he is a conservative Republican because he does not "like people who try to take advantage of things and take, take, and give nothing back." Some, like Tony Sansone, object to the idea that we have collective responsibility toward the needy and lament that "there are a lot of hard-working people out there and [Democrats] take [all their] money and spend it on all these stupid things." Liberals also share the view that the role of the state is to help create conditions for self-sufficiency. John Bridges, the warehouse worker, asks "Is it cheaper to raise three children on welfare to age 18 or to pay for the mother's education when she's 12 years old?"

White workers do not privilege structural explanations to account for the predicament of the poor. While a few white workers mentioned the role of bad luck, downsizing, and the flight of capital to the Third World, none provided a full-fledged structural explanation of poverty or of the precariousness of the condition of workers.[48] They take a more individualist perspective, which has resonance for them: in their own self-identity, and given their living conditions, struggles to pull one's weight and remain self-sufficient against all odds are central. In this context, they particularly resent that others receive help from the state. In the words of Tim Williams, the laborer, "Everything I got now I made myself. Nobody gave it to me. And anybody can do it." By morally condemning the poor, workers may improve their own social integration at the symbolic level by voicing support for one of the central tenets of the American dream, namely, that those who want to succeed, can.[49] However, as we saw in the previous discussion, workers also take critical and alternative stances toward the American dream.[50] Hence, their attitude toward the American dream is paradoxical: they can uphold the individualistic beliefs at the heart of the American dream when it comes to evaluating people below but not believe in equal opportunity when it comes to explaining their own position.[51] While this stigmatizing rhetoric maximizes the differences between the poor and the rest of the population, studies show that the values of the underclass are very similar to those of other Americans.[52]

Earlier in the century, the moral failures of the poor were often blamed on genetics and "feeblemindedness." Since the sixties, a "culture of poverty" explanation pointing to the perpetuation of a pathological culture across generations has gained wide currency.[53]

"Attitude" explains it all, and workers borrow from this widely available rhetoric because, according to historian Michael Katz, "The moral redefinition of poverty followed from the identification of market success with divine favor and personal worth. Especially in America, where opportunity awaited anyone with energy and talent, poverty signaled personal failure."[54] As James Patterson argues, this rhetoric posits "that many, if not most, of the destitute are undeserving; that large numbers of poor people exist in an intergenerational 'culture of poverty'; that social insurance is preferable to welfare, which is wasteful and demoralizing; that wise public policy seeks to prevent destitution, not to provide income maintenance; that work, not welfare, is the essence of the meaningful life."[55]

At the time I conducted the interviews, the view that poverty results from laziness was readily available from the media and from conservative and liberal politicians alike.[56] The conservative rhetoric, which has a stronger behavioral bent,[57] gained much influence during 25 years of almost uninterrupted Republican control of the White House and had marginalized the view that we have collective responsibility toward our less fortunate fellow citizens. Accordingly, the National Election Study "feeling thermometers" reveal that attitudes toward the poor became more polarized between 1972 and 1994.[58] The deterioration of the situation of the poor added further evidence to their unworthiness, especially given the widespread recognition that public resources have been used to improve their plight.[59] The general conditions that led to a retrenchment in welfare benefits also contributed to the rise of a moralistic antipoor rhetoric, as the declining influence of unions and left-of-center organizations and parties reduced the salience of solidaristic discourse in the United States as elsewhere.[60]

We saw in Chapter 1 that self-reliance, laziness, and responsibility are important in framing whites' moral stigmatization of blacks. We also saw in Chapter 2 that some white workers associate African Americans with laziness and welfare dependency. As Edsall and Edsall suggest, "welfare" has become a code word for blacks:[61] while only 37 percent of AFDC recipients are black, there is in the American population a widely shared perception that blacks make up the vast majority of welfare cases.[62] While blacks make up only 33.4 percent of the American poor,[63] the average respondent to a 1991 national survey believed that they made up 50 percent.[64] This association between race and poverty fosters political attitudes centered on the view that white racial and middle class solidarity go hand in hand. And indeed, white support for social spending that implicitly or explicitly benefits blacks primarily is considerably lower than white support for other programs.[65] Whites' opposition to welfare is strongly associated with blaming the character of blacks for racial inequality.[66]

Finally, how can we account for this association between blackness and poverty? Blacks are indeed overrepresented among the poor in this country,[67] but the discrepancy is not large enough to explain such a high level of association. Here again, media representations have an important impact: 62 percent of the people represented in a sample of news stories about the poor from 1988 to 1992 were blacks, at a time when this group made up only 29 percent of the American poor.[68] The Republican Party is often viewed as responsible for diffusing negative images of blacks. By equating blacks with welfare dependency and crime, Republicans have been able to attract the racially resentful—particularly the populist white working class.[69] Linking welfare programs to blacks was key to the decline of popular support for further governmental intervention.[70] By diffusing the notion that blacks and welfare are associated, Republicans legitimized a view of the Democratic Party as caring more about the needs of minorities than about those of ordinary workers. This had devastating effects because programs aiming to help minorities were construed as ineffective and discriminating against whites. In fact, the Clinton administration has paid more attention to economic issues, such as free trade and deficit reduction, than to income inequality, succumbing to pressure from business interests.[71]

PART-TIMERS AS A POLLUTING CATEGORY. While social scientists have paid considerable attention to the stigmatizing rhetoric aimed at the poor, the homeless, and welfare recipients in particular,[72] they have neglected that aimed at part-time workers.[73] This rhetoric was salient in my interviews with white workers, but it was absent among professionals and managers. Working class men with stable employment frequently distinguish themselves from part-time workers. Their work conditions, benefits, the simple fact of having a full-time job, and the fact that they can keep material needs at bay and have greater financial security place them above part-timers in a Malthusian hierarchy of producers. While Stan Morley, the pipe fitter, may be indifferent to "whether you have a college degree or not," he feels superior to the part-time workers employed by the perfume manufacturing company where he works: "I feel maybe superior to them in that respect that I have full-time gainful employment and they're only here today and gone tomorrow." Also, the tin factory foreman, Jim Jennings, puts himself above part-time workers, whom he views as "dummies. They have to struggle through life to get to where it's to live week by week off a paycheck." Similarly, when drawing comparisons, Michael Brandon, the Exxon supervisor, singles out "laborers in the yard. They're not Exxon employees, but if you have really dirty work like cleaning out the inside of a tank, they'll bring laborers in . . . They're not making the salaries that we're making. So I mean the evidence is, when the people walk around every day, they see what a laborer does. We're not all equal in this world."

This rhetoric is particularly vivid, perhaps because of the liminal status of these part-time workers: they occupy morally ambiguous positions, and as a result workers may use a more rigid system of moral designation to evaluate them and to keep them at bay.[74] They are singled out as having particularly low moral standards (they indulge in sexual promiscuity, alcohol, and drugs) and as being "nothing but trouble," as if their part-time employment was to be explained in part by their instability, lack of character, or inability to handle responsibility. Johnny Page, the printer, expresses his views clearly: "I don't like people who hold temp jobs, or who work a job just to get unemployment, so they can live off unemployment all summer long, so they can ride their motorcycles around. Who get into fights, who beat on people because they said something to somebody's girlfriend, stuff like that. Most of the population would agree with me, that's not the type of person to hang around with." Billy Taylor, the cosmetics company foreman, also points to the low morals of part-time workers. He notes that the hourly wage offered by the company fluctuates:

At the lower economic level, there were fights. There were lots of times when knives came out and stuff like that. When [the pay rate] was low, that's when we had all the dregs of society coming through. It created a lot of problems in the workplace . . . There's a lot of threats and subversive things going on . . . Homosexuality and you have no idea what goes on with some of these brothers. Everything would be bought and sold around here. Next thing you know, you got a couple guys loading the truck, and you don't see them for a little while. You go walking into the truck and there's a lot of overt action occurring, which you wouldn't expect. You would have a girl wearing a winter jacket in July because she had tracks all the way up and down her arm. In order to get the stuff, she was doing things in the back of the warehouse.

Jimmy Brown, the born-again truck driver, singles out the moral character of part-time workers who steal when given the opportunity:

All they are interested in is making money for the day, so they can drink it or smoke it, or whatever they do with it. And they come back the next day, lots of times, some of them, not all of them, but some of them, they're wearing the same clothes and they were out all night and they don't have any money and the next morning they're looking for you to buy them cigarettes or breakfast or lunch or whatever . . . But there are some guys that come down that work nights to make a couple of extra bucks on the side, and they're decent guys, they're good guys to work with.

Part-timers embody the moral threat that so concerns the workers I talked to, who regard a stable job and being hardworking as essential tools for keeping this danger at bay.

INTERPERSONAL ALTRUISM AND THE POOR. It has been argued that the recent conservative turn against social spending and entitlement, and the simultaneous stigmatization of the poor, emerged largely from corporate America: businessmen succeeded in convincing politicians and the public that they could not afford to support social programs while facing the financial pressures of economic globalization, and that it was in the national interest to reduce taxes.[75] While this view has gained popularity, large groups of Americans still believe that too little is being spent on assistance to the homeless, the poor, and the unemployed, and this group continues to favor more social spending on their behalf.[76] Nevertheless, of all the programs that are part of the United States welfare state—including education, health care, and benefits to the elderly—the least popular are those that provide help to poor families (such as "Aid to Family with Dependent Children" (AFDC), general assistance, and food stamps).[77] In comparative perspective, support for collectivism and egalitarianism in policy preferences is much lower in the United States than in other advanced industrial societies.[78]

We find in the literature contradictory evidence concerning the relationship between attitudes toward the poor. Surveys show that negative attitudes toward the homeless are found among almost half of the population and are more frequent among older, less educated, and poorer people.[79] However, the public redistribution of income appeals more to workers than to professionals. Fifty percent of workers and 41 percent of professionals responding to a 1984 survey agreed with the view that "it is the responsibility of government to meet everyone's needs, even in case of sickness, poverty, unemployment and old age."[80] Yet in my interviews I encountered only a few white workers who explicitly expressed compassion toward the poor, who questioned the equation between moral value and socioeconomic standing when it came to "people below," or who refused to blame welfare recipients for their fate.

What distinguishes these compassionate men from those who do not broaden their definition of "us" to include the poor? They mentioned the potential precariousness of their own economic status by reminding me that there is little social distance between their station in life and the nightmare of homelessness. In the words of Tim Williams, the laborer, "right under lower middle class is poor, and right after that is homeless, you know"; for Jack Getty, the stage technician, "there is a part of me that thinks, 'Well, you know, you're only that far away from becom[ing homeless] at anytime . . . Things could go very wrong really fast.'" For Dennis Young, the Bayonne firefighter, "If you goof off, you're without a job, and then you find out how easy it is to be homeless. It happens every day. Somebody loses a job and they're homeless in a month, when the rent is due again." These workers can imagine how homelessness can result from bad luck rather than moral failure.

Research on attitudes toward poverty also shows that personal contact with the poor increases support for welfare and changes how people understand the sources of poverty. Personal contact is associated with the use of structural, as opposed to individualistic and moralistic, explanations of poverty.[81] Accordingly, among my interviewees, the workers who are most accepting of the poor are those who have experienced poverty or have been exposed to it.[82] For instance, the receiving clerk, Murray DiPrete, recalls his own experience with unemployment: "I can understand [the poor] better now because I was in that type of situation where I didn't know what I was gonna do next. I was so poor. I was only getting like $310 every two weeks. If it wasn't for my mother feeding me, I don't know how the hell I would have survived, O.K.? I mean, I couldn't afford to do the job search. I had to go buy stamps in the post office—$5.80 for a book. That was a lot of money to put out for these stupid stamps!"

Stan Morley, the pipe fitter, also understands the position of welfare recipients. At one point he had to "suck in my pride" and take welfare because he had a new baby and was unable to find a job. He says, "People like [short-term recipients], I have no problem with. They're using it as it is supposed to be used. But the people where whole generations of families are on welfare, I'm sorry, I don't go for that. Something should be done."

According to historian Michael Katz, in America "considerations of productivity, cost, and eligibility have channeled discourse about need, entitlement, and justice within narrow limits bounded by the market. In every era, a few people have counter-posed dignity, community, and equality as standards for policy. But they have remained outsiders."[83] The idea that we belong to a common humanity, and that we have an obligation to help the less fortunate of our peers, simply has little currency among the workers I have interviewed, whereas we will find the opposite among French workers. As compared to American workers, French workers are more likely to posit that the poor have a right to receive assistance and that "needs arise as a result of misfortune for which society, in an act of justice, not charity or mercy, ha[s] to assume responsibility,"[84] thus drawing from the Judeo-Christian tradition of giving distinct meaning to poverty. Unlike their American counterparts, these workers borrow from a socialist or social-democratic rhetoric that

romanticizes the poor and legitimizes redistribution in the name of social justice. In the United States, the very same factors that have facilitated the triumph of neoliberalism in the eighties and nineties can
account for these glaring absences among American workers. Had I
conducted interviews in the seventies, such themes might have been
more salient.

What we do have among American workers, however, are references
to person-to-person assistance that resonate with the altruism discussed
in Chapter 1: gratuitous acts of kindness are often mentioned and are
generally carried on outside formal organizations. Dennis Young, the
Bayonne firefighter, randomly gives small change to children "just to
show them that everyone is not rotten in this world." With biking bud-
dies, Tim Williams, the laborer, has started a fund-raising program to
help needy children. Richard Wrong, the car mechanic, explains what
it means to be working class by referring to such acts of kindness, implicitly distinguishing himself from "people above" who are more selfish. For him "working class" means that "we don't get wet when it
rains" and that he has occasionally invited homeless men to sleep on
his living room couch:

> I've been kind of fortunate on that one too because we managed
> to come down in the morning and the place was straightened up,
> cleaned up, and they took care of themselves. They still had a lit-
> tle bit of their own self-respect. And whether they just led us to
> believe that or whether that was the way it is, they went off and
> you know, hopefully, they'll be all right. But what else can you
> do? You can't do shit . . . So that's the working class . . . You've
> got a place, when you've got people out there that are cold and
> hungry all by themselves and you can do something about it,
> you can invite them in, and you open the couch and let them sit
> down . . . and when they overcrowd you, you've got the author-
> ity to go ahead and tell them to hit the road.

Note that these white workers are quite different from professionals
and managers, who rarely mention welfare recipients or people who
"give up" in their descriptions of feelings of superiority and inferiority.
They are more concerned with measuring themselves with people

closer to them. They compare how much money they make, the quality of the neighborhood in which they live, which colleges their children are accepted to, and who is the smartest and most successful. In other words, for upper middle class people as compared to workers, the most salient category of "people below" are not the homeless or the poor but less successful professionals and managers. They are less concerned with people below than with people above because keeping danger at bay is less of a daily challenge for them than it is for workers.

Blacks Who Are against "Nothing Going Nowhere" Types

Black workers set limits to racial solidarity when they discuss the "no-good niggers," who, in the words of a paper quality inspector, "have no morals, no respect, no plans, no hopes, no outlook" and who "don't want to go out there and get a job, or when you do get a job, you don't keep a job."[85] For Art Mann, the former drug addict and maintenance worker, the kind of people he used to hang out with are the type he wants to stay away from. They are people who "just couldn't seem to get out of that deviant type of character . . . They didn't want to do things in life, in terms of bettering themselves or their families, or anything like that . . . Partying, just being out there, surviving on strength type of thing. But basically nothing, nothing, just the bottom line . . . They didn't have stable jobs. Basically nothing going nowhere types. They'd rather be out there with their friends, hanging out in the street, not having a purpose or a direction."

For these respondents their positions as black stable working men presume taking a different route than the one they believe the poor take, and which they view as readily available in the neighborhoods they live in. In the words of a black x-ray technician, "If [you] want responsibility, in order to get to the things [you want] in life, you have to go to school and learn it, and have to be honest, and have to go the normal route, and study, and get to where you're going, and know what your priorities are. Whereas in the black neighborhood you are led to drugs. Your priorities right now should be your family, but let's spend it on drugs and good time, and when you spend it on drugs and having a good time, you start not having any money, so you start robbing people for it."

Blacks draw boundaries against the poor for different reasons than do whites. On the one hand, because of their own experience with racism, black workers have a more structural understanding of the causes of poverty and are more compassionate and supportive of the poor and of welfare programs. Also, their own experience with poverty or familiarity with the poor help them understand better the structural mechanisms by which one gets there.[86] As a consequence, they are less likely to associate success with moral superiority. They are also less likely to stigmatize welfare recipients for their dependency than whites. On the other hand, black workers also say that they keep their distance from the poor for fear of being pulled down—a concern that is not shared by white workers. Given the dangers associated with the poor (for instance, the availability of drugs), it is imperative for black workers to maintain a clear boundary between the "mainstream" and the "non-mainstream."[87] For black workers, poverty is a more ambivalent issue than it is for whites.

COMPASSION AND THE STRUCTURAL UNDERSTANDING OF POVERTY. It is well established that American "low-status" groups—blacks, women, Catholics, Democrats, and "have-nots"—have a more structural understanding of the causes of poverty while college graduates, Protestants, professionals, the elderly, Republicans, and the more affluent tend to explain poverty by individual causes, pointing to character flaws that put the blame on the poor themselves.[88] In my interviews, black workers contrast their own understanding of poverty with those of middle class people and/or whites who they believe tend to be naive or misinformed. This is expressed clearly by Tony Clark, a black medical supply worker who works in a white environment:

> At my job, people say "Why is this person homeless? Why can't he get a job at McDonald's or something like that?" They can't see why a person would be homeless. I say that the person is probably homeless because they lost their job that was paying good, and they could no longer keep the house they had, so those things kind of fell down. Working in McDonald's won't be able to give them a place to keep a roof over their heads. That would put them back in the bracket where they will be taxed and

be way down. It would be better for them to be homeless . . .
People have a hard time seeing why that is. Or they have a hard
time seeing why people sell drugs . . . It's about surviving . . .
These people buy a new car every two years. They have no concept of what being poor is about . . . I knew what it was like not
to have. I knew what it was like to be hungry or weak . . . Without having the experience of being there, you know, and working
your way through it, you lose out on that educational experience.

Bill Washington, the UPS mail sorter, points to how whites' perceptions of poverty are shaped by their lack of experience with the poor,
and he links racism to these perceptions: "If you were born rich and
grew up in a rich community, you tend to believe the world as you see
it on TV . . . The rich community looks at TV and sees a poor person,
poor, grungy, dirty. Not healthy, not sanitary. Basically, this is where
some racist themes come from."

This structural understanding of the causes of poverty dissociates
moral worth and income and avoids stigmatizing the poor. For instance, Craig Patterson, the assistant cable splicer, says that he does not
feel superior to people who did not succeed as well as he did. He just
feels sad for them because "I realize that some people get bad breaks
. . . You never know why they do what they do unless you get to really
talk with them to know what happened." People like Craig do not condemn the poor for their lack of self-sufficiency, their "giving up," or the
fact that they use welfare unfairly.

Because of their more structural understanding of poverty, many
black workers advocate compassion and social solidarity, in keeping
with their emphasis on the collective aspects of morality discussed in
Chapter 1.[89] As documented in the literature, compared to whites,
blacks are more supportive of income redistribution and public spending aimed at improving the situation of the poor.[90] This racial difference is added evidence that blacks adopt a collective understanding of
morality that stresses solidarity and generosity. Another study finds
that blacks discriminate little toward people poorer than themselves.
Working class blacks feel considerably closer to people below themselves than to those above, while middle class blacks express a prefer-

ence for the poor and the working class over their own class.[91] Accordingly, several workers expressed support for greater income redistribution. Tyrone Smith, the chemical plant operative, puts it this way: "I'm not for the person that helps the rich get richer and the rich maintain their riches. If that keeps happening we'll eliminate the middle class in society. Now we have the 'haves' and the 'have-nots.' I don't think it should be like that in America. That's for European countries." This greater collective orientation is reflected in the political party affiliations of workers: among whites, 33 percent are Democrats, 20 percent are Republicans, and 36 percent are independents. Among blacks, 76 percent are Democrats, none are Republican, and 10 percent are independents.

TACTICAL DISTANCE TOWARD THE POOR: STAYING CLEAR OF "THE HANDS THAT PULL YOU DOWN." To the extent that black workers draw boundaries against the poor, they stigmatize them not for their lack of work ethic but for their low moral standards. They also focus on the issue of substance abuse. They contrast work ethic and responsibility with lacking direction and seeking pleasure, pointing to the broader moral failings of the poor. For instance, a black building inspector who works for Jersey City criticizes some people he knows for their self-indulgence when he says, "What most of them have done is really compromise what their abilities are. It's hanging out, it's going to bars, it's, you know . . . To me they are frivolous kinds of things for adults to be [doing]."

Blacks say that friends, neighbors, and family in need can put enormous demands on one's resources and limit one's chances to "move up." This is compounded by the fact that the likelihood of downward mobility is greater for blacks than for whites.[92] Thus, although black workers have a more structural and compassionate understanding of the position of the poor, many said they hesitate to become close to them for tactical reasons. While white workers, like white professionals and managers, never discussed the importance of staying clear of people who can put too many demands on one's resources, blacks discussed this frequently. Tony Clark, the medical supply worker, uses poignant language: "If I try not to let the hands pull me down, then I could get that American dream . . . Friends, family, it's just the extra weight. It is another hand that's keeping me from getting something. If somebody needs help with something, then that's another hand that's keeping me back. I feel that once I can get some of those hands off of me, then I could run."

A number of workers maintain distance from friends in need because their own position in the working class is precarious, and their resources could easily be drained. Tyrone Smith, the chemical factory operative, says of his friend Jim: "He's a nice warm guy. Our goals are a little different right now. He's not working. He's unemployed for about three years now. I guess he's looking, but if he could find something that he really wanted . . . My philosophy is that misery loves company and he really don't have too many goals right now and I can't let him turn me from my goals." Bill Washington, the UPS mail sorter, says, "I never stay friends with or become a friend with anyone who can mess up your career." These limits of collective solidarity are dictated by personal self-interest and by the concrete situation in which black workers find themselves.[93] These respondents confirm that the boundary between the mainstream and the deviant is to be vigilantly guarded by the black working class.[94] Because whites readily associate poverty with blacks, African-American workers may want to refute this stereotype by keeping their distance from the poor. This may help explain the strength of the boundaries that blacks draw against the poor, despite their more structural understanding of the causes of poverty.

THE POLICING OF CLASS BOUNDARIES

This chapter has offered an understanding of the boundaries that white and black workers draw within the American national community through their discourse on "people above" and "people below." As was the case for racial boundaries, we see that the class boundaries workers draw are a direct extension of their broader moral worldview, which is organized around keeping the world in moral order: being hardworking, self-reliant, caring, and having integrity are at the center of the distinctions that whites and blacks draw toward other classes.

For many professionals and managers I talked to, socioeconomic success and moral worth go hand in hand, the former confirming the latter.[95] In contrast, when evaluating the upper half, most workers disentangle socioeconomic and moral worth. They accomplish this by (1) elaborating a detailed critique of the moral character of upper middle class people, mostly by pointing to their lack of personal integrity, lack of respect for others, and the poor quality of their interpersonal relationships;[96] (2) adopting alternative definitions of success.[97] In so doing, they locate themselves above, or side by side with, "people above."[98] This was the case for 75 percent of the white workers I talked to and for 50 percent of their black counterparts.[99] I conclude that workers are not condemned to think of themselves as losers due to their failure to realize the material version of the American dream.[100] They strive to maintain a sense of self-worth and dignity, and to achieve this, they develop alternative measuring sticks that can be viewed as key elements in a culture of resistance. Unsurprisingly, whites mobilize a wider range of evidence of equality across classes, than they use to demonstrate equality across races. Being respected despite their social status is a challenge for them, whereas being respected as whites is not. This explains why they adopt many more alternative definitions of success than the literature indicates.

We saw that more blacks than whites identify with middle class values and that, as compared to whites, blacks more highly value certain middle class attributes, such as leadership, goal orientation, and money because they provide, and help them demonstrate, social membership. However, blacks are more likely than whites to decouple economic success from moral character due to their experience with racism. They also draw stronger boundaries against the middle class than whites do. Just as they criticize whites for their dominating tendencies, they point to the exploitative tendencies of middle class people, criticizing them for their lack of caring.

White and black workers are less likely to mobilize alternative measuring sticks to evaluate "people below" than "people above." Here, many whites especially do not hesitate to equate socioeconomic standing and moral worth, as they describe the poor, the homeless, and the unemployed as lazy and as having no dignity because they are not self-reliant. Just as black workers often take white and middle class to be synonyms, white workers often equate being poor with being black. This combination may explain that the boundaries blacks draw toward the upper half are stronger than those whites draw, and that the boundaries whites draw toward "people below" are stronger than those blacks draw.

In contrast to working class men, professionals and managers are primarily concerned with comparing themselves to people like themselves, which goes along with their desire to ensure the material comfort and self-actualization of their children and to maintain a secure position in their work environment through conflict avoidance. Our qualitative comparison of workers and upper middle class people reveals that for the latter group, the most salient category of "people below" are not the homeless or the poor but less successful upper middle class people. Also, they may be less concerned with people below than with people above because keeping danger at bay is less of a daily challenge for them than it is for workers.

This chapter also suggests that we need to rethink how we conceptualize workers' class consciousness and the thesis that class is not a very salient dimension of identity in postmodern societies.[101] Workers repeatedly refer to class when they define who they are in contrast to other groups, by pointing to "Ken and Barbie" people or to employers. Many also adopt a critical stance toward the upper half, but this differs from that predicted by Marxist theory. Although blacks mention exploitative behavior, overall workers are particularly concerned with the arrogance of people above and with their lack of respect for workers' dignity. Also, the comparative study of boundary work suggests that workers are very aware of the distinctive disadvantages of their position. They empower themselves not by supporting a socialist alternative but by using measuring sticks that dissociate worth and respect from social status. This, of course, has limitations: race and poverty still trace the limits of "us" for the workers I talked to, despite the centrality of the themes of egalitarianism and populism in American civic culture.[102] The next chapters will show that French workers emphasize different aspects of morality than their American counterparts, which lead them to draw stronger boundaries toward "people above" and weaker boundaries toward "people below."

PART II

The United States Compared

"MEMBERS OF national communities often believe that 'the world' . . . is filled with people who do not deserve . . . communal support. They do not want to 'save' such persons. They do not wish to include them, protect them, or offer them rights because they conceive them as being unworthy, amoral, and in some sense 'uncivilized.'"[1] Like the United States, France has a black population. Unlike American workers, however, French workers do not single out blacks and the poor as particularly unworthy. Instead, they point to the growing number of Muslim immigrants originating from North Africa.

Part II introduces cross-national comparisons that shed light on the American case by revealing French workers' taken-for-granted conceptions of people's worth. The analysis will follow the same order as that used for American workers: I first discuss the standards French workers use to assess the worth of people and then examine how they use these criteria to draw racial and class boundaries. In line with French usage and for convenience, I will use the term "French workers" to describe *white* French workers, whom I compare with white American workers.[2]

Chapter 4 sets the scene by sketching the French context. Like their American counterparts, French workers value keeping the world in moral order and believe that a strong work ethic and a sense of responsibility are essential to reaching this goal. However, dissimilarities are also found. For instance, French workers more readily subordinate material interests to integrity. They are more likely to value "civility" than traditional morality. Like African Americans, they also stress solidarity more than white Americans do.

Chapter 5 parallels Chapter 2, examining how French white workers extrapolate moral boundaries to draw racial boundaries. More so than blacks, "immigrants" (by which workers generally mean "Arabs" and "North Africans")[3] are viewed by the French respondents as (1) lacking in a work ethic and a sense of responsibility; (2) incompatible with the French culturally, as exemplified by their lack of civility and criminal inclinations; and (3) refusing to assimilate. In contrast, blacks are constructed as more similar to the majority, although they are phenotypically more distinct from this majority than North African immigrants who are white; this latter group is often thought of as a "quasi-race" on cultural and biological grounds (they present strong South Mediterranean features, with dark eyes, dark frizzy hair, and olive skin). The smaller number of blacks, their greater religious heterogeneity as compared to North Africans (who include few Christians), and the particularly violent decolonization process in North Africa combine with specific features of the political culture of republicanism to make blacks less salient than North Africans in French workers' definitions of "us" and "them." Moreover, a large number of blacks are French citizens from the Caribbean and as such are easily made part of "us." While, as we will see, republicanism has traditionally been an important tool of integration for assimilated blacks and others, it is also ammunition for racists who oppose immigrants who "refuse to assimilate." The ideals of republicanism posit a strong boundary between insiders who share this political culture and outsiders who do not.

Chapter 5 also compares the standards of worth French and white American workers use to establish that African Americans and North African immigrants are equal to the majority group. Unlike white Americans, French workers never posit that money makes races equal. In fact, some posit that people are equal despite their economic inequality. Also, unlike white American workers but like black Americans, French workers ground racial equality in a moral language stressing the themes of solidarity and humanism, in line with their conception of moral worth.

Finally, Chapter 5 also compares how African Americans and North African immigrants establish that they are as worthy as the majority group. North Africans resemble French workers in that they also eschew economic arguments. They prefer to point to work as evidence of equality. Moreover, like African Americans, they rebut racism by showing their moral superiority over the majority group.

Chapter 6 parallels Chapter 3 in its focus on the class boundaries drawn toward the upper half and the poor by French workers. Here as well, striking differences appear. French workers use a repertoire of class struggle to trace stronger boundaries toward the upper and middle classes than American workers do. It seems that despite the decline of left-wing parties and organizations in France (most notably, the French Communist Party and unions), this repertoire remains readily available in French political culture. Instead of associating high socioeconomic status with moral worth as do some, but not all, American workers, French interviewees often associate the upper half with exploitation and dehumanization. A few even suggest that ambition and upward mobility are incompatible with the cherished values of solidarity and integrity. However, compared with American workers, French workers more readily legitimize high socioeconomic status by the intellectual superiority of the upper half. Finally, in stark contrast to their American counterparts, French workers rarely express feelings of superiority toward the poor. This group is simply absent from their descriptions of boundaries. To the extent that they are present, they are portrayed as "part of us," as workers who are having temporary problems and should be helped.

This comparative analysis provides evidence that French and American workers promote different definitions of "us" and "them": French workers draw strong lines between the French and "foreigners," creating a clear boundary between the national symbolic community and the external "other" (although this other, "immigrants," is located physically within France). In contrast, we saw that in the United States, boundaries against immigrants were weaker, as most interviewees were indifferent to them. Simultaneously, French workers downplay important lines of division within the national citizenry—that American workers stress—and particularly those distinguishing the poor and blacks from "us." Hence, in the two societies, workers define their identity through very different models of exclusion.

For the reader, such differences may beg the question: given these patterns of boundaries, which country is most egalitarian and least racist? Here again, very different answers are likely to emerge from the two sides of the Atlantic. On the one hand, Americans often invoke Europe's feudal past and hierarchical class relations (particularly in France and England) to uphold their self-image as the utmost defenders of universal values, including equality. Also, American intellectuals often scorn France's disregard for cultural diversity (as it pertains to race, ethnicity, and gender) as evidence of America's greater egalitarianism—which stands as a form of moral superiority.[4] On the other hand, because of the American history of racial segregation and discrimination, and of what they believe to be the inhumanity inherent in the market principles that drive American society, the French portray themselves as the true guardians of equality and denounce America's moral self-righteousness as unjustified.[5] French intellectuals and politicians often sing the merits of their own assimilationist political culture for downplaying cultural differences between groups: they believe that this political culture allows them to avoid the racial polarization, balkanization, and social strife that plague the United States, and they readily cite American race riots as symptoms of the endemic crisis of a profoundly sick society.[6]

Conflicts surrounding the merits of these two systems tend to be fed by nationalistic rhetoric. The role of social scientists should be less to fuel such conflicts than to propose means of making sense of how national differences are constructed. Analyzing national boundary patterns or national models of cultural segmentation shifts the focus away from judgments concerning the overall fairness and goodness of societies and places it on the location, dynamic, and content of different types of boundaries and the principles of membership that they presume.[7] Before turning to the substance of our discussion, some background information on the men that I interviewed is needed.

4

Workers Compared

LIKE THE American economy, the French economy has moved away from manufacturing and toward services. Total employment in manufacturing had dropped from 25.8 percent of the labor force in 1980 to 21.3 percent in 1990 (compared to a fall from 22.1 percent to 18 percent in the United States).[1] In the early 1990s, France faced one of its most serious recessions and lost some half million jobs, primarily in the manufacturing sector. Accordingly, between 1990 and 1993 alone, there was a 9 percent decline in the absolute number of workers in manufacturing among all wage earners and salaried employees.[2] The unemployment rate hovered around 10 percent, as compared to 7 percent in the United States.[3]

This decline has gone hand in hand with changes in the socio-demographic composition of the working class and in industrial politics. Over the last decades, the composition of French workers has become more diverse: female labor force participation increased from 28.2 percent in 1960 to 36.3 percent in 1990 (when it was 44.1 percent in the United States).[4] As for industrial politics, at a time when firm-level bargaining gained in importance, the unionization rates fell from 21.5 percent in 1970 to 9.7 percent in 1989 (as compared to a decline from 25.9 percent in 1970 to 15.4 percent in 1989 in the United States).[5] However, although French trade union membership is now the lowest in Europe, the French labor movement retains considerable influence in workplace politics, in the management of workers' benefits,[6] and in building political mobilization. While strikes had declined to a historical postwar low in 1992, 1993 saw several major 24-hour strikes in transportation and other public services, and 1995 saw the longest and most important general strike since 1968 (in defense of the right of subway conductors to retire at age 60).[7]

Whereas in the United States, economic restructuring led to greater inequality, this was not the case in France.[8] In fact, wealth is now less concentrated and income inequality is smaller in France than in the United States.[9] For instance, from the seventies through the mid-eighties, the college wage premium and the nonmanual/manual differential expanded dramatically in the United States, while the differential narrowed in France during the 1980s at a time when a high and pervasive French minimum wage prevented the relative wages of the unskilled from falling significantly.[10]

Because the United States is less the land of equality than it was just three decades ago, it is particularly interesting to compare how French and American workers understand standards of worth, especially in the context of their evaluation of the upper half. The literature often describes French workers as particularly radical, whereas American workers stand as the epitome of a middle class-identified proletariat.[11] Do the economic changes I just described translate into a convergence in the boundaries drawn toward the upper half in the two countries? In particular, does the decline of working class organizations in France translate into a weak opposition to the upper half? These questions will be addressed in Chapter 6. First, we must compare the characteristics of the French and American workers I talked to.

PROFILE OF FRENCH WORKERS

The French and American men I interviewed are similar in a number of dimensions. I selected respondents to produce samples matched, as closely as possible, on length of full-time employment, age, occupation, and level of education. However, there are some unavoidable differences between the two groups that result from cross-national differences in the structures of income distribution and of secondary and post-secondary education. Median household income among French workers was lower (at $28,000) than among Americans (at $49,000).[12] Nevertheless, the two groups may be similar in terms of disposable income because the French welfare state and unions provide health care, day care, rent allowances, family allowances, and, in some cases, food subsidies to many middle income workers.[13] Moreover, income is distributed differently in the two countries, with French workers controlling a slightly larger share of the national disposable income.[14] Note, however, that the income differential between the two groups of interviewees can be explained in part by differences in their spouses' occupations: 35 percent of the French partners work in lower white-collar occupations, which rarely pay well, compared to only 13 percent of the American partners.[15]

The French men I interviewed have less formal education than their American counterparts: while almost half of American workers have some college education, this is the case for only 4 of the 75 French interviewees. This reflects important national differences in tracking systems at the secondary school level. While there are virtually no venues for individuals who have graduated in a vocational track to pursue post-secondary education in France even those who have obtained a General Equivalency Degree (GED), as opposed to a standard high school degree, can obtain a college degree in the United States. Hence, in France, a smaller proportion of the population obtains higher education than in the United States, which translates into lower possibilities for mobility.[16] However, while France offers comprehensive vocational education programs for manual workers, the United States does not, though two-year college degrees can provide an opportunity for Americans that parallels that provided by vocational education for French workers.

There exist other differences between the French and American workers I talked to. In the Introduction, I suggested that American interviewees are tightly inserted in densely structured working class social networks at home, in their neighborhood, and at work. Most have grown up in or near the town where they now live, and they know many people in the area from school, work, or through their involvement in church, sports teams, or volunteer groups. Not so in France. Scholars have noted the decline of traditional networks of sociability in the French working class due to the decline of key working class institutions (in particular, the Communist Party) and to a crisis in the intergenerational transmission of working class culture.[17] Hence, workers are more isolated than their American counterparts.

Half of the French workers I talked to were born in the "provinces," which is fairly typical for workers in the Paris region.[18] Many maintain strong personal attachments to their region of origin. They often express nostalgia about these places, dream of retiring there, and complain of the anonymity of the Paris suburbs. They find companionship in their workplace and leisure activities instead of in their neighborhoods, which they often describe as soulless and uninviting.[19]

Finally, as is the case for French and American workers in general, only a minority of French and American interviewees are unionized. This is the case for 22 percent of the white French workers[20] as compared to 30 percent of the white American workers (but note that it is the case for 70 percent of African-American respondents). We find stronger contrasts in the political orientation of workers: a slight majority of French workers are left-leaning whereas only 33 percent of white American workers support the Democratic Party (76 percent of black American workers support the Democratic Party). That only half of French workers define themselves as left-leaning is unsurprising given the dramatic decline of the French Communist Party—the traditional party of the French working class—over the last 30 years.[21] This parallels the low political involvement of French interviewees. While only three are currently active in left-wing organizations, six have been active as political militants in the past.[22] In contrast, none of the white American workers are active in political parties.

PROFILE OF NORTH AFRICAN IMMIGRANTS

To complement the interviews I conducted with African Americans, I interviewed North African immigrants residing in the Paris suburbs; like African Americans, they occupy the lowest status position among workers and are the prime victims of racism in their country of residence.

Eleven percent of the 57 million individuals living on French soil in 1990 were born outside France.[23] Due to labor shortages, France has historically been one of the European countries with the highest immigration rate.[24] It also has a longer history of immigration than any other country in Western Europe and the second largest foreign population.[25] North African immigrants come from the former colonies of Algeria, Morocco, and Tunisia, and today they make up approximately 40 percent of the foreign population living in France[26] but less than 5 percent of the French population.[27] In comparison, black immigrants to France represent only 5 percent of immigrants.[28] Considered together with black French citizens, they made up less than 2 percent of the French population in 1990.[29]

North Africans arrived in large numbers in the sixties and seventies. Once in France, many were given short-term renewable work permits and were directed into the worst paid, least desirable jobs in manufacturing, mining, and public works. Since at least 1918, foreign workers living in France have had a quasi-monopoly on the most painful and dirty jobs.[30] They were attracted to France largely because of former colonial ties, economic opportunity, geographical proximity, networks, and familiarity with the French language. Moreover, French firms aggressively pursued these workers in their home countries to solve the problems of labor shortage that plagued the French economy and to have access to cheap labor.[31] These firms often benefited from special programs created jointly by the French state and the governments of the migrants' countries of origin. As is now the case, legal immigrants were given roughly the same civic and social rights as French citizens. While in earlier decades, immigrants would leave their families in their country of origin, more have settled with their children on French soil since the end of the open immigration era in 1974.

The North African men I met include 13 Algerians, 15 Moroccans, and 2 Tunisians.[32] As with all interviewees, they were chosen randomly from phone books of working class towns. However, for this group I drew Muslim names only. I met these men in cafés, parks, other public places, and, in a few cases, their homes. This small group did not allow access to the full diversity of North African immigrants living in France. However, the in-depth interviews I conducted provided a solid base for understanding the parameters by which immigrants assess the worth of people in general, as well as that of the French and members of other classes. Because of limitations of space, I focus on how North Africans rebut French racism, but the analysis is informed by my understanding of their views on these larger issues.

Most of the 30 men I talked to are solidly settled in France: all but a few have been in France for more than 20 years.[33] While a third own property in their country of origin, two-thirds have brought their families to France.[34] However, none has taken French citizenship, and all declared that they are legal immigrants.[35] Several have children who are French or who plan to claim French citizenship when they turn 21. At the time of the interview, six were between 34 and 39 years of age, twelve were in their forties, and twelve were in their fifties.[36]

These North African immigrants are better described as working poor than as solidly lower middle class. Their median annual family income is 100,000 francs (or $17,491) per year.[37] Seventy percent of them have no academic degree, which is not atypical: among Algerians, Moroccans, and Tunisians living in France, 69 percent have no degree, 8 percent have only an elementary school degree, and 14 percent have a professional high school degree.[38] Like 76 percent of all first-generation North African immigrants, they are mostly working in manual occupations and are employed in construction and manufacturing industries.[39]

Most of these men reside in old working class towns with heavy industry, which are located on the outskirts of Paris. Several of these towns have been under the control of Communists since the beginning of the twentieth century. While some live in old downtown areas in unsanitary apartments, others live in large public housing complexes that are in need of repair and that have higher than average vandalism and crime. These public housing complexes, known as *HLM (habitations à loyer modique),* are widely perceived as centers of social problems, where violence is particularly salient.[40] They offer little privacy and racial tensions often occur between various immigrant groups and low-income French residents.

The position of these immigrants in French society is highly paradoxical because of the experience of French colonialism in the Maghreb. They are tied to France by family history; many have fathers, uncles, and grandfathers who worked for colonists in Morocco, Algeria, or Tunisia or who died fighting for France in Indochina or Germany. Despite their strong ties to France, they face mounting racism. The far-right National Front consistently captures 10 to 15 percent of the French vote since it had its first major breakthrough in the 1984 European parliamentary election.

Founded in 1972, this party pits the French against the non-French—one of its main slogans is "Les français d'abord" (the French first). Its program has supported law and order along with "a definitive stop to new immigration . . . the cancellation of all laws and rulings that create legal equality between the French and immigrants, and the definitive, and progressive, expulsion of all immigrants—with immediate expulsion of those whose aggressive behavior, permanent hatred, and illegal acts are not worthy of French hospitality."[41]

The electoral success of the National Front suggests that racism is common in France. This is confirmed by a Eurobarometer survey conducted in 1997, which showed that among all European Union countries, France ranked second in terms of the percentage of respondents supporting a number of racist propositions.[42] Along the same lines, 34.5 percent of the French respondents to a 1988 survey revealed that they would object to having a North African supervisor, while 44.4 percent would object to having a family member marry a North African of the same social class.[43] Racist attitudes are found among individuals throughout the political spectrum: 45 percent of respondents to a 1995 national survey, when asked whether they are racist, replied affirmatively. Of these individuals, the following percentages defined themselves as sympathizers to the main political parties: Communists, 35 percent; Socialists, 38 percent; National Front, 86 percent; Ecologists, 41 percent; center parties (Union pour la démocratie française (UDF) and the Rassemblement pour la République (RPR)), 58 percent.[44]

Since 1985, the National Front has grown largely at the expense of the right, but it has also gained support in the former "bastions of Communist strength."[45] The support it receives from workers is growing at a fast pace: while only 19 percent of workers voted for the National Front in 1988, 30 percent did so in 1995.[46] The workers I interviewed share many of the characteristics of French racists as documented by surveys: the latter tend to be primarily manual workers, people with low socioeconomic status, and individuals with a vocational (as opposed to an academic) high school degree.[47] This suggests the importance of examining closely how workers' definitions of worth support anti-immigrant racism. For that, we need to look at the definitions of worth themselves.

WORKING CLASS MORALITY

Eric Dupuis works for a heater repair shop in Ivry-sur-Seine, an old working class suburb in the south of Paris. His job consists of servicing residences in the Paris metropolitan area. He defines himself as a hardworking person, and his condemnations of lazy people are vehement ("laziness is the mother of all vices"). He loves his work in part because there is a good atmosphere among workers: they constantly tease one another and they like to give a hand. Also, they have built a large aquarium together as a common project; they all bring in various objects to decorate it, and the aquarium stands as a symbol of the fun they have together.

Eric believes that friendship is one of the most, if not the most, important aspects of life. He explains his philosophy concerning friendship in the following terms: "When you like someone, one does not calculate what one gives . . . If it was not for friendship, it would not be worth living. You can make yourself happy by going to the movies, but I put movies in their place. It is not like the presence of a friend: it is not living, it does not give warmth." Eric describes his best friend as someone who has a big heart, wants to grow, devotes a lot of energy to what he wants, and is a hard worker. He believes that what he and this friend can do for one another is limitless.

When asked to describe the types of people he likes, Eric points to people who are straightforward, who "call a cat a cat." He also values personal integrity: "When I shave in the morning, I look at myself in the mirror and am happy. I don't understand how [people who screw others] can live with themselves, respect themselves." When asked what kinds of people he dislikes, Eric gives the example of his brother-in-law who lives at the expense of others. For him, being responsible means taking one's life in hand, adopting a line of conduct, being able to stick to it, and doing what is needed to achieve one's goals: "If you get off the rails, you will hurt yourself. You have to be responsible and go on working." This belief sustains Eric's poor opinion of people who drink too much. He is proud that "my wife has never seen me drunk, never." Nevertheless, Eric refuses to feel superior to people—drunks or others—because he thinks it is dishonest. He does not like it when people feel superior to him and is upset at the thought that he could feel superior to others.

Like his father before him, Eric Dupuis is part of a strong leftist tradition. Not only does he value the solidarity he shares with his coworkers; he also talks about himself as part of "the backbone of the French working class," which fights to keep alive the torch of working class struggle against the bourgeoisie. He spends days working on his income tax report in order to send as little money as possible to the French state: it is a matter of principle. He also hopes that one day he will be the "president of all the French workers"; he has no interest in being the president of the French Republic.

Like American workers, French workers put considerable emphasis on morality when defining the value of people.[48] However, French workers are both alike and different in the aspects of morality they value most. If they value the "disciplined self," appreciating hard work and taking on responsibility, they also value the "caring self," as they put much emphasis on solidarity. In this, they resemble African Americans more than white American workers.

Work Ethic, Responsibility, and Personal Integrity

Work is absolutely central to the life of Louis Lebleu, a steam engine operator who is employed by the national gas and electric company. I interviewed him at the kitchen table in his small apartment in Nanterre, a modern town in the western suburbs of Paris. This small, skinny man smokes and talks nonstop. Quick-witted, he is a master of banter and gladly describes himself as a *gueulard:* he gets what he wants by being a pest. He is extremely proud of his work because he believes that, through their manual labor, people like him make a real contribution to society ("when I go to bed and I see the lights outside, I think, 'The guys are at work'").

Louis grew up in a family with strong working class roots, which he cherishes. Because solidarity among workers is of utmost importance to him, he nourishes a deep hatred for slackers at work who "live at the expense of others. We are all in the same boat, so we should all put our share into it." While pulling one's weight goes to the heart of his conception of morality, he does not believe people should be fired because of their incompetence: he privileges job security over efficacy and explicitly advocates subordinating market imperatives to humanitarianism. In this, he differs from his American counterparts, whose defense of competence and efficacy is often at odds with collectivist principles.

❖ ❖

French workers resemble their American counterparts when they equate a strong work ethic with moral character. Take, for instance, Jules Auclair, an aircraft technician who lives in Nanterre and works for a multinational firm that has laid off many workers over the past five years. Like Eric, he believes that unemployment leads to vice: "The person who does not work necessarily ends up doing stupid things, like stealing. People who are not lazy can always find a way to get money by redoing an apartment, for instance . . . Work is really a fundamental value."

Workers time and again celebrate the *courageux*, that is, people who are able to sustain efforts even in difficult circumstances. This quality is given value by individuals who describe their work as dirty and physically demanding or as requiring particular willpower and perseverance (often because it is boring and repetitive). Jean-Luc Derain, an auto painter who has been elected to the Communist city council of his town, says that it is especially important for people who are not highly educated to be hardworking: hard work allows you to demonstrate your worth "even if you are not very intelligent . . . It's not because you don't have a *bac* [academic-track high school degree] that you have to stay with your arms crossed, waiting for something." Thirty-four percent of the French workers said "lazy" is a quality they dislike greatly, compared to 44 percent of the Americans. Although the French scores are lower, being hardworking remains one of the qualities French workers value most.[49] The French may place less emphasis on this trait because some French workers have always celebrated laziness as a matter of principle, due to anarchist influences.[50] As for American workers, their discourse on the importance of work may be viewed as a script of self-presentation composed for the interview; after all, stealing time from employers has always been a central component of working class culture. Nevertheless, what is key here is that, as we will see, French workers use this self-presentation to distinguish between their virtuous selves and other less worthy groups.

French workers also resemble their American counterparts in attaching great weight to having a sense of responsibility. When asked to describe people he dislikes, François Noyant, a policeman in his mid-thirties and a National Front sympathizer, singles out young people who destroy the environment with their graffiti and refuse to take responsibility for what they do. He is exceptionally vehement against delinquents who do not respect private property:

> Young people who do nothing and who just go around and break everything. If you catch them, they say "it is not me"—although you have seen them do it. They do not take responsibility. These people are really not worth much . . . They do not even deserve that I look at them. They just deserve that I hit them. These people, I call them the small ones, the minuscule ones. They are to be eliminated, out of my sight. They are worthless people, worth absolutely nothing, they are lower than the ground. I would walk on them . . . Either they are stupid and should be put in the mental hospital, or they should not be on the street.

Gaston Roger, a pastry maker, is also pestered by irresponsible people. In his view, there is little worth in people who do not struggle in life, do not take responsibility for their actions, and do not contribute to the proper functioning of society. Although responsibility is one of the qualities that French workers value most highly, they emphasize it less than their American counterparts: only 38 percent chose "irresponsible" as a quality they dislike, compared to 58 percent of Americans.[51]

French and American workers also resemble one another in the emphasis they put on personal integrity, which they define as "being your own man" and standing on principles. A draftsman employed by the printing office of a small municipal government stresses this very dimension when he defines success as "being myself all the time, having central values, guidelines, and trying not to get very far away from them. I want to do only a minimum of concession to these values." Similarly, Jules Auclair, the airplane technician, says, "It is important to be able to look at yourself in a mirror when it comes to your views in life, your attitudes toward others. We should not change our orientation as the wind blows, put ourselves in this or that position in an opportunistic manner. It is important to have your own opinions."

French workers resemble their upper middle class counterparts, putting integrity above conflict avoidance.[52]

One of the most important differences between French and American workers is that the French believe that personal integrity often requires one to put principles above material interests. They resist the profit motive more than American workers, as illustrated by Louis Lebleu, who believes that slackers should not be fired even though they are not cost-effective. This is also illustrated by Roland Sorel, a wood salesman, who explains that "personal integrity is what we have deep inside of us, at the level of our code of conduct. We have to stay in line with what we really think, not adapt to outside constraints, not go beyond what we really believe in. If I were asked to do something that is incompatible with my values, I would most certainly refuse even if it meant losing my job."[53] Similarly, Marc Bataille, a railway technician, says that although he has often been penalized at work for his honesty, he always says what he has to say because this allows him "to walk with your head high [which] means not owing anything to anybody. This is something that is worth something." Clearly, the defense of personal integrity and dignity are linked in the minds of workers. This requires a certain courage and heroism because it may require losing material advantages and fighting against the forces of domination, sometimes for the benefit of the group.[54]

As we will see in the next chapters, this antimaterialism is associated with the lasting influence of socialism and with the presence of a strong welfare state that provides workers with a safety cushion or a security blanket. These factors encourage workers to think about the profit motive as a negative force that should be resisted. The same trend was present among French professionals and managers who defined personal integrity in terms of "intellectual honesty"—which also has an antimaterialist component.[55]

Traditional Morality, Religion, and Civility

Although French workers share with their American counterparts the goals of keeping the world in moral order and protecting their personal integrity, they are less committed to the defense of traditional morality. Several workers express a strong dislike for people who are perceived as disturbing the social order or as polluting agents (like drug addicts).

However, they very rarely mention the importance of following the Ten Commandments, a concern of American workers. The consumption of alcohol in particular is very much at the center of their socializing and is also construed by workers as a form of resistance to attempts by the bosses to discipline and control them.[56] National surveys as well as my comparison of French and American professionals and managers also suggest that the French pay little respect to traditional morality.[57]

This cross-national difference can be accounted for in part by the presence in France of a strong antireligious tradition among workers—to the extent that traditional morality and Catholicism are associated.[58] Few French workers value religion: 84 percent are either atheists or not involved in a religious organization.[59] A few of them even draw on Marxist themes to describe religion as a scam created to keep workers in their place. A boiler-smith, for instance, believes the Catholic Church is inhumane and discriminatory because it imposes rigid rules on people—"they ask for money but refuse to bury you in the cemetery if you have not been baptized." The atheism long promoted by the Communist Party continues to have an influence on French workers.

Another factor reducing the likelihood that this group would emphasize traditional morality is that the workers live in relatively secure environments, compared to their American counterparts, and may be less concerned with promoting rigid moral rules to ensure their safety and that of their family. Indeed, the level of urban violence is much lower in France than in the United States, as a result in part of much stricter gun control.[60] Moreover, the French welfare state provides workers a safety net against the risks of illness, accident, and old age. This increases the overall level of security for the less affluent.

For French workers, the focus on respect for traditional morality is partly substituted by a concern for civility defined largely in terms of "having a good education" (i.e., having good manners and respecting others). This theme is especially apparent when workers describe the type of people they like and what they try to teach their children. The association between manners and respect is best expressed by a train inspector, who says, "Good manners are very important in terms of knowing to respect people. Good manners mean offering someone a drink [when he comes to your home]. It is always important to respect other people, to know how to address them, to say good morning in the street or on the train. It is the consequence of a good upbringing." A bellman also points to the importance of "having a good education" when he says, "I would feel superior to people who have no education, who don't know how to behave, people who are egotistic. I would feel superior to them because I have had an education. This means not to steal from your neighbor, respecting everyone, your neighbor, and the traffic regulations. Everything that is normal for me."

In contrast, the American workers rarely mention the importance of civility, perhaps reflecting a regional trait specific to New York as opposed to, say, the South or the Midwest. That civility is more salient among French workers may also suggest an upper middle class influence: French professionals and managers spoke much more on this issue than their American counterparts.[61]

Altruism and the Collective Dimension of Morality: Solidarity

Social scientists ranging from William Sewell, Jr., to Duncan Gallie have time and again noted the centrality of solidarity in French working class culture.[62] In line with this literature, the French workers I interviewed differ from at least white American workers in putting a premium on solidarity. Laurent Larue, an automobile technician who lives in Nanterre, illustrates the importance attached to solidarity. He describes the values he wants to teach his children thus: "In the society in which we live, there is too much individualism, and I want to avoid this. It would be better both for professional life and for the leisure life. I want to teach [my children] solidarity with their friends at school: if they don't understand French or if they make mistakes, they should try to help them. It is quite simple: try to work with others. Don't have in mind to only take care of yourself."

Along these lines, 39 percent of French interviewees mentioned "shows solidarity" as one of the five qualities they value most. Among African Americans, 37 percent chose this trait; this was also the case for 28 percent of white Americans.

Many associate solidarity with the most pleasurable dimensions of life. This solidarity is what many workers value most, what gives meaning to their dreary lives. It takes the shape of a strong camaraderie, which is often a form of resistance that coworkers develop. Engaging in fun projects (like jointly building an aquarium in Eric's case), controlling the workplace by tacitly agreeing on the pace of work, and organizing gargantuan collective cookouts are illustrations of this. It gives the workers a warm feeling that helps them to go on. As explained by Robert Renan, a photographer, "in the morning, [my coworkers and I] all go to have a coffee together. We talk about work, but we also laugh a lot. At noon, we all go to eat together also, and it is the same thing. We talk about work, but we tease one another a lot." Similarly, a boiler-smith explains: "With my coworkers we celebrate everything together. We have lunch together everyday. One just bought a new car and we had a drink to celebrate that together. We are all there for half an hour: the foreman, the technicians, the workers, everyone is there. Once a year, we celebrate the patron of boiler-smiths and goldmakers, St. Eloi. We get together all of us and we make a great meal that begins at 10 A.M. We prepare the meal ourselves and we serve it in the shop on an improvised table." In contrast, American workers appear to lead more isolated lives and to take less pleasure in the time they spend together in their workplace.

Solidarity also means sharing equitably the most painful work tasks and pulling one's weight. The premium placed on solidarity helps explain why the lazy and those who take undue advantage of collective goods are particularly despised. When asked what kinds of people they find despicable, French workers often point to the profiteer. He is defined as an egoist who takes advantage of others and who has the ulterior motive of using others to improve his position instead of valuing relationships for themselves. This includes those who barge in, invite themselves for dinner, and receive advice and help, but do not reciprocate. People like Roland Sorel, the wood salesman, dislike this type of person: "Egoism is something that hurts me. I think that is something that is truly awful for others . . . It is a really bad quality, it always works against you because you find yourself alone at the end. It pushes you aside little by little. It is never good to be alone . . . Egoism is something that makes me truly very sad."

When asked what kind of people he likes, Louis Lebleu, the steam engine operative, points to people who help others not because they expect something in exchange but because it pleases them.

Finally, solidarity is also understood to mean standing up against injustice at work or elsewhere for the benefit of others. This principle is deeply internalized and defended by many workers, including a union official who says, "I cannot stand injustice, . . . social injustice, injustice at work. Injustice can break people down; it can have dramatic consequences." Along similar lines, Henri Beliveau, a draftsman who grew up in a rather homogeneously left-wing environment, explains that he wants to give his children the values he received from his own Socialist father, mainly, the importance of struggling for justice, of feeling responsible toward society, and of not forgetting that we are able to shape the world that surrounds us. Like the defense of personal integrity, the defense of solidarity is viewed as requiring courage, as it is often done at the expense of one's individual interest (economic or noneconomic).

The Policing of Moral Boundaries Compared

This chapter has suggested that there are differences and similarities in what French and American workers define as morality. Most important, French workers more readily put personal integrity above material interest as they resist actively the profit motive, perhaps because of the influence of socialism combined with the greater security offered to them by a strong welfare state (as compared to American workers). Their moralistic rhetoric centers more around civility and respect for others than around traditional morality, in part because they associate the latter with Catholicism. Finally, like African Americans, French workers put considerable emphasis on a collective dimension of morality, solidarity, which, as we will see, is valued by socialism and republicanism alike. This study also finds similarities between French and American workers in their emphases on a work ethic, responsibility, and personal integrity as central dimensions of their definitions of worth. Hence, like African Americans, French workers appreciate both the disciplined and the caring self. We will now turn to the ways in which these moral boundaries shape racial boundaries.

5

Racism Compared

ERIC DUPUIS' apartment building in Ivry is inhabited by a number of Muslim immigrants. This building is owned by the state, which subsidizes rents and ensures a "proper" ethnic mixture among the resident population, which means in principle a maximum of 15 percent immigrants.[1] These Muslim neighbors define the limits of Eric's working class solidarity, he says, because they are slothful and irresponsible. In one of his diatribes against laziness, Eric echoes almost word for word what some white American workers said about African Americans:

> Parasites . . . I hate all of them. All those people who don't have a sense of responsibility. We work so hard to support them. When you look at your pay stub and you see all that is taken away! How can I explain it? When you go to welfare offices, it is not Gaulois [descendants from France's original settlers in Roman times] who take advantage of it. French families with fourteen children, I have not seen many.[2] Two or three, maybe. And we break our backs for these people. I am very familiar with them. They don't work. They only know the way to the unemployment insurance office, the ASSEDIC [the acronym for this office, which he pronounces with a North African accent].

Later in the interview, Eric describes himself as someone who spends his life busting his chops, and he explains that he resents having to do it for the benefit of others, immigrants in particular. In his view, there are too many North Africans in his neighborhood, and the French end up feeling like they are not at home. Yet in the building where he lives with his wife, Eric often talks to the children of immigrants and tries to give them guidance and to help them in ways both small and large. He dreams of leaving the housing project and of buying a little house with a small garden in the countryside, where he could go fishing at the end of the day. But he can't afford it; it would mean dispensing with all the pleasures of life. Instead, he bought a big motorcycle, which he likes to drive at high speeds. The noisy presence of immigrants in his neighborhood acts as a reminder of his blocked mobility. At the age of 30, he is already running out of realizable dreams and talks about his future retirement.

❖   ❖

This chapter denaturalizes American racism by revealing a different kind of racism, one where blacks are not salient and North African immigrants are. Although French workers live in conditions not unlike those of their American counterparts, they have access to very different cultural resources that lead to distinct ways of drawing boundaries. I first examine the French rhetoric of racism (a term also used in reference to xenophobia in France)[3] to determine why some French workers view North Africans as unworthy. While social scientists have paid considerable attention to the rhetoric of racism produced by politicians associated with the National Front,[4] but for a few exceptions the racist rhetoric used by lay people has gone largely unstudied. I fill this gap by adopting a more exhaustive and systematic approach than the few available studies.[5] I am more concerned with describing and explaining the content of this rhetoric than with explaining why specific individuals are (or are not) racists, a topic that is also the object of a large and sophisticated literature.[6] Among French workers, only 20 percent of the lower white collars and 50 percent of the blue collars made subtle or blatant racist statements, fewer than in the United States where 60 percent of the white-collar and 63 percent of the blue-collar workers made racist statements.[7]

French workers resemble American workers in that the two groups are concerned with keeping the world in moral order and criticize the minority group for lacking a work ethic and sense of responsibility. In the two countries, at the time of the interviews an economic recession and anxieties concerning loss of national status fed into racist feelings. However, we will see that French workers differ from American workers in that (1) they are less concerned with the lack of self-reliance among immigrants than by their benefiting from governmental favoritism, which threatens workers' sense of their group positioning relative to immigrants; (2) they are less concerned with immigrants' violation of traditional morality than by their lack of civility; (3) they provide mostly cultural explanations for ethnoracial differences that stress cultural incompatibility;[8] and (4) they find resistance to assimilation more intolerable than Americans do. Moreover, French workers draw weaker boundaries against blacks than Americans do, in part because blacks are not religiously homogeneous (as are Muslims) and because many of them are French, which works against a clear polarization between "us" and "them." Also, blacks are a smaller group than North Africans; they better master the French language and are not perceived as violent as North African immigrants.

While French intellectuals generally present republicanism as the key to French equality, in fact this political ideology contributes to erecting a clear boundary between "us" and "them." Indeed, (1) it requires sharing a uniform national political culture; (2) the privileged republican bond that links French citizens, independently of skin color, entails a lower status for the non-French. In the case of North Africans, this lower status is reinforced by a caste-like relationship that the French maintain with members of their former colonies and particularly with Muslims.[9] However, this culture also downplays the significance of internal boundaries within the citizenry and particularly that of race: it accounts in part for the fact that blacks were not salient in the interviews I conducted with French workers.

The second part of this chapter turns to the rhetoric of antiracism, in a structure parallel to that of Chapter 2. This section sheds light on values taken for granted by American and French workers. The two groups similarly privilege antiracist arguments that point to the universality of human nature over cultural relativism and multiculturalism. However, while Americans believe that money can make people equal, the French are more concerned with the potentially leveling role played by work: they also assert that some North Africans who are good workers are accepted and equal. Moreover, unlike white Americans, French workers affirm the importance of fighting racism in the name of the collectivist dimension of morality that they value most, solidarity. They assert that people are equal as human beings despite their uneven socioeconomic status. In doing so, they draw on different cultural resources than do their African-American counterparts, who also stress solidarity. More specifically, they draw on elements of the cultural repertoires of republicanism, socialism, and Catholicism, which are not as readily available in the United States.

The last section of this chapter illuminates African-American responses to racism by comparing them with those of North African immigrants. When this latter group discusses what defines for them the value of people, they often implicitly or explicitly rebut racism. Unlike blacks, they often blame members of the minority group for the racism of the majority group. However, they resemble African Americans in a few respects: they point to human commonalities to demonstrate equality and describe their own culture as superior to that of the majority group because it is warmer and more caring toward the poor and the elderly. Like blacks, some North African immigrants also use particularistic arguments—for instance, the fact that, like the French, they also drink alcohol—to show their proximity to the majority group, as if their everyday experience led them to view universalism as a fantastic ideal.

FRENCH WORKERS ON MUSLIMS

Work Ethic, Parasitism, Group Positioning, and Displacement

We saw that French workers value the work ethic and stigmatize their coworkers who are perceived to be slackers. This distinction is extended to immigrants. Although some observe that their North African coworkers are diligent, many argue that on the whole North African immigrants want to do as little as possible.[10] To add insult to injury, French workers believe that Muslims appropriate an inordinate proportion of social benefits (family allocations, subsidized housing, and so on).

In Chapter 4 we met Jules Auclair, who works as an aircraft technician for one of the main French aircraft builders. Over the past five years, this firm has laid off many of its employees, and this has destroyed the good spirit that used to be found on the shop floor. It is against this backdrop that Jules echoes Eric's view of immigrants: "What I don't like about foreigners is that they don't work and they want everything. They want an apartment even if they don't work. They want unemployment benefits." At the same time, Jules explains that this judgment does not apply to all: "Two North Africans work with me. They work hard to do what they have to do. I respect them like I would a Frenchman because they are people who are working. They are not going around stealing radios."

In a more radical vein, François Noyant, the policeman in his mid-thirties who is a National Front sympathizer, suggests that French society needs "a strong electrical shock" to be put back in order, beginning with immigrant populations who take but contribute little. Enamored of authoritarianism, he dreams of various methods for "forcing people back to work":

> Especially young people who are just hanging out, we need to pull them by the hair and put them back to work. Instead of creating new hairstyles and working on their looks, they should be laboring. [I would tell them:] "You will work hard, and if you are not happy, I am going to hit you in the face, and I will do it until you start working." And then they would work. They would break stones on the road, but at least they would be working, and doing something that is useful for everyone. These people, I find them really disgusting!

Noyant is particularly concerned with the idleness of second-generation immigrants and he does not distinguish between what their inactivity owes to moral failure as opposed to an unemployment rate that reaches almost 50 percent within this group.[11] His account resonates with that produced by French colonial soldiers, missionaries, and farmers who occupied Algeria for over a century and who viewed the North African male as "incorrigible, idle, and incompetent; he only understood force; he was an innate criminal and an instinctive rapist."[12] Colonials construed the moral character of Muslims in contradistinction to that of whites, Europeans, Christians, and the French, who incarnated civilization and especially the control of reason over nature (and over natural indolence in particular).[13] This historical baggage continues to permeate French collective memory.

French workers associate the alleged weak work ethic of Muslims with a parasitic nature. Like Eric Dupuis, some believe that the money taken every month from their own paycheck goes directly into the pocket of a North African. That so many North Africans have several children is taken to be a proof of the connection between laziness, indulging in sex, and hoping to live at the expense of others. This is why an electrician believes that, although North Africans make little effort to become part of French society, they are very savvy when it comes to understanding how to get the most out of the French state: "They don't understand French, but when they look at their pay stub, they understand. Numbers, they understand well [when it is time to] receive family subsidies and this and that advantage. When a franc is missing, they know, but everything else, they don't know." François Noyant echoes this perspective when he says:

> You go to the street and you see that they don't work. They live from public support. They don't speak two words of French, but when it's time to find money, they know how to do it. They even have a right to get the minimum guaranteed income ["revenu minimal d'insertion"]. They bring in the whole family to have more money; the children of their brother-in-law become their children. They declare ten children, even if they are not their own. And with ten children, they live well. They all do that.

Immigrants are viewed as the ultimate slackers who take from the collective pot but contribute little. This is particularly objectionable because it offends French workers' solidaristic impulses. Accordingly, 59 percent of the Frenchmen surveyed by the National Commission on Human Rights in 1995 declared that in their view immigrants are a burden to the French economy.[14] Their discourse on these themes is often inspired by the National Front, which was frequently cited with approbation during the course of the interviews.

We saw that American racists criticize blacks for not being self-reliant and for depending on welfare, while arguing that they themselves have never received any help. In contrast, French racists are mostly critical of North Africans because they receive more than their share of the pie, which violates the French workers' sense of their own position in the national pecking order. They seem less concerned with critiquing welfare programs per se—they too are the beneficiaries of many public programs.[15] In France support for welfare programs is strong on the left and the right (the largest increase in social spending occurred under right-wing presidents).[16] Hence, welfare reform holds a minor place in electoral politics in France as compared to the United States, and is not as emotionally charged for French workers as it is for American workers.

French workers focus their attention on what they believe to be the state's preferential treatment of immigrants through policies aimed at fighting social exclusion (to be discussed in the next chapter), which violates the workers' sense of group positioning.[17] Because the state plays a crucial role in the distribution of resources in France,[18] the allotment of welfare benefits is more readily interpreted as indicative of relative positioning of groups than in the United States. This resentment was exacerbated by a prolonged economic recession that destabilized the position and collective identity of French workers.

A feeling of displacement adds to this threat to group positioning. This is expressed by George Desjardins, a firefighter who supports the National Front. He resents that the children of immigrants are the primary users of a new soccer stadium:

> When I was young, we did not have so many things to play with, but them, they have a lot, and we have to give them more. We have to give them a stadium. But the stadium is there and it is totally destroyed . . . And you should see who plays at the stadium. Only immigrants; they don't accept French kids . . . At the school here, there was a team for older kids. Someone tried to have his kid play in the team, but he was refused because he was told that the boy was not good enough. There are only a few French kids, well I don't know if they are French but they are whites . . . I feel invaded.

The issue of distribution of state resources to immigrants and the French is nowhere more sensitive than in educational matters, perhaps because of the downward mobility and threat to intergenerational class reproduction that workers experience under the high unemployment that prevailed in recent decades.[19] Explicitly critiquing the solidaristic policies of the government under the Socialist President François Mitterand, one respondent complains that children of immigrants are given priority by the Ministry of Education because they are viewed as a problem group. Similarly, Vincent Lortie, an electronic chipmaker who voted for the National Front, complains that his daughter's education suffers because most of her classmates are immigrants. For an electrician the preferential treatment that immigrants receive is also apparent in the legal realm: Vincent complains that a policeman he knows tolerates vandalism by North Africans because his higher-ups want to avoid making waves with immigrant communities. He believes that the republican principle of "one justice for all" should be maintained, defending political ideals against the state itself: "It is always the same ones [who cause problems]. At City Hall, they say that it is not true. They treat them well because they might vote one day. There is the same law for all in France . . . And the authorities are not taking care of anything."

At the political level, the hesitation of successive Socialist governments to address fears about immigrants and these governments' open condemnation of racism have heightened popular concerns about Muslims.[20] At the time of the interviews a long-lasting economic recession was exacerbating workers' resentment, while they found themselves caught between the daily challenge of making ends meet while becoming more dependent on subsidies to maintain their standard of living. Their anger was also exacerbated by the decomposition of the French working class, a factor linked to a shrinking labor market. The deterioration of living conditions and labor market position, as well as a greater sense of competition, weakens social bonds between the have-nots, and workers are pushed to draw stronger boundaries toward people who are simultaneously worse off and culturally different from themselves.[21] Hence, we see a greater fragmentation of the working class, including a greater exclusion of immigrant workers.

The fears of workers concerning displacement are also fed by simultaneous demographic and cultural changes. In their eyes, the urban landscape unmistakably reveals that Muslims "want to take over." For instance, Richard Jalmain, a subway conductor, points out that "you walk on certain streets, certain avenues, and they are dominant. You see them all day long, sunbathing. It hurts me, and I wonder what they do to make a living." Echoing Richard's concerns, a recent poll shows that 57 percent of the French think that "we don't feel at home like before."[22] Political scientist Florence Haegel explains these feelings of displacement by the fact that North Africans are viewed as breaking the rules of communal life and as "overextending French hospitality"—another breach in civility.[23]

These feelings are coupled with impressions of loss generated by the destruction of working class culture mentioned above, which is concomitant with the decline of working class organizations such as unions and the Communist Party. The workers' feelings of isolation and powerlessness are accentuated by the fact that in their environment the cultural and religious institutions of immigrants are gaining in visibility. French workers discover the existence of dense Muslim communities where individuals can find various forms of support and space for expressing their collective identity.[24] They experience this as a threat to their political culture. As suggested by Pascal Perrineau, these feelings of loss are also accentuated by the perception that France is going downhill, due largely to the presence of immigrants.[25] In this, French workers resemble American workers. For instance, Vincent Lortie, the electronic chipmaker, points to North African immigrants as the greatest source of stress in his life because they affect the health of the nation: "It is dirty everywhere. I rarely take the subway, but when I do, I feel that it is a real garbage can. In the neighborhood, we still have our little world, so it is OK. But wherever they [the immigrants] go, there are graffiti everywhere, it is full of garbage. Americans are used to it, but not us. Little by little it comes here. Everyone thinks that what happened in LA could happen here." Vincent adds that he votes for the National Front because he likes its political program:

> For instance, there are too many immigrants. Now everyone is aware of it and people talk about it, but [the National Front] is organizing things to fight against it . . . We need to give France back to the French and to defend their rights. It is OK to help people solve their problems in their country, but to bring them

here and to have French people pay for it, no, I don't agree with this. And any foreigner who comes here has three times more power than we do here . . . I agree with the idea of sending everyone back to their country, absolutely.

French workers deeply resent this perceived loss of national status, given that their nationality is one of their rare high-status characteristics. Political scientist Pascal Perrineau even argues that workers experience this loss as emasculation.[26]

To summarize, French workers resent North African immigrants because of their alleged laziness and parasitism. Their economic dislocation and a sense that their superior group positioning is not being recognized by the state heighten their anger. We will see that this anger is also worsened by a perceived cultural incompatibility between the workers and immigrants.

Cultural Incompatibility, Civility, and Violence

Whereas many American workers believe and accept that they live in a cultural world separate from that of blacks, a sizable group of French workers believe that their culture is fundamentally incompatible with that of North Africans.[27] While American workers offered a multicausal explanation of black inferiority that pointed to nature, history, psychology, and culture, French workers' racism focuses more exclusively on cultural factors as they single out religion to explain differences between Muslims on the one hand, and Christians, Catholics, and the French on the other. Whereas Americans stress what they believe to be blacks' violations of traditional morality, French workers are more concerned with the lack of civility of North African immigrants.

Several workers describe Muslims and Christians as separated by an unbridgeable cultural fault line, which leads them to attach different weight to transcendental values such as human life and peace. Pierre Beleau, an electrical appraiser who lives in a town with a large North African population, describes these cultural differences thus: "They don't have the same religion. I have tried to read about how they live, to be informed, to see the history of their cult, how they interpret things. They say that they want peace, but they like to fight and they are the first ones to commit murder. So, there is clearly something wrong with them." A railway technician also points to a fundamental Christian/Muslim cultural fault line concerning the transcendental values of human life and equality, and even the maternal feelings of Muslim women:

> We have to be honest. The problem is that they don't have the same education, the same values as we do . . . Most of the French do not believe in God but they all have a Christian education that regulates our relationships. But the Koran doesn't have the same values at all. They send children to get killed in the mine-fields of Iraq. In France, if you kill children, it is really a scandal. But in those countries, social things are not as important. The mother is happy to send her child to go get killed in the mine-fields. She will cry, it is true, she will have the same pain as a European mother, but it is not the same thing . . . And there is also the respect of the value of life itself. Women in the Muslim world have no place. Whereas here in France, I have washed dishes . . . At some point, my wife had a depression, and I stayed with my children.

Particularly crucial cultural differences are believed to exist in the teaching of civility to children. Proof of the lack of civility among Muslims is found in barbarian habits, such as "spitting in front of you if they feel like it, whether they are a man or a woman" or pushing people around in the subway "and they don't apologize. They are very proud." A pastry maker also mentions the Muslims' strange customs, such as killing a sheep at Ramadan, which is done in bathtubs or on the balconies of apartments. He is also disgusted that Muslims hang sheep-skins outside to dry in the sight of everyone. Many French workers reminisce nostalgically about the more homogeneous, integrated, and caring communities in which they grew up, where Islamic veils would never have been seen on the street. The invasion of their immediate environment by immigrants symbolizes for them the collapse of the working class neighborhood, working class culture, and France more generally.[28]

The challenge of living with immigrants, and of having to put up with their different mores, is magnified by the physical proximity imposed by public housing projects where a sizable proportion of the workers in this study reside, and where immigrants compete for the symbolic control of public space by, for instance, blasting Arabic music—another proof of incivility. Richard Jalmain the subway conductor, who lives in a high-rise project, complains, "Some evenings, it is unbelievable the noise they make. One had a whistle the other day and he whistled every few minutes. It lasted for an hour at least. There were 20 of them down there, between 17 and 20 years old, so it was difficult to attempt to stop them . . . So the problem is a lack of respect. It was 10 or 11 P.M. and here there are thousands of people who were trying to sleep."

As was the case for American workers, much of the workers' anger crystallizes around criminality and the immigrants' lack of respect for private property. For instance, in the words of François Noyant, the policeman, "With experience you are forced to become racist because it is always the same race that creates problems. Always, always. You have no idea what crooks they are." François also links lack of civility to delinquency and criminality when he says, "They tend to live at night whereas the Frenchman, at night, he sleeps because he has to work the next day . . . They have no manners . . . They are very aggressive and they don't say 'good morning.' And they break everything they touch. I am lucky because I have a garage, but three or four of our neighbors got things stolen from their cars. The only problem I ever had is that they sometimes throw stones at me while I jog. Also when I compete in cycling races, they throw stones at me."

The personal experiences that workers and their friends and family have had with vandalism and violence increase the likelihood that they will adopt anti-immigrant positions that stress cultural incompatibility.

The experience of colonization and the Algerian War have contributed to constructing North Africans as violent and criminal. A French colony for 130 years, Algeria had played a particularly important role in the making of French prestige and grandeur because of its size, natural resources, and geographic proximity to France. For their part, Morocco and Tunisia were given the status of "protectorates" and were able to maintain their monarchies and a certain level of political autonomy. Whereas the decolonization process was gradual in these countries, the violent Algerian War of 1954–1962, which killed 600,000 people, left deep scars on both sides, as the opposing countries felt mutually betrayed.[29] This war also left scars within the French nation as the population came to be deeply divided around it. However, unlike the Vietnam War in the United States, the Algerian War has been downplayed in French collective memory. This has led some experts to argue that the racist violence against North Africans expresses the "return of the repressed" in a particularly virulent form because this war symbolized the end of France's status as an imperial power and marked the beginning of a crisis in French national identity.[30] Frequent associations between Islam and violence in recent years (for instance, the Iranian revolution, the Gulf War, Algeria's Front Islamique du Salut (FIS), bombings by Islamic militants on French territory, international terrorism, and Islamic fundamentalism more generally) have kept fears and resentments alive. These associations could only harden the boundaries that are erected against North Africans and nourish the view that they are violent and prone to crime.

North African immigrants themselves have experienced a variety of problems—crime, drug and alcohol abuse, alienation—that are associated with poverty and poor housing and that feed into racist attitudes. Although foreigners are not overrepresented in French prisons (when age, class, and sex are controlled),[31] many French citizens blame crime on foreigners, just as American racist stereotypes blame crime on blacks. Economic precariousness adds to the workers' fear of loss of national identity and to a sense of threat. This leads them to exaggerate differences between themselves and North Africans and to adopt a homogeneous view of the "other."[32] Hence, a growing number of French people conclude that the religion and customs of North Africans are not compatible with theirs.[33]

How can we account for the cultural character of racist explanations? The genetic and biological explanations found in the United States are simply absent in France, perhaps because they are illegitimate in France's republican political culture, which posits the equality of citizens participating in the social contract.[34] Hence, explanations of racial inequality shift toward cultural arguments. North Africans can be construed as truly "other" in cultural terms because they are a priori defined as having a strong allegiance to Islam. One worker explains that Muslims are incompatible with the French because religion dictates all aspects of their lives. In fact, this question has been much debated throughout Islamic history. The fundamentalism that is culturally influential today subordinates the political to the religious, and posits that the Sharia, the sacred law, should regulate all aspects of social, political, and religious life and must be given precedence over civil law.[35] Among North African immigrants themselves, there is considerable variation in level of religious participation—although this diversity is systematically downplayed in media representations of the group.[36]

When workers describe North Africans as fundamentally different and as having barbarian habits that include spitting on people and killing sheeps in bathtubs, they draw on taken-for-granted cultural repertoires that construe Islam as a "religious other." Islam has been the nemesis of Catholic France, and of Christian Europe, for more than a millennium—after all, the history of France, the Catholic Church's "oldest daughter," is marked by crusades and wars against Muslims in the name of the Pope.[37] The majority of the population remains Catholic, and although religious practice is very low,[38] Christianity continues to be an important cultural referent.[39] Christianity has given Muslims the lasting label of "barbarians" and has construed Europeans as the sole proprietors of civilization.[40] The National Front works assiduously toward maintaining these distinctions, multiplying efforts to "re-Islamize North Africans in the political imagination," which have succeeded in part because they coincide with a renewal of Islamic fundamentalism.[41] Hence, it is not surprising that workers readily draw on this prominent aspect of the national cultural repertoire to frame their understanding of differences between themselves and immigrants as unbridgeable, particularly in the realm of civility. Although highly contested, the national identity of France as a Catholic nation is defended by a sizable segment of the French right.[42]

How do these views on Muslims compare with those held in the United States? There as well, Muslims are viewed as "other," especially since the end of the Cold War, which brought about the disappearance of communism as the nation's favorite enemy. However, Muslims are less vilified in the United States than in Europe. First, Muslim immigrants to the United States have less rural backgrounds, have higher occupational and educational status, and are less religiously oriented than Muslims living in France,[43] which works against a clear dichotomization between "us" and "them." Second, the presence of many other immigrant groups in the United States detracts attention from Muslims, as they are viewed as one immigrant population among many others. Third, whereas the United States offers immigrants the American dream as an alternative ideology, France does not have an equivalent, and Islam is always available as an important fallback private identity attractive to immigrants who are not well integrated socially.[44] Finally, as we will see now, there are important differences in the way immigrant assimilation is understood in the French and American contexts.

The Challenge of Assimilation

While French workers believe that the sources of the differences discussed above are to be found in the culture of origin of the North Africans, they also insist on the importance of cultural assimilation. Immigrants are viewed as breaching national values because they refuse to integrate and downplay their cultural distinctiveness. For Pierre Beleau, the electrical appraiser, this is linked to fundamental differences between Islam and Christianity. He explains the situation thus: "I used to know a lot of Polish people who worked in the mines [in the north]. They were also Catholic and they could become integrated. If you come from a foreign land, you shut your mouth and you learn the habits and customs of people. [Muslims] are the ones who want to come here and impose their customs to us. You go in their country and they cut off your hand for stealing, and here they come, steal, and keep their hands. This is impossible: everyone mixes and we will all end up mixed-blood."

Luc Laurent, a bank clerk, concurs when he says of immigrants: "We don't know them, in part because they don't try to make us know them. We only see the negative side and say that we are not at home anymore in France. But the foreigners make no effort to assimilate themselves, to change their culture. If there is no effort, there will be a rejection." Yet Luc explains that he likes the Arab who operates the corner store and who is assimilated. He also asserts that he would come to his defense were he to be attacked by a Frenchman. Consequently, Luc concludes: "it is not a question of race, purely of race."

Louis Lebleu, the steam engine operator, elaborates on what he believes to be the most important aspects of assimilation: "I would say that the difference between us and them is fundamental. When they come to France, they keep their culture and do not try to become more European, but if we go there, many things are forbidden. This is not normal. If they want to come to work here, they have to try to respect the rules. They could keep the essentials of their culture concerning food or even how they dress. This does not bother me. But to see children of eight or ten years old in the street at one in the morning, I cannot accept this."

This criticism is accompanied by growing skepticism regarding immigrants' ability to assimilate. While in 1985, 42 percent of the French thought North African immigrants would not be able to integrate into French society because they are too different, in 1989 the same sentiment was expressed by 51 percent.[45] A content analysis of two newspapers also reveals that left-wing and right-wing journalists alike construct the problem of immigration in terms of the inassimilability of North Africans immigrants, who are contrasted with other assimilable immigrants—notably, Europeans.[46]

Other institutions add strength to this view of Muslims as inassimilable because they are fundamentally "other." One cannot neglect the cultural influence of the National Front in diffusing a view of North Africans as inassimilable and in lamenting the disappearance of the old Catholic, white, and culturally homogeneous France, one where neighborhoods were safe and French, and where collective life was truly organic.[47] Anti-immigrant movements elsewhere in Europe also nourish a view of immigrants as fundamentally different and/or as morally lacking in a work ethic. The European Union reinforces external continental boundaries, contributing to institutionalizing a definition of Islam as homogeneous and truly "other" to Europe.[48]

In fact, North Africans are more highly assimilated than the media and other organizations suggest. An exhaustive survey of immigrants to France leads Michèle Tribalat to conclude that these populations are not noticeably less integrated than other immigrant populations.[49] The integration of the beurs (that is, second-generation children of North African immigrants) is particularly high. In a recent survey, when asked the question "Do you feel closer to the way of life and to the culture of the French people than to that of your parents?," 71 percent of a sample of beurs answered "yes." Concerning properly religious issues, a 1983 survey of all immigrants revealed that "virtually all fathers of North African origin declared themselves to be Muslim, while over a quarter of their children refused to identify themselves with Islam. Almost half of the parents said they continued to perform the daily prayers as against only 3 percent of the children."[50]

The belief that immigrants should assimilate is grounded in a historical understanding of France and of French culture. Catholic ethnocentrism, discussed above, is reinforced by a French ethnocentrism that goes back to the Revolution and to the Napoleonic Code, which is grounded in the view that France has civilization and modernity to offer the world, first in the form of an inherently superior culture and technology and, second, in the form of democracy and republicanism.

As historian Gérard Noiriel argues, because France's national unity was constituted before important waves of immigration in the nineteenth century, immigrants were never construed as agents of national construction as they were in the United States.[51] They had to fit into a preconstituted organic national entity, defined by quintessential qualities.[52] These qualities are embodied in France's contributions to world culture in gastronomical, literary, intellectual, political, and other realms. France's sense of cultural superiority is sporadically reaffirmed by the French government. For instance, the Mitterand government officially placed at the top of its program the promotion of the rayonnement of French culture in the world, with the view of "reasserting France's rightful place among the great nations of the world" and especially in the eyes of the United States and Japan.[53] France's cultural prestige is affirmed by Jocelyn Lavigne, a policeman who began emphatically singing the merits of French cuisine (which he compared to the poor taste of American hamburgers) in the course of our interview.

This belief in the superiority of French culture has been maintained through colonialism via France's *mission civilisatrice*—its mission to carry civilization to such less-developed regions as North Africa.[54] French culture was imposed on Asian and African elites at a time when France's empire was second only to Great Britain's. By contrast, the British colonial project supported the cultural autonomy of its subjects.[55] For the French, barbarians could become part of humanity by assimilating. This idea was part of an evolutionary perspective that was central to eighteenth-century thought—de Tocqueville shared it with

French proponents of biological racism such as Joseph Arthur de Gobineau.[56] Although in the twentieth century the assimilationist position was abandoned in favor of "associationism,"[57] assimilation has continued to shape through republicanism how the French interpret the position of workers from former colonies. Hence, I discuss French republicanism in some detail, although only two workers referred to it explicitly in their discussion of racism.

Republicanism as a Condition for Anti-Immigrant Boundaries

In line with the central tenets of liberalism, republicanism posits citizens who have equal political rights and enter voluntarily and explicitly in a covenant by which they delegate their political sovereignty directly to the state, whose role is to define and promote the common good.[58] The state stands above particular interests as a neutral agent embodying universal reason and acting for the benefit of an undifferentiated mass of equal citizens.[59] What distinguishes this form of republicanism from its American cousin is that, as exemplified by the *Federalist Papers* (notably *Federalist 10*), the American system recognizes and legitimizes natural and social inequality.[60] In the United States, although individuals are at the foundation of the political system, a pluralistic logic prevails, and groups make claims in part based on their cultural identity.[61] For the French, this is the path to be avoided at all costs because it has led to the destruction of the American social fabric—as exemplified by the Los Angeles riots, pervasive poverty, ethnic conflicts, and identity politics.[62]

Hence, in France (1) intermediary bodies are not recognized; (2) citizens participate in the public sphere as individuals, not as group members; and (3) individuals are considered to be equal citizens, independently of their cultural, natural, or social characteristics. This means that ethnic, racial, religious, regional, and corporate groups cannot use their distinctive identities as bases for making claims in the public sphere. They also face pressure to assimilate in the name of a universalistic polity[63] and do not get the benefit of American-style pluralism.[64] Thus, officially France does not have a North African minority, but it shelters "aliens" who are defined not in reference to their cultural identity but to their economic status.[65] It does not have a category of "blacks," since a 1978 law prohibits the collection of ethic and religious statistics.[66] Finally, it has weak antidiscrimination laws, as the logic of republicanism is taken to be a powerful warranty against discrimination.[67]

Historically, centralized institutions such as the army and the school system played important roles in transforming republican principles into reality: they turned peasants, immigrants, and everyone else into French people by teaching them the rules of cultural membership, including the downplaying of particularistic identities.[68] The goal was to produce a national community with largely overlapping cultural and political boundaries, such that political culture acted as the line separating the national in-group and the out-groups.[69] For the last 20 years, French academics and politicians have been concerned with the crisis of this republican model, as schools have come to be perceived as failing to perform their traditional assimilation functions. Important debates have arisen between those who maintain their faith in the system and those who, while remaining wedded to republicanism, preach multiculturalism and communalism.[70]

This crisis has been particularly vivid in the policy arena and has been articulated around three issues that have exerted an impact on assimilation and have acted as lightning rods for political conflict (much like affirmation action has in the United States). Most notably, (1) the issue of immigration control has gained visibility, expressing fears concerning the growth of a destructive and inassimilable body within the nation;[71] (2) the 1993 reform of the Code of Nationality has generated considerable debate by replacing an automatic *jus soli* (citizenship based on territorial birth) with a law making the acquisition of French citizenship conditional upon actively requesting it at age 21, that is, upon expressing explicitly a will to assimilate and be part of the republican social contract;[72] (3) the 1989 debate about whether symbols of religious identity such as the Islamic scarf should be allowed in secular public schools became the occasion for a collective reflection on the place of multiculturalism in French society. Some approved of the idea in the name of the right to be different while others opposed it in the name of lay education. The republican model was reaffirmed by what came to be known as the *affaire du foulard* ("the scarf affair"). While in the eighties, many on the left rallied behind the "droit à la différence" (the right to be different), in recent years they have come to reaffirm the principle of assimilation that has provided the cement of French society since the Revolution.[73] In 1991, the socialist government created a "Ministère de la ville" (Ministry of Urban Affairs), now called "Ministère chargé de l'intégration et de la lutte contre l'exclusion" (Ministry in charge of integration and the fight against exclusion). The latter deals de facto with immigrants by focusing on their economic, as opposed to their cultural, integration. However, in line with the basic tenets of republicanism, it does not recognize group-specific problems.

One worker, Arthur Mineau, a phone salesman, explained that he opposes the National Front because he "believes in republican values" and thus refuses to make distinctions based on race. For similar reasons, many French academics and politicians continue to uphold republican values as the best guarantee against racism. Yet because it is based on assimilation, the French political culture of republicanism provides special ammunition for arguments against North Africans: it presumes (and aims to achieve) a national community with overlapping cultural and political boundaries, such that all members of the national community share the same political culture, which de facto distinguishes the national in-group from out-groups. As such, republicanism draws strong boundaries against immigrants: they can only become part of "us" by ceasing to be "them."[74]

The lower status of immigrants is reinforced by the caste-like relationship that the French have historically maintained with members of former colonies, which was justified in part by the ideology of French cultural superiority discussed above. In the case of Muslims, this caste relationship is particularly strong because of the traditional salience of Islam as a French nemesis. Against this backdrop, it is not surprising that French workers could have benefited from the presence of North Africans who took on the most painful and most exploitative jobs.[75]

It is only with the permanent settlement of North African immigrants after 1974 that the strengths of anti-immigrant boundaries inherent to republicanism were brought vividly to the surface.[76] In the past, immigrants were accepted because as temporary workers, most would not reside in France for long—although many extended their stay.[77] Others were accepted because they were not "them" for long, being "digestible" Polish, Jewish, and Italian immigrants.[78] Today, Maghrebis are defined in opposition to Jews and to immigrants from former Asian colonies who followed the path of their European predecessors in assimilating and accepting republican values.[79] And, indeed, none of these groups were salient in my interviews. This pattern perhaps suggests that we should not conclude that Muslims are to France what Hispanics are to the United States: French political culture requires assimilation in a way that American political culture does not.[80] Moreover, as Muslims and formerly colonized people, North Africans violate French rules of social membership more radically than do Hispanics in the United States.[81]

It has been argued that in France, racism does not pit the French against immigrants but pits unemployed youth (French and foreign) against everyone else.[82] My interviews suggest that the most salient boundary line is not an intergenerational one but a racial one. While some workers are concerned with youth in general, others single out beurs as posing a problem. For instance, an automobile painter explains: "Immigrants who came to France after the war in 1950, '55, '60, they came here to work and they worked . . . But their children, they don't know who they are because they have both nationalities. They don't want to go back home, and there is a big problem of unemployment." However, my interviews also provide clear and abundant evidence of the importance of racism directed not only at second-generation children of immigrants from the Maghreb but at all North African immigrants because "Muslims are Muslims." For these workers, "otherness" comes in a bundle—they are not preoccupied with making the fine distinctions between civic, ethnic, and religious dimensions of identity that are the object of social science writings.

Republicanism and Blacks

More French than American interviewees adopt antiracist stances: statements pointing to the equality between groups were made by 20 percent of the American lower white-collar respondents and 13 percent of their blue-collar counterparts. In France, such statements were made by 73 percent of the white-collar workers and 23 percent of the blue-collar workers.[83] Accordingly, more French workers view racism as a negative trait.[84] A 1997 national poll on racist attitudes in France suggests that blue-collar workers and lower white-collar workers are equally distributed between racists and antiracists, while professionals and managers were overrepresented among the antiracists. Thirty-three percent of respondents to this pool were classified as antiracist, 18 percent as racist, and 49 percent as somewhat racist, based on the extent to which respondents support a number of "racist positions."[85]

The lower salience of racism in France can be attributed in part to the impact of republicanism, particularly on the social meaning attributed to blackness. Indeed, if republicanism strengthens the boundary between a French "us" and a foreign "them," it also has had a powerful effect in downplaying the salience of skin color in the French public sphere: it presumes a voluntaristic or contractual approach to political participation that posits that anyone can join in the polity as long as he of she comes to share a political culture based on the universal (and superior) values of reason and progress. This principle has applied historically to members of colonies, including blacks. It has made it possible for a culturally and politically assimilated black Senegalese, Blaise Daigne, to be elected to the French National Assembly as early as 1914. As one of the main theorists of French colonialism put it, colonized people were considered "a *tabula rasa* onto whom the French could write French values. Thus transformed Africans would then be accorded the full political rights and responsibility of French citizens."[86] However, these inclusive rules of political membership prevailed simultaneously with the "code noir," which, in France as elsewhere, limited intimate relationships between blacks and whites.[87]

Republicanism shapes how workers talk, or do not talk, about black cocitizens and immigrants. Blacks were never mentioned by my interviewees, with three exceptions. Two workers made comments concerning the laziness of blacks.[88] A third, Roger Renault, a phone technician, explicitly distinguished between alien blacks originating from sub-Saharan Africa and French blacks originating from French territories such as Guadeloupe and Martinique in the Caribbean (also called the "Dom-Toms" or the "Départements d'outre-mer" and "Territoires d'outre-mer"). He criticized a neighbor for yelling at noisy black children from Guadeloupe, objecting that "these children are at home like we are" and should be treated accordingly. In so doing, Roger appropriates one of the central tenets of the French republican ideology, color-blindness, and accordingly downplayed one of the dimensions of differentiation that could stratify French society from the inside, skin color.[89] Paradoxically, he also supports the view that French society maintains a caste relationship with its former colonies.[90] He intimates that the privileged bond that links French citizens, irrespective of skin color, entails a lower status for the non-French. Accordingly, a national survey reveals that as compared to first- and second-generation North Africans, fewer black citizens from the Dom-Toms say that they have been victims of racism. Thirty-nine percent of the French from the Dom-Toms say that they have been victims of racism in contrast to 65 percent of the French of foreign origin (which includes mostly beurs) and 46 percent of immigrants from the Maghreb.

This is not to say that phenotypes are not used as a basis for discrimination in France. The police routinely check the legal status of blacks on the street, inferring their possible illegality from their skin color. North Africans are also victims of such operations, as most are distinguishable phenotypically from the majority group.[91] However, the official illegitimacy of skin color as a basis of differentiation is repeatedly reaffirmed publicly by intellectuals and politicians, and in this France is strikingly different from the United States.[92] As we saw, it even led to a law forbidding the collection of racial statistics. Those who refer to skin color, racial differences, or biological explanations, such as National Front leaders, are severely criticized for it by the media, intellectuals, and politicians. And the French do not perceive their society as racist. A survey conducted for the *Nouvel Observateur* in 1995 showed that very few French people view racism as one of the main threats faced by French society; respondents were more concerned with unemployment, poverty, AIDS, drugs, economic insecurity, and pollution than they were with racism. In contrast, foreigners and immigrants view racism as the first or second most important threat facing French society.[93] The illegitimacy of race as a basis for differentiation influences the boundaries drawn by workers. Some, like Julien Latige, a union representative, can be National Front supporters, castigate North Africans for taking advantage of welfare benefits, and still describe themselves as not racist because they like North Africans who are assimilated. This suggests a relative decoupling of racism and blackness—the presence of a kind of racism that is different from that found in the United States.

The decoupling of racism and blackness is found within the population at large: surveys are uniform in revealing that negative feelings toward blacks (as well as other racial minorities and European immigrants) are weaker than those toward North African immigrants. In a 1988 study of attitudes toward out-groups, North Africans were found to be the most disliked of all groups, after Northern Europeans, Southern Europeans, Jews, West Indians, Southeast Asians, black Africans, Indo-Pakistanis, and Turks.[94] That survey suggests that the French establish proximity primarily on the basis of Europeanness, shared citizenship, and, to a lesser extent, whiteness. Along these lines, a 1989 survey reveals that, when asked which category of immigrants poses the greatest difficulty for integration, 50 percent mentioned North Africans, 19 percent mentioned black Africans, and 15 percent mentioned Asians.[95] A 1984 survey on the degree of integration of various groups in French society reveals similar trends. The groups received the following scores on an index of opinion concerning degree of integration: Algerians (–49), Gypsies (–43), Turks (–24), Moroccans (–15), black Africans (–12), Tunisians (–5), Armenians (+9), Asians (+22), Yugoslavs (+23), Eastern European Jews (+33), Antilleans (French blacks from the French West Indies) (+37), "Pieds Noirs" (former French colonials from Algeria) (+45), the Portuguese (+52), the Poles (+67), Spaniards (+72), and Italians (+72) (with a mean of +18).[96] This ranking reveals the absence of a sharp racial line.[97] The opposition between the Judeo-Christian identity and Islam best accounts for the ranking of these groups.

A number of factors combine with the culture of republicanism to downplay the boundary against blacks. First, most North Africans are first- or second-generation immigrants. Blacks are more heterogeneous: while some are recent immigrants from sub-Saharan Africa, those from the Dom-Toms have been French for several generations. This works against defining "us" in opposition to "blacks" and partly trumps the low status of blacks as formerly colonized people. Second, blacks living in France are more heterogeneous in their religious self-identification than North Africans—for instance, the Senegalese are predominantly Muslim while the Congolese are Catholic.[98] While North Africans include a small Jewish population, they are often presumed to be homogeneously Muslim. Third, North Africans are more salient to French workers because they constitute a larger group than blacks (they make up almost 5 percent of the French population as compared to less than 2 percent for blacks).[99] Fourth, the process of decolonization was much more peaceful in French sub-Saharan Africa than in North Africa, and this produces fewer negative stereotypes of blacks than of North Africans. Fifth, historically a sizable proportion of black African immigrants came to France to be educated.[100] This population was more assimilated than the North Africans, who included more low-skilled workers; low-skilled black Africans had less easy access to France than North Africans due to geographical distance.[101] The more recent waves of sub-Saharan African immigrants are often better educated than earlier waves, and they have a better control of the French language than North African immigrants.[102] The policy of family reunification that was put in place after 1974 brought in large African families. These changes generated a backlash: they made Muslim African migration more visible and focused public attention on polygamy and traditional female genital mutilation.[103] However, overall the characteristics of blacks living in France work against a clear polarization between "Frenchness" and "blackness." Other racial groups, such as Asians, have assimilated quickly. They contribute to the playing down of race in French definitions of cultural membership.

This pattern of weaker boundaries toward blacks and stronger boundaries against immigrants (as compared to the United States) may be in the process of changing, as sub-Saharan African immigration grows and as highly publicized protest movements against repatriation have received much media coverage. We may also be witnessing an accelerated process of the "blackening" of immigration, as more non-Caucasian immigrants come to France. African-American popular culture, which is widely appropriated by youth, increases the salience of blacks as victims of racism—with French rappers borrowing directly from their American predecessors. Moreover, black Africans are joining North Africans at the bottom of the social ladder. Consequently, in the future, French definitions of social membership may be less likely to downplay skin color. It remains to be seen whether the republican myth and the presence of black French citizens from the Dom-Toms will remain powerful enough to trump the association between blackness and outsider status.

French workers and professionals and managers have access to similar cultural repertoires that facilitate this boundary pattern toward blacks and immigrants. The historical conflict between Christians and Muslims, the colonial past of France, the violent Algerian War, the notion of France's cultural superiority, and the National Front's racist messages are cases in point. However, in the interviews I conducted with French professionals and managers, neither race nor immigration was salient, perhaps because like their American counterparts, they seldom come into contact with immigrants or blacks. Or the explanation may be that, in France as elsewhere, the better educated use subtle rather than blatant forms of prejudice.[104] However, a number of structural factors may prompt workers, but not professionals and managers, to draw boundaries against North Africans. In particular, globalization, economic slowdowns (such as the recession of the early 1990s, the time of the interviews), and the breakdown of traditional French working class culture may heighten workers' concern about their group positioning and lead them to resent that immigrants receive more than their share of welfare benefits at a time when left-of-center organizations are weakened and less able to diffuse solidaristic messages than they were in the past. Hence, specific structural factors increase the likelihood that available cultural repertoires will lead workers to limit the community of "people like us" to the narrow confines of their national community.

FRENCH WORKERS' ANTIRACISM: EGALITARIANISM AND SOLIDARITY

George Lheureux is a bank clerk who has been employed for the last 15 years by the Société Générale. I interviewed him in his apartment in Créteil, a suburb located south of Paris. Tall, strong, with a big mustache and longish hair, he expresses himself eloquently. His wife left him three years ago and he has been raising two teenagers by himself. He defines the values he wants to pass on to his children as "the ideals of socialism: sharing, helping others, the abolition of the death penalty, solidarity . . . It is unbearable that some people can work as much as they want while others are unemployed." These are the values he received from his own parents: "socialism, republican values, such as freedom, and work."

Although he loves to read, George did not go far in school because he was unruly as an adolescent. Now he seemed himself a "prisoner" of blocked mobility at work and does not see a way out. He has taken an exam for promotion three times, but he has failed each attempt. He pours his energies into Amnesty International. He detests people who only talk about money: he believes it is more important to volunteer one's time to change the world. George has always been interested in politics and was for a while active in the Socialist Party. Struggling against injustice, including racism, is one of the big motivations in his life. He has a deep hatred for hierarchy and particularly racial hierarchy. He views inequality as contradicting everything he stands for and defines his goal in life as the "struggle for justice."

❖   ❖

To illuminate how moral boundaries shape racial boundaries, I now turn to an unexplored topic, the antiracist rhetoric of French workers. As in the United States, the antiracism of the men I interviewed is starkly different from that of intellectuals and activists.[105] But for one exception, French workers do not refer to cultural relativism or multiculturalism—that is, to the notion that all cultures are equally valuable—to demonstrate the equality of North Africans. Like their white American counterparts, French workers are more likely to justify their belief in racial equality by pointing to the fact that in their experience there are good and bad people in all races—that human nature is universal. Others point to the universality of human needs, as does an old mason when he says, "we are all there to work together and everyone has to eat." Unlike American workers, French workers do not use money as a means of establishing racial equality. George Lheureux readily upholds egalitarian and solidaristic principles to provide a powerful alternative to the National Front, which rejects human solidarity in the name of national solidarity. Thus, French workers draw not only from republicanism but also from socialism and Catholicism in their arguments for equality. Their accounts of cultural differences are more structural and less individualistic than those of Americans. They point to the living conditions of North African immigrants to explain their deviance from mainstream norms and hence denaturalize the characterization of this group.

Principles of Solidarity and Equality as an Antimarket Position

We saw that for white American antiracists and for some African Americans, class can trump racial inequality: money makes black people equal to white people. This argument is foreign to the French workers I talked to. None of them took socioeconomic success as a criterion of social membership and none argued that the market adjudicates the value of people. Instead, drawing somewhat differently on republicanism, workers affirm the existence of equality despite social differences, as opposed to conceiving it as resulting from such differences, that is, from purchasing power.[106] This appears in denunciations of inequality and injustice that are associated not only with racism but also with ageism and sexism. A draftsman, for instance, says, "Wherever I go, the secretaries I see are always pretty and young. I ask myself where are the old ones now? It is a form of racism. There is not only the racism of color." Others affirm the principle of equality in the face of cultural diversity and suggest that all should be treated equally "whether they are Buddhist or Catholic."

French antiracist arguments persistently referred to the principles of solidarity and its natural complement, egalitarianism—principles ignored by American workers.[107] For instance, draftsman Henri Belliveau, who is a long-term militant in the French Communist Party, explains that we cannot be racists if only because we are all workers and should stand by one another. These principles are connected to the way French workers draw moral and racial boundaries: we saw that solidarity was particularly central to workers' definitions of worth and that they readily put personal integrity above profit motives. Railway technician Marc Bataille says that racism is a disposition that he does not like because "it is the lack of respect for the other, and the person who is racist against black people or Arab people can also be racist against the butcher or the sweeper, against anyone." Marc affirms the importance of recognizing the dignity of people regardless of their labor market positions. He inverts one of the main principles of equality used by American workers.

Equality and solidarity are held sacred by some of the workers, especially in the face of practical considerations. Like their upper middle class counterparts who value intellectual honesty,[108] these workers define themselves against the type of moral pragmatism advocated by some American workers. A few justify such principled positions by their past experiences of injustice. For instance, Laurent Larue, the automobile technician, reaffirmed the importance of humanism as a way to fight against "the dark side of human nature" that is represented by racism and that inevitably leads to oppression. He described his sensitivity to the misery of others as overpowering and recalls that, as a child, he attacked an adult who was hitting his North African friend. He believes this reaction to be deeply ingrained and to reveal how he understands his place in the world. In fighting injustice, he affirms that personal dignity and personal integrity (his and that of others) are to be placed above selfish interests, including improving one's social position.

In proclaiming their obligation of solidarity with the unfortunate, workers draw on a solidaristic discourse central to Catholicism,[109] which is reinforced by France's strong tradition of state interventionism by the right as well as the left. Some also appeal to the principle of international solidarity among workers, which is central to the socialist tradition, to justify their antiracism. The French labor movement sustains these solidaristic attitudes with its historically internationalist and anticolonialist orientations. It promoted solidarity between nationals and colonial workers, and later between French workers and immigrant workers.[110] These forms of antiracism are also shaped by the antiracist social movement that emerged in response to the National Front and that put solidarity at the center of its agenda. It brings together traditional antiracist organizations such as the "Ligue des droits de l'homme" (LDH) and the "Movement contre le racisme et pour l'amitié entre les peuples" (MRAP) with "SOS-racisme," which in 1985 organized an antiracist concert that attracted 300,000 people.[111] SOS-racisme, which recruited students, socialist activists, and minority youth, has popularized the famous slogan *touches pas à mon pote* ("don't hurt my pal")—an important rallying cry against the National Front. In recent years the antiracist movement lost much of its influence and came to adopt a more conciliatory tone in line with the dominant republican themes of French political culture.

Work Ethic and the Structural Explanation of Differences

Work is what brings the French and immigrants together—the workplace provides the opportunity to learn about and appreciate one another. Antiracist workers extend the logic of the universality of human nature to the realm of work, affirming that there are good and bad workers in all races, just as there are good and bad people in all races. Richard Marois, a locksmith, exemplifies this. After explaining that the day before our interview, he had watched from his window as beurs set a car on fire, he says that he likes the Maghrebis he knows: "they are people who work and who are serious. These are people that I like and have respect for. There are French kids who are into delinquency, who steal, who attack old ladies, and who break things. And for me, whether they are black or yellow or red, it is the same thing." Similarly, concerning North Africans, a 50-year-old carpenter explains that "we cannot be racist at work because we work with them, and they are people like others. There are some good ones and some bad ones. They work."[112] From this observation, he attempts to understand the distinctive characteristics of North Africans in sociological terms. He says, "There are some cultural differences. North Africans are from countries that are underdeveloped . . . They have not been to school, but those who are my age, you can see that they are not able to make it. A lot of them don't know how to write." Richard Marois similarly sociologizes criminality and deviance when he says of North Africans that "these people often are unskilled and unemployed. They don't have money. They are depressed and end up taking drugs." Finally, after praising the merits of tolerance, a warehouse attendant who works in a multiracial milieu at the Charles de Gaulle Airport explains that it is important to try to understand the position in which people find themselves.

By providing a structural explanation for social differences, these workers denaturalize differences and offer a powerful counterargument to the notion that Muslims are fundamentally "other." They are less likely to blame minority group members for their plight, in line with the discourse of solidarity discussed above. Such structural explanations were absent from the discourse of white American antiracists. They were common among African Americans, although they have access to different cultural resources than French workers (for instance, the discourse of solidarity produced by the black church versus that produced by left-wing parties). The French may more readily adopt structural explanations because of the socialist tradition, which popularized a materialist understanding of the world as a means of raising class consciousness. Coupled with highly influential and visible antiracist organizations, this tradition plays an important role in sustaining the diffusion of antiracist ideas.

NORTH AFRICAN RESPONSES

Omar Ankli is an Algerian who works as a quality controller for the French automaker, Citroën. I interviewed him in his apartment in Clichy, located at the back of the interior court of an old building covered with peeling greenish paint. While his wife, who cleans offices and barely speaks French, was busy preparing a meal, his 20-year-old daughter was doing her homework, sitting at a corner of the kitchen table. Birds in a cage were singing at the window. The dark and tiny apartment is so overcrowded with overstuffed furniture that one can barely move about. Emerald and ocher wallpaper adorns the walls, and it appears to have been there for several decades.

Omar came to France "in search of a better life" and "to take charge of his destiny." He left Algeria in 1962, in the aftermath of the Algerian War. When he first arrived, he took night courses to learn French as well as to learn to read and write—he started working at the age of 5 as a shepherd and had never attended school. Through his union, he also received some training in welding but was not allowed to complete the course, though his French coworkers did. Consequently, he was never able to move up and improve his situation. He reiterates several times that for the management at Citroën, he is there only to fulfill "a production quota." The only immigrants who move up are those who get brainwashed and who accept being used to get other immigrants to work harder—"they have to become the worst of all, mere objects, robots who bark orders. They must also change their nationality to move ahead." He hopes that his daughter will, one day, be in "a better situation to fight in life," that "she will have more of a chance to penetrate society."

Omar is a very handsome man. He confesses that sometimes he dresses well and sits at the terrace of a café where he meets French women. He talks to them, but after a while he runs away because he does not want these women to see what he calls his "weakness," his poverty. He also feels handicapped because he is not educated ("it hurts me because I did not have the chance to discover many things, to understand them"). Yet he says that he has very little contact with French people: "We don't see them. At work there are only foreigners. My boss is Italian, the other one is Spanish . . . The French are very far from us. They are in the countryside, where there are only other Frenchmen, unlike here in the large cities where there are foreigners."

When reflecting on his experience in France, Omar remembers nostalgically that in Algeria "there was human warmth. It was limitless. There was contact with others, although work was very hard. There was a time for work and a time for pleasure, and there was also a pleasure found in working . . . People would take the time to live . . . Here there is no life." He believes that most French people do not try to understand immigrants: "They only judge by the language or the look. They say, 'This one is dirty, this one is a bad person, this nationality does bad things.' But when they take the time to penetrate our milieu, they appreciate it. They find a kind of human warmth that they cannot find in their own environment and that they appreciate . . . Human warmth is what gives us a taste for life, what helps us avoid being sad . . . It helps us forget our worries, it helps us forget hunger, it help us forget the cold."

In Omar's view, North Africans are better than the French in several respects. For example, they are much more altruistic. To illustrate this, he describes how on a rainy night he gave a hand to an old Frenchman who had fallen on the ground. While thanking him, the old man said, "'It takes a North African to come all the way to Paris to help me when all these Frenchmen did not even look at me' . . . I felt bad for this guy, I felt that he was old and weak and I had to help him. In contrast, the French people who were passing by thought, 'He must be drunk, too bad for him.'"

Omar thinks poorly of the French because he believes that the French treat old people badly. Their children put them in nursing homes because they do not want to be bothered, and they forget to pay them visits. In contrast, in Algeria parents live with their children who "help them be happy" and "give them human warmth," so that they are not lonely.

❖ ❖

By looking at the main strategies used by North African workers to rebut the notion that they are inferior to the French (or to Christians), I provide a comparative lens though which to examine the antiracism of American blacks. Of the 30 North Africans I interviewed, all but five said that they had been victims of racism.[113] A large number were concerned with proving their symbolic fit or legal membership in society by describing their moral behavior as that of a "good Arab" or by showing proof of their right to be in France, in the form of work permits or pictures of children born in France. Our interactions illustrate vividly how precarious they consider their presence in France to be in the context of the growing influence of the National Front, which calls for their rapatriation. Unlike African Americans, as noncitizens some North Africans went as far as to argue that it is the privilege of the French to be racist because, after all, they are at home. Unlike blacks in the United States, some blame members of their own group for the racism that victimize them.

A second strategy used by North Africans and African Americans alike to establish equality between themselves and the majority group is to point to human commonalities found in their daily life. Like African Americans, North Africans point to common human characteristics—common physiology and needs, differences in intelligence within groups. However, North Africans discuss a wider range of universal commonalities, pointing to universal moral rules and our shared cosmic destiny.

A third approach used by North African immigrants to deal with racism is to provide evidence of their superiority to the majority group. They do so by using arguments about the "caring self" that are similar to those used by their African-American counterparts. For instance, they view themselves as having a higher quality of interpersonal relationships, stronger family values, and greater moral and physical resilience than the

French. The arguments provided by Omar Ankli concerning the human warmth found in North Africa is an example of this.

Several immigrants share with African Americans the assumption that the world is based on particularistic as opposed to universalistic rules. Concretely, this means that North Africans point to privileged connections between themselves and the French to demonstrate equality between the two groups.

"The Straight Path" of the "Good Arab"

North Africans rebut racism by providing evidence of personal goodness. In interviews, they demonstrate that they personally conform to what they perceive to be moral criteria highly valued by the host society. This strategy involves abstracting oneself from one's race/nation/religion in order to show that a member is not necessarily defined by the group to which he or she belongs or to argue that judgments about a group cannot be extended to each of its representatives. "Following a straight path" is an important leitmotiv in how workers demonstrate their personal goodness. This is illustrated by Kaibi El Jouhari, a mason from Kabylia who came to France in 1953 to work with his father, and who was joined by his family in 1972. He says he has done all he could to become part of French society. He explains his attitude thus: "I tell you the truth, I am like Switzerland: I go one way. I don't go here and there. I am straight, neither left nor right. The only thing I look for is my bread, that's it . . . I only do my work and take care of my children, that's it . . . I have been in France for many years and I don't pay attention to politics . . . I don't go to bars, I don't walk around. Before my family came, I used to go to movies, but since they are here, I don't anymore."

All but two interviewees volunteered that they are not interested in politics, as if they wished to give me evidence that they mind their own business. Similarly, a warehouse worker, a gold-plating craftsman, an electrician, and a dressmaker explained that they have no dealings with racist people because they go directly from work to home and see no one. They attribute the fact that they have always worked and have never experienced problems with the police to their seriousness and commitment to "following the straight path."

Work is central in the way workers demonstrate their moral character: one belongs because one is a hard worker. To counter the French perceptions that immigrants are parasites, several reminded me that, after all, French entrepreneurs came to North Africa to find immigrants to work in the plants when there was a labor shortage.

While asserting that they are "good Arabs" because they follow the straight path, some immigrants blame the victims of racism for their situation. They justify French racism by the fact that immigrants are intermingling with French society in a way that they should not be, instead of doing what they are supposed to do, which is to work. Assan Zenine, a roofer, lives in a tiny bedroom located in a public housing building constructed expressly by the state to house single immigrant men. He explains that foreigners make the French racist because "they bring their children here, foreigners, blacks, Arabs, and they do anything they want, write on walls. This is not normal. If you give your child paint and he writes on the walls and you say nothing, it is you who make the French racist." Assan left his family in Morocco and is now saving every penny he makes for them. He describes his life as organized by seriousness and thrift. He says, "I have been here for 24 years and I have never been arrested by the police on the street. They never asked me to show my identification papers. It is because I come to my room directly and I don't look for fights."

The control that one can exercise on one's children is particularly crucial for immigrants. They see it as a religious obligation. Yet this control is not easily established, given that children often master French society and language better than their parents and often do not identify with Islam.[114] Those who have control over their children talk with pride about the fact that their children would never light a cigarette or watch people kiss on television in the presence of their father.

Another worker who blames North Africans for French racism is Ayadi Matoub, an electrician for whom working also goes hand in hand with "seriousness," which he defines as follows: "It means not hanging out with just anybody, with people who drink too much. I never smoked or drank, and I think it has helped me a lot because I never had any problems. I have always found work [because] I make a good impression on people. I have never done anything bad to anyone." Indeed, seriousness has high moral standing for him. It is an orienting feature of his life: "Seriousness is my model. If you compare people who live here in this public housing project with my friends, there is a big difference. The French are racist and it is normal when you see people who destroy everything, who are aggressive . . . I am Arab, but when I see an Arab who is destructive or aggressive, it makes me racist toward him. Normally I should not be racist toward someone who is from my country or race, but I become racist." Only three interviewees blamed North Africans for the racism of which they are victims. None of the African Americans blamed other African Americans for white racism, although many defined themselves by their hard work and marked distance toward other blacks they considered amoral.

The North African workers I talked to were quick to point out that the moral traits they value are emphasized in the Koran, which provides guidelines for all aspects of everyday life. "Tranquillity" and "following the straight path" are not especially valued in the Christian tradition, but they are prized in the Koranic tradition—for instance, "following the straight path" is mentioned in the first sura of the Koran.[115] Hence, North African workers ground their equality in particular dimensions of morality that are central to their own religious tradition.

Human Commonalities: Physiology, Human Needs, Intellectual Differences, Cosmic Destiny, and Moral Rules

North Africans also rebut racism by showing that all human beings share something essential. They point to the universality of our physiological characteristics ("we are all nine-month babies"; "we all have ten fingers") and to the universality of human needs. This is true for Mohamed Aboul, a forklift operator who says that "everyone goes to get bread at the bakery for dinner, and everyone has to put their coat on to go to work in the morning, whether you are Arab or French. Everyone is the same, it is the same thing." Similarly, a plumber, Said Ben Massoul, says, "We all have to work, Algerians or French, we all work the same, there is no difference."

However, North Africans point to a broader range of universal characteristics than do other groups in the study. Some focus on the universality of human destiny: an auto factory worker stresses our fragility and relative insignificance in the universe when he mentions that we all "pass like clouds" over the earth. Others ground equality in the fact that there is the same distribution of intelligence across all groups. Indeed, Kaibi El Jouhari, the mason, believes that "there are intelligent people in all [groups], whether it is in the police, in society, in all races." Moreover, Abdelaziz Bouabdallah, a mechanic, explains that "the Canadian who is an idiot will be viewed as a Canadian imbecile because there is this symbol of the flag. And the Algerian idiot will be viewed as Algerian because there are other symbols. But stupidity is the same when we take everything else away." Yet others use arguments having to do with universal moral rules of behavior that should guide everyone, independently of race, nationality, or religion.[116] In doing so, however, they refer implicitly or explicitly to the Koran. For instance, after explaining that he is very concerned about having his children likened to young North African deviants, Abdelaziz refers to Koranic rules to say that for all races it is important to "play the card of respect . . . Whether you are Algerian or French has no importance because people will judge you on the basis of your behavior. We find this rule everywhere, independent of time and space. It is not because you are old or because it is the year 2000 that this rule does not apply. Respect is an immutable rule."

This type of argument was frequently made by North African workers to rebut the notion of racial inequality. In contrast, black Americans do not refer to this kind of universal theme, for example, that the Golden Rule applies to all, independently of color.

North African workers are often less concerned with demonstrating equality per se than with establishing equivalence, similarity, or compatibility between themselves and the French. To achieve this, they point to constant "facts," which are frequently drawn from concrete naturalistic images (for instance, "we all pass like clouds"), as if naturalistic metaphors carried ahistorical truth. This is in line with the Koran, in which nature is often presented as evidence demonstrating the essence of things.[117] This "naturalistic" antiracism contrasts with the multicultural and relativistic approaches used by academics, as did ordinary theories of antiracism in the United States.[118]

Muslims above the French

Just as some African Americans rebut the notion of white superiority by showing that they are superior to whites, some immigrants argue for the superiority of Muslims, or of their own national group, over the

French. By using such moral arguments, North Africans, like African Americans, place themselves above the dominant group. Most important, they point to the moral values of Islam as evidence of the superiority of their own tradition over Christianity.[119]

It has been argued that postcolonial ideology contrasts community with capitalism and defines colonizers as antithetical to love, kinship, and collectivism.[120] This observation holds for the men I interviewed: they describe Muslims as superior to the French because they are more moral, by which they mean less individualistic and more altruistic. They explain that one of the five pillars of Islam (Islam's basic rules) requires them to give to the poor and take care of the weak. Ali Ben Aour, a skilled worker who specializes in air conditioning, explains that "here in France, if you have nothing to eat, you will cross your hands, stay with your wife at the table, look at one another, discuss, watch TV. In Algeria, if we have nothing in the house, it is not shameful . . . My wife or I, we will go to see a neighbor and say, 'Give me this!' and he will give it to me."

Some of these men describe their own culture as more humane, and therefore richer, than that of the French. This was also a recurrent theme among African Americans. Omar Ankli best illustrates this perspective. Speaking about French people who take the risk of penetrating his milieu, he says, "they appreciate a kind of human warmth that does not exist among them." This echoes the theme of the "caring self" that was common among blacks discussing whites and among white American workers discussing the upper half.

In line with this appreciation of altruism and warmth, immigrants are critical of the individualism found in French society.[121] A packer in the textile industry who is in his early thirties, Abdelsalem Antri equates individualism with a low quality of life. This became apparent when he told the story of a neighbor who disappeared. He says, "I had never seen her, never, and I have lived there for five or six years. In my country, [my neighbors] would know my grandfather, my great-grandfather. There, it is not the same, and this has a lot of value. We don't run as much, we see life more. Life is longer, the days are longer too." He contrasts French individualism with the tightness of networks of support that he knew in Algiers. He finds it impossible to get to know his neighbors and coworkers in France because anonymity prevails everywhere.

This focus on altruism and warmth also shapes North Africans' view of the quality of family life in France. Like Omar Ankli, Ali Ben Aour, the skilled worker who specializes in air conditioning, is critical of the fact that in France people put their parents in nursing homes so that they will be free to go to the movies: "Old people are badly treated and their children don't come to see them. In contrast, in our country, we live in the milieu, the old people stay with their children. We have to help them, live with them, and this is human warmth. Although the parents are old, they don't feel alone, they are there among their children and grand-children."

Abdelsalem Antri, the packer in the textile industry, also argues that the French lack family values: "Here, we often hear that a father has slept with his daughter. This is a catastrophe for us. Our parents have never heard of such a thing. If someone tells them there is a father who slept with his daughter, they become sick, they go crazy. This is how I react when I hear that a father slept with his daughter. I see this as an enormous earthquake."

Another realm in which workers believe that the French are inferior to Muslims is that their modernity is destroying their quality of life because it gives them too much freedom. Islam can better protect individuals against dangers because of its traditional character. In this spirit, Abdelkader Kantoui, a Tunisian screw cutter, criticizes modern societies: "Contemporary civilization has given us nothing, absolutely nothing. On the contrary, before it was much better . . . before, when you ate a fruit, it really tasted like something . . . people knew how to taste life." He believes that in France there are too many temptations, which reduces the value of things. He also believes that there are advantages to being from a poor country: he explained to me that whereas I can buy what I want, he gets to desire what he wants more than I do, which makes it more valuable. In his view, the French only brought decadence to Tunisia (in fact, his family lost land to the colonizers). Nevertheless, he believes that "life has more quality" in his country, as exemplified by the fact that people do not kiss on the street. He hopes to return to his country, and to this end he had a villa built near the sea in Tunisia. This antimodernist discourse, which sociologist Riva Kastoryano calls "defensive traditionalism" ("traditionalisme de defense"), is not available to African Americans.[122]

In a few cases, this antimodernist discourse is used to ground the intellectual and moral superiority of North Africans over the French. In particular, although he is critical of Islam fundamentalists, Abdelkader Kantoui explains that he feels superior to the French because all that the French know is included in the Koran: "The Koran speaks of the knowledge of life. It speaks of the sun, it speaks of the wind, it speaks of plants. It [also] speaks of all the sickness that you can think of, and that doctors are trying to find remedies to, but you won't be able to find [these remedies] because you don't read the Koran." In his view, whereas Westerners have to work hard to discover knowledge, Muslims "know everything in advance" because everything there is to know is revealed in the holy book. Abdelkader also mentions that the Koran recognizes knowledge and wisdom as the only legitimate bases of inequality: all men are equal, says the Prophet, except in learning.[123]

Finally, it is interesting to note that like African Americans, some North African workers ground their superiority in their physical (and, indirectly, moral) resilience. For instance, a gold-plating craftsman argues that Arabs are superior to the French because they are less lazy and do not tire as quickly. Echoing the African-American worker who believes that blacks are superior because interracial breeding generally produces black offspring, a laborer believes that Muslims are superior as a group because they make up a larger part of the world population than Christians do.

These arguments about the superiority of Islam have to be understood in the context of a global renewal of Islam, one in which immigrants are now more interested in religion than they were in previous generations. Incidents such as the *Satanic Verses* affair in Great Britain and the *affaire du foulard* in France embody the politicization of Islam. The Bosnian War and the conflict between Israel and Palestine dramatize the complex relationship between the Muslim and Western worlds as seen through the media.[124] These developments make their common identity as Muslims more salient to them and encourage them to affirm it in the face of French pressures to downplay it. For unskilled immigrants in particular, their Islamic identity can provide a community and

social network that they do not find at work.[125] It can also play a particularly crucial role for younger workers, who tend to be more militant
politically than older ones and who have not learned to downplay their
cultural distinctiveness.[126] It is in this context that many North Africans
appear to view themselves as fundamentally different from the French,
paralleling the view that the French have of them.

Particularistic Ties and the Myth of Republicanism

In Chapter 2, we saw that although African Americans often use universalistic arguments to establish their equality with whites—based, for instance, on money and human nature—some also believe that
particularism is how the world works: their confrontations with discrimination are living proof that people try to help people like themselves. A number of North African immigrants appear to share these
assumptions concerning the prevalence of cultures of particularism, but
in a different manner than African Americans. They attempt to rebut
racism by pointing to concrete historical and sociocultural ties between
the French and their own groups (Moroccans, Tunisians, Algerians, or
Kabyles). In doing so, they establish that they engage in a privileged relationships with the French. None of the African Americans attempted
to show that they had a privileged relationship with whites. Their
strong notions of racial solidarity may have worked against it.

An Algerian laborer provides a prime illustration of how this process
operates among North Africans. He explains that Moroccans are close
to the French because "when there were French people in my country,
Moroccans would give them gifts, so the French came to like the Moroccans." Similarly, a Moroccan painter says, "Moroccans say that the
French are good, France is good, there is no problem. For us immigrants, we would say that they are like brothers. There is no problem
between the two governments and when the French went there, Moroccans protected the French. It was normal." A third worker, who is em-
ployed as a phone booth cleaner, argues that "Algerians are used to the
French because almost three-quarters of us have learned French.
Whether you are French or Algerian, it is the same thing." Kaibi El
Jouhari, the mason, explains that Kabyles are closer to the French than
Algerians are because, like the French, they eat pork and drink alcohol.
Here again, evidence of similarity is taken not from formal political ide-

ologies like republicanism but from daily experience. This is consistent with findings from a study of the Moroccan identity that shows that the cultivation of particularistic ties and the resources these give access to are key to how Moroccans define their own identity, and how they are defined by others.[127]

The complement to—or justification of—this culture of particularism is that some workers believe that the republican view of French society is a fantastic ideal with little connection with reality. For instance, Abdelmajid Lahou, a civil servant, explains, "We say that [in France] segregation does not exist, but it is not true. That it is the country of universal human rights, but it is false, completely false. Nothing is respected, there is no country that can criticize the other without seeing its own wrongdoing." Abdelaziz Bouabdallah, the mechanic, observes, "They said that France equals liberty, equality, fraternity. They used to tell us that when they needed soldiers to fight for France all over the world. But when it was time to share the cake—to create schools for us in Algeria—they were not saying it anymore." Because they are skeptical of the ability of republicanism to foster solidarity and humanitarianism, these workers celebrate particularism as a more effective antiracism.

The antiracism of North Africans is shaped by the cultural repertoires that are readily available to them. Islam provides them with the main cultural tools they use to think about the value of human beings. This is suggested by the salience of themes such as "following a straight path" and altruism in the interviews, and by the fact that some mention that wisdom and knowledge are the only principles of inequality recognized by the Koran.[128] The antiracism of North African immigrants is also shaped by French racism: that some of them are willing to blame North Africans for French racism suggests the extent to which immigrants have been put on the defensive by racist organizations.

North Africans' structural position also helps to explain the distinctive features of their antiracism. Immigrants do not formally claim equal status in part because many perceive their legal status to be precarious despite having legally resided in France for many years and having children who are French citizens. They have limited occupational mobility and a rate of unemployment higher than that of any other ethnic group in France;[129] this situation is likely to dissuade them from taking strong dissenting positions and claiming rights. It contrasts starkly with the antiracism of African Americans, who claim full social and legal citizenship.

THE POLICING OF RACIAL BOUNDARIES COMPARED

In this chapter, I sought to accomplish several goals. We saw that French workers construct North Africans as violating their standards of worth. These immigrants are criticized for lacking a work ethic, sense of responsibility, and civility, and are described as parasites that have invaded the country. Unlike American racists, French racists are more concerned with the fair distribution of the social welfare pie than with self-sufficiency and responsibility. They view immigrants as culturally incompatible with the French—because they are Muslims—and their alleged inability to assimilate is offered as evidence of fundamental differences. Some white Frenchmen perceive North Africans as violating the spirit of French republicanism.

In the United States, white workers defined blacks as the prime violators of morality, while immigrants were much less central to the boundaries they drew. In France, we find the opposite pattern, as blacks are absent from the mental maps of white workers. Several factors work against defining blacks in opposition to "us": they are viewed as closer to the French than North Africans because many of them are Christians, French citizens, and/or highly educated. The country of origin of most black immigrants has experienced a relatively peaceful decolonization process compared to that of North African immigrants. Blacks are less visible than North Africans because they exist in smaller numbers in France.

There are also important differences in the antiracism of French and American workers. I found that French workers who hold antiracist positions point to the moral importance of the principles of solidarity and egalitarianism to rebut racial inequality, drawing on a key dimension of their conception of moral worth. Like their American counterparts, they emphasize the universality of human nature in demonstrating racial equality and do not use arguments having to do with cultural relativism or multiculturalism. However, unlike Americans, they do not believe that the market makes people equal; instead, they believe that people are equal despite differences in socioeconomic status. This is in line with their belief that the profit motive is a negative force that should be resisted.

A comparison of the antiracism of North Africans and African-American workers shows that North Africans do not consider earning capacity to demonstrate racial equality the way African Americans do. North Africans assert that they, personally, are good people, offering as evidence the fact that they work. They stress that they "follow a straight path" and the rule of respect, drawing on important themes in the Koranic tradition. They also blame members of their own group for the racism they encounter, something that African Americans do not do.

Both groups evoke evidence ranging from the universality of human nature to common physiology and human needs to demonstrate similarities between all human beings, independent of race. Like African-American workers, North Africans resist intellectual explanations grounded in the logic of multiculturalism and cultural relativism in favor of arguments grounded in their daily life. The culture of republicanism does not appear to have penetrated their milieus significantly. Instead, universal arguments are described by some as fantastic standards that have no impact on reality.

Sometimes both groups also place themselves above the majority group by arguing that they have better interpersonal relationships. The greater altruism of North Africans, their warmth, and the strength of their family ties are offered as evidence. In this, they resemble African Americans who perceive themselves to be more caring and humane than whites.

French social scientists often argue that the French political culture of republicanism produces a low level of racism because it delegitimizes the salience of ascribed characteristics in public life, hence facilitating the integration of racial minorities. In contrast, my analysis suggests that republicanism has a contradictory impact: it delegitimizes one form of racism but also strengthens another by drawing a clear distinction between those who share this universalistic culture (French citizens) and those who do not (immigrants). This boundary is reinforced by traditional anti-Muslim feelings found in Christian France, by a lasting historical construction of French culture as superior, and by a caste-like relationship that often characterized the relationship of the French with members of their former colonies. This situation contrasts with that found in the United States, where concern for the assimilation of immigrants is much less acute. While immigrants follow different patterns in adapting to life in the United States,[130] in principle they can participate in civil and political society without having to abandon their culture of origin and identity. This model sustains weaker boundaries toward immigrants than the republican model in France.[131] Such differences are particularly striking given that among European countries, France has the largest proportion of inhabitants with a parent or grandparent of foreign origin.[132] While it has been suggested that advanced industrial societies are converging in how they integrate immigrants,[133] the American model remains markedly different from the French model, with important consequences for the permeability of the external boundaries of the community. These differences are likely to persist although globalization increases the extent to which French society borrows cultural patterns from American society in particular.

This chapter has discussed how available cultural repertoires shape national differences in the way racism is conceptualized. We saw that some French workers ground their racism in part in republicanism and that antiracists also draw on solidaristic traditions that emerge from this tradition as well as from socialism and Catholicism.[134] In contrast, American racists and nonracists alike are more influenced by market ideology, as evidenced by the fact that they ground racial equality in socioeconomic equality. National differences in the use of market arguments can be explained by how such arguments speak to central themes in political and civic cultures. In contrast to the United States, the market is not viewed in France as a legitimate mechanism for the distribution of resources and positions.[135] Instead, it is construed as producing inequality, and its pernicious effects are perceived as correctable through state intervention.[136] In this context, liberalism is understood as "incompatible with the maintenance of a 'French exception' which is expressed in particular in the French public conception of public service and therefore of collective solidarity."[137]

One of the main challenges that French and American societies face at this point is to succeed in simultaneously maintaining a strong sense of collective identity while reducing the boundaries that they erect against the "other." As noted, there are important movements toward the recognition of the multicultural character of both French and American societies.[138] The broadening of cultural repertoires might show the way toward a happy compromise between exclusion and self-actualization through a collective project.

It is telling that in the United States the main policies developed to deal with racial inequality are affirmative action programs aimed at creating equal opportunity, whereas in France the government has promoted a policy of social solidarity to fight exclusion. White Americans defend egalitarianism by supporting the creation of equal opportunity programs aimed at creating equal conditions of competition as opposed to equal outcomes,[139] while elite and popular antiracism in France draws on universalistic principles informed by the Enlightenment and republican precepts that stress equality of conditions. The presence of a mainstream and openly anti-immigrant and racist political party in France leads us to believe that blatant racism has more legitimacy there than in the United States.[140] Because of the lasting impact of the civil rights movement, the United States does not, and probably could not, have a mainstream political party whose leaders make public statements in support of biological racism, as is the case for the National Front.[141]

Throughout this chapter, I have pointed to structural factors that explain the rhetorics of racism and antiracism that I have documented. I have mentioned in particular the impact of economic restructuring and globalization on the working class, and that of European integration on a sense of national threat and downward mobility. I now turn to how workers understand their place in the class structure. We will see that this is also acutely influenced by structural changes, and that workers' class boundaries draw on similarly broad definitions of worth as their racial boundaries.

6

Class Boundaries Compared

CLASS BOUNDARIES IN A DYING CLASS STRUGGLE

DOES CLASS figure differently in how white French workers and American workers evaluate others? French workers are much more likely to put themselves above the upper half and much less likely to equate worth with socioeconomic status.[1] Like their American counterparts, they believe that their interpersonal relationships are warmer than those of middle class people. However, unlike white Americans, they borrow from an entrenched rhetoric of class struggle to depict "people above" as morally unworthy. Many also scorn ambition and the desire for upward mobility as incompatible with personal integrity and solidarity—two valued dimensions of morality. Moreover, like African Americans, French workers often view the upper half as exploitative and inhumane. Hence, while social scientists argue that the opposition between the working class and the bourgeoisie has become less salient in France since 1980 due to the decline of unions[2] and of the French Communist party,[3] I find that this division remains alive and well among the men that I interviewed, and that many continue to draw on a language of class struggle and on France's revolutionary tradition in defining their relationship with the upper half.[4]

French workers draw much weaker boundaries toward "people below" than Americans do. Their understanding of the place of the poor is shaped by the solidaristic tradition inherited from socialism, republicanism, and Catholicism discussed in the previous chapter. In interviews, they often express solidarity with the poor, stating, for instance, that "we are all wage earners, we are all exploited." Or, as was the case among French professionals and managers, the poor are simply absent from workers' descriptions of the kinds of people they like and dislike or feel superior or inferior to. Boundaries drawn against the poor, like those against blacks, are much stronger in the United States than in France.

The first part of the chapter focuses on workers' attitudes toward the upper half, while the second part centers on their attitudes toward people below. I first describe the handful of French workers who identify with the middle class. In the United States, 25 percent of white workers identified with the middle class, as did 40 percent of blacks. In France, only a few French workers identified with the middle class. Although a larger number of French than American workers link social position with intellectual ability, a large majority of French interviewees are quite critical of the upper half.

WORKERS ON "PEOPLE ABOVE"

The Exception: In Support of "People Above"

THE MIDDLE CLASS IDENTIFIED. I met Claude Rieux in the backyard of his brand-new white bungalow in the suburb of Stains, by the Charles de Gaulle Airport. Although the neighborhood includes several public housing projects, Claude lives on a quiet street lined with small houses built in the fifties. We are sitting comfortably in his neatly kept backyard as departing airplanes travel over our heads. This otherwise bucolic and sunny setting suggests serenity and small-scale prosperity.

In his mid-thirties, Claude works as a bank clerk, but he changes employers regularly, which is highly unusual in his line of work. He explains that one needs to move often in order to climb up professionally. The risk is well worth it because he avoids being trapped in the type of dead-end positions that are omnipresent in the banking world. He started at the bottom of the hierarchy as a bank teller, but he now works in a loan department and supervises several people.

Claude's hero is the French professional skier and Olympic gold medal winner, Jean-Claude Killy. Claude admires Killy because he has demonstrated that "it is possible for people without diplomas to move up even if they start very low." He identifies with Killy because they share the same orientations toward competitiveness and competence. Moving up is important to Claude and he is obviously very proud of his sparkling bungalow. However, he explained that he would not want to become a manager. This would mean working more than 35 hours per week and his family would inevitably suffer. He does not like the idea because he considers his spouse and toddler to be the most important things in his life. He is ambitious but will not sacrifice his quality of life. Nevertheless, he defines success in professional terms: his goal is to make himself a place in the sun.

❖ ❖

Very few French workers I talked to identify with the middle class—with its attributes, such as success, power, and money, or with its values, such as ambition. Those who admire the ambitious include Roger Callon, who works as a foreman in a lamp factory. He says that he feels superior to people who have no goals, who do not attempt to improve their future, "who are just living to follow the shepherd. We have objectives and we are trying to achieve them. Mine [he says with a grin] is not to stay here for the rest of my life to answer your questions." Others, like Eric Dupuis, the heater repairman who dreams of becoming the president of all the French workers, share this appreciation of ambition: "Some people want a little easy job, a little easy life, and to live like this until the end. Me, personally, I try every day. It is not an obsession either. No, but every day, I try to see where I am going, if I am improving."

Like Claude Rieux, most workers who identify with middle class values set clear limits on their investment in upward mobility and success. They largely define their own worth and happiness by the quality of their interpersonal relationships and of their family life in particular. As Lucien Maroix, a radar technician, puts it, "Family goes before work . . . because at work things could always go wrong. They could let people go."

I found only one French worker who explicitly measures human worth on the basis of socioeconomic success. He talks about success and goal orientation in terms reminiscent of the language of some

American workers. His name is Jean-Jacques Neveu and he is employed as a "railway technician" by the Société nationale des chemins de fer (SNCF). In his mid-thirties, he comes from the provinces—from the Massif Central. He grew up in a small village, in an environment where money was scarce. Several of his brothers and sisters still live in poverty. Determined to find his way out of that miserable environment, Jean-Jacques worked hard and steadily for the national railway company. He started as a train controller on local lines and was rapidly promoted to the national lines, the only path to mobility. A few years ago, he was again promoted and asked to "come to Paris" where he now supervises a small group of train controllers. He makes a good living and was able to buy a cozy home in Ivry, south of Paris, where he lives with his wife and two children. I interviewed him in an immaculate living room. The white carpet and heavy wood furniture give the room a quasi-bourgeois atmosphere.

Jean-Jacques attaches enormous importance to his achievements. He says that he feels superior "to people who started like me and did not go as far. It makes me feel good inside." He is not egalitarian and in this he is different from many of the other French workers I talked to. In his words, "We need differences. Even if I lean toward the left, [I believe that] you need people who have money—this is for sure. I would say that it is normal to want to limit differences, but we cannot reach equality. We are equal in front of death alone. In life, we are not. To each his own luck. Each does what he can, what he wants. If he wants to live in an apartment, fine. If he wants to save to buy a house, he will make some sacrifices . . . One has to take responsibility for one's choices."

In describing the values he received from his parents, Jean-Jacques says, "It is important to respect money, not to spend it carelessly. I was taught that you have to work hard to make your money in a clean way, not to steal, to deserve it, not be a parasite." The humiliations he experienced as he was growing up led him to value money. He explains that "those who had money would put you down, when, for instance, we had an outing at school. They would always throw their money in your face. It was the clothes they had, their ways of doing things. I had nothing. I could not dress like them. I could not do the same things and I just had to put up with the situation." A desire to never again be in that position motivates him to work hard.

However, Jean-Jacques is the only French worker I met who identifies fully with middle class values. Other workers resemble Claude Rieux in their ambivalence toward work and their desire to protect their private worlds from the invasive sphere of work. They view these two worlds as antagonistic and rarely equate familial bliss with middle class consumption. The thinness and scarcity of the pro-middle class discourse among these French workers contrast starkly with the picture that emerged from interviews with American workers. In France, statements against the middle or upper middle class are multifarious, rich, and abundant. Similarly, in earlier research, I found fewer professionals and managers who expressed unqualified support for materialism and ambition in France than in the United States.[5]

INTELLECTUAL INEQUALITY LEGITIMATES SOCIAL HIERARCHIES. French workers who identify with middle class values more often justify the position of the upper half in terms of the rewards of intelligence than do their American counterparts. This is one of the few instances where they appear to be under the spell of middle class culture, in line with the legitimist theory of working class culture.[6] Men like Jean-Luc Derain, the auto painter, explain their status in life by their limited knowledge and innate intellectual inferiority:

> There are some people who are born to be powerful, who are born to be at the top of the hierarchy, and there are people who are born to be in the pyramid but not at the top of it. It is in the nature of people. I could not be at the top. I don't know why. I would see myself in the middle of the pyramid; this would be good enough already. I don't have the education, the knowledge, the intelligence maybe. You have to know your limitations. You cannot just say, "I would like to be there." You have to be able to do the job, and this is not easy.

Jean-Jacques Neveu, the train controller we just met, also believes that one's social position is proportional to one's intelligence. Reflecting on his own social trajectory, he concludes, "I feel that I did well, but I know my limits . . . I think that I deserve to be a manager as much as [my boss] does. He does nothing and I do everything, so I wonder why I am not in his position. But I also know my intellectual limitations. I would not know how to analyze files the way [executives do]. I know what I am capable of. I cannot go very far."

French workers are also more likely to express feelings of inferiority about cultural knowledge. A bank clerk says that he "feels inferior to people who are very cultivated on everything, on many topics . . . It is particularly the ability to remember everything. For instance, on the games on TV where people are asked general questions, you have people who can answer in one second questions on all kinds of topics." Like French workers, French professionals and managers are much more attuned to cultural distinctions and cultural capital than their American counterparts.[7]

A few interviewees downplay intelligence as a principle of hierarchy, arguing that while they may be inferior intellectually, they are superior in other dimensions. However, in general, French workers offer a stark contrast to American workers who more often refuse to explain their low social position by their lower ability or lack of cultural knowledge. In the United States, the American dream and its corollary, populism, are pervasive cultural repertoires that lead workers to believe in limitless possibilities and the power of self-determination.[8] This simply has no equivalent in France, where the educational system is particularly efficient at legitimating social differences and where higher education is less democratized and is more elitist than it is in the United States.[9] As we saw in Chapter 1, American workers often legitimize authority by competence, but they are more likely to think that those who want something can get it, and that one's intellectual level is a characteristic that can be improved through schooling.[10]

The tendency to explain inequality as a consequence of innate differences in intelligence is reinforced by the fact that French educational certification and promotion in public sector jobs are largely based on standardized examinations, which are viewed as uniquely meritocratic. Many workers I interviewed explained that they have never performed well on exams, which they take to be objective measures of their abilities. Hence, they internalize their inferiority and are less likely to believe they can improve their situation. This adds to the experience of blocked mobility, which was exacerbated at the time of the interviews by the economic recession.[11] Others believe social position is largely inherited, and they think it ludicrous to organize one's life around a project of social mobility. As Yvon Lahire, a warehouse keeper in his early thirties, suggests:

> There are people who are rich and others who are poor, people who are lucky and others who are not lucky. There are people who have had the chance to be raised in a rich family, and those who grew up in working class families who have to fight to survive . . . Those who grow up in a richer family have the chance that all doors are open to them, whereas we have to discover all kinds of things ourselves. This is like union membership: if you don't have the card, everything is closed for you. When you don't have a name, no one gives you a break . . . They treat you like a peon: "You will do this. Now, stop! This one is good at this, we don't take a risk. Let's leave him there."

American workers also believe that middle class people have all kinds of breaks along the way but not to the same extent as do French workers. We will see that in France more than in the United States the association between social position and social origin works against equating socioeconomic status and moral worth.

Against "People Above"

The French workers I talked to draw much stronger boundaries against the upper half than do their American counterparts. Many believe in a persisting class struggle and view money and power as evils. Accordingly, they view the "bourgeois," "bosses," or "higher-ups" as exploitative and dehumanizing—a sentiment shared by some African-American workers but absent among white American workers. French workers condemn profit-making rather than praise it. They associate ambition and upward mobility with moral corruption and see it as incompatible with personal integrity and solidarity—dimensions of morality that they value. They also believe that snobbishness is incompatible with civility.

Like their American counterparts, French workers perceive their quality of life to be better, and their interpersonal relationships to be

221

warmer, than those of the upper half. Like African Americans, they also emphasize the "caring self." The moral flaws of the upper half and their poor quality of life help French workers place themselves above "people above."

THE CLASS STRUGGLE. Study after study has found that French working class culture is in a state of advanced decomposition, brought about in part by long-term unemployment and the decline of working class organizations.[12] Concomitantly, a declining percentage of the population identifies itself as working class.[13] Yet many of the French workers I talked to continue to identify themselves as such and remain, in their minds at least, deeply engaged in class struggle. In this, they are markedly different from American workers. This concern with the class struggle is illustrated by Robert Renan, the photographer. He contrasts his working class humanitarian orientation to middle class materialism, conformism, selfishness, and exploitation:

> I cannot stand the petit bourgeois . . . They are social climbers and I am disgusted that they have made it by the sole fact of being born. They only think about money. They all dress the same . . . They live in a system where they are unable to make things improve. They have received an education where they learned that they had to think like this, this, and this [hits the table]. They are prisoners and their field of vision is very narrow . . . I come from a working class milieu, and I cannot stand people—the bourgeois—who dominate. It is disgusting what they do. They succeed in creating conditions that make people hungry while they make a fortune . . . Social injustice is something that I find enormously disturbing. The top boss of my firm makes what someone at the minimum wage takes his whole life to make. Is it necessary that he make so much money? Could the minimum wage guy make a little more, so that he can take vacations once in a while, buy books for his kids, and succeed a little better in life?

Yvon Lahire, the young warehouse worker, is less concerned with the zero-sum aspect of class relations than with comparing his work conditions and rewards with those of bosses:

Being a worker means that I wake up very early in the morning, and I spend my whole life working for just a little bit of money. Others work too, but there are days when I start at 5:00 A.M., so I get up at 3:30, and I bring in only 6,000 francs per month. The manager, he gets up at 8:30 and makes at least 25,000 francs per month. When he gets to the office, he goes to say hi to this one and this one . . . Me, when I come back from work, I am very tired. I sit on the couch to watch tennis and within an hour I fall asleep. The manager, when he comes home, he does not watch tennis on TV. He goes [to see the tennis matches] at Roland-Garros because he can get a ticket. Do you see the difference? This is it.

Interviewees also explicitly ground their oppositional attitude in the traditional working class culture they inherited from their families. René Saumier works for a firm that installs undersea phone and electrical cables. He is one of the most upwardly mobile of the men I talked to: he started as a worker but has been promoted to the rank of technician despite his lack of formal education. He explains that he remains wedded to the working class values he inherited from his family and neighborhood:

Because of my family, I was always very much to the left. Now I am less so, but I have always kept the same left-wing sensibility . . . I would never vote for the right . . . It does not correspond to my values. The right are those who made us suffer . . . It was very hard for workers during the De Gaulle period. There was an economic boom. Towns were growing and bosses were getting rich at the expense of the workers . . . De Gaulle for me represented an ability to get control over people, over little people, to exploit them for the benefit of the bosses . . . I was fed these ideas from an early age because I grew up in a working class environment. This was all around me, all the people I knew.

René Saumier alludes to the fact that, until the mid-sixties, the state-led economic development of French society took place at the expense of workers' wages, rights, and benefits. Due in part to delayed modernization,[14] they did not grow as much as they did in the United States and in other European countries.[15] This situation sustained polarized class relations, which were reinforced by the presence of "one of the more uncooperative business classes in any advanced capitalist society" that was particularly unwilling to "tolerate workers' demands and [that] granted a legitimate identity only to citizens who accumulated capital and property."[16]

Indeed, the class struggle also manifests itself in an authoritarian work culture and a climate of distrust that has characterized French labor relations for decades.[17] Although, paradoxically, some older workers are nostalgic about authoritarian relationships in the workplace,[18] others point out that their persistence exacerbates class antagonism.[19] Ironically, several workers say that they do not want the more open relationships at work that are being introduced as new management techniques: in their experience, bosses often use information gained from workers to reduce worker autonomy.[20] The conflictual character of class relationships is not identified only by workers but also has been historically recognized by the French state. The functions of the French administration include mediating between workers and employers, and this helps to institutionalize class conflict.[21] Hence, the view that interclass relations are exploitative is more readily available in popular discourse in France than it is in the United States.

French unions have historically played an important role in sustaining class antagonism.[22] In particular, the influential Confédération générale du travail (CGT), the union close to the French Communist Party, opposes cooperation with management,[23] building on a tradition of defense of workers' autonomy.[24] Along with other left-wing organizations, this union has romanticized the history of class struggle—the crucial role played by the "sans-culottes" during the French Revolution of 1789, for instance[25]—as well as a tradition of successful mass mobilization (or general strikes) that is still part of workers' familiar cultural repertoires.[26] These collective memories remain alive, although, since it came to power in the early eighties, the Socialist Party has shifted attention away from the promotion of workers' interests and toward the priority of economic competitiveness.[27]

Even today, working class militancy remains important in the lives of some workers. I interviewed Luc Larada, a train ticket salesman, at work in the ticket booth of a subway station. He lives in Ivry, a southern sub-urb of Paris that has elected Communist mayors for the last 90 years. He has always been involved in local politics. He says that in his envi-ronment people mobilize frequently: "When there is something [like] the closing of a plant, there is always a big fight . . . an old tradition like this does not disappear easily." Drawing on the language of class strug-gle, Henri Beliveau, the draftsman, stresses the importance of fighting against materialism, power, institutions, and conformity. He describes the kinds of people he likes as "the rebels, those who in relation to in-stitutions do not accept established rules, like marriage. Those who can by their work, their activities, their actions, try to stop a little bit this trend toward economic profit, speed . . . who are breaking the mold. People who fight, who do not accept society as it is, who refuse a num-ber of things, like watching television." Yet others echo recent sociolog-ical analyses and mourn the decline of working class culture and solidarity. A draftsman, for instance, says that there are no workers any-more "the way it was during my father's time—it was another time." Similarly, in the opinion of Eric Dupuis, the heater repairman, the working class movement is over and is no longer worth fighting for. Speaking of the government, he says, "they have tried to destroy the tools that the workers had and now they want to destroy [solidarity in] the family."

All in all, though workers believe that the class struggle has eroded, it continues to shape their critical view of the upper half. It is also a cru-cial piece of evidence that French workers identify less with the middle class than do their American counterparts.

EXPLOITATION AND DEHUMANIZATION. In Chapter 3, we saw that white American workers admire entrepreneurs, dream of being in-volved in moneymaking schemes, and view profit-making as a worthy and legitimate venture. In contrast, among African Americans, a sizable subgroup described interclass relationships in terms of exploitation. French workers expressed similar sentiments: many believe that the quest for wealth involves exploitation and dehumanization.

First, exploitation: time and again, workers explained that there is a zero-sum relation between their employer's profits and workers' wages.

Justin Lagneau, a garbage-recycling specialist, says that "if there was honesty, a boss would not keep 95 percent of his salary for him and give 5 percent to the workers. He would divide it fifty-fifty . . . Or at least there would be a little more sharing." Justin suggests that making a profit is essentially dishonest. This notion is foreign to American workers, but it was espoused by several French workers. For instance, for Jules Auclair, the aircraft technician, "It is always the little ones who pay for the others . . . It is people who have the most money who are most able to get more than they deserve." Similarly, Richard Jalmain, the subway conductor, explains that he does not respect the notions of profit or opportunity. For him, making a profit is akin to trying to move in front of others when waiting in line: it implies a lack of respect and benefiting at the expense of others.[28] By emphasizing the exploitative character of capitalism, some workers borrow explicitly from Communist ideology. For instance, George Desjardins, the firefighter who is also a National Front supporter, says of workers, "We all have the same value, we are just exploited differently."

Other workers are concerned less with unequal exchange than with dehumanization in the workplace. This manifests itself in the prevalence of purely instrumental relationships between managers and workers, the poor quality of communication between hierarchical levels, the deterioration of working conditions, and the lack of appreciation experienced by workers. In the eyes of Jean-Luc Derain, the automobile painter, dehumanization is illustrated by the fact that most of the time bosses barely greet workers, but when they need something done they are very solicitous. Eric Dupuis describes dehumanization in these terms: "Some bosses have been killed by money. They are only thinking about it, about their lifestyle. They don't pay attention to workers and are only concerned with whether or not they are profitable. My boss, we can share things with him, but he shares nothing with us . . . He is on the top of his ladder . . . He never puts his feet on the ground. This is disrespectful toward the people who get the work done." Eric concludes in graphic terms: "They have us crawling in the mud. When you come up to breathe a little bit, they put your head in it again. Their motto is 'shut up and swim.' You never see the end of it. The more you think about it, the more difficult it gets."

Like Eric, many believed that the recession that was going on at the time of the interviews had worsened the situation, as workers had to put up with more while owners' profits increased. Jules Auclair was particularly sensitive to this situation because his employer, Boeing, had fired many employees and had put more pressure on those who remained: "They just reduced the workforce from 1,600 people to 1,100 people in a year and a half. There is too much pressure. Before, there was a very friendly atmosphere—it was like working with family. Now it is really inhuman, and this is also the case in many firms in France today." When Jules protested against deteriorating work conditions, he was told that he was free to leave. Collective means of pressure were unavailable because "if we went on strike now, the bosses would be very happy because they would not have to lay people off."

THE DOWNSIDE OF MONEY AND POWER. Unlike the Americans, few Frenchmen dream of becoming entrepreneurs or of joining the upper half. Marc Bataille, the railway technician, believes that "people who have too much money don't know what to do with it . . . I have fewer problems than them. I would not like to take the place of an Arab emir." Marc values money to the extent that it translates into personal comfort. He explains that "money does not have great importance. It is important in terms of doing certain things. It is important to build a house, but money itself is not really the most important thing." Accordingly, more French workers than Americans criticize materialism; my previous study showed that, similarly, French professionals and managers are much more critical of materialism than are their American counterparts. A bank clerk describes a widely held view when he says that "I don't like people who only talk about money . . . People who always ask you how much you have paid for this or that drive me crazy . . . I don't spend my time trying to find ways to have more money. I don't recognize myself in this. It is really not me."

More French than American workers are also critical of power: they equate it with domination and experience it negatively, as coercive and repressive instead of empowering (this was less the case among French professionals and managers). A wood salesman says that he does not like power because all it does is make one afraid to lose it and because people never have enough of it. Similarly, a painter believes that power is not always achieved honestly: "Most people who are powerful today, they obtain power through money, and people are often ready to do anything to get it, to get what they want, at the expense of others. And this I cannot stand . . . It is true that there are some exceptions . . . It depends on how it is done."

THE IMMORALITY OF AMBITION, UPWARD MOBILITY, AND SNOBBISH-NESS. Consistent with their antimaterialism and criticisms of power, French workers also view ambition and the quest for upward mobility as immoral. In fact, while only a third of American workers were critical of ambition, many French workers criticized this trait. When choosing from a list the qualities they value highly, none of the French chose "successful" and only four chose "ambitious." In contrast, a fifth of the American workers chose "successful" and a quarter chose "ambitious."

In Chapter 4, we saw that French workers value personal integrity, solidarity, and civility. Many perceive the ambitious, the upwardly mobile, and the snobbish as lacking in these characteristics. For instance, when questioned about his child-rearing values, Henri Beliveau, the leftist draftsman, explains that he does not want to teach his children the importance of becoming "someone" in life. For him, remaining faithful to oneself is more crucial. He views upward mobility as incompatible with integrity because one obtains it by agreeing to follow orders blindly. For Eric Dupuis, the heater repairman, those who move up are "yes-men. They have completely subordinated any values they may have to the good of the wallet. The wallet is not everything."

The opposition between ambition and solidarity is illustrated by the fact that a number of workers believe that accepting a promotion would force them to put an end to their closeness with coworkers.[29] Others describe ambition as antithetical to good interpersonal relationships. For instance, Gaston Roger, the pastry chef who is in his early thirties, says, "Many people who really want to succeed are willing to hurt others. Like this one chef, Christopher, he wanted to be at the pinnacle. He wanted to turn the other cooks into workhorses who would work all day with their heads down. No contact, no feeling." The rigid hierarchical relationships that characterize the French workplace may sustain this view of ambition as incompatible with solidarity and empathy.[30]

The fact that some French workers view social ambition as largely re-lated to social origin works against the glorification of ambition. Adopting a stance never encountered among American workers, Roger Renault, the phone technician, says, "I know that our children will be approximately what we are. I don't have any illusions socially. The sons of low-level civil servants will become middle-level civil servants . . . I am lower than my father. He was a mathematics teacher in a high school ['lycée']." Similarly, a draftsman says of the engineers that he works with: "It is logical that they graduated from the top schools. Al-ready their fathers were quite high . . . It is not about to change . . . They were raised for that." Thus, as compared with American workers, very few French workers view themselves as ambitious or regret lacking ambition. The attitude of Lucien Maroix, the radar technician, is typi-cal: "My wife has told me that she thinks that I lack ambition, which is true, completely true. I don't find this interesting."

Ambition is also rejected as offering false or shallow rewards. Work-ers such as Laurent Larue, the automobile technician, contrasts worldly pursuits with other goals. He thinks ambitious people end up facing ex-istential crises because their lives ultimately have no meaning. A phone technician rejects ambition because "the end of the world could hap-pen anytime" and "the world will subsist for many billions of years after us. We have time. These people [who are ambitious] are unable to see beyond their death, as if we were the end of it all." To ambition some workers oppose the more satisfying goal of self-actualization. In particular, Henri Beliveau describes people who are social climbers as "small. What I am interested in is the discovery of my self . . . We only live once, there are so many things to discover on earth, things to do! Why spend one's life consulting one's career, trying to have a nice car, a social status above others? Really, I don't see the purpose."

French workers also reject people who are overly concerned with so-cioeconomic status as lacking in civility—they point to those "who ex-aggerate small [social] differences," "who drive nice car and believe that they are above others [for that] while in fact they are not better," "who go on expensive vacations when they cannot afford it," "who [are] al-ways trying to sell themselves and are not sincere." Time and again, they defined the people they appreciate, as opposed to snobs, as unpre-tentious, natural, and simple.[31] Justin Lagneau, the garbage-recycling specialist, defines "having good manners" in terms of not bragging, not trying to "impress people because you are an engineer," being natural. For him, it also means respecting other human beings and having friends. These definitions of manners center more on interclass decency than on "knowing which fork to use," which some workers described as a class-based behavior.[32] Even Jean-Jacques Neveu, the train controller who grew up poor and does equate worth with socioeconomic status, says that he dislikes snobs: "I prefer people who are natural, who don't need to have nice clothes to conceal who they are, or to hide behind nice words." Lucien Maroix, the radar technician, contrasts the simplicity he appreciates with snobbishness when he says, "The only thing [snobs] have in mind is to impress others. We can easily laugh at them . . . [I prefer] people who although they have to wear their ties [at work], would rather wear shorts." He explains that he does all he can to avoid contact with pretentious people: "It is at the level of the chromosomes. It really tires me to have to interact with people who are like that. The only thing I want is to go in the opposite direction."

This dislike for snobbishness extends to very critical attitudes toward conspicuous consumption that were not found among American workers. Wearing clothes with designer labels is particularly looked down upon. Marc Bataille, the railway technician, says that he cannot stand people who are overly concerned with themselves and with what they consume: "'I wear a Lacoste shirt, I wear Lacoste socks, I have a Christian Dior belt' . . . These people, I don't like them. I don't even try to get to know them." Similarly, Eric Dupuis says that he cannot accept seeing young people "who are 18, know nothing about life, go around in expensive cars, and who have shoes—'if it is not Weston, it is not good' . . . This is exactly what I reject. A pair of shoes is a pair of shoes, and it is made to walk in. But to buy a pair of shoes for 300,000 francs [$5,000] so that it looks good [is unacceptable], if only out of respect for those who have no shoes to wear."

ALTERNATIVE DEFINITIONS OF SUCCESS: PERSONAL LIFE AND SOLIDARITY. Like American workers, some French workers look down on the upper half because they believe their own quality of life is superior: they spend more time with their families and their lives are less driven by work. In the words of Gaston Roger, the pastry chef, although bosses make more money, "my advantage is that I have my weekends free." For an electronic chip maker, a manager's "goal is work . . . I prefer to put a lot of energy into my personal life." Accordingly, protecting family time is often offered as a justification for not taking courses or preparing for a promotion exam. Yvon Lahire, the warehouse worker, says that he does not want to prepare for exams because "I would have to work at it 3 or 4 hours a day, and it is too difficult given my circumstances. I spend a lot of time with my children. It is very important for me, and if I took classes, I would have to work a lot because I have not been in school for at least 15 years . . . I prefer to just have a little job in the office with 6 or 7 thousand francs a month. Of course, I would prefer to make 15 or 20 thousand a month, but I know that I will not be able to make it."

Yet Yvon describes his milieu as one of "small salaries, small employees, small ways of thinking. We are going in circles in there, and we get stuck easily. There is a state of mind that is not very healthy. In France, many people are very lazy, and laziness is the mother of all vices. When I come home at night and I analyze what I have done, I see that I could have done more, but there is no way to go forward."

Others refuse promotions because they want to protect their quality of life by avoiding stress. Paul Dubois, an electrical appraiser, explained: "I make a good living. My boss told me, 'If you want an increase, you have to do this or that.' I refused! The system is totally destroyed by responses like mine . . . I don't want to be more interested in my work because it creates too much stress." People like Paul value having fun in life, "laughing a lot, being calm, and not stressed" over making money. They share the philosophy of police officer Jocelyn Lavigne, who says that it is better to make less money and have a good spirit among workers: "you touch your paycheck only once a month, whereas you see your coworkers every day."

Like Americans, French workers look down on the upper half because they believe that working class solidarity allows them warmer interpersonal relationships. In Chapter 4, we saw the importance workers attach to solidarity. In the present chapter, we have seen that some believe that managers and bosses have to be uncaring, cold, and inhumane. In contrast, they perceive their own environment as one of warm camaraderie. When asked to describe the types of people they like, they repeatedly oppose the "bon vivants" ("jolly fellows") to people who are "coincés" (constipated), a term they often apply to managers—that is, those who have less fun at work and are less jovial. They associate "joie de vivre" with the absence of stress that characterizes their own lives. For instance, a shy electronic chip worker who comes from a Communist milieu but is also a National Front supporter, says, "For someone like me, from a working class background, I am sorry that there are fewer workers nowadays, fewer Communists. When you think about it, you think about this warm feeling that [workers] have and that many people don't have . . . People who work in bureaucracies, normal people, are much less fun. At noon in the cafeteria, I see the [manual] workers. They have a good time, they tease one another . . . They have their wine on the table."

Workers associate this warmth with solidarity, which some describe as a distinctively working class virtue, grounded in a community of class interest and collective misfortune.[33] This is expressed by René Saumier, the cable technician, who defines the working class in these terms: "It is first solidarity, a political commitment with specific objectives, it is becoming aware of your condition and feeling that you are with others in the struggle . . . People who have been raised in a working class milieu never completely lose this state of mind. It is not possible to forget the problems that you have known, the things that you have seen."

The centrality of solidarity in working class culture is also noted by a pastry chef, who explains that blue-collar workers "work hard but we know how to find compensation . . . There is much more solidarity than you find in offices." Others point to the importance of showing solidarity by sending toys to children of strikers or, as a draftsman notes, organizing a concert "just to warm up [the strikers'] hearts." In France, fully half of workers talked about the importance of workers' solidarity, whereas in the United States just over a third of workers mentioned it. Moreover, American workers were much more likely to criticize labor unions or worker solidarity.[34]

As noted by historian Gérard Noiriel, since the end of the nineteenth century, French workers have repeatedly mobilized symbols such as the red flag, May 1 (workers' day), and songs like the "Carmagnolle" and the "International" to express this solidarity. In turn, these symbols have sustained the ability of workers to mobilize collectively, precisely because they embody a collective identity and common "tradition de lutte,"[35] which has very deep roots in the collective memory of the working class. Events such as the massive strikes that in 1936 brought 2.4 million workers to the street and paralyzed the country are brought up to keep alive the view that one should fight for worker dignity and against capitalist abuse.[36]

These themes of solidarity survive in the worldviews of the men I talked to, although those men also mourned a growing individualism and indifference. They pointed out time and again that bosses were taking advantage of the recession that was occurring during the period of the interviews to undermine solidarity. Some noted that warmth and camaraderie at work are declining, and that workers are barely saying "good morning and good night" to one another.[37] A car painter, for instance, explains that "workers who had been there for 23 years had created a style in the plant. They knew everyone—who worked with whom—whereas now it is more anonymous and people don't necessarily work faster than they used to. Also the foremen are more arbitrary than they used to be, favoring some more than others, which breaks down solidarity."

What is most striking is the extent to which French workers remain under the spell of socialist ideologies—in contrast to their American counterparts—despite the decline in France of working class culture and institutions, such as unions.[38] This finding supports work showing that class voting has not declined in France: in recent years, France has returned to the high level of class voting of the 1940s and 1950s. In contrast, in the United States class voting has declined markedly.[39] There is also a sharp increase in class differentials in turnout, with a large decline in working class turnout between 1980 and 1988.[40] We will now see that these arguments about solidarity have a direct impact on how workers understand the place of the poor in their society and their responsibilities toward them.

SOLIDARITY À LA FRANÇAISE: AGAINST "EXCLUSION"

Being poor is worse in the United States than it is in France. First, the French poor are less poor: the French welfare state is better equipped to redistribute income, and it has not experienced the rise in poverty seen in the United States in recent years.[41] Second, poverty is mostly associated with long-term unemployment in France, whereas in the United States the minimum wage is so low as to create a large segment of impoverished workers.[42] Third, the French poor are less isolated than the American poor because the French public housing projects are more racially and ethnically diverse and bring together employed and unemployed people.[43] By contrast, American public housing projects tend to contain a relatively homogeneous population of unemployed urban blacks. French workers also have a less negative image of the poor than their American counterparts, given the presence among the poor of many native-born whites, their lesser geographic concentration, and the weaker stigmatization of public project dwellers. Also, American mass media reinforce the association between poverty and blackness by underrepresenting whites in reporting on the poor.[44] It is against this backdrop that we examine the boundaries that French workers draw toward the poor.

Anger toward the poor was seldom expressed in any interviews with French workers. This contrasts sharply with the case of white American workers. [45] In France only 7 percent of the white-collar and 37 percent of the blue-collar workers I talked to had a negative view of the poor. By contrast, in the United States this was so for 67 percent of the white-collar and 50 percent of the blue-collar interviewees. The majority of French workers—and especially white-collar workers—were supportive of the poor. French workers drew on a discourse of human solidarity, equality, and humanitarianism to denounce those who reject the poor because they perceive them as immoral. Like African Americans, some French workers offered explanations for poverty that, instead of placing moral blame on the victim, identified social mechanisms that lead to poverty. Hence, solidarity and a critique of the exploitative dimensions of capitalism shape workers' understandings of the place of the poor in French society and of society's responsibilities toward them.

The discourse in favor of the poor draws on a logic of egalitarianism that was alluded to in our discussion of French antiracism. Workers reject the idea of denigrating the poor for the same reason that they believe that old secretaries should be hired as frequently as younger ones or that butchers should be given the same respect as people who wear ties: their common humanity confers equal dignity on them as a matter of principle. Hence, Eric Dupuis, the heater repairman, explains that, for reasons of personal integrity, he refuses to feel superior to people: "I think it is dishonest [to act superior to others]. I don't like that people do it to me. So you have to be honest with yourself. Either you don't like people to do it to you and you don't do it to others, or you are hypocritical . . . You have to decide what should guide your behavior."

Only three French blue-collar workers and four French white-collar workers adopt explicit nonegalitarian positions toward the poor. For instance, Jean-Jacques Neveu, the train controller we encountered at the beginning of this chapter, makes passing comments signifying his superiority to those who did not go far ("they put me above . . . It makes me feel good inside"). François Noyant, the racist policeman we encountered in Chapters 4 and 5, also attacks the poor. He is highly critical of the unemployed. He associates them with criminals and, perhaps implicitly, with the North African youth who, he says, haunt the streets and engage in vandalism. He stresses the importance of taking responsibility for one's actions. As we saw in Chapter 4, when asked about the kinds of people he does not like, he points to "young people who do nothing and who just go around and break everything . . . They do not take responsibility. These people are really not worth much . . . They do not even deserve that I look at them. They just deserve that I hit them . . . I call them the small ones, the minuscule ones. They are to be eliminated, out of my sight. They are . . . worth absolutely nothing, they are lower than the ground."

François says that he would kill himself if he were to become unemployed because he believes that it is not worth living if you fall so low. Following the British political economists Ricardo and Malthus, he believes that public assistance breeds laziness.[46] He does not question the welfare state but believes that some get more than their share of the pie. Pointing at immigrants who are not truly part of the collective "us," he reaffirms that these immigrants are the cause of the high unemployment rate among the French, for some of them are lazy and take advantage of the system. He also points out that the unemployed "get 6,000 francs of unemployment [insurance per month] and work at night and make 10,000 francs per month, which means that they are not interested in working in a plant . . . I feel sorry for saying this, but it might be better not to help people . . . We should have the lazy Frenchmen put to work. They don't feel like working because they make too much money. I know a lot of people who are in this situation."

We saw that in the United States poverty is understood by workers as a matter of individual responsibility.[47] In contrast, French workers draw mainly on structural explanations. Luc Larada, the train ticket salesman, had to leave his small town in the south of France to find a job in Paris. He argues that "we cannot condemn or judge [the poor] without knowing what happened. There is always a reason . . . We have to know why things are the way they are." Luc is very politically involved—one of the two or three workers who are true political militants. At the time of the interview, he was participating in the organization of one of the legendary subway strikes that would paralyze the system the next day. He takes a resolutely egalitarian position toward the poor in the name of quality of life because he thinks that feeling inferior or superior to others "makes relationships impossible; it destroys all spontaneity." Similarly, bank clerk George Lheureux, a longtime leader in Amnesty International, explains that instead of feeling superior to people who take drugs, it is important to understand the conditions that lead to drug abuse. Even workers who are less supportive of the poor do not place full blame on the individual. For instance, a railway technician says, "It is true that people don't all have the same chances, but people can make their own luck. We should not wait there with our arms reaching out . . . Maybe it is a little bit their fault if they need things, but often it is not entirely their fault."

It has been argued by historian Giovanna Procacci and others that in France, from the Revolution on, poverty was not conceived as a matter of personal failure; instead, it was explained as the result of forces inherent in the social system and—following Marx—as an unavoidable by-product of a capitalist system that requires a reserve army of workers.[48] This representation has been kept alive by left-wing organizations[49] and has been diffused in mainstream political culture to the point that it has become widely accepted that "equality meant that the Republic must promise citizens subsistence or assure them the right to work."[50]

It is against this background that several workers offer a general critique of the capitalist system and of the system of distribution of resources. Anticipating a 35-hour-week law passed in 1999, some actively support policies to reduce the length of the work week in order to distribute work more equally. For example, a bank clerk explains, "I think it is unacceptable that some people are unemployed while others can work as much as they want." Roland Sorel, the wood salesman, concurs. He criticizes the impact of market mechanisms on the distribution of resources: "People who have top responsibility often get extremely high salaries for what, after all, remains only a job. I think this is not normal, although some people do have responsibilities over the lives of others. I think all workers should be reasonably well paid." Both men promote egalitarianism in response to problems inherent in capitalism, such as unemployment. In sum, the poor were taken by many French workers to be part of "us"; few drew strong boundaries toward the destitute.

As sociologist Hilary Silver points out, French discourse on poverty draws heavily on a social-democratic emphasis on social rights and on the political culture of republicanism. By contrast, the American discourse on poverty is shaped by liberal themes relatively absent in France.[51] Furthermore, as historian Herrick Chapman argues, in France "[f]ew people sp[eak] of the 'undeserving poor' as in the United States"[52] in part because means-tested social benefits are rare, and "the French system averted the political danger that came with . . . distinctions that might divide better paid workers from the poor." In other words, here as elsewhere, universal social programs discourage the denigration of the poor.[53] In particular, the French tradition of collective health and risk insurance, which is based on a desire to lower social conflicts by protecting people against dangers that are shared by all, has had the unintended consequence of lowering the stigmatization of the poor.[54]

In conclusion, it is worth mentioning that French workers' inclusion of the poor as "part of us" parallels France's policies toward the poor. With an unemployment rate that has hovered around 10 percent for at least a decade,[55] the French government has put together a complex apparatus aimed at alleviating the social marginalization and stigmatization of the "exclus." The term "les exclus" is important because it stresses that poverty leads to social isolation and drives people out of social institutions, including the family, neighborhood life, social associations, work, and politics.[56] Instead of blaming the poor for their situation, this term points to social processes that lead to poverty, as well as to collective responsibility for the reintegration of the excluded.[57]

It should be noted that poverty is identified by politicians as one of the most pressing social problems in contemporary French society. Interestingly, the administrative unit in charge of reintegration is called the "Ministère de la solidarité." Governmental efforts culminated in a 1998 antiexclusion law explicitly created to reinforce the social integration of 10 million "extremely deprived people" through programs that would improve access to employment, training, credit, housing, health care, culture, and citizenship, as well as through a guaranteed minimum income (created in 1988).[58]

In stark contrast with the predominant American governmental approach to the poor, the presence of such a large number of "exclus" is explicitly construed by the French government (and by a wide range of civic and political associations) as a serious symptom of the degeneration of social life as a whole and of a deep crisis in French society.[59] Left- and right-wing parties alike adopt the view that ensuring the reintegration of the poor is a matter of moral duty, in part because misery is asocial and ungovernable.[60] They also agree that the task of alleviating poverty should not to be left to private philanthropy, and that the state has a responsibility to carry out social justice.[61] The state's role is to step in to maintain the social link ("lien social") when the economy is unable to perform this role. Hence, social benefits bring some 12 to 13 million French people above the poverty line.[62] In contrast, "the United States is consistently at the bottom in its support for different kinds of social welfare benefits,"[63] with the exception of education.[64] Accordingly, some French workers view the treatment of the poor in the United States as inhumane, thereby implicitly equating the United States with immorality.

Several factors sustain weak boundaries toward the poor in the French context, namely, the republican tradition, the lasting influence of left-wing parties and unions, and the presence of a strong governmental discourse on, and policies for, integrating the poor. The remarkable visibility of public associations created in the mid-1990s to defend the "exclus" (the homeless, the unemployed, the immigrants, youth, and so on) also plays a role. These associations have organized successful events aimed at increasing media coverage of these groups and publicizing their plight.[65] The rhetoric used by these associations often taps directly into feelings of solidarity, since they openly appeal to "people's hearts," as is the case for the famous soup kitchens "les restos du coeur" (the "restaurants of the heart"). Their impact in sustaining an organic view of French society—that is, one where all members have moral obligations toward one another—should not be underestimated.

THE POLICING OF CLASS BOUNDARIES COMPARED

This chapter fleshes out the argument that French and American workers define "people like us" on the basis of different principles of division. We have seen that in France strong boundaries are erected toward Muslim immigrants, whose particularistic culture is viewed as fundamentally incompatible with France's universalistic culture. In this chapter we saw that French workers also draw strong boundaries against the upper half while they draw weaker boundaries toward the poor. In contrast to the United States, the boundaries against people above are framed in terms of domination and exploitation. Yet, while French workers do not associate high socioeconomic status with moral worth, they are more likely than their American counterparts to explain inequality by differences in levels of intelligence. Republicanism and a well-entrenched socialist tradition have historically played key roles in diminishing boundaries toward the poor, given the ideals of social justice, equality, solidarity, and civil rights.[66] Republicanism and socialism have been fused in the history of French working class radicalism.[67]

In Chapter 3, I suggested that the drawing of strong boundaries against the poor in the United States resulted in part from the recent hegemony of neoliberalism. In France, neoliberalism has also grown in influence, but instead of resulting in social welfare cuts, it has produced a shift in focus from income redistribution to fighting the social exclusion of the poor. The left has interpreted this as undermining the social-democratic ideals characteristic of French society until 1983. But Socialists and right-wing politicians alike have justified these changes by appealing to economic imperatives—in particular, French economic competitiveness[68]—and to the importance of trimming the national deficit in order for France to join the European Union.[69]

These changes have had a powerful impact on workers. The unemployment rate rose, as did the number of temporary and part-time workers.[70] Simultaneously, these changes have accentuated the national boundary patterns that have been described in the last two chapters (in particular, solidarity toward the poor), just as economic changes in the United States may have accentuated the patterns found on this side of the Atlantic. In the final chapter I will return to the explanations of these patterns and reflect on the social and political implications of these changes for French and American society.

Conclusion: Toward a New Agenda

MY AIM HAS been to explore the criteria working men use to define worthy and less worthy people and to draw racial and class boundaries. To this end, I explored workers' views on the meaning of work, responsibility, success, power, money, solidarity, and so forth. Building on my earlier study, *Money, Morals, and Manners,* this book lays the foundations of a comparative sociology of group boundaries and of ordinary models of definition of community. This sociology documents patterns of inclusion/exclusion based on various bases of societal segmentation (such as class, race, and citizenship) across groups.[1] It also offers a multifaceted theory of status that centers on the relationship between various standards of evaluation—morality and socioeconomic standing—within national repertoires.

The white American workers I interviewed primarily use moral standards ("the disciplined self") to distinguish between "people like us" and others: they distance themselves from the upper half, who lack integrity and straightforwardness, and blacks and "people below," who are lazy and hold wrong values. Similarly, the moral standards privileged by African Americans ("the caring self") overlap with the criteria they use to evaluate the upper half, whom they consider exploitative and lacking in solidarity, and whites, whom they regard as domineering and lacking in human compassion. Although in principle universal, these moral criteria are unevenly valued across groups and thus particularistic. Workers often judge members of other groups to be deficient in respect to the criteria they value most. This paradox helps us understand how moral criteria can generate strong intergroup boundaries.

Yet moral criteria also serve as tools for bridging group boundaries ("there are good and bad people in all races").

These moral standards provide workers with alternative definitions of success and perceptions of hierarchies of worth. However, while white American workers view socioeconomic status as an indication of moral worth when evaluating the poor and blacks, many abandon this standard when evaluating the upper half. In contrast, black workers are less prompt to assess moral worth in terms of wealth and social status in part because their own battles with racism teach them that the most deserving do not always get their just rewards. Hence, some also draw stronger boundaries toward the upper half than whites. At the same time, they identify more with middle class values because they symbolize cultural membership in American society.

This study also compared the United States with France and showed that racial and class divides are articulated differently across national contexts and that we should not take the white/black antagonism as universal. In France, by contrast to the United States, the white workers I interviewed define the poor and blacks as "part of us," using the language of class solidarity. They accept these groups but reject North African immigrants, who, they say, lack civility, violate the principles of republicanism, and are culturally incompatible with the French. Amidst laments for the decline of working class culture in France, these workers continue to draw on the language of class struggle to define their relationship with the upper half, whom they view as exploitative and dehumanizing. Even more than American workers, they adopt alternative definitions of success to locate themselves above, or next to, "people above." This allows them to guard their own self-worth and dignity, even though they fare poorly on traditional measures of success.

The study did not draw on original survey research to establish whether these patterns are generalizable to the French and American working classes at large. However, secondary survey data were discussed in detail, and I pointed to many instances where such generalizations appear to be called for.

The explanatory framework I deploy can be contrasted with the standard framework used to study national cultural differences—the "modal personality" and "national character" frameworks—that stress psychological traits shared by all members of a society.[2] Whereas this approach accounts for cultural orientations by childhood socialization, I account for French and American patterns of boundaries toward blacks, immigrants, the upper half, and the poor by available cultural repertoires (such as a prominent discourse on solidarity) and the structural conditions in which workers live (such as the availability of important welfare benefits). I understand these patterns of boundary work not as essentialized individual or national characteristics but as cultural structures, that is, institutionalized cultural repertoires or publicly available categorization systems.[3] My framework can explain intranational variance that is ignored by culturalist approaches. Indeed, it accounts for patterns of boundaries across groups within a nation—white and black workers—as well as for patterns across nations—the United States and France. Also, unlike culturalist approaches, this framework takes into consideration cross-national similarities, such as the weak boundaries that white French workers and African-American workers draw toward the poor.

Because cultural repertoires, like structural conditions, change,[4] the patterns of boundaries that I have documented should be regarded as historically contingent. A dramatic increase in the number of blacks in France could lead to a strengthening of antiblack boundaries, especially if combined with other structural and cultural changes (for instance, a sharp decline of the left and a greater availability of neoliberal ideas that would make solidarity less salient).[5] A more detailed and dynamic account of causal factors would include a description of mechanisms of change, such as the path-dependent transformation of repertoires.[6] It remains to be seen whether further economic and cultural globalization will bring about a general convergence of national models of cultural membership, with perhaps the French model coming to resemble the American model with its strong boundaries toward the poor and blacks.

The use of a comparative approach to working class cultures and racial and class boundaries makes explicit many taken-for-granted levels in boundary work. This study thus makes a contribution, or serves as a corrective, to several wider American and French literatures.

Specifically, my inductive research provides an empirical assessment of postmodern theories of identity. My findings support the postmodernist view of identity as constructed, as opposed to "primordial," essential and fixed in time. In particular, we saw that French and American workers define who they are in opposition to different "others"— the straightforward workers versus the snotty professionals. However, my findings also undermine some postmodernist assumptions. Like Freud, Lacan, and other theorists of identity, postmodernists understand personal and collective identity as being defined relationally, in opposition to other meanings, against which they take on their own significance.[7] They assert that this relational principle functions in an undifferentiated manner across settings, and that identity is multiple, problematic, fluid, self-reflexive, "plural," and "decentered."[8] Instead of asserting this principle and/or illustrating it with anecdotal evidence, I traced systematically a wide range of arguments that individuals use to define their self and "the other" across contexts (i.e., for white and black workers, for American and French workers, and so on). Also, instead of positing that this process is open, fluid, plural, and decentered, I showed that it is tied to the cultural resources workers have access to and to the conditions in which they live, which, for instance, make workers less likely to define themselves in opposition to the poor versus blacks or immigrants across contexts. In other words, instead of positing that identities are unstable or fragmented, I establish empirically that some patterns of self-identification and boundaries are more likely in one context than in another. This is not to deny the importance of individual agency but to stress the fact that it is bounded by the *differentially structured* context in which people live.[9]

Postmodern writings have also asserted the declining significance of class as a basis of identity.[10] In contrast, my research suggests that it remains an important basis for collective identity among workers: Chapters 3 and 6 showed that many workers define who they are in opposition to hierarchically defined groups ("people above" and "people below" broadly defined), and that they identify with people who share similar living conditions ("nothing is easy for people like us") and similar cultural definitions of "who we are not." In fact, these working men use a rhetoric of class to talk about differences between "our kind of people" and others. Their definitions of social membership are one of the cultural roots of inequality because, like racial identity, class identity is expressed and tied to the criteria that workers use to evaluate others. The study thus confirms that we should study class consciousness by not focusing solely on explicit class conflict or on position in the system of production.[11] We also need to look at workers' sense of *worth* and more broadly at their social identification and group categorization as workers.[12] Hence, the greater radicalism of French workers, as opposed to American workers, is best understood in the context of their wider moral worldviews, which play an important role in making this radicalism possible.

The issues discussed here have implications for a question to which American social scientists have devoted an inordinate amount of attention: "Why is there no socialism in the United States?" It has been argued that, unlike workers in other advanced industrial societies, American workers have not developed a socialist alternative because they have bought into the American dream. Among the causes are the economic prosperity of the nation; the existence of a frontier that opened alternative routes for upward mobility; the absence of a feudal past; and racial and ethnic diversity, which curtailed class solidarity.[13] The notion of American exceptionalism has been challenged by scholars because it implies that the German, French, or British patterns of working class formation are modal.[14] Nevertheless, authors continue to contrast the United States with European societies, where class hierarchies are thought to be more rigid, and social mobility more limited.[15] The argument I have proposed can be of equal use to the proponents and opponents of exceptionalism. My findings suggest, in line with proponents of exceptionalism, that, indeed, the American pattern of exclusion toward the poor, blacks, and immigrants is different from patterns elsewhere, or at least in France. However, they also suggest, in line with opponents of this thesis, that the American pattern is not less exclusive than the one found in France. Moreover, instead of viewing the American and French working classes as radically different from one another, I show that their worldviews overlap. For instance, workers in both countries emphasize the importance of hard work, responsibility, and keeping the world in moral order.

Sociologists have argued that alternative moralities are grounds for struggles of classification and forms of cultural resistance. My findings suggest, unlike standard approaches, that resistance is often the unintended consequence of workers defending their dignity and attempting to gain respect. One aspect of this process is the valuing of morality as a dimension of self-worth. Social psychologists have shown that those groups that are in positions of dependency or with limited access to power most often value morality and/or collective over individualistic aspects of morality. This is the case not only for blacks as compared with whites but also for workers as compared with professionals[16] and for women as compared with men.[17] This may point toward a more general theory of boundary work among groups in subordinated positions.[18] However, instead of understanding the relationship between morality, self-worth, and hierarchical position in terms of the universal disposition of all low-status individuals, as social psychologists tend to do, I emphasize the relationship between these agents' stress on morality and the context in which they live—blacks' emphasis, for instance, on the caring self. I explore how conceptions of self-worth are shaped by the broader context of political and social relationships and by institutionalized definitions of cultural membership that people have access to—a topic rarely visited by social psychologists working on the self and identity.[19] I also historicize patterns of inclusion and exclusion by analyzing how these conceptions of morality are shaped by changing political traditions.

There have been important debates, in French sociology in particular, concerning whether the working class is under the spell of a dominant culture.[20] Chapter 1 suggested that, at least as far as conceptions of morality are concerned, workers inhabit worlds that partly overlap, but are largely different from, those of professionals and managers. They do not oppose upper middle class definitions of the world as much as emphasize different aspects of reality. For instance, they are more exclusively concerned with moral criteria of evaluation than are professionals and managers. However, the extent of these class differences cannot be easily measured because they take place within distinct schemes of reference.

Finally, I explore much uncharted territory here. In particular, I contribute to the sociology of racism and antiracism by (1) analyzing racism in the context of individuals' broad moral worldviews and bringing to light their inner logic through comparative lenses—the concern white workers have for providing for their families helps us understand the centrality of self-reliance in the boundaries they draw against blacks; (2) documenting inductively which norms the majority group

perceives the minority group to violate (for instance, traditional morality but not straightforwardness) and thus complementing the literature
on symbolic racism; (3) providing evidence about the antiracism of ordinary white Americans and French men—white American workers
offer less evidence of racial equality than of their equality with "people
above"; and (4) analyzing how ordinary blacks construe whites and understand the differences between blacks and whites—blacks challenge
dominant white representations of blacks as morally lacking when they
emphasize their greater generosity and caring and contrast themselves
to whites.

❖   ❖

At a normative level, my analysis suggests that American workers are
better off doing precisely what they do: not buying too wholeheartedly
into the American dream with its unrealistic promise that anyone can
achieve material success if he or she is willing to work hard. In fact, as
we saw in the Introduction, only 20 percent of working Americans have
the college degree necessary to become part of the professional-
managerial class. Yet the professional-managerial class is the very group
whose lives are described by the media and other cultural institutions
as the model to emulate.[21]

The dispersion of wealth is now greater in the United States than it is
in several European countries, while intragenerational mobility is comparable.[22] Yet many continue to believe that only in America can you
"be what you want." The disarticulation between opportunity and belief speaks volumes about the power of the myths that the United
States continues to generate about itself. For American workers, these
myths have provided stimulating but hollow promises. Ultimately
more self-validating are measuring sticks less in line with middle class
values: by keeping a healthy distance from the American dream, and by
defining their worth in realms other than that of economic success,
workers are able to maintain a sense of personal dignity.[23] American
blue-collar workers still need this kind of distance because they have a
greater sense of personal distress than their counterparts in countries
such as Poland and Japan—while, by contrast, professionals have higher
self-esteem here than elsewhere.[24] Just as black pride increases self-

esteem, especially among younger blacks,[25] a greater consensus concerning the value of alternative measuring sticks among American workers may lead to an increased sense of self-worth within this group and to the preservation of dignity, that is, of a space for expressing one's own identity and competence.

❖ ❖

This book also has implications for social change. By reconstituting workers' worldviews and considering the racial boundaries workers draw within this context, we are better able to understand the conditions that legitimize these boundaries for workers and to move beyond viewing racism as an aberration or a sign of working class ignorance. In other words, by gaining a better grasp of the inner logic of racism, we can develop more effective tools to fight it. This is a particularly urgent task, given that antiracist arguments based on multiculturalism and cultural relativism, which are particular popular in academic circles, have little currency with workers. My most egalitarian respondents never made such arguments.

A number of issues remain to be addressed, such as gender differences and the dynamic character of boundaries and repertoires. I want to bring this book to a close by highlighting questions that I perceive to be particularly pressing.

The patterns of opposition by which workers define their collective identity are an intrinsic part of the process of class formation.[26] More work needs to be done on precisely how contemporary working class identities express themselves through the very types of boundaries that are documented here, and how these identities have shaped working class politics. We also need to understand better the specific mechanisms by which these shared definitions of cultural membership can be articulated by political institutions to produce more or less inclusive national policies toward the poor. Studies of social exclusion neglect definitions of collective identities and imagined communities to focus on institutional factors. This needs to be corrected.

The book as a whole has focused on the subjective worlds of workers. The natural complement to this approach would be to look at the making of objective boundaries through the distribution of resources—

for instance, through hiring and firing.[27] In my earlier work, I described subjective boundaries as a necessary but insufficient condition for the construction of objective boundaries.[28] This may provide us with directions for the study of boundaries in the making. It would also be important to produce a much more detailed analysis of the ways in which institutional forces, history, and material factors shape boundaries. We need to analyze more closely the process of institutionalization of symbolic boundaries, that is, how workers come to take them for granted and give them objective reality.

Finally, the book has examined the process by which workers build bridges, as opposed to draw boundaries. This issue was at the center of the discussion of the rhetorics of antiracism and, to a lesser extent, of solidarity toward the poor. For instance, we found that common lineage or physiological similarities ("we all need to eat") were used to rebut racism or to show that the poor are "like us." We know very little about how individuals produce universalism and promote forms of cosmopolitanism in different settings—at work, in kinship networks, and so on. We need to study the extent to which professionals and workers consider it natural to first help "their own kind" and how they reconcile meritocratic norms in the workplace with clientalistic practices. While in recent years, political philosophers have given considerable attention to questions of community boundaries[29] by discussing tribalism, patriotism, cosmopolitanism, communalism, particularism, and universalism, much work needs to be done before we can understand how ordinary citizens conceptualize these questions. Pursuing such an intellectual agenda would move us closer to one of the main objectives I have pursued here: to break the path-dependent ways in which social scientists think about issues. I have tried to identify and make the reader aware of other, alternative ways of thinking about the world that rarely register with academics, policy makers, and the educated reader. It is my hope that this book will broaden the horizons of an increasingly narrow uppermiddle class and hence contribute to the widening of our communities.

Appendix A: Methods and Analysis

CROSS-NATIONAL comparisons reveal otherwise invisible patterns, making national contexts useful sociological laboratories.[1] Hence, this research is designed to explore differences across several groups, which yield information both on themselves and on their perceptions of others. In the United States, these groups are black and white blue-collar workers and white lower white-collar workers. In France, I focus on parallel groups but consider North African immigrants in lieu of blacks. Respondents in the two countries are compared with college-educated professionals, managers, and entrepreneurs interviewed in a previous study.

Though the United States is increasingly multiracial, the black/white divide has had a foundational and pervasive role in American history.[2] Scholars ranging from Gunnar Myrdal to Winthrop Jordan have repeatedly buttressed the view that black/white relations here are unique due to the country's racial history and lasting racial discrimination.[3] Patterns of racial intermarriage remain much lower for blacks than for any other group, while patterns of residential segregation remain much higher.[4] Accordingly, sociologist Herbert Gans convincingly argues that American society is moving toward a racial divide opposing all non-blacks to blacks.[5] It is only recently (perhaps since the Los Angeles riots) that the awareness of a multiracial America has become acute.[6] However, demographers show that as a whole, the nation remains largely white.[7] The black/white divide continues to shape the American social fabric deeply, if unevenly across regions, and as such it is an unavoidable focus of study. Given that New Jersey and New York are among the five states with the highest rates of immigration (see Chapter 3), multiracialism is at least as likely to shape the black/white dynamics there as it would almost anywhere else.[8]

Research Procedures

The sampling procedures parallel those used for my study of professionals and managers in France and the United States in *Money, Morals, and Manners: The Culture of the French and the American Upper-Middle Class:* I constructed random samples of individuals fitting certain age, occupational, and educational levels. Respondents were chosen from the suburbs because a growing proportion of the working class population lives in these environments. It is notably the case for black workers living in New York suburbs[9] and for French and North African immigrant workers in the Paris area; although factories have been located on the outskirts of Paris since the beginning of the twentieth century, workers are increasingly being pushed outside the city limits by the climbing price of real estate.[10]

Using census information, I identified several towns in the suburbs of New York and Paris that include large numbers of working class individuals.[11] I identified American towns with white and/or black populations and French towns with French and/or Muslim populations. Next, I sampled names randomly from phone directories for these towns and sent prospective participants a letter of introduction on Princeton University stationery. The letter described the project and informed individuals that they would be contacted to ascertain eligibility and willingness to participate. Based on the socioeconomic profiles of potential interviewees, as ascertained by a short phone interview conducted by a research assistant, I decided whether to include interviewees in the sample. When possible, I created parallel samples across sites by matching respondents in terms of occupation and age.[12] This sampling method is costly because many of the individuals contacted do not meet the specific criteria of the study.[13] However, this method does allow one to tap a diverse range of respondents and avoid the limitations of site-specific research and community studies.[14]

Characteristics of the Respondents

In order to qualify for the working class sample, individuals had to (1) be employed in a blue-collar or low-status white-collar job; (2) have a high school but not a college degree;[15] (3) supervise no more than

10 people, if at all; (4) show continuous full-time participation in the labor force for at least five years; (5) describe themselves as black, for the United States, or white; (6) have resided in the study area for at least five years; (7) be a native of the United States (for American interviewees), France (for French interviewees), and Morocco, Tunisia, or Algeria (for North African interviewees); and (8) be a man between the ages of 25 and 65. The first four criteria aimed at producing a sample distinct from both the upper middle and the lower classes. The other criteria aimed at tapping relevant variations concerning race and nationality and at keeping constant other socio-demographic variations (length of residence, place of birth, gender, and age) to facilitate the comparison. I use education instead of income to separate the upper middle class from the lower middle class because having a college degree is a strong predictor of high socioeconomic status and is one of the most powerful variables shaping life chances. Hence, I consider individuals in different income categories to belong to the "working class" or "lower middle class." These criteria were also used to identify North African interviewees except for the criterion of level of education.[16] *Beurs*—children of North African immigrants born in France or having French nationality—are excluded from the sample because they are French citizens.

Racial self-identification is used to qualify white and black respondents for the samples because (1) it is more accurate than racial identification by the interviewer; (2) it does not exclude African Americans of multiracial descent if they identify themselves as African American. All immigrants are excluded from the American sample to keep socio-demographic dimensions that do not pertain to occupation/education and race constant and to make comparisons meaningful. This decision is justified because my primary purpose is not to study the black population or the American working class in their full complexity.

In the upper middle class study, only professionals, managers, and entrepreneurs holding a four-year college degree (in the case of American respondents) or "bac + 4" (in the case of French respondents) were interviewed.[17] Restrictions concerning numbers of employees did not apply. Only self-identified whites born in the United States or France were interviewed. These respondents had to meet the same criteria as did lower middle class interviewees concerning length of full-time employment, length of residence, gender, and age.[18]

THE INTERVIEW

Each in-depth interview lasted approximately two hours—long enough to develop a complex view of the ways in which these men understood the similarities and differences between themselves and others. Each was confidential, tape-recorded, and conducted at a place and site chosen by the respondents.

The main point of entry into the world of these men were questions that identify how they define and discriminate between worthy and less worthy persons, that is, between "their sort of folks" and "the sort they don't much like." I asked interviewees to describe people with whom they preferred not to associate, those to whom they felt superior and inferior, and those who evoked hostility, indifference, and sympathy. I also asked them to describe the negative and positive traits of some of their co-workers and acquaintances, regarding these descriptions as templates of their mental maps. More specifically, I scrutinized symbolic boundaries—the lines they drew when they categorized people—and how they ranked others on these bases. My goal was to obtain a picture of the labels participants used in describing people whom they consider to be above and below themselves.

The questions exploring feelings of superiority and inferiority were as follows: "Whether we admit it or not, we all feel inferior or superior to some people at times. In relation to what types of people do you feel inferior? Superior? Can you give me concrete examples? What do these people have in common?" To explore likes and dislikes in others, I asked participants "What kinds of people would you rather avoid? What kinds of people leave you indifferent? What kinds of people attract you in general? Can you give me specific examples? Which qualities do these people have in common?" I also asked them to describe their perceptions of the cultural traits that are most valued in their workplaces. Finally, to identify the interviewees' definition of high-status signals, I explored their child-rearing values, asking them to describe the values they try to impart to their children and to explain in detail the meaning assigned to each value. For instance, the participants were asked to explain what they mean by "honesty" or "respect," and why these values are important to them. (The interview schedule is available on request).

In this process, I often asked respondents to explain their standards and guide me toward a greater understanding of their cultural categories.[19] In the majority of cases, I did not ask respondents to define themselves in relation to, or describe their feelings toward, a specific group, precisely because I was interested in the relative salience of groups within workers' mental maps. Reactions to various categories of people, including "people above," "people below," "immigrants," and racial minorities, generally emerged spontaneously during the course of the interview as workers answered the general questions listed above.

THE CHARACTER OF THE DATA

All data-gathering techniques favor or hinder the emergence of particular forms of discourse. As a researcher, one should try to be aware of these effects instead of dissimulating or ignoring them.

I decided to conduct all the interviews myself. The main advantage of this choice is that interviewees are all offered the same "stimulus" and hence adjust their responses to the same person. The main drawback is, of course, that interviewees might have shared more easily controversial opinions on racism and class differences—not to mention gender differences—with members of their own groups. This is particularly important in a study bearing on racism. Respondents adapt their discourse to their audience, and the discourse they produce for each category of audience partially reveals aspects of their worldviews, but none of these discourses exhaust their worldviews.[20]

I hope that the openness of respondents was increased by my in-between status: as a native French-speaking Québecois, I am a foreigner both in France and the United States. By my accent, I am readily located somewhat outside of the national racial conflicts I am studying. I believe that on some occasions this in-between status encouraged respondents to offer revealing explanations of notions they take for granted because they assumed that I had little knowledge of their cultures. Furthermore, the effect of my own identity on the interviews was to some extent minimized by my attempt to present myself with a blurred national and professional identity.[21]

By drawing on interviews instead of observation, I privilege breadth over depth: interviews make it possible to gather data from a larger number of individuals than does observation, thereby improving the reliability of the comparison. However, this data-gathering technique does not provide the kind of in-depth behavioral information that could be obtained from participant observation.

In interviews, individuals are likely to provide what they believe are the most socially desirable answers to questions, particularly in a face-to-face situation. Hence, one might expect moral discourse to be made particularly salient in this context. This is in line with the objectives of the research, which is to document high-status signals—or what respondents perceive to be the most desirable attitudes and behaviors. This signaling is viewed as a form of behavior (i.e., as performance) and not uniquely as an attitude or discourse.

Finally, interviews cannot tap class consciousness "in action."[22] However, they can tap broader cultural frameworks that are transportable from one context of action to another, providing a template of the contours of mental maps. As such, they are useful in documenting and comparing the saliency of various types of arguments across populations. Moreover, interviews are better suited than surveys to document mental maps because they do not require predefinition of key status dimensions, and thereby give the researcher access to a more subtle and inductive understanding of the standards interviewees use to assess status.

Data Analysis

The criteria of evaluation behind responses were systematically compared to recreate a template of the grammar of evaluation used by each interviewee. I distinguish between the differences that are at the center of the respondents' individual maps of perception and the differences that are not salient. I am particularly concerned with the types of superiority that people operate with and how they rank others on these bases.

To analyze the interviews, I summarized them in a 13-page document including socio-demographic information as well as information on the boundary work of the interviewees. To facilitate comparisons, I noted some of the respondents' answers on grids and summarized these on matrix displays using techniques suggested by Miles and Huberman for standardizing and processing qualitative data.[23] Interviews were also analyzed one by one, with a focus on the criteria that each respondent mobilized for the evaluation of status. Moreover, I located each interviewee on several five-point scales pertaining to the most significant dimensions they use to evaluate status. I also compared individual interviewees with respondents who were similar to and different from them, both within and across samples. Finally, I classified all the transcripts thematically to perform a systematic analysis of all the important themes that appear in the interviews, approaching the latter as data against which theoretical questions can be explored. As was the case for my study of upper middle class culture, I expected the most central symbolic boundaries to emerge gradually during the interviewing period. Despite its limitations, the analysis presented here provides an important step in this direction because, unlike survey research, I attempted to identify inductively as clearly as possible the principles of organization, both implicit and explicit, for workers.

Appendix B: The Context of the Interview: Economic Insecurity, Globalization, and Places

> The pressure was building on me . . . The boss said "If you don't like it there's the door because there are other people waiting to take your job" . . . A lot of companies are looking for the give back. Give me back! Give me back! The company kept expanding but they never gave you any more help. That's why I got out. If I didn't get out I would have had a nervous breakdown or shot somebody. That's how bad it got. I'll be very, very honest with you: they couldn't care less about you anymore. You're just a number. In a small group, it's a warm feeling, a family, you give 110 percent. Once you started getting too big, they don't say "How the hell are ya? How ya feeling? How's the wife? How's the baby?" Those days are gone . . . Since the economy crisis started five, six years ago . . . everybody was survival, survival . . . I've seen a complete change, a complete change. (White warehouse worker)

MY INTERVIEWS were conducted in the early nineties, at a time when workers were facing important challenges that redefined their position in the national and international economy. Changes in occupational structure and rising unemployment increased global competition, froze wages, and widened inequality. A growing number of women and immigrants were entering the workforce, while new technologies were requiring higher skilled workers. Also, labor relations were greatly affected by a decline in union membership, with the number of temporary jobs tripling between 1979 and

1992.[1] Discussion of these changes and how they were experienced by my interviewees will help put their lives in context.

GLOBALIZATION AND ECONOMIC TRANSFORMATION

In the last 20 years, the American economy has been reshaped by globalization. American workers have had to compete with nations whose workforces receive lower wages for work done under different rules. Globalization has affected sectoral shifts, unemployment, wages, benefits, and unionization.[2] Between 1950 and 1990, the service sector expanded while the manufacturing sector shrunk.[3] This resulted in higher unemployment for workers in general, and for blue-collar workers in particular, at a time when jobs requiring the least education were growing less rapidly than other jobs.[4] In the United States, the 1993 unemployment figures were 6 percent for whites and 13 percent for blacks.[5] Part-time work increased despite efforts by unions in the manufacturing sector to limit use of the contingent workforce.[6] In 1991, 18 percent of workers thought they would be laid off temporarily and 17 percent thought they would lose their jobs permanently in the following year. This is the context in which I interviewed workers: the experience of job loss was having profound psychological effects on a significant segment of the working class, and many workers, like the one quoted above, felt acutely the many pressures associated with increasing competitiveness.[7]

The trend toward higher unemployment has been accompanied by falling or stagnating median family income, despite the increased participation of women in the labor force. Measured in 1990 dollars, the national median family income for whites declined from $37,076 to $36,915 between 1973 and 1990. For blacks, there was a tiny increase from $21,398 to $21,423 by 1990, with the racial income gap remaining relatively stable at 71 percent.[8] The gap between rich and poor was increasing sharply. This has remained true through the late 1990s, although the economy is more healthy now than it was a decade ago; the median worker's wage fell 5 percent between 1989 and 1997, and increased only 0.3 percent in 1997 while the stock market was reaching new heights. Some argue that wage stagnation is artificially maintained to limit inflation.[9]

France has experienced similar deindustrialization. Displaced workers have been somewhat less penalized than their American counterparts because of a more generous state contribution for income maintenance.[10] However, the French state has been an active agent of deindustrialization through industrial planning, capital investment financing, nationalization of corporations, and layoff facilitation via training and job creation.[11] As a result, the French government has had to contend repeatedly with social movements contesting specific policies.

NEW JERSEY–NEW YORK AND PARIS METROPOLITAN AREAS

The New York City metropolitan area has been affected strongly by the changes just described—it has become a global city functioning as a highly concentrated command point in the organization of the world economy and a key location for finance and specialized service firms.[12] In the last 20 years, the area has also experienced a massive decline in manufacturing, a large loss of corporate headquarters and accompanying office jobs, and a deteriorating fiscal situation.[13] The ratio of low- to high-wage jobs is much greater now than it was when manufacturing was the leading sector. Existing manufacturing jobs have been downgraded from the middle-income category (such as construction jobs). Here also, the result is an increase in income polarization.[14]

New Jersey, where the majority of the American interviewees resided, has a relatively healthy economy with a per capita income 29 percent above the national average in 1994.[15] Favorable state policies regarding business taxation have played an important role in attracting employers from New York City.[16] However, the lowest employment during the recession was reached in May 1992, a few months before I conducted my interviews. Fifty-seven percent of the lost jobs had been restored by March 1995, with growth of service sector and construction jobs offsetting manufacturing job losses.[17] During this period, factory job losses continued, declining from an average of 33,500 a year from 1989 to 1992, to 5,400 a year in 1994.[18] Below the national average from 1982 to 1992, the New Jersey unemployment rate rose to 7.4 percent in 1993 (compared to 7.7 percent in New York state), with a rate of 12.9 percent for African Americans.[19] The largest growing service-based industries demand semiskilled literate workers and are not very attractive to displaced blue-collar workers.[20]

Paris has a much more central role in the French national economy than does New York in the American economy. In 1990, the Île-de-France region, which includes Paris, had 18.8 percent of the French population but 23 percent of the jobs. In the 1980s, this region attracted half of the new jobs and 26 percent of the demographic growth of the nation.[21] Over the last decades, Paris itself attracted 40 percent of all new jobs in financial and high technology services, while its share of industrial jobs declined to 17 percent.[22] The Seine-Saint-Denis, the department to the north of Paris where most of the industrial jobs of the region are concentrated, lost 29,437 blue-collar jobs between 1982 and 1990, at a time when 50,000 such jobs were lost elsewhere in the Île-de-France. In fact, suburbs adjacent to Paris, including those where I conducted my interviews (in what is called "première couronne"), lost half of their production-related jobs.[23] In contrast, during the same period, 186,610 new "professions intermédiaires" (technicians and semiprofessionals) and 293,148 new professional and managerial jobs appeared.[24] Nevertheless, the economy of this region is more diversified than that of London or New York, though this diversity is decreasing rapidly.[25]

These infrastructural changes have a strong impact on the sociopolitical outlook of the region. In the last decade, the Paris metropolitan area has become more polarized socially, with managers and professionals increasingly concentrated in the southern and western suburbs, and productive-sector employees concentrated in the northern and eastern suburbs.[26] The suburbs are also divided politically, as was shown in reactions to the Maastrich agreement of 1992; poorer suburbs opposed Europe vigorously while richer suburbs supported Europe.[27]

THE PHYSICAL LOCATION OF WORKERS

In the New York suburbs, workers were chosen from the following New Jersey towns: Bayonne, Elizabeth, Hillside, Irvington, Jersey City, Linden, Orange, Paterson, Rahway, Roselle, Roselle Park, South Orange, and Union City. To increase diversity, I also chose interviewees from Hempstead and Uniondale on Long Island. In the Paris suburbs, workers were chosen from the following towns: Aubervilliers, Bobigny,

Clichy, Créteil, Gennevilliers, Ivry-sur-Seine, La Courneuve, Nanterre, Puteaux, Stains, and Vitry-sur-Seine. Below, I describe the areas where workers reside; descriptions of the areas where professionals and managers live are provided in the appendixes of *Money, Morals, and Manners.*[28]

Essex County, where Hillside, Irvington, and the Oranges are located and where I conducted a few interviews, includes Port Newark and the Newark International Airport, making the county a major trade center with an important concentration of goods-producing and service jobs. Of the three New Jersey counties where I conducted interviews, Essex contains the smallest proportion of foreign-born residents (18.6 percent of the population in 1990).[29]

Union County, where I conducted most of the interviews, is the industrial heart of the region, with a strong presence of industrial research and development and chemical and pharmaceutical production. This county, including the towns of Elizabeth, Linden, Rahway, Roselle, and Roselle Park, has strong manufacturing industries that employ most of its residents. In 1990, 15 percent of its population was foreign-born (with 37 percent in the town of Elizabeth).[30] Nineteen percent was black of non-Hispanic origin (as compared to 13.4 percent for New Jersey as a whole).[31]

Hudson County, where Bayonne, Jersey City, and Union City are located, has been an important industrial center historically. Twenty-five percent of its land is covered by roads, highways, and railroads. Jersey City's population declined during the seventies and eighties with the downturn of the economy; 25 percent of its active labor force is involved in blue-collar occupations.[32] Local governments have organized economic rehabilitation projects such as Liberty State Park on the waterfront. Bayonne has a more stable economy with Standard Oil as an important employer; 36 percent of Bayonne's active labor force is in blue-collar occupations.[33] However, the 1989 per capita income of $18,440 in Hudson County was nearly last in the state, and the 1991 unemployment rate of 6.4 percent was well above the state average. Finally, with 30.6 percent of its population foreign-born, Hudson County has one of the highest proportions of foreign-born in the country; in Union City, 55.1 percent of the population is foreign-born, as is 24.6 percent of Jersey City's population.[34]

I also conducted interviews in Hempstead and Uniondale, located in Nassau County on Long Island, about 22 miles east of Manhattan. These are commuter communities with some light industry. The population of Nassau County is relatively well-off, ranking eleventh in the nation in personal per capita income. In 1990, blacks represented 9 percent and Hispanics 6 percent of the county's population.[35] Uniondale includes a higher proportion of blacks (46 percent) and Hispanics (14 percent). Per capita income is lower in Uniondale than in the county as a whole ($14,850 compared to $23,352). In contrast, the population of Hempstead is 12 percent black and 6 percent Hispanic. Hempstead's per capita income is $13,294 a year.[36]

The French "communes" where I conducted interviews are mostly old working class towns with heavy industry dating from the beginning of the twentieth century. Peasant workers forced to leave their provinces came to towns like Ivry, Saint-Denis, and Aubervilliers to work in large chemical or metallurgical plants. These towns were homogeneously working class for most of this century.[37] Several are part of the *banlieue rouge,* the set of communes surrounding Paris where city government has been controlled by the French Communist Party for the better part of the century. Others, such as Créteil and Nanterre, have developed more recently and are less clearly associated with the working class.

On average, the populations of the communes where I conducted interviews were 22 percent foreign and 15 percent blue collar. In 1993, the average annual income was 81,379 francs, compared to 86,889 francs for all of France, and 116,391 francs for the Île-de-France, the Paris metropolitan area.[38]

Some of these communes are classified as "grands projets urbains" (GPU). These suburbs have been identified by urban experts and policy makers as "problem" areas posing risks of social explosion. Clichy, Aubervilliers, Gennevilliers, and La Courneuve, all located north of Paris in the Seine-Saint-Denis department, have been identified as such as a result of their large public housing projects and high concentrations of young people.[39] Historically, these towns have been industrial centers specializing in chemical products, tires, and similar industries. Now they experience unemployment rates as high as 19 percent in some areas. These communes also have more immigrants—on average

20 to 30 percent of the population compared with 10 to 12 percent for the Île-de-France as a whole. Finally, their populations have lower per capita incomes and include a higher percentage of blue-collar workers (22 percent in Aubervilliers and Gennevilliers) than does the Île-de-France.

Some of the towns where I conducted interviews are more prosperous and serve as important regional commercial and administrative centers. These include Bobigny (the center of the Seine-Saint-Denis, the industrial department located north of Paris), Créteil (the center of the Val-de-Marne department located south of Paris), and Nanterre (the center of Haut-de-Seine, located west of Paris). The population of Créteil is 13 percent immigrant and 10 percent blue collar. In 1958, Créteil was identified as a "zone a urbaniser en priorité" (ZUP), and consequently became the site for the construction of many new apartment buildings. These buildings came to be associated with modern anomie and decadence—they have not aged well and their large size was not conducive to nurturing local communities.

Nanterre also received many such buildings. However, it has more of an industrial character than Créteil. Nanterre is also an important port and contains a Citroën automobile plant as well as a large university and cultural institutions. Nanterre is located near Puteaux, which is the site of the La Défense complex, France's response to Manhattan's skyscrapers. Among the communes where I conducted interviews, Nanterre is second only to Créteil in income.

Ivry-sur-Seine, like Vitry-sur-Seine, is separated from the south of Paris only by the "périphérique," a highway circling the city proper. Historically, these two towns have been important industrial centers and a ground for working class resistance. Indeed, their local governments have been under Communist control for most of this century. Ivry has a large recycling plant. It is here that the national electric utility company, Electricité de France (EDF), has located subsidized housing for its workers. This suburb used to have a large number of Italian immigrants. Now Ivry and Vitry both have relatively small immigrant populations (19 percent and 18 percent, respectively).

This brief panorama provides the urban contexts in which the French and American workers I interviewed live.

Appendix C: Interviewees

Table 1   Occupation and age of Caucasian blue-collar workers

FRENCH		AMERICANS	
OCCUPATION	AGE	OCCUPATION	AGE
House painter	30	Printer	31
Automobile painter	39	Mechanic	40
Mason	45	Ironworker	43
Carpenter	47	Construction worker	38
Automobile technician	35	Security system installer	51
Locksmith	39	Plumbing inspector	35
Boiler maker	32	Plumber	32
Electrical technician	42	Heating system specialist	59
Electronics operative	35	Electrician	31
Heater repairman	30	Electrician	34
Warehouse attendant	31	Stage technician	34
Electrical appraiser	46	Warehouse worker	30
Railway technician	30	Warehouse worker	35
Railway technician	35	Train conductor	39
Railway technician	37	Pipe fitter	58
Subway conductor	30	Petroleum company foreman	45
Garbage recycling technician	38	Tin factory foreman	46
Tire technician	54	Automobile assembly line	
Steam engine operative	35	worker	45
Radar technician	31	Foreman, cosmetics plant	45
Shop foreman, lamp		Truck driver	34
factory	41	Truck driver	44
Bellman	32	Tool and dye maker	49
Phone technician	40	Postal service sorter	45
Cable technician	36	Firefighter	33
Pastry maker	30	Firefighter	50
Policeman	35	Policeman	34
Aircraft technician	36	Policeman	54
Pastry chef	31	Warehouse worker	63
Butcher	55	Letter carrier	39
Cook	42	Letter carrier	48
Average age	37	Average age	41

Table 2   Occupation and age of minority blue-collar workers

NORTH AFRICANS		AFRICAN AMERICANS	
OCCUPATION	AGE	OCCUPATION	AGE
Mechanic	37	Painter	46
Mason	59	Car inspector	49
Painter	42	Equipment operator	62
Painter	57	Machinist	46
Operative, car factory	46	Union rep., car factory	53
Operative, car factory	50	Health inspector	38
Gold-plating craftsman	50	Plumber	32
Plumber	45	Assistant cable splicer	36
Skilled worker, car factory	52	Phone technician	25
Electrician	34	Maintenance worker	32
Warehouse attendant, petroleum company	55	Warehouse attendant	53
Warehouse attendant	50	Letter carrier	57
Laborer, construction industry	53	Newspaper worker	33
Yard worker, railway	41	Truck driver	35
Bus driver	33	Recycling plant worker	31
Meat delivery man	60	Operative, chemical company	30
Warehouse attendant	33	Chemical operator	53
Skilled worker, air conditioner	50	X-ray worker	33
Roofer	51	Foreman, bindery	59
Screw-cutter	49	Worker, health industry	27
Truck driver	44	Shear operator	31
Phone-booth cleaner	47	Fumigation technician	55
Packer, textile industry	34	Sorter, mailing company	26
Handler, textile industry	34	Phone technician	44
Metalworker, car factory	56	Paper quality inspector	31
Hotel handyman	47	Security supervisor	36
Operative, telemechanics	54	Photo technician	45
Worker, pharmaceutical industry	37	Operative, textile company	59
Laborer, road construction	48	Park maintenance worker	44
Dressmaker	42	Hospital orderly	61
Average age	45	Average age	42

Table 3 Occupation and age of Caucasian lower white-collar workers

| FRENCH | | AMERICANS | |
OCCUPATION	AGE	OCCUPATION	AGE
Bank clerk	34	Bank clerk	45
Bank clerk	39	Receiving clerk	53
Bank clerk	40	Civil servant	52
Bank clerk	44	Civil servant	54
Civil servant	42	Draftsman	38
Draftsman	39	Electronics technician	38
Electronics technician	31	Postal clerk	35
Postal window clerk	30	Hotel industry salesman	30
Railroad-ticket clerk	33	Paper goods salesman	32
Wood salesman	40	Bank supplies salesman	60
Phone salesman	41	Insurance salesman	52
Charcuterie salesman	51	Clerical worker	53
Aircraft technician	36	Broadcast technician	47
Photographer	35	Audio technician	29
Draftsman	44	Electronics technician	28
Average age	39	Average age	43

Table 4   Occupation and age of Caucasian professionals and managers

FRENCH		AMERICANS	
OCCUPATION	AGE	OCCUPATION	AGE
Public school administrator	50	Public school administrator	58
Academic administrator	57	Academic administrator	50
Music teacher	41	Earth science teacher	46
Priest	43	Minister	51
Museum curator	53	Museum curator	44
Musician	42	Artist	48
Science teacher	46	Science teacher	53
Professor of architecture	31	Professor of social work	49
Literature teacher	57	Professor of theology	57
Social worker	35	Recreational professional	33
Diplomat	55	Civil servant	58
Computer specialist	33	Computer specialist	34
Professor of accounting	39	Applied science researcher	42
Human resources consultant	38	Human resources consultant	41
Psychologist	44	Psychologist	50
Hospital administrator	60	Hospital controller	39
Dentist	34	Statistics researcher	46
Physician	46	Computer researcher	36
Architect	43	Economist	52
Human resources consultant	59	Labor arbitrator	53
Business management		Investment advisor	31
specialist	46	Chief financial officer	56
Senior executive, manufacturing	58	Banker	44
Banker	45	Banker	59
Investment banker	40	Insurance company VP	44
Insurance executive	42	Plant facilities manager	40
Corporate attorney	36	Corporate attorney	41
Computer engineer	51	Computer specialist	52
Marketing executive	55	Marketing executive	45
Electrical engineer	42	Computer software	
Tourism executive	43	developer	53
Lawyer	39	Lawyer	39
Lawyer	45	Lawyer	42
Lawyer	47	Portfolio manager	46
Accountant	57	Computer consultant	46
Architect	46	Realtor	51
Insurance broker	45	Custom house broker	57
Proprietor, printing firm	56	Wholesale distributor	55
Proprietor, engineering firm	47	Proprietor, broadcasting company	49
Accountant	37	Proprietor, car leasing company	45
Accountant	40	Machine tool distributor	35
Average age	46	Average age	47

Notes

Introduction

1. Freeman (1996).
2. In the 1990 U.S. census, 40 percent of the currently employed population over 25 years of age were high school graduates employed in a blue-collar or lower white-collar occupation—47 percent of whites and 52 percent of blacks. These figures are based on the standard 1 percent unweighted sample of the decennial census and include individuals with associate degrees. Blue-collar and lower white-collar occupations correspond to the following occupational census categories: technical, sales, and administrative support occupations, service occupations, precision, production, craft, and repair occupations, operators, fabricators, and laborer and military applications. Workers with college degrees make up 7 percent of the population (8 percent of whites and 6 percent of blacks) while workers without a high school degree make up 11 percent of the population (12 percent of whites and 21 percent of blacks). Professionals and managers with college degrees make up 15 percent of the population, while professionals and managers with high school or associate degrees make up 10 percent of the population. Figures based on Ruggles et al. (1997).
3. "The sharp swings among the non-college-educated whites include a decline of 21 percentage points in support for George Bush between 1988 and 1992, a decline of 13 points in support for Democrat House candidates between 1992 and 1994, and a decline of 14 points in support for Bob Dole between early 1995 and mid-1996" (Teixeira and Rogers 1996, p. 1). See also Hout, Brooks, and Manza (1995).
4. Whereas in 1970 the typical affluent person lived in a neighborhood that was 39 percent affluent, in 1990 she or he lived in a neighborhood that was 52 percent affluent. Affluent neighborhoods include families whose incomes are at least four times the poverty level (Massey 1996, p. 398). On upper middle class consolidation, see also Kalmijn (1991), who shows that educational endogamy is higher than racial endogamy among the college-educated.
5. Between 1985 and 1989, wages went down 5 percent (7 percent for men) for the non-college-educated but increased by 2 percent for college graduates (4 percent for men with advanced degrees) (Teixeira and Rogers, 1996, p. 22). The rise in inequality between 1983 and 1989 was particularly striking; the share of wealth controlled by the top 1 percent of the population rose by 5 percent while the wealth of the bottom 40 percent showed an absolute decline (Wolff 1995, p. 2). Domestic

household wealth is more concentrated now than at any point since the 1929 crash.

6. Krueger (1997) reflects on the 1992–1997 economic upswing: "Rapid economic growth has not been sufficient to lift real wages. We are in danger that when this economic upswing ends, it will be the first recovery on record in which the real wage of the median worker fell." Between 1989 and 1998, wages increased by 0.3 percent for low-wage workers (20th percentile), decreased 0.2 percent for "typical workers" (50th percentile), and increased 0.4 percent for high-wage workers (90th percentile). During this period, the consumer price index increased by 3.2 percent (Mishel, Bernstein, and Schmitt 1998, table 1).

7. Hochschild (1995a, pp. 58–59) cites detailed figures on "How Good Are Your Chances to Pursue the American Dream?" from 1947 to 1991. Responses to questions pertaining to perceptions of one's own prospects indicate an overall decline, as do responses pertaining to the likelihood that one's children will have a better opportunity to succeed.

8. The concept of "imagined community" is borrowed from Anderson (1991, pp. 6–7), who argued that most communities are imagined because community members never know most of their fellow members. He also characterizes communities as involving deep, horizontal comradeship and as limited—they have external boundaries and are not coterminous with mankind.

9. In Lamont (1992) I use "boundary work" to designate the process by which people differentiate themselves from others. In contrast, Gieryn (1999) uses this concept to designate "the discursive attribution of selected qualities to scientists, scientific methods, and scientific claims for the purpose of drawing a rhetorical boundary between science and some less authoritative residual non-science" (p. 4; see also pp. 15–18).

10. See Chinoy (1955), Lane (1962), and Rubin (1976). Rubin (1994) also presents workers as passive victims of broader social forces. By comparison, I show that workers find meaning, value, and worth in their own lives by downplaying status criteria that are the dominant currency in the upper middle class world. These discrepancies are worth exploring although they might be explained by time lag and differences in the socioeconomic status of interviewees. Rubin's respondents are poorer than the men considered in this chapter: their median family income was $31,500 in 1992 (p. 32) as compared with $49,000 in the present study.

11. I draw on Hodson's (1996) definition of dignity as having autonomy for defining one's identity and protecting oneself from abuse. Also, see Hodson (1991) for a useful typology of resistance.

12. Massey and Denton (1993) showed that in 1980 the average black person in any of the ten largest U.S. cities lived in a neighborhood that was at least 80 percent black; the vast majority resided in areas that were 100 percent black (p. 160). However, network data do suggest a higher level of social interactions between whites and blacks. While 45 percent of blacks responding to a 1992 national survey said they are close friends with several whites, 10 percent described themselves as close friends with one white, 37 percent described themselves as having white acquaintances, and 7 percent described themselves as having no white acquaintances. Re-

ported black contacts among whites are also high, with 30 percent of whites describing themselves as having several close friends who are black, 17 percent reporting having one close black friend, 36 percent reporting having black acquaintances, and 16 percent reporting having no black acquaintances (Anti-Defamation League 1993, pp. 73–75).

13. Changes in the size of the gap are being debated. For example, see Patterson (1997).

14. This inductive approach to symbolic boundaries contrasts with that of Bourdieu (1984), who predefines categories of evaluation/identification. On this point, see Lamont (1992, chapter 7).

15. While interviewees use a multiplicity of sometimes contradictory standards, I focus my attention on the standards they emphasize.

16. The concept of mental maps is derived from Geertz (1973, p. 220), who understands culture as the ways people construct meaning to make their way through the experienced world. I make this concept of culture mine. I also understand boundary drawing as a form of social practice, in response to anthropologists who are calling for a practice-oriented approach to culture (Ortner 1984). Finally, I am concerned with the relative availability of various themes within mental maps. Drawing on Aristotle who defined rhetoric as the art of discovering available means of persuasion in a given case (Perelman and Olbrechts-Tyteca 1969, chapter 1), I want to describe the *established rules* of upholding claims or the *conventional and widely shared mental maps* that people mobilize to demonstrate an idea. Ultimately, this endeavor aims to document alternative systems of thought that organize discourse and guide the formulation of new arguments. It also aims to establish a "storehouse of codified ways of thinking, seeing, and communicating that may be tested for goodness-of-fit to the matter at hand" (Simons, 1990, p. 11). Note that I build on a strong postwar tradition of primarily British scholarship that aimed at analyzing the shared creation of meaning or "habits of thoughts" in working class communities (Hoggart [1957] 1992, Thompson 1966, Goldthorpe et al. 1969, and Grignon and Passeron, 1989). In the last decades, this tradition has given birth to important books in labor history, including Sewell (1980). For a review of this literature, see Critcher (1980). I also build on the Durkheimian tradition in cultural sociology, including Douglas (1966). For a review, see Lamont and Fournier (1992). Finally, I draw on more recent European literature that studies the repertoires of claims that people mobilize to justify their actions and the criteria they use to evaluate the worth of people and things in situations of crisis (Boltanski and Thévenot 1991). In contrast to these authors, I pay attention to the cultural and structural conditions that lead individuals to use some criteria of evaluation instead of others. For a description of the two approaches, see Lamont and Thévenot (2000).

17. This method resembles that of W. Lloyd Warner and associates in their Yankee City study. This research asked "What similarities exist among the members of the same class in the social hierarchies? What differences are found among the members of different classes?" (Warner and Lunt 1942, p. 3.) Through interviews, these sociologists collected behavioral and attitudinal data concerning the struc-

ture of social class defined as "two or more orders of people who are believed to be, and are accordingly ranked by the members or the community, in socially superior and inferior positions" (Warner et al. 1969, p. 36). They were particularly concerned with the criteria according to which status is attributed. Similarly, Young and Willmott (1956) considered the weight given by manual workers to "social contribution" as a criterion for ranking the prestige of occupations.

18. I share the usual reservations concerning the notion of national "model": that it downplays the importance of international influences, variations internal to specific societies, and the impact of reform on traditions. For a critique of this concept, see Kastoryano (1996); Favell (1998, p. 27); and Feldblum (1999, chapter 1).

19. This book shares its focus on broad national patterns of inclusion and exclusion with other recent works. In particular, Marx (1998) suggests that "state-imposed exclusion of a specified internal group, used to reinforce the allegiance and unity of a core constituency, may be a more pervasive pattern" of community than an all-inclusive imagined community (p. 25). Similarly, Skrentny (1996) analyzes how shared moral models that determine who is deserving and undeserving shape policy-making. Gerstle (1997) analyzes the place of immigration, citizenship, social welfare policies, and race in the American "communal imagination." He is particularly concerned with the dynamic between two nationalist traditions, one civic and one racial, and in demonstrating the undue neglect of the latter in historical scholarship. Gerstle (2001) provides an important analysis of the conditions under which the contemporary community boundaries I document developed during twentieth-century American history.

20. To mention only some of the most important ones: Gans (1962), Kornblum (1974), Halle (1984), and Rubin (1976).

21. These include the excellent studies of Noiriel (1996) and Brubaker (1992).

22. Here, as elsewhere, translations from French to English are mine.

23. Marshall (1950, pp. 1–85, especially pp. 28–29) suggests that members of a society attribute rights to one another based on a sense of solidarity and moral community, which is what I mean by cultural membership. More specifically, I am concerned with the content people give to "people like us," the definition of which often posits moral commonalities. On social and cultural membership, see also Walzer (1983) and Alexander (1992).

24. I view these boundaries as indicative of exclusionary behavior and as leading to the construction of objective boundaries. On the relationship between symbolic and objective boundaries, see Lamont (1992, chapter 7). I suggest that symbolic boundaries are a necessary but not sufficient condition for objective boundaries. The connection between attitudes toward categories of individuals and discriminatory behavior is documented in the literature on homophobia; it has been shown, for instance, that negative attitudes toward homosexuality shape exclusionary behavior such as avoidance and discrimination against homosexuals (DeCecco 1984).

25. See, for instance, Inkeles (1979). For a critique of this literature, see Lamont (1992, chapter 5). See also Corse (1997) and Griswold (1981).

26. This multidimensional approach to explaining how people draw boundaries is presented in Lamont (1992, chapter 5).

27. For a cognate perspective on the use of cultural repertoires in the creation of identity, see Somers (1994), who is concerned with how the use of available narratives in the construction of identity is shaped by contexts or relational settings defined more or less broadly as "institutions, public narratives, and social practices," including social networks (p. 626). On repertoires more generally, see Swidler (1986) and Tilly (1995, p. 16).

28. One of the advantages of this approach is the diminishment of contrast between national and intranational differences. I consider elements of repertoires to be present across analytical units such as class, races, nations, or regions, but in varying proportions. For instance, as we will see, cultural repertoires prevailing in the United States make market references more readily available to Americans and enable them to resort to such references in a wide range of situations. French repertoires, on the other hand, make principles of solidarity more salient and are accessible to a larger number of French people, often in those situations in which Americans would resort to market principles. This does not mean that market criteria of evaluation are absent from the French repertoires, but only that they are used in a small number of situations by a smaller number of people. As is often argued in the comparative literature, generalizations concerning national differences can be dangerous, as they lead researchers to overlook variations and the specificity of structured contexts in which people use principles of evaluation. They can also lead to confirmation of a view of differences as national character traits attributed to almost all the citizens of a country and expressed in a heterogeneous range of situations. I believe that my distinctive approach avoids such pitfalls. On these issues, see also Lamont and Thévenot (2000).

29. Moreover, this comparison does not posit nations as places of agreed-upon meeting that would be unitary or strongly bounded. The cultural distinctiveness of the two nations is constructed partly in relation to one another, and has to be understood as national narratives developing historically. For a critique of the traditional "culture and places" approach in anthropology, see Gupta and Ferguson (1997).

30. Cited by Lind (1995, p. 231). Pierre Nora also writes that the universal values that characterize France have been able to "make of a particular national adventure the emancipatory avant-garde of humanity" (cited by Kastoryano 1996, p. 45).

31. Hunter and Bowman (1996a, p. 4).

32. Smith (1997, p. 14).

33. Perrineau (1997, p. 186) estimates this percentage at 25 percent of the French voters. Martin Schain, a key American expert on the National Front, estimates it at 28 percent based on figures on party loyalty from year to year (personal communication).

34. There is no data available on interracial marriage in France. However, Tribalat (1995) observes that if binational marriage represents "a very small share" of all marriages in France, it represents a "substantial proportion" of immigrants' marriages (p. 111). In 1984, 7.6 percent of all marriages in France were binational, compared to 7.3 percent in Germany (Barbara 1994).

35. On Americanization, see Kuisel (1993); on the threat to French economic sovereignty, see Cohen (1996); on the impact of Europe, see Birnbaum (1998); on the

tensions surrounding the construction of the European Union, see Williams (1995).

36. I am referring specifically to the 1998 movement of solidarity with the unemployed, and to strikes of almost a million people that paralyzed Paris over a two-month period at the end of 1995. Although the primary goal of the movement was to oppose a reform of social security benefits for state employees, it rapidly came to embrace larger purposes such as the defense of public services and the support of republican principles like equality and solidarity against short-term profit-making and the European Union.

37. In 1975, 24 percent of French workers were unionized. This figure had fallen to 10 percent by 1992 (Upham 1993, p. G-20). In the United States only 15 percent of the active labor force in the public and private sector workforces were union members in 1994 (Bureau of National Affairs, 1996, p. 9). In 1975, this figure was 29 percent (United States Bureau of Census of the Population, 1988, table 666, p. 401).

38. See Skocpol (1995) and Quadagno (1994). Skrentny (1996, pp. 237–238) notes that these books point to, but do not elaborate on, the importance of moral communities in policy-making. Sociologists have contrasted the French and American welfare systems: whereas the American system provides programs that are often means-tested and offer comparatively few benefits to narrow sectors of the population, French welfare programs are generally universal. For a historical discussion of French welfare benefits, see Chapman (1995).

39. In contrast, recent studies of welfare retrenchment policies tend to focus almost exclusively on institutional factors. See Pierson (1994). For a more synthetic approach, see Noble (1997).

40. Ellwood (1988). For an analysis of the place of resonance in the institutionalization of meaning, see Schudson (1989).

41. As pointed out by Offe (1987, p. 528), advanced industrial societies face increasing skepticism concerning the notion that social policies and welfare provisions are "public goods," as individuals come to evaluate them in terms of gains, losses, and free-riding. He writes: "The disorganization of broad, relatively stable, and encompassing commonalties of economic interests, associational affiliation, or culture values and life-styles is in my view the key to an adequate understanding of the general weakening of solidaristic commitments. If it no longer 'makes sense' to refer to a broad and sharply delineated category of fellow citizens as 'our kind of people,' the only remaining interpretive referent of action is the individual who refers to her or himself in rational-calculative terms" (p. 527).

42. Lamont (1992) analyzed the boundary work and mental maps of college-educated professionals and managers living in Indianapolis, New York, Paris, and Clermont-Ferrand. The main findings of the book were that moral criteria of evaluation were as salient in France as in the United States, cultural criteria were most important in France, and socioeconomic criteria were most important in the United States (p. 130). However, I also found that standards of prestige vary nationally in a marginally significant fashion.

43. The median family income of white respondents is $50,000 a year compared to $45,500 for blacks. These figures compare with 1993 national median family in-

comes of $39,300 for whites and $21,542 for blacks (U.S. Bureau of Census 1993, in current dollars). These figures are close to the average median family income of $48,000 for the counties where I conducted interviews (based on information gathered in the *County and City Data Book 1994* on the 1989 median income in the counties where interviewees reside). This figure is considerably higher than the national median income of $35,000. However, note that in 1991, the composite cost of living index for the New York metropolitan area (PMSA) was 213.3 percent higher than the national average of 100. The second highest cost of living index in the nation (at 148) is that of Nassau-Suffolk County on Long Island where a large portion of my respondents reside (United States Bureau of Census of the Population 1992, table 745, p. 475). The per capita family median income in the New York–New Jersey area is 29 percent higher than the national average (Appendix B, note 15). The racial inequalities in income between the white and black samples reflect broader trends in the American population (Farley and Allen 1987). In our sample, they are also compounded by the fact that 24 percent of the spouses of white respondents work in high-status white-collar occupations, compared to 4 percent of the spouses of blacks. Furthermore, African Americans have more expenses because they have more children: 36 percent have four or more children compared to only 8 percent of the white interviewees. Thirty-five percent of whites do not have children compared to 26 percent of the blacks.

44. Twenty-two percent of white families make $39,000 or less a year compared to 36 percent of black households.

45. For heuristic purposes, "class" is defined here in terms of (1) level of education, contrasting individuals on the basis of their highest degree (college vs. high school); (2) type of occupation (professionals and managers vs. lower white-collar and blue-collar workers); (3) employment status (full-time vs. others); and (4) the exercise of supervisory functions (supervise 10 people or more vs. supervise fewer than 10 people or none). The conception of class that undergirds the analysis is a relational (as opposed to a gradational) schema that focuses on degree of economic security, sources of income, workplace authority, and prospects for advancement (hence the focus on degrees). This schema is akin to that developed by Erickson and Goldthorpe (1992) and revised by Heath et al. (1991, p. 66) and by Hout et al.(1995). I also follow the important work of Grusky and Sorensen (1998) by focusing less on class than on occupation as the locus of identity. Drawing on the literature, these authors provide persuasive evidence of the lasting centrality of occupations as bases for self-identification, social closure, collective action, and lifestyles and dispositions. Class remains a significant symbolic community in American society to the extent that individuals belong to class-related occupations with shared market power and subcultures (due to training, socialization, and self-selection, as suggested by Van Maanen and Barley 1984).

46. Individuals working in managerial and professional occupations included 23 percent of the active population in l992, the year I conducted most of my interviews (United States Bureau of Census of the Population l993, table 644, p. 405). Also in 1992, 21 percent of Americans 25 years old and over had received a four-year college degree. Sixteen percent had completed some college but had not received a

degree, and 6 percent had received an associate degree (United States Bureau of Census of the Population 1993, tables 232–234, pp. 153–154). On the recent growth of professional and managerial categories, see Hodson and Sullivan (1990, p. 74).

47. This contrasts with the proportion who identified themselves with members of other classes: 7 percent as lower class, 45 percent as middle class, 3 percent as upper class, and 1 percent as "other." The cumulative percentages for the 1972–1996 period are comparable (46 percent working class, 45 percent middle class). See note 2 for demographic information on the size of this group.

48. While all American respondents are high school graduates or have completed a GED, 30 percent of the whites have completed some college as compared with 50 percent of the African Americans. In 1992, 22 percent of white Americans of 25 years of age and more had a college degree in contrast to 12 percent of blacks; 59 percent of whites had a high school degree but no college degree, as compared with 56 percent of blacks (United States Bureau of Census of the Population 1993, table 233, p. 154). In 1990, 86 percent of young American adults had completed high school, and 45 percent had completed at least a year of college (Jencks 1996, p. 90).

49. Gusfield (1975, pp. 34–37) suggests that members of a symbolic community have both common categorization systems to differentiate between insiders and out-siders and common vocabularies and symbols through which they create a shared identity. Individuals can be members of the same symbolic community even if they have no face-to-face interactions and if their work situations vary greatly. Def-initions of this community vary across generations, as these definitions are in part shaped by common experience and collective memories. On this topic, see also Noiriel (1986, chapter 7), Jenkins (1996), and Melucci (1996).

50. This is also documented in Halle's (1984) excellent ethnography of New Jersey chemical plant workers.

51. For instance, for a white warehouse worker, being working class means "I have to get up every morning and sit in traffic. If I don't get up and go do it I won't get my money. It's not like people who own companies: 'Maybe today I'll just get up and go fishing because everybody else is working. The store's open and the sales people are there.' [They have] less headaches and aggravation . . . They can spend time mak-ing friends with people that can lead them to different things or different directions. You're not stuck in the same rut all the time." Similarly, while a black shear opera-tor describes living conditions across classes when he says "Gotta work hard. Gotta keep going. Can't afford these long trips around the world," a white train conductor says "Most of us have to work at it. Do different things, maybe get real estate, but life is basically sometimes a struggle. Sometimes we give a struggle. Sometimes we're saved from a struggle. Every day is a struggle." He contrasts this destiny with that of middle class people who always get breaks; he adds that nothing is given to workers: "We are not all blessed with silver spoons." Finally, a white warehouse worker also compares in evocative terms how class conditions affect survival: "In general, work-ing class people have a shorter life span. Their bodies are more abused from the things they have to do. Working class people, and I am one of them, are bottom feeders. The trout and the gang fish are at the top. I wouldn't say the professionals,

I would say the big business people don't want to give anything to us . . . Bottom feeders means that our future and how well we do depends on the top feeders . . . What they don't swallow up, we get."

52. On the distinction between "model for" and "model of," see Geertz (1973, pp. 93–94). On the importance of social identity in the formation of personal identity and, more generally, on the use of publicly available categories in the construction of the self, see Somers and Gibson (1994), Turner et al. (1994), and Burke (1980). From 1990 to 1995, major American newspapers published 258 articles that included references to "America[n]'s working class" or "America[n]'s working man[men]" and approximately 10,000 stories that included references to "America[n]'s workers." These data were found using the Nexis database. A comparable data bank is not available for French newspapers. However, a search of *Le Monde* indicates that 40 stories including references to "classe ouvrière française," "ouvriers français," or "travailleurs français" were published between 1990 and 1995.

53. Fifty-four percent of the Americans interviewed for this study have fathers who were blue-collar workers, 18 percent have fathers who were in a lower white-collar occupation, and 9 percent have fathers who were in a high-status white-collar occupation. Information is missing for 17 percent of the American interviewees.

54. Among African-American respondents, 16 out of 30 individuals were born in the New York/New Jersey area and 13 elsewhere (with data missing for one case). Among whites, 39 out of 45 respondents were born in the New York/New Jersey area, and only 4 were born elsewhere (with data missing for two cases). A large portion of those born in the New York area were born in proximity to their current place of residence.

55. A few studies are available, including Duneier (1992) and Anderson (1990). In contrast, the black "underclass" and middle class have been the object of considerable scholarly attention. A few examples include Landry (1987); Stack (1974); and W. J. Wilson (1996).

56. While black blue-collar workers represent 2.3 percent of the total U.S. population, they make up 32 percent of the black labor force and 36 percent of employed blacks. In contrast, white blue-collar workers make up 16 percent of the U.S. population. They represent 27 percent of the total U.S. labor force and 29 percent of the employed white labor force. Forty-six percent of blacks and 41 percent of whites work in service and salaried (low-status) white-collar occupations (United States Department of Labor 1989).

57. A survey published by the Commission Nationale Consultative des Droits de l'Homme shows that in 1990, 85 percent of the French thought the main victims of racism in their country were North Africans, and 59 percent thought that *beurs* were the main victims—this term is widely used to designate the children of North African immigrants who were born or are growing up in France. Respectively 42 percent and 37 percent of the respondents to the survey expressed antipathy toward these groups (Policar 1991).

58. In 1986, black American families with incomes between $10,000 and $35,000 represented nearly 50 percent of all blacks; those with incomes of less than $10,000 a year represented 30 percent of blacks, and those with incomes of more than

$35,000 represented 21 percent (Jaynes and Williams, 1989, p. 275). Similarly, in France, the index of disparity between the mean income of immigrants in 1994 as compared with that of French nationals (before taxes) was 62 percent for Algerians, 58 percent for Tunisians, and 51 percent for Moroccans (as compared to an average of 73 percent for all foreigners) (INSEE 1994, p. 91). Twenty-nine percent of the French and 67 percent of the North African populations are workers (p. 71).

59. In 1992, the U.S. unemployment rate was 6 percent for whites, 10 percent for Hispanics, and 11 percent for blacks (United States Bureau of Census of the Population 1993, table 629, p. 398). In France, the unemployment rate for the same year was 10 percent for French, 19 percent for all foreigners, and 30 percent for North African immigrants (INSEE 1994, p. 83).

60. While at the onset of the research I planned to interview minority white-collar workers, this proved to be impossible because of their small numbers in the population and the difficulty of identifying qualified respondents through random sampling. In 1990, only 16 percent of all Maghrebis living in France declared they had been hired as "employés" (clerical workers) (INSEE 1994, p. 71).

61. Information on the sample of professionals and managers is presented in the appendixes of Lamont (1992).

62. In 1992, blacks represented only 6.5 percent of American workers located in managerial or professional occupations (United States Bureau of Census of the Population 1993, table 644, p. 405). A natural extension of this research would compare white and black upper middle class cultures and the extent to which they are distant from black and white working class cultures. Annette Lareau's ongoing research on children's socialization across race and class will provide important information on this topic, particularly on differences between white and black upper middle class cultures (for instance, Lareau and Howley-Rowe 1995).

63. A subsample of interviews with 15 upper middle class women revealed interesting differences in the boundary work of men and women. Most important, women tended to put more emphasis on the cultural and moral criteria of worth and to downplay socioeconomic standards more than men (Lamont, 1992, pp. 133–134). On the changing social, occupational, and economic characteristics of the working class, see Esping-Anderson (1993); Dudley (1994); and Rubin (1976).

64. For a very informative study of the gendered aspect of American working class culture, see Kefalas (forthcoming). Note that in this book I do not analyze all the boundaries that workers drew toward women (including myself) in the context of the interviews. Comparing French and American conceptions of gender differences and gender relations is a complex topic that should be the object of a separate study. Very promising research directions are offered by Saguy (2000) in her study of French and American conceptions of sexual harassment.

65. Kocka (1980, p. 11) argues that historically the occupational line between white- and blue-collar workers has been relatively insignificant in France and in the United States, given the "lower level of organization of the French working class and the much less unified (if sporadically more radical) character of the French labor movement [compared to the German]" and the countervailing impact of ethnic divisions in the United States (p. 275). The distinction between these

groups is losing importance as the groups become more alike in terms of income, work satisfaction, skills, and work conditions, due in part to the decline of the situation of white-collar workers (Braverman 1974, pp. 297–298 and 355).

66. This tactical decision should not be taken to indicate that I adopt an essentialist view of the groups under study. For a critique of essentialism in the study of working class culture, see Fine and Weis (1998, p. 4).

1. The World in Moral Order

1. The names of all interviewees are pseudonyms used to ensure each man's anonymity.

2. Defining what morality consists of is an arduous enterprise that occupies entire scholarly fields. Without entering in the debate, I will define morality as norms and prescriptions thought of as having universal value and pertaining to personal responsibilities and duties toward others (as described by the Decalogue, for instance). In contrast, ethics refers to prescriptions particular to specific groups and having to do not with their status as human beings but with their distinctive responsibilities (as is the case for professional ethics). Descombes (1998, p. 41) discusses these definitions.

3. These responses were given to open-ended questions. Seventy-eight percent of the whites and 75 percent of the blacks appreciated moral values in others. Less than 10 percent of each group put a premium on cultural and socioeconomic values together. Similarly, 75 percent of the whites and 65 percent of the blacks stressed moral values when discussing the traits they dislike in others; less than 10 percent of both groups referred to cultural and socioeconomic traits when asked to describe traits they dislike. Here and elsewhere, figures comparing whites and blacks refer to blue-collar workers only.

4. Moral criteria are also at the center of workers' descriptions of the values they hope to pass on to their children (such as "being hardworking," "avoiding trouble," etc.). Indeed, among the men I talked to, 76 percent of the whites and 67 percent of the blacks stress morality in their discussions of child-rearing values. In contrast, only 1 percent of whites and 7 percent of blacks stressed socioeconomic achievement. Twelve percent of whites and 22 percent of blacks stressed education. In these discussions, workers most often define the transmission of traditional morality as a top priority (14 percent), followed by the transmission of education (12 percent), a work ethic (8 percent), and religion (8 percent).

5. Only 8 percent of the whites and 11 percent of the blacks use cultural criteria to define success (for instance, "he is well educated").

6. "In 1986, over two-thirds of whites and three-fourths of blacks [of all classes] agreed that good relationships with family and friends, commitment to religious beliefs, and social utility are all 'very important elements of success.'" Roper survey cited by Hochschild (1995a, p. 60, note 13). When asked what qualities they value in a personal friend, 98 percent of the non-college graduates questioned for the 1993 General Social Survey said that honesty is extremely or very important for them; 90 percent described responsibility in these terms (my analysis).

7. This inductive approach departs from that adopted by Wolfe (1997), who sets out to explore whether middle class Americans still "believe in middle class morality," which he predefines as "the values of those people who strive to earn enough money so that they feel that their economic fate is in their own hands, but who also try to live by principles such as individual responsibilities, the importance of family, obligations to others, and a belief in something outside oneself" (p. 5). Instead of predefining middle class values in order to explore whether middle class people still uphold these values, I analyze how middle and working class members define their values. I find that several of Wolfe's "middle class values" are in fact more cherished by the workers than the professionals I interviewed. Note that he defines the middle class as people who reside in "middle class suburbs" and have "middle class incomes." The majority of his respondents reside in regions with relatively low costs of living, and 66 percent have family incomes of more than $50,000 a year. More than 50 percent of his respondents have at least a college degree (p. 29). My approach similarly contrasts with Hunter and Bowman (1996a), who posit a middle class morality to explore whether it is adopted by a loosely defined "social elite."

8. On American individualism, see McClosky and Zaller (1984); Coughlin (1980); and Kluegel and Smith (1986).

9. For comparative purposes, I follow procedures described in the methodological Appendix A by locating each of the interviewees on several five-point scales. These scales pertain to the frequency and strength with which they draw moral, cultural, and socioeconomic boundaries. I also rank interviewees by the extent to which they draw racial boundaries against blacks, and class boundaries against middle class and poor people. This ranking was done on the basis of answers that respondents gave to a wide range of questions pertaining to the attributes one appreciates in friends, values regarding child-rearing, and feelings of inferiority and superiority vis-à-vis others. While this is only an approximate ranking, it provides useful information on the importance of various types of symbolic boundaries and on the magnitude of cross-national differences. White blue-collar workers score 3.8 on the moral scale, 2.5 on the socioeconomic scale, and 2.6 on the cultural scale. Their lower white-collar counterparts score 3.7, 3.0, and 3.4 on these scales, respectively. Overall, blacks score a little lower on the moral scale, with an average of 3.4. They score higher on the socioeconomic scale at 3.7, and near the white average (3.0) on the culture scale.

10. This is confirmed by national survey data: the 1993 General Social Survey reveals that non-college graduates value honesty and responsibility roughly as much as college graduates do. Ninety-six percent and 97 percent of the groups, respectively, consider honesty "extremely" or "very" important in friends, while 83 percent of professionals and 90 percent of workers describe responsibility thus.

11. See note 9 for the scores of white and black workers. In contrast, white American professionals and managers score 3.4 on the moral scale, 4.0 on the socioeconomic scale, and 3.1 on the cultural scale (Lamont 1992, table A5, p. 232). Additional evidence of the relationship of workers to socioeconomic status will be provided in Chapter 3 when I discuss the value workers ascribe to middle class attributes like power, ambition, and higher education.

12. To describe their fathers, they use terms such as "hardworking," "family-oriented," "caring," "provider," "standard-bearer," "strong," "evenhanded," and "helpful." In contrast, professionals and managers rarely point to their fathers in response to this question. Among 45 white workers, of those who have a hero, 10 mentioned their fathers and 18 mentioned someone else. Among the 30 African-American respondents, these proportions are 5 and 18.

13. Rodgers (1974, p. 35).

14. The commitment of many American workers to hard work per se is revealed by a 1992 national survey in which a surprisingly high percentage (51 percent) expressed admiration for someone who works hard and earns little (69 percent expressed admiration for someone who works hard and earns a lot of money). Cited in Wuthnow (1996, p. 408, note 37).

15. Students of working class culture have compared workers who have settled lives with those who are hard living (for instance, Gans 1962, Rubin 1976). Note that most of the workers who agreed to talk to me have settled lives, perhaps because they are more likely to want to participate in a study of this type.

16. On the place of work in the liberal ideology that has shaped American society, see Smith (1997, p. 37). For an extensive discussion of the literature on the American national character, see Wilkinson (1988). On Protestantism and the work ethic, see Weber (1958).

17. On the place of this republican vision in the labor movement, see Fink (1994, pp. 26–27, 179).

18. On American individualism and the lower middle class, see Gans (1991) and Bellah et al. (1985); McClay (1994) offers an historical account of the impact of religion on American individualism.

19. Willis (1977, chapter 4, especially p. 104) shows how being hardworking is equated with being attractive as a male in the British youth working class culture of the seventies. On the relational process of definition of masculinity versus femininity, see Connell (1995, chapter 3).

20. In a 1992 national survey of randomly sampled full-time and part-time workers, only 43 percent of working class respondents had high job satisfaction scores, compared to 66 percent of professionals (Wuthnow 1996, p. 404, note 13). On the impact of workplace organizational factors on job satisfaction, see Hodson (1996), who shows that craft workplace organizations continue to provide more job satisfaction than workplaces organized under alternative principles (direct supervision, assembly line, bureaucratic, and worker participation).

21. In the last decades, "nationwide, the average real wages of male college graduates rose 8 percent but the wages for male high school graduates fell by 40 percent . . . Real wages for young high school graduates at the 10th percentile of the work force's income distribution were almost 20 percent lower in the late 1980s than in 1963." Figures cited by Newman (1999, chapter 3, p. 343, note 3).

22. On these changes, see Appelbaum and Batt (1994). The General Social Surveys conducted in 1990–1994 reveal that 12 percent of workers believed it likely or very likely that they would be laid off in the next 12 months (9 percent for whites and 15 percent for blacks; my analysis).

23. Jencks (1994) shows that the nation's shelter population grew by a factor of five between 1980 and 1990 (p. 9). During this period, the number of poverty-wage workers (defined as full-time workers unable to support a family of four) increased from 9.7 to 11.5 percent of the labor force. Among whites, this rate increased from 8.4 to 9.7 percent; for blacks, it changed little—from 18.7 to 18.6 percent (Swartz and Weigert (1995, p. 51). On the downsizing of welfare benefits, see Watts (1997).

24. For details, see the Introduction, notes 5 and 6.

25. The importance of work for black workers is also noted in Duneier (1992, chapters 8 and 9) and in Anderson (1990). Newman (1999) also argues that work provides these individuals with a structure of social insertion, a valued social identity, and a sense of moral worth that helps them withstand ridicule for holding low-paying jobs.

26. The proportions agreeing with this statement are 61 percent of black workers and 55 percent of the black middle class (National Conference 1994, p. 45). Note that the theme of "survival" is a central part of the literature on self-concepts among blacks (Akbar 1994, p. 111).

27. This was documented by comparing systematically the meaning attributed to success when respondents discussed it in the context of the interview.

28. An update and critique of Goldthorpe and Lockwood's work is offered by Devine (1992), who suggests that the British working class is less privatized than they had suggested.

29. Young and Willmott (1974). However, Pleck and Lang (1978) report evidence of little class difference.

30. There is a large literature on work satisfaction that offers limited information on the importance of providing for leisure and family needs as an extrinsic reward of work (Brief and Nord 1990, pp. 38–41).

31. Lamont (1992, chapter 4). On this topic, see Lamont, Kaufman, and Moody (2000).

32. On class differences in the importance attached to formalized leisure activities and self-actualization, see Lareau (1998); Lareau and Howley-Rowe (1995); and Lareau and Berhau (forthcoming). Lareau's work suggests that upper middle class children learn to manage their leisure activities in such a way that they develop time-management skills, which can be used in school and future work settings. They "perform" frequently to gain poise and learn how to "negotiate institutions," while working class children tend to "hang out" in unstructured settings. On class differences in the importance attached to self-actualization and intellectual development in child-rearing values, see Gecas (1979, p. 460).

33. Similar results were obtained from questions on the importance of having a self-fulfilling job in the culture module of the 1993 General Social Survey. When asked whether "having a fulfilling job" was "one of the most important or very important" aspects of their lives, 90 percent of professionals and 81 percent of workers responded affirmatively. Similarly, 11 percent of professionals described "having a fulfilling job" as "somewhat, not too, or not at all important," compared to 19 percent of workers (my analysis).

34. There was a significant increase in concern for safety and fear of crime between 1989 and 1994. While in 1989, 34 percent of the individuals surveyed were "truly

desperate" about crime, this figure had increased to 62 percent in 1994. Survey cited by Haghighi and Sorensen (1996, p. 17).

35. Skolnick (1998, p. 92). However, research shows that fear of crime is more connected to media coverage of high-visibility events than it is to changes in crime rates (Gans 1995, pp. 78–79).

36. One Jersey City firefighter illustrates this by saying, "I know when someone is trying to pull the rug, the wool, over my eyes. I am not gullible to anyone . . . That's the difference between me and my wife. See my wife is only book-smart. You could sell her a box of bricks, tell her it's a VCR and she would never open it, she'd trust you."

37. This was true of John Lamb, one of the few single men I interviewed in his home. As a black 31-year-old who works in a recycling plant and resides in a town next to Newark, he explained: "If I had your job, I don't think I could just walk into anybody's house and interview them like that. I mean some people you might be able to trust, but you got a lot of weird people out there. A lot of things . . . There's no way in the world I'd go into a house like that."

38. On differences in the labor market positions of blacks and whites, see Farley and Allen (1987).

39. At the end of the eighties, "on any given day, approximately one in four African-American men (ages twenty to twenty nine) is either in jail, in prison, on probation or on parole while for white men the same age, approximately one in sixteen is under such state control." Figures cited by Messerschmidt (1993, p. 184). Many of these crimes are directed at other blacks.

40. Anti-Defamation League of B'Nai B'rith (1993, p. 57).

41. These men represent 60 percent of the American sample. Thirteen percent of whites and 3 percent of blacks are divorced, while 25 percent of whites and 36 percent of blacks have never married. In the national population, black men over 18 years of age are also more likely to have never married than are white men (38.5 and 24.1 percent, respectively, in 1990). The proportion of married men is also lower among blacks than whites (49.4 percent compared to 66.2 percent in 1990 (United States Bureau of the Census of the Population 1996, table 58, p. 54).

42. In this disjunction between the ability to perform the provider role and beliefs concerning its desirability, the men I interviewed resemble those studied in national surveys (as in Hood 1986).

43. One of the few recent studies of the role of father/husband in intact low-income black families suggests that men "indicate clearly that they are the main provider for their families." They are also involved in decision-making concerning purchasing appliances and selecting a residence, contradicting the "matriarchy" thesis that puts decision-making power in the exclusive hands of women (Robinson, Bailey, and Smith, Jr., 1985, p. 147).

44. Malson (1983, p. 132). On the prevalence of traditional gender roles among whites as opposed to blacks, see Hood (1986, p. 354) and Blee and Tickamyer (1995).

45. Hood (1986, p. 350).

46. For a comparison of the dual careers in working class and middle class families, see Ferree (1987). Workers are less likely to share household work than are middle class men. More generally, "the larger the proportion of family income the wife

contributes, the more likely it is that her husband will contribute housework and child care to the family economy" (p. 290). However, survey research shows convergence in the conception of gender roles across classes (DiMaggio, Evans, and Bryson 1996, p. 739).

47. Rose (1992, chapter 6) shows how working class men gain self-respect by supporting a family through their work. On the importance of providing to the identity of working class men, see Rubin (1976, chapter 9). For a more general analysis of the role of breadwinner in masculine identity and the difficulties breadwinner status poses in the context of a multiplication of available masculine roles in relation to the family, see Gerson (1993, chapter 4). See also Epstein (1992) on the construction of gender differences.

48. Based on an historical analysis of the meaning of manliness, Mosse (1996, chapter 1) identifies as manly virtues competitiveness, quiet strength, stoicism, sang-froid, persistence, adventurousness, independence, sexuality, virility tempered with restraint, and dignity.

49. Bellah (1992, chapter 2). In a national survey on American political culture conducted in 1996, Hunter and Bowman (1996b, table 13) found that while 55 percent of all Americans believe "the United States is the greatest country in the world, better than all others," 59 percent of high school graduates and 49 percent of college graduates believe this.

50. Hunter and Bowman's (1996a, p. 3) survey on American political culture reveals that 87 percent of respondents believe it is important to teach children that America "has had a destiny to set an example for other nations." Ninety percent of high school graduates and 79 percent of college graduates believe this (figure cited in Hunter and Bowman 1996b, table 23J).

51. Nagel (1998).

52. Kanter (1977, p. 63). In general, highly educated people have higher rates of informal social interaction than do less educated people (Curtis and Jackson 1977, p. 173).

53. Lamont (1992, chapter 2). Professionals and managers also value competence and competitiveness. These traits will be discussed in Chapter 3.

54. On various aspects of southern culture, see Reed (1983); Nisbett and Cohen (1996). On differences in conceptions of morality in Indianapolis and New York, see Lamont (1992, chapter 2).

55. Rieder (1985, p. 37).

56. Phonies are defined as people who are not sincere, have no substance, and pretend to know more than they do or be something they are not (Lamont 1992, p. 26). Like professionals and managers, workers are very critical of social climbers and use a moral language to critique them. For the sake of simplicity, this category will be discussed when we address how workers relate to "people above."

57. Milkman's (1997, chapter 3) description of the "culture of grievance" that organizes the relationship between management and workers at the Linden GM plant is an illustration of how conflict avoidance is antinomic to the blue-collar workplace.

58. On this issue, see Kochman (1981, p. 18). His book compares the role of cultural differences in interracial communication, and the meanings and cultural conven-

tions that whites and blacks use as implicit standards (pp. 7–8). Unfortunately, the author confounds racial and class differences, using the word "white" "to represent the cultural patterns and perspective of the dominant social group, also called in other studies white mainstream, white middle class, Anglo, Anglo-American." He uses "blacks" to "represent the ethnic patterns and perspective of black 'community' people called elsewhere ghetto blacks, inner-city blacks, or Afro-Americans" (pp. 13–14). Kochman finds that blacks perceive themselves and are perceived by whites as being the more argumentative group (p. 18). Blacks are also perceived by blacks as being more sincere because they are less dispassionate and less involved in "fronting." Finally, blacks also attach great importance to personal integrity and believe that "core beliefs" should be personal (p. 22).

59. These topics are also discussed in Williams's (1987) ethnography of a suburban blue-collar factory community, focusing on the dynamics of in-group/out-group struggles (pp. 164, 172).

60. Tocqueville ([1835] 1969); Lipset (1979).

61. Results concerning religious affiliations are based on a comparison of the effects of belonging to a mainstream Protestant denomination with belonging to no denomination or to other denominations (Lamont et al. 1996, p. 46). On traditional sexual mores, see Cochran (1991).

62. Three white and four black workers are Evangelical (including Jehovah's Witnesses). In addition, five whites and seven blacks say that religion has an important place in their lives. The percentage of individuals for whom religion is very important is much smaller in my sample than in the American population as a whole. Fifty-eight percent of respondents to a 1990 national Gallup survey described themselves as belonging to this category (Kosmin and Lachman, 1993, p. 9). However, 94 percent believe in God or in a universal spirit, and 71 percent believe in life after death.

63. Fifty-five percent of white and only 6 percent of black interviewees are Catholic. Fifty-six percent of blacks are Evangelical, compared to 3 percent of whites; 3 percent of blacks and 10 percent of whites are mainline Protestants. Altogether, the worker group I interviewed is 35 percent Catholic, 36 percent Protestant (including 25 percent Evangelical), 2 percent Jewish, and 11 percent "others." Fifteen percent declare no religious affiliation. In 1993, 26 percent of the American population was Catholic, 57 Protestant, 1 percent Jewish, 8 percent "others," and 8 percent declared no religious affiliation (United States Bureau of the Census of the Population 1998, table 88, p. 70). See Binder and Reimers (1995) on working class Italian and Irish descendants in the New York area.

64. For a summary description of this historical process, see Davis (1986, chapter 1). Katznelson (1981) offers an alternative explanation having to do with the fragmentation of the work, community, and political universes of workers. For a description of such tightly knit communities, see the classical ethnographies on the American working class, especially Gans (1962) and Kornblum (1974). The working class character of these enclaves is well established. For instance, Glazer and Moynihan (1963) show that in New York City in 1950, two-thirds of second-generation Italian men worked in blue-collar and service positions (p. 206).

65. On symbolic ethnicity, see Gans (1979) and Waters (1990).

66. Note that contrary to Rieder (1985) and others, I do not predefine my object as "white ethnics." Instead, I use an inductive approach, which suggests that the ethnic dimension is not very salient in these workers' collective identity.

67. The 1990 National Survey of Religious Affiliation provides us with data on the religious self-identification of a representative sample of the adult African-American population. Nine percent of the individuals surveyed were Catholics, 82 percent were Protestants, 6 percent declared having "no religion," and the remainder refused to respond or were sprinkled among other religions. Among Protestants, 50 percent were Southern Baptists, 9 percent were Methodists, and the rest belonged to smaller denominations, including Pentecostal (4 percent), Disciples of Christ (4 percent), and Jehovah's Witnesses (2 percent). Figures cited by Kosmin and Lachman (1993, p. 131).

68. These denominations include the African Methodist Episcopal (A.M.E.) Church, the African Methodist Episcopal Zion (A.M.E.Z.) Church, the National Baptist Conventions Incorporated (NBC) and Unincorporated (NBCA), and the Church of God in Christ (COGIC) (Lincoln and Mamiya 1990, p. 1). Black churches, like white churches, attract members of different classes, with the African Methodist Episcopal Church having a larger middle class constituency than do Baptist and Pentecostal churches.

69. Higginbotham (1993) includes a chapter on "The Politics of Respectability" in the black church. She writes: "The church played the single most important role in influencing normative values and distinguishing respectable from non-respectable behavior among working-class blacks during the early twentieth century. Indeed, the competing images of the church and the street symbolized cultural divisions within the mass of the black working poor" (p. 204). Kelley (1994) also points out that the National Baptist Convention has played an important historical role in advertising the importance of hard work and morality as keys to respectability for the race as a whole (p. 24).

70. Along these lines, recent surveys find that blacks embrace religious commitments more than whites. See Smith and Seltzer (1992, p. 30).

71. On these points, see Nelson (1997) and Hannerz (1969, p. 52).

72. Menninger (1973).

73. One would expect these Christian respondents to support traditional morality because "moral asceticism" in sexuality and other realms is still a major principle of inclusion and exclusion in this group. See Ammerman (1987); Hunter (1987); and Roof and McKinney (1987).

74. Brint (1985, p. 389). Church attendance is also a more significant predictor of opposition to premarital sexuality and homosexuality among non-college than college graduates (Lamont et al., 1996, p. 43). This analysis used the 1983 General Social Survey to compare individuals with lower and higher incomes (using a log of annual family income as a continuous measure). I found that individuals with higher incomes are less likely to value the importance of God and to oppose homosexuality than are individuals with lower incomes. Contrary to predictions,

higher-income individuals emphasize children more than lower-income individuals.

75. Wood and Hughes (1984, p. 89). A previous study has also found that the defense of traditional sexual morality (opposing premarital sex and homosexuality, for instance) is more important for working class men and the non-college-educated in general than it is for college graduates (Davis 1982). On moral reforms and moral panic, see Gusfield (1963); Luker (1984); and Cohen (1972). For a short review of the recent literature on the topic, see Cauthen and Jasper (1994).

76. See Lipset (1976, chapter 4). For a critique and reassessment of the working class authoritarianism thesis, see Hamilton (1972).

77. Tony Sansone, the warehouse worker, says he likes people who don't "shyster" you: "They don't tell you one thing and then turn around and totally disregard what they said. Like I say, 'I need a favor: could you pick me up at 10:00?' And they say, 'yeah, yeah' and then 10:00 comes and they're hanging out with their friends. You know, head games." For John Smith, an ironworker, "What really gets on my nerves is people that are deceptive. People that you don't know if they're cheaters or liars. People that lie without fazing them."

78. Lamont (1992, p. 27).

79. A number of authors have stressed the importance of alcohol consumption in male working class culture. This cultural practice has been interpreted alternatively as a form of resistance (Willis 1977), a way of affirming masculinity (Messerschmidt 1993), and a way of coping with the limitations and stresses of working class life (Rubin 1976). Others discuss the topic in the context of primary group formation (Kornblum 1974). Halle (1987) suggests that alcohol consumption is spread widely enough in this group to require distinguishing between alcoholics and hard drinkers.

80. On cultural behaviors as pollution, see Douglas (1966).

81. A bank supply salesman, who describes himself as a supporter of human decency, says he will respect you if you "behave in a law-abiding way to gain what you acquire. If you figure that the end justifies the means, then no." Similarly, when asked what values he received from his parents, a mechanic said "normal American. A little respect for the other guy. Follow the rules. Obey the police, follow the Ten Commandments. That's about it."

82. For other workers, vulgarity is the trait they dislike most. A fireman says he dislikes people who are vulgar, that is, "curse a lot, hand signals, you know, say inappropriate things to people," while a civil servant defines vulgarity as using "foul words" that are not in the dictionary. Attitudes toward women are also mentioned frequently as a sign of moral character. A man who works in a recycling plant criticizes a former friend, saying "he had a real nice girlfriend, and he treated her like a dog, he got two kids from her, and he wouldn't marry her . . . they lived together, but he still treats her [badly]. He's like using her . . . He'd do a lot of things that would make her get mad at him to get in an argument for her to leave."

83. Along these lines, see the study of everyday understanding of legality provided by Ewick and Silbey (1998). They suggest that low-status individuals, including blacks,

are more likely than others to define themselves as "against the law" and to be aware of the inner workings of the legal system (chapter 7).

84. The percentage of drinkers with dependence problems is slightly higher among high school graduates and individuals with less than a high school diploma than it is among those with some college education or a college degree (Hilton and Clark 1991, p. 117).

85. On this concept, see Jackall (1988, p. 101). Baumgartner (1988) has proposed the notion of "moral minimalism" to discuss morality in the context of conflict avoidance (pp. 124–129).

86. This form of moral pragmatism is analyzed as a form of workplace resistance by Wellman (1995).

87. On this topic, see Gilman (1985) and Stoler (1991).

88. Specialists of regional cultures in the United States provide evidence that southerners generally attach more importance to traditional moral values than do residents of other regions (Reed 1983). In particular, they have been shown to be more oriented toward home, family, and church (Marsden et al., 1982).

89. This is confirmed by Kochman's (1981) classroom study of interpersonal style among black and white students, which showed that blacks put much more emphasis on egalitarianism and downplay status differences among group members (pp. 66 and 76). Surveys also show large black/white differences in support for social responsibility, defined as a concern for limiting inequality and meeting basic human needs. This buttresses the idea that blacks value solidarity and generosity more than whites (Bobo 1991, p. 80).

90. On this issue, see Stack (1974).

91. According to Nelson (1997), "Conditions of oppression and marginality often produce an exploitative individualism as people try to get as much as they can from one another without themselves appearing vulnerable to manipulation." In his ethnography of a mostly African-American housing project in St. Louis, Lee Rainwater (1970) observed that "[t]echniques of relating to other people are markedly defensive: individuals manipulate and exploit others where possible and at the same time try to ward off manipulation and exploitation by others. This contributes a pervasive tone of guardedness and mistrustfulness to interpersonal relations within the community" (p. 174).

92. Regarding black working class men, Franklin (1992) writes: "I am convinced, because of numerous conversations I have had with black men on street corners and in parks, barbershops, and other gathering places, that these men's friendships are warmer and more intimate than the ones reported by upwardly mobile black men and those reported in the literature. I contend that the sources of warmth and intimacy may lie in their shared political ideology" (p. 206). On intimacy in black culture, see also Williams (1988, p. 4) and Mithun (1973, p. 28). Also, at the social-psychological level, comparative analyses of the cognitive styles of black and white children conclude that blacks are more other-oriented than whites: they are more emotional, more proficient in nonverbal expression, and have keener senses of justice and altruism and lower object orientations than whites (Hale 1982, pp. 42–43, 69).

93. These range from the anecdotal (in, for instance, the childhood memories of Henry Louis Gates 1994) to organizational forms described in writings on movements to uplift the race (Meier, Rudwick, and Broderick 1971; Gaines 1996; Van Deburg 1992).

94. For example: Fordham (1996, p. 71). On the concept of "imagined community," see Introduction, note 8. See also Stack (1974); Malson (1983); Staples (1974); Fordham (1996, pp. 72–73); and Taylor (1990). On fictive kinship as a medium of boundary maintenance vis-à-vis whites, see Fordham and Ogbu (1986, p. 185).

95. Data cited in Jackman (1994, pp. 122, 186–187). Experimental social psychologists have found that when black identification competes with one or two other identifications, black identification tends to be the strongest. Also, age identification is stronger than sex and class identification for this group (Gurin, Miller, and Gurin 1980, p. 37).

96. Dawson (1994) uses the term "black utility heuristic" to point to the importance of racial status group interests in individual political evaluation. On the larger question of shared racial interest, see Chapter 2. On the origins of a sense of community of interest for blacks, see Chapter 3. Dawson links these common interests to the shared experiences of economic disadvantage, discrimination, and segregation.

97. On shared memories of oppression, see Harris (1998). When asked "what are the things about black people that make you feel the most proud," 24 percent of respondents to the 1980 National Survey of Black Americans chose "group pride, identity, togetherness, and mutual support," and 22 percent chose "endurance, striving, and progress made"–these are the items that were chosen most frequently. Similarly, in explaining to their children what it is to be black, 26 percent have told them about the importance of racial pride and heritage, and 23 percent have told them about the necessity to "excel and survive." Jaynes and Williams (1989, p. 198).

98. But some black workers put human solidarity above racial solidarity. It is the case for Larry Wright, a black park maintenance worker, who is a quarter white and a quarter native American. A Vietnam veteran, he says that for him "solidarity means you love everybody . . . After you've seen as much death [in Vietnam] and stuff as I did, you just leave [racial differences] along. You try to get along with everybody, that is the bottom line."

99. Drake and Cayton (1962, pp. 394–395).

100. Thompson (1998).

101. On Afrocentrism and black nationalism as worldviews, see Omi and Winant (1986, pp. 92–95). Fifty-six percent of African-American respondents to a 1980 survey disagree that parents should give their children African names, 51 percent that black women should not date white men, and 51 percent that blacks should always vote for black candidates when they run. Also, 47 percent believe that blacks should shop in black-owned stores when possible, and 42 percent believe that black children should learn an African language. Jaynes and Williams (1989, p. 198).

102. Wilson (1978).

103. Along these lines, Wuthnow (1991) and Ostrower (1995) provide detailed analyses of the individualistic rationales developed by ordinary and wealthy citizens for giving or engaging in institutionalized philanthropic activities; the evidence they present suggests that the discourse on civic solidarity is marginal among available American representations of giving.

104. These collectivist and individualist types of altruistic actions are key components of what Ammerman (1987) describes as middle class "Golden Rule Christianity" (p. 198).

105. This is not surprising because involvement in formal organizations in general tends to be correlated with level of education. See evidence cited by Wilson and Musick (1997, p. 699). The college-educated tend to attend church more frequently than do the non-college-educated (p. 700), and religiosity increases the likelihood of providing help to others through religious channels (Wuthnow 1994, p. 253).

106. Blacks spend more time than whites helping their friends but slightly less time helping primary kin and engaging in formal volunteering, due in part to a lack of resources and time. See Gallagher (1994, p. 573). However, evidence concerning the relative importance of the involvement of blacks and whites in formal volunteering organizations is mixed. After socioeconomic status is controlled, some studies find no race difference (notably Carson 1989 and Latting 1990, while others find that blacks engage in more volunteering than whites (for a review, see Smith 1984, p. 249). Still others find that blacks engage less in formal volunteering than do whites (Wilson and Musick 1997, p. 706).

107. Lincoln and Mamiya (1990, p. 5).

108. In the words of Lincoln and Mamiya (1990), "the core values of black culture like freedom, justice, equality . . . and racial parity at all levels of human intercourse are raised to ultimate levels and legitimated by the black sacred cosmos. Although this cosmos is largely Afro-Christian in nature due to its religious history, it has also erupted in other black militant, nationalistic and non-Christian movements" (p. 7).

109. Among the whites in this study, 13 are union members, 30 are not, and information is missing for 2 interviewees. Among blacks, 20 are union members, 3 used to be, 5 are not, and information is missing on 2 respondents. Half of the black workers who are union members are active as shop stewards. That fewer white than black interviewees are unionized might account in part for (and be the effect of) the hold of individualism on their worldviews: union jobs often involve job security, which is likely to facilitate collectivist strategies. However, roughly the same percentage of white and black workers (a fourth) work in the public sector, which generally offers more job security.

110. On the changes in popular opinion that have accompanied these strategic reorientations, see the analysis by democratic pollster Greenberg (1995).

111. Portes and Sensenbrenner (1993).

112. A survey conducted by Rokeach (1973) at the end of the sixties shows differences in values between whites and blacks that overlap with my results; he finds that equality is ranked considerably higher by blacks than by whites. Other less impor-

tant differences are that blacks rank higher than whites in having a comfortable life, social recognition, and in being clean, ambitious, and obedient. Whites rank higher than blacks in having a sense of accomplishment, mature love, family security, national security, and in being logical, loving, and responsible (p. 69).

113. A 1990 New York Times/CBS News poll asked a sample of New Yorkers if "the government deliberately . . . investigates black elected officials in order to discredit them," if "the government deliberately makes sure that drugs are easily available in poor black neighborhoods in order to harm black people," and if "the virus that causes AIDS was deliberately created in a laboratory in order to infect black people." Over three-quarters of black respondents, but only one-third of whites, thought the first charge was true or "might be true"; 60 percent of blacks and less than 2 percent of whites found the second charge plausible or convincing. Finally, 30 percent of blacks, but only 5 percent of whites, were willing to entertain the third charge. Cited by Hochschild (1995b, p. 6). Other authors argue that poor blacks are now more culturally distinct from "mainstream America" than they were 30 years ago (see Anderson 1990 and Massey and Denton 1993, chapter 6).

114. For instance, 85 percent of blacks, compared to 34 percent of whites, agreed with the decision of the jury in the O. J. Simpson trial (data cited by Hochschild, 1995a, p. 11). White respondents to a 1995 national survey believed that blacks represented 23.8 percent of the U.S. population while blacks thought they represented 25.9 percent of the population in the United States. In fact, they represented 11.8 percent at the time of the survey. When asked whether they agree that "people of other races can't really understand the way my race sees things," 35 percent of whites and 57 percent of blacks agree (cited by Hunter and Bowman 1996a, p. 40). While 41 percent of high school graduates agree with this statement, only 29 percent of college graduates agree (Hunter and Bowman 1996b, table 41b). Furthermore, 27 percent of blacks and 18 percent of whites agree that "in political discussion, a person's ethnic or group identity is more important than the things [he or she says]" (table 41f). Twenty-three percent of low- to middle-income laborers and 17 percent of professionals share this view. Finally, 61 percent of white respondents to a 1992 national survey believed that whites and blacks have "more common ground," while 54 percent of blacks believed this. A large minority of 32 percent of whites and 39 percent of blacks believed that the two groups have more that is not in common (Anti-Defamation League of B'Nai B'rith 1993, p. 43).

115. My conclusions coincide with those of Sigelman and Welch (1991), who end their study of white and black explanations of racial inequality with the verdict that the two groups occupy separate but largely overlapping worlds. This position is different from that of Hochschild (1995a), who concludes her extensive review of research on black and white attitudes toward the American dream by stating that the two groups resist separatism and uphold similar values (p. 248). My position is also different from that of Labov (1986; 1993), who documents a divergence in linguistic patterns between whites and blacks, suggesting that the cultures of the groups are increasingly differentiated.

Other studies find racial divergence particularly on issues that involve the treatment of blacks by American society. For instance, a 1994 national survey on intergroup relations found that while 63 percent of whites are convinced that blacks "really suffer from a lot of discrimination," 76 percent of blacks believe that whites "are insensitive to other people and have a long history of bigotry and prejudice" (National Conference 1994, pp. 6, 14). Moreover, attitudinal survey research shows that blacks and whites agree on what contemporary American society should be but not on what it actually *is* (DiMaggio, Evans, and Bryson 1996, p. 741). Convergence is found on feelings toward liberals, conservatives, and the poor, and on views on aid for minorities, crime, justice, and abortion (p. 723).

116. This portrayal of blacks as immoral reappears intermittently in the media and popular opinion in such instances as the Hill-Thomas hearing, the O. J. Simpson trial, and the association between crime and blackness suggested by the use of the Willie Horton ad during the 1988 electoral campaign (for instance, Mendelberg 1997). On the broader issue of the media's role in diffusing images of social groups, see Gilens (1996) and Entman (1992). Examples of American politicians portraying blacks as immoral were found in the "Contract with America" (which aimed at restoring American family values to lower the increased crime rate, illegitimacy rate, and homosexuality) and in the Welfare Reform Bill of 1995 (Watts 1997, p. 409).

Note that my findings also offer support to important recent studies of black working class culture that have documented the centrality of decency and responsibility in the worlds of black workers. In particular, Duneier (1992) shows the importance of respectability for the black working class (chapters 8 and 9), and Anderson (1990) demonstrates the importance of decency and of establishing respect in black communities. Also, see Anderson (1978) on respect (i.e., a shared sense of who can say what to whom) as the basis for the social order in the black community.

117. This confirms earlier predictions (Lamont 1992, p. 192).

118. Hunter and Bowman's (1996a) study suggests that the American middle class is not especially worried by the economy, their jobs, or their finances; "rather, what they fear and what upsets them is the sense that everything they have lived for—their Judeo-Christian God, their family life, their moral commitments, their work ethic, and the public school system that would pass their beliefs on to their children—is in decline and possibly disappearing. It's not a 'fear of falling' that haunts the middle class but a fear of the curtain falling upon their way of life . . . due to developments in the culture they feel but do not quite understand . . . and is being taken away—in part by the ineptitude of the nation's political leadership; in part by the machinations of the governing elite" (pp. 12–13).

119. Hunter and Bowman (1996a, chapter 2) and Jackall (1988).

120. Between 1970 and 1990, convergence was found in attitudes toward women's roles and feelings toward conservatives, abortion, sex education, and legal restrictions on divorce (DiMaggio, Evans, and Bryson 1996, p. 723).

121. For instance, Davis (1982) uses the 1972–1980 cumulative General Social Surveys to investigate whether educational attainment, respondent's occupation, and father's occupation affect a variety of attitudes and behavior. He finds that occupational stratum has nontrivial associations with about one-third of the items, but the magnitudes are small and the associations are concentrated in two clusters, cyni-

cism and job-related topics. Education is stronger than class as a net predictor for most associations. Davis concludes that the notion of class culture receives little support, given the weak magnitude of association, the disappointing effect of occupation, and the lack of agreement between occupational and educational effects. As argued in the Introduction, the close association of education, life chance, and class makes me reluctant to come to such a strong conclusion.

122. See Beck (1992). Other factors include the decomposition of class hierarchies (Clark and Lipset 1991), the greater availability of high culture across regions (Blau 1989), the impact of the media that define their audience in terms of lifestyles (Crane 1991), the omnivorousness of the college-educated population (Peterson and Kern 1996), the increasing importance of race, gender, and age as alternative bases of stratification (Hall 1991), the weakened link between structural position, consciousness, and political action (Hobsbawm 1981), and the impact of high social and geographic mobility and political decentralization on weakened high-culture tradition (Lamont and Lareau 1988).

2. Euphemized Racism

1. Racism is defined here as "an ethnic group's assertion of . . . a privileged or protected status vis-à-vis members of another group or groups who are thought . . . to possess a set of socially relevant characteristics that disqualify them from full membership in a community or citizenship in a nation state" (Fredrickson 1997, p. 85). Goldberg (1993, p. 98) defines racism similarly, as a rhetoric aimed at promoting exclusion based on racial membership and produced by a dominant group against a dominated group. I use the term "racist rhetoric" broadly to refer to exclusive discourse aimed at racial or ethnic groups.

On racism and the boundary between in-group and out-group or between "us" and "them," see Sumner (1906); Merton (1972); Banton (1983); Guillaumin (1972); and Memmi (1965). Social psychologists working on group categorization also focus on "us" and "them" segmentations (for instance, Moscovici 1984 and Tajfel and Turner 1985). The works of Barth (1969) and Horowitz (1985) also center on the strength of boundaries and on how feelings of communality are defined in opposition to the perceived identity of other racial and ethnic groups.

This relational approach is akin to closure approaches in the fields of nationalism, citizenship, and immigration, which attempt to establish rules of membership and boundary work (for instance, Brubaker 1992; Favell 1997a; and Zolberg and Woon 1999). This approach is also close to that of sociologists who, following Herbert Blumer, understand racism as resulting from threats to group positioning. This approach "shifts study and analysis from a preoccupation with feelings as lodged in individuals to a concern with the relationship of racial groups . . . [and with] the collective process by which a racial group comes to define and redefine another racial group" (Blumer 1958, p. 3). Influential scholars using related approaches include Bobo and Hutchings (1996); Sidanius (1993); Feagin and Vera (1995); Rieder (1985); Roediger (1991); and Wellman (1993). On race and cultural membership, see Praeger (1987).

2. This is part of an internal identification process, which, along with group categorization, are the two processes central to the formation of group identity (Jenkins 1996).

3. Weber (1978, vol. 1, p. 42).

4. Following Patterson (1977, p. 197), I define the tradition of universalism as "the idea of the brotherhood of mankind, the psychic unity of the human race, and the equality of [people's] worth."

5. A similar argument is made by Wellman (1993) and Feagin and Vera (1995).

6. Following Sniderman and Hagen (1985), I consider these descriptions of categories of individuals to be revealing of broader social and political attitudes. They write: "The average citizen, though he (or she) may know little about politics, knows whom he likes, and still more important perhaps, whom he dislikes. This can be a sufficient basis for figuring out a consistent policy stance" (p. 16). In their view, this is particularly true of racial attitudes and of race-targeted policies.

   Again, the bulk of the interviews I have conducted concern how individuals draw boundaries between the people they like and dislike, feel inferior and superior to, and feel similar to and different from. Respondents were encouraged to answer these questions in reference to people in general and to concrete individuals they know at work and elsewhere. Discussions of racism generally emerged while exploring these issues, but some interviewees were also probed specifically on racial differences and racism at the end of our meeting.

7. This focus on evidence is inspired by the work of Boltanski and Thévenot (1991). They are concerned with the arguments used by members of political communities to establish that particular positions serve the common good. In this context, the definition of the boundaries of a community of reference and the principles upon which similarity between members is established (for instance, morality, genetic features, intelligence) are important (Thévenot and Lamont 2000; Benatouil 1999). The concern with the mobilization of evidence in the establishment of facts is also inspired by the work of Latour (1987) and Callon (1986).

8. I use Aptheker's (1992) definition of antiracism as rhetoric aimed at disproving racial inferiority.

9. However, we do have a survey-based literature on whites' and blacks' accounts of racial inequality (Schuman et al. 1997); a historical literature on the struggle against racism in the abolitionist and the civil rights movements (Aptheker 1992; McAdams 1988; and McPherson 1975); and a study of contemporary antiracist organizations (Omi 1998).

10. Essed (1991) analyzes perceptions of racism among 50 academic and professional Surinamese women in the Netherlands and African-American women in the United States. Her analysis of cultural racism shows that white middle class standards are imposed on blacks and define minority culture as cultural deficiency, social inadequacy, or technological underdevelopment (p. 14). Another notable study was performed by Wetherell and Potter (1992); they combine a discourse analysis approach with a concern for the larger script offered by Australian society. Also, see Van Dijk's (1993) study of racism in elite discourse for its focus on

discursive aspects such as the structure of models in memory, semantic macro-structures, and argumentative structures.

11. The social-psychological and survey-based literatures on race exhibit a clear bias toward examining whites' stereotypes of racial minorities. This point is made by Sigelman and Welch (1991, p. 3); Roediger (1998); and hooks (1997). I am not aware of any contemporary ethnographic and interview-based studies of blacks' perceptions of whites beside Fordham (1996), which deals with this topic only tangentially.

12. For the purpose at hand, I classified workers as "racist" or "antiracist" despite the fact that most people exhibit both racist and antiracist sentiments (on this topic, see Wetherell and Potter 1992, p. 197). I categorized them based on the preponderant type of argument they made concerning racial differences during the course of the interview: if they argue that racial groups are unequal, I classified them as racist, whereas if they mainly argue that racial groups are equal, I classified them as nonracist or antiracist. For the purposes of this book, I do not use the world "racism" to refer to blacks' negative statements concerning whites. I prefer to reserve this term to designate a rhetoric contributing to the reproduction of unequal relationships between a dominant and a dominated group—which, of course, is not the position of blacks toward whites in the contemporary United States.

13. I particularly point to competing historical frames that are part of the rhetorical resources that American society makes available to its citizens. In this, I follow Wetherell and Potter (1992, p. 197), who write that social scientists should focus not on whether there is conflict "between a feeling and a value, or between psychological drive and socially accepted expressions, or between emotions and politics, but between competing frameworks for articulating social, political, and ethical questions," such as those offered by liberal and egalitarian ideologies. Jackman (1994, p. 268) is also concerned with the importance of available repertoires for analyzing racism.

14. This argument resonates with that of Rubin (1976, p. 7), who argues that many of the behaviors and attitudes of working class individuals are realistic responses to, and results of, their structural position.

15. Using the 1990 General Social Survey, Smith (1990, p. 90) shows that blacks are perceived by whites and members of other ethnic groups as being most different from whites in their ability to be self-supporting. Along the same lines, 21 percent of nonblacks who participated in a 1993 national survey agreed that African-American men enjoy living on welfare (National Conference 1994, p. 72).

16. Kinder and Mendelberg (1995, p. 407). In the early seventies, a considerably higher percentage of the population perceived blacks as being lazy: 69 percent of whites surveyed in a 1972 national study considered blacks' continued disproportionate poverty a result of their not trying hard enough; 52 percent of whites explained black poverty by the dysfunctionality of black culture (Sniderman and Hagen 1985, p. 30).

17. Similarly, Wellman (1993) shows that white racist rhetoric describes properties blacks are lacking, calls blacks responsible for current problems, and demands

changes in blacks (not in whites). Contrary to Wellman, I emphasize workers' affirmation of their identity by blaming blacks rather than their defensive responses.

18. On the central role of "passing on advantages" in the reproduction of racial and class inequality, see the ongoing work of DiTomaso (2000).

19. Figures cited by Patterson (1997, p. 148).

20. Sixty-one percent of white respondents to a 1992 national survey believed that whites and blacks have "more common ground," while 54 percent of blacks shared this belief. A large minority of 32 percent of whites and 39 percent of blacks believed that the two groups have more that is not in common (Anti-Defamation League of B'Nai B'rith 1993, p. 43).

21. See Bennett (1993). For a discussion of this literature, see Sandel (1996, pp. 324–328).

22. Hunter (1991; 1994) argues that American society is deeply divided between relativists and traditionalists. In contrast, sociologists like Wolfe (1997, p. 276) and DiMaggio, Evans, and Bryson (1996) argue that although Americans have moral principles for themselves, they are fairly tolerant on most moral issues. The latter study concludes that any culture war that exists in American society is largely a creation of the media and not of irreconcilable moral differences among citizens.

23. For a description of debates about family values during the Clinton administration, see Stacey (1996, chapters 3 and 4). For an analysis of the impact of conceptions of family morality on the conservative/liberal political divide, see Lakoff (1996).

24. Roediger (1991, pp. 13–14).

25. Kinder and Mendelberg (1995, p. 407).

26. In surveys cited by Sigelman and Tuch (1997, p. 88), 50 percent of respondents considered blacks to be aggressive.

27. Rieder (1985) understands the moral criticisms of blacks by middle and working class white ethnic Italians in terms of resistance to black demands. He views these criticisms as expressions of a defense of traditional values, family, and neighborhood (p. 42), a form of nostalgia (p. 93), and a desire to defend their territory in the context of more frequent physical encounters that are perceived to threaten law and order (p. 67). He suggests that for these white Italians, race is a "metaphor for vague indignities" (p. 93), which are considered to be incompatible with family life and patriotic devotion. The presence of blacks threatens their precarious middle class status (p. 97). A similar argument is made by Rubin (1994). She explains white workers' racism as a result of the anger and resentment generated by the deterioration of their condition (p. 239). See also Bobo and Hutchings (1996). My explanation for white racism is more multidimensional than those proposed by these authors as it takes into consideration the supply of cultural repertoires as well as the structural conditions that push workers to draw on aspects of these repertoires.

28. Sidanius et al. (1997, p. 118).

29. Kinder and Mendelberg (1995, p. 407).

30. The tendency of blacks to rank other blacks on a scale of prestige based on skin color has also declined since World War II (Blackwell 1975, p. 70).

31. For an interesting analysis of the conditions explaining the success of *The Bell Curve,* see Fassin (1997).

32. Accordingly, Simmel (1978, pp. 442–443) wrote that money is a "basically democratic leveling social form" that functions in "complete indifference to individual qualities."

33. Wellman (1993, chapter 6) remarks that several of his respondents view market position or consumption as racial equalizers. For instance, home ownership is considered to make people equal. Market arguments posit that people are responsible for their lower position in a hierarchical system (p. 57); these arguments valorize the achievements of individuals who have a certain level of socioeconomic success (p. 168) and reinforce faith in the American dream notion that a person's success should be a prime criterion of evaluation.

34. See Wilentz (1984b).

35. Esping-Anderson (1990).

36. In contrast, nonracists are not willing to generalize from the individual to the entire race—a categorization process typical of racial stereotyping (Hamilton and Trolier 1986). For a more general review of the literature on stereotyping, see Stangor and Lange (1994).

37. This position is different from rationalist universalism, which considers people to be equal because of their perfectibility and ability to make moral judgments. Patterson (1977, p. 215) links rationalist universalism to the Stoics and Alexander the Great; Alexander would have developed this notion to ground the unity of a multitude of people and races in their perfectibility through rationality.

38. On cultural relativism, see Lévi-Strauss (1973, pp. 367–422) and Taguieff (1988). On multiculturalism, see Taylor (1992). For an excellent overview of American debates surrounding multiculturalism, see Lacorne (1997).

39. Along these lines, fully 65 percent of the respondents to the 1993 General Social Survey conducted by the National Opinion Research Corporation agreed or strongly agreed with the statement that "it is a shame when traditional American literature is ignored while other works are promoted because they are by women or by members of minority groups" (DiMaggio and Bryson 1995). Verter (1994) finds that the majority of Americans uphold a traditional canon to the exclusion of alternatives.

40. On race recognizance as a form of multiculturalism, see Frankenberg (1993). Her book uses interviews with 30 Bay Area white women to contrast three types of discourse about racial differences: essentialist racism, stressing biological inequality; color evasiveness, promoting assimilation and downplaying cultural and biological differences; and race cognizance, affirming the cultural autonomy of blacks and recognizing that race makes a difference in people's lives. Frankenberg argues that of these three types of coexisting discourse, color evasiveness predominates. Her typology is not detailed enough to describe the antiracist arguments that emerge from my data, such as the claim concerning the universality of human nature. She attaches great importance to race-recognizance arguments affirming the "differentness" of people of color (pp. 13–14)—again, a type of argument absent from my interviews. This might be due to her purposeful overrepresentation of

women involved in feminism and antiracism movements. Her 30 respondents, all of whom live in San Francisco and Santa Cruz and 8 of whom are lesbian, might be involved in a distinctive radical subculture in which race recognizance is particularly valued.

41. On tolerance and the broad range of taste of the college-educated, see Lamont (1992, p. 105) and Bryson (1996). Peterson and Kern (1996) coined the term "cultural omnivorousness" to label this latter phenomenon.

42. Symbolic racism "represents a form of resistance to change in the racial status quo based on moral feelings that blacks violate such traditional American values as individualism and self-reliance, the work ethic, obedience and discipline" (Kinder and Sears 1981, p. 416).

43. Pettigrew (1989).

44. This notion refers to whites' convictions concerning fairness, justice, and racial equality, as well as whites' feelings of discomfort, uneasiness, disgust, and fear toward blacks, occurring commensurately with an aversion to racism because of their commitment to equality (Dovidio 1998).

45. McConahay (1986) defines the principal tenets of modern racism as follows: "(1) Discrimination is a thing of the past because blacks now have the freedom to compete on the marketplace and to enjoy those things they can afford; (2) blacks are pushing too hard, too fast, and into places where they are not wanted; (3) these tactics and demands are unfair; (4) therefore recent gains are undeserved and the prestige granting institutions of society are giving blacks more attention and the concomitant status than they deserve. Two other tenets are added to this psychological syllogism: Racism is bad and the other beliefs do not constitute racism because these beliefs are empirical facts" (pp. 92–93). In an earlier text McConahay and Hough (1976) associated this form of racism not with a sense of threat to the personal welfare of whites but to fears for the survival of the nation. These fears translate into symbolic acts like voting against black candidates. For these authors, American civil Protestantism (hard work, individualism, sexual repression, delay of gratification), negative feelings toward blacks, and socialization in laissez-faire political conservatism are central in defining that which is rejected by modern racism.

46. Bobo and Smith (1998, pp. 20–21) also proposed the term "laissez-faire racism" to label new patterns of belief that involve "acceptance of negative stereotypes of African-Americans, a denial of discrimination as a current societal problem, and attribution of primary responsibility for blacks' disadvantage to blacks themselves."

47. Using Lickert scales, theorists of symbolic racism measure how strongly people believe in certain statements representative of symbolic racism. McConahay and Hough (1976) identify several dimensions of symbolic racism without providing empirical evidence of their levels of salience. Elsewhere, Kinder and Sears write that symbolic racism rests on traditional Protestant values, including "hard work, individualism, thrift, punctuality, sexual repression and delay of gratification, as opposed to laziness, seeking favoritism and handouts, impulsivity, and so on" (1981, p. 72). However, the importance of these values is not documented within

the context of a broader set of racial representations. In their more recent work, Kinder and Sanders (1996, p. 106) prefer the concept of racial resentment to that of racial symbolism, highlighting the notion that whites resent blacks for wanting favors while not trying hard enough. Symbolic racism is contrasted with "old-fashioned racism" through the ideas of the divine origin of racial differences, lower ability of blacks, support for housing and school segregation, and opposition to interracial marriage (p. 26). One of the many criticisms of this theory is that "the traditional American value of individualism does not foster either antipathy to blacks or opposition to public policies intended to help them: on the other hand, traditional authoritarian values like obedience and conformity promote both" (Sniderman and Piazza 1993, p. 6).

48. Sears et al. (1997, p. 49) recognize that they have yet to unravel which nonracial dispositions are involved in symbolic racism.

49. Thompson (1998).

50. Ehrenreich (1989, chapter 3) has also argued that the Republican Party has fueled working class resentment of the new class by bringing together racism, anti-intellectualism, and populism while promoting the moral concerns of the New Right relative to family values, abortion, patriotism, private schooling, and religion.

51. See also Entman (1992).

52. McClosky and Zaller (1984, p. 83). The authors do not provide information concerning the year the survey was conducted. On this topic, see also Hochschild (1981).

53. Schuman et al. (1997, pp. 104–105). This figure is for 1972, the last year that the question was included in the General Social Survey. Nevertheless, questions that pertain to the implementation of antidiscrimination policies "always reveal a much lower level of support than for the principles themselves" (p. 197).

54. Roediger (1991, pp. 13–14) explains white workers' construction of blacks as libidinous by their need to cope with fear of dependency. In this account, workers' fear is not sufficiently grounded in the cultural and structural context in which workers live.

55. On the importance of perceptual salience in framing comparisons, see Stanger and Lange (1994). On the isolation of professionals, see Laumann (1973). Note that upper middle class isolation can encourage tolerance, indifference, or stereotyping, as it may leave individuals "susceptible to propaganda, rumor, and their own stereotypes—to 'fears of imagination,'" as Gordon Allport once put it (Kinder and Mendelberg (1995, p. 420).

56. Meertens and Pettigrew (1997, p. 67).

57. In a 1992 national survey of 800 American adults aged 18 and older, the least prejudiced group included 67 percent of those with post-graduate degrees, 54 percent of those with college degrees, and 38 percent of those with high school degrees or less (Anti-Defamation League of B'Nai B'rith 1993, p. 19).

58. Bobo and Kluegel (1993).

59. On consumption and cultural membership, see Ong (1996). See also Molnar and Lamont (2000). On the importance of consumption for cultural membership among poor black residents of Philadelphia, see Nightingale (1993).

60. For political philosopher Judith Shklar (1991, p. 3), American citizenship has primarily involved the right to earn a living.

61. Hochschild (1995a, p. 26) describes this as a tenet of the American dream: "people start the pursuit of success with varying advantages, but no one is barred from the pursuit."

62. These contested meanings of racial uplift are the object of Gaines (1996).

63. Cited in Meier, Rudwick, and Broderick (1971, p. 5).

64. Meier, Rudwick, and Broderick (1971, p. 11).

65. Van Deburg (1992, p. 195). This soul style is also defined in opposition to the "robot-like mannerisms of 'uptight' white people" (p. 197). On the meaning of "soul" as an expression of essential black identity and belonging, see Hannerz (1968).

66. The Washington, D.C., African-American high school students studied by Fordham and Ogbu (1986) also point to the disciplined self of whites when they define the meaning of "acting white." Indeed, these students view the following behaviors as distinctively white: spending a lot of time in the library studying, working hard to get good grades in school, getting good grades in school, and being on time. Other cultural practices labeled "acting white" include listening to white music, classical music, and white radio stations, having a party with no music, going to the opera, ballet, and the Smithsonian, reading and writing poetry, going to a Rolling Stones concert at the Capital Center, doing volunteer work, camping, hiking, or mountain climbing, having cocktails or a cocktail party, speaking standard English, and putting on airs. The authors of the study argue that blacks "develop a sense of collective identity and a sense of people-hood in opposition to the social identity of white Americans because of the way white Americans treat them in economic, political, social, and psychological domains." See also Fordham (1996).

67. Crocker and Major (1989, p. 616). I thank Nancy DiTomaso for bringing this literature to my attention. Sidanius (1993) also discusses strategies that are not relevant here, such as defection, social competition through mass movement and rebellion, and avoiding comparison with the high-status group.

68. Van Deburg (1992, p. 260).

69. Sigelman and Tuch (1997, p. 88). These beliefs are shared across the population. However, the belief that whites have positive stereotypes of blacks (pertaining to religion, athletic abilities, and parenthood) is more widely spread among black men, older blacks, and lower-income blacks than among black women, younger blacks, and higher-income blacks (p. 96). Along these lines, a few authors have noted that historically blacks have often lived in the shadow of whites and been witnesses of their character. This experience has led them to associate whiteness "with the terrible, the terrifying, and the terrorizing" (hooks 1997, p. 170). Citing Aptheker, Roediger (1998, p. 10) also discusses the importance of studying myths of African-American superiority to whites, constructed around themes such as "the lynched above the lyncher" or "the Crucified above imperial Rome."

70. The National Conference of Christians and Jews (1994, p. 15).

71. Cited by Sigelman and Welch (1991, p. 184).

72. Jaynes and Williams (1989, p. 198) also note that blacks believe endurance and making progress are among the qualities that set their group apart and that are worth preserving. Other such qualities are group cohesion and striving.

73. Classical discussions of resistance in the context of black/white relations are found in Levine (1977); Lewis (1991); and Stuckey (1987). Building on the work of Williams (1980), it has been suggested that black popular culture is more alternative than oppositional, since it generally does not attack the social hegemony of whites.

74. My findings complement those of historian Robin Kelley, Jr.(1994) and others who have advocated the importance of analyzing black identity by considering how feelings of mutuality and fellowship were constructed and what is viewed as distinctively black by blacks. This includes pleasures derived from black popular culture (p. 45).

75. Brewer's (1986) social identity theory suggests that "[p]ressures to evaluate one's own group positively through in-group/out-group comparison lead social groups to attempt to differentiate themselves from each other." This process of differentiation aims "to maintain and achieve superiority over an out-group on some dimension" (Tajfel and Turner 1985, pp. 16–17). Sidanius (1993) argues that this in-group bias operates more for higher status groups than for lower status ones.

76. This resonates with Newman's (1993) study of downward mobility among New Jersey residents. She writes: "American culture is allergic to the idea that impersonal forces control individual destiny. Rather we prefer to think of our lives as products of our own efforts. Through hard work, innate ability, and competition, the good prosper and the weak drop by the wayside. Accordingly, the end results in peoples' lives—their occupation, material possessions, and the recognition accorded by friends and associates—are proof of the underlying stuff of which they are made. Of course, when the fairy tale comes true, the flip side of meritocratic individualism emerges with full force. Those who prosper—the morally superior—deserve every bit of their material comfort" (p. 89).

77. Du Bois (1935, p. 124). Cited by Kelley (1994, p. 42). See also Harding (1981).

78. Condit and Lucaites (1993, p. 192).

79. Lincoln and Mamiya (1990, p. 4) describe differences in emphasis in black and white worship by pointing to "the greater weight given [by blacks] to the biblical view of the importance of human personality and human equality implicit in 'children of God.' The trauma of being officially defined by the U.S. Constitution as 'three-fifths' human and treated in terms of that understanding, the struggle of the African-American people to affirm and establish their humanity and their worth as persons has a long history."

80. Lincoln and Mamiya (1990, p. 4) suggest that blacks consider their Christianity to be more Christian than that of whites because it is based on "the rock of anti-discrimination" and oriented toward the search for freedom. For more on the relationship between religion and the struggle against racism, see Baer (1984); Baer and Singer (1992); and Wilmore (1983).

81. In pristine Christianity, "the divinity of each person makes evident not only his or her worth but makes it necessary to treat each human being as an end in himself or herself" (Patterson 1977, p. 226).

82. Readings of the Bible were widely used to justify white racism by feeding the notion that Americans are chosen people especially favored by God. See Smith (1997, p. 24).

83. Miles (1989, chapter 1) suggests that this account gained in popularity between the sixteenth and nineteenth centuries, after which it was superseded by scientific racism viewing the human species as divided into permanent and discrete groups.

84. Condit and Lucaites (1993, p. 6).

85. The term "universalism" is used differently across sociological literatures. The functionalist literature compares cultural orientations cross-nationally using the "universalistic/particularistic" pattern variable. Universalists believe that "all people shall be treated according to the same criteria (for instance, equality in and before the law)," while particularists believe that "individuals shall be treated differently according to their personal qualities or their particular membership in a class or group" (Lipset 1979, p. 209). In the French literature on racism, universalism is opposed not to particularism but to differentialism. For instance, Taguieff (1988, p. 164) opposes a universalistic racism (which posits that *we* are the humanity) and a differentialist racism (which posits that *we* are the best). The anthropological literature opposes a universalism that declares an absolute and shared human essence—including the Enlightenment notions of freedom and equality—to a relativism that affirms the diversity of cultural identities. Finally, the philosophical literature juxtaposes a universalism defined through shared moral orientations or Platonic ideals (the good, the right, the just) and communitarianism, which stresses moral norms that emerge from the collective life of groups (see, for instance, Rasmussen 1990).

86. This may also hold among white workers. A number of them also share this culture of particularism. For instance, a white printer explains that he has never met anyone who is 100 percent comfortable with someone not from their race, "because you have to watch what you say and in interracial dating, people behave like they always have to prove that they are not racist."

87. This is in accord with Smith's (1990, p. 11) analysis of images associated with ethnic and racial groups in the United States. He shows that blacks are consistently rated as further from whites than members of other minority groups, including large numbers of immigrants.

88. Fix et al.(1994). While the absolute number of foreign-born is at an all-time high of 19.7 million in 1990 (34 percent more than in 1980), their share of the total population is much lower than it was from 1879 to 1920 (8 percent in 1990 compared to 15 percent in 1890) (p. 21).

89. Commission on the Future of Work-Management Relations (1994, p. 14).

90. Together, these groups make up nearly one-fifth of the total population (Zolberg and Woon 1999, p. 11).

91. Four percent come to New Jersey and 14 percent come to New York.

92. Commission on the Future of Work-Management Relations (1994, p. 253).

93. United States Bureau of the Census of the Population (1990a, table 1).

94. Computed from United States Bureau of the Census of the Population (1992).

95. Espenshade and Belanger (1998).

96. Harwood (1986, p. 205), cited by Espenshade and Belanger (1998, p. 21).
97. Espenshade and Belanger (1998, p. 19).
98. Martin (1994, p. 87).
99. Freeman (1995, p. 89).
100. Schneider (2000).
101. Lapinski et al. (1997, p. 367).
102. Only in 1953 did more than 10 percent of U.S. residents surveyed in an opinion poll favor increasing immigration levels. Freeman (1995, p. 91).
103. Fernandez-Kelly and Curran (2000); Espiritu (2000).
104. This is suggested by the preliminary findings of the study conducted by Philip Kasinitz, John Mollenkopf, and Mary Waters on models of incorporation for various immigrant groups in the New York metropolitan area (personal communication with Philip Kasinitz). See also Nelkin and Michales (1988). These authors propose that eugenics arguments were still present in the anti-immigrant rhetoric of the 1980s.
105. Kennedy (1996, p. 58) points to episodes of "nativism, anti-semitism, anti-Catholicism, and anti-foreign radicalism, from the know-nothing movement of the 1850s to the American Protective Association of the late nineteenth century and the revived Ku Klux Klan of the early twentieth century."
106. Sahlins (1997) provides a hagiographic description of this myth; he focuses on the American experiment's uniqueness, moral superiority, and centrality of immigration (see especially chapter 4). See also Jasper (2000).
107. Kallen (1924, p. 124); Walzer (1992, p. 15).
108. Hunter and Bowman (1996a, p. 3). There are no differences between high school graduates and college graduates.
109. Also, the majority of the population, and probably several of my interviewees, thinks of itself as from immigrant origins: when questioned on their ancestry, only 6 percent of the total U.S. population prefer "American" over other ethnic labels (Lieberson and Waters 1988, p. 265). Figures obtained from the 1980 Census.
110. Zolberg and Woon (1999, p. 6).
111. Bach (1993, p. 36).
112. Ibid., p. 34.
113. Fix et al. (1994, p. 31).
114. Kennedy (1996, pp. 6 and 63). Welfare recipients total only 2.0 percent of those who immigrated during the 1980s versus 3.7 percent of working-age natives. Among longer-resident immigrants, 3.2 percent are on welfare, still below the proportion of working-age natives (Passell and Edmonston, 1992).
115. For a review, see Lapinski et al. (1997). Anti-immigrant attitudes are most common among older and less-educated people (see Espenshade and Calhoun 1994 and Espenshade and Belanger 1998, p. 3).
116. Espenshade and Belanger (1998, pp. 8 and 16).
117. It has been suggested that racial and anti-immigrant prejudice increases with threat to group position, measured by the relative size of the subordinated group and the national economic situation (Quillian, 1995).

118. Quillian (1995), Cornelius (1982), and Higham (1955). Hollifield and Martin (1996) show that support for Proposition 187 was strongest in counties with high levels of unemployment, especially those on the southern border of California.
119. Commission on the Future of Work-Management Relations (1994, pp. 300–302).
120. Portes (1994; 1995).
121. Kennedy (1996, p. 56). See also Higham (1955). American immigration policy has been shaped by "contending forces advocating that the nation should serve as a refuge for the world's dispossessed and those who believe that immigration policy should seek to sift the wheat from the chaff–to admit the immigrants who add to the U.S. economy and society and exclude those who may become a burden" (Fix et al. 1994, p. 9).
122. Espenshade (1997) suggests that immigration proceeded more smoothly in New Jersey than elsewhere. See also Waldinger (1996).
123. Only two of the black workers made spontaneous derogatory comments about immigrants. This nonsalience of immigrants for blacks contradicts other studies that document strong tensions between blacks and immigrants in cities that have exceptionally large immigrant populations (Miami and Los Angeles in particular) (see Portes and Stepick 1993, chapter 8; Park 1996; 1998).
124. As suggested by Scott (1985), morality provides individuals in dominating positions with suitable tools to confront and adapt to their situations.
125. For a discussion of the meaning of egalitarianism in American political culture, see McClosky and Zaller (1984, chapter 3). These authors show that even in the late seventies Americans tended to interpret the egalitarian principle as having more to do with equality of opportunity than with equality as resulting from a common humanity (p. 74).
126. See the coverage of the Hill-Thomas hearing and the O. J. Simpson trial and the use of race in political campaigns (for instance, the Willie Horton ad in 1988 and the 1994 "Contract with America" that aimed at restoring American family values against crime, illegitimacy, and homosexuality; on these topics, see Mendelberg 1997). On the broader issue of the role of the media in diffusing images of social groups, see Gilens (1996) and Entman (1992).
127. See Watts's review (1997, p. 409).
128. This point is made concerning rates of black and white teenage pregnancy by Luker (1996).
129. Kirschenman and Neckerman (1990).
130. In a survey based on a large sample of whites, blacks, Hispanics, and Asians residing in Los Angeles, respondents were asked to rate each ethnic group according to these criteria, with a high score reflecting more prejudice. Blacks rate themselves at 3.60 for "unintelligent"; blacks received scores of 3.77 from Hispanics, 4.05 from whites, and 4.27 from Asians. On the welfare issue, blacks gave themselves a score of 3.98 and received scores of 4.10 from whites, 0.84 from Asians, and 5.22 from Hispanics. In terms of difficulty to get along with, blacks gave themselves a score of 3.57 and received scores of 3.81 from whites, 4.02 from Asians, and 4.55 from Hispanics (Bobo and Zubrinski 1996).

131. Jackman (1994, pp. 73–93 and 314). For this analysis as it applies to reactions to the civil rights movement, see Omi and Winant (1986, p. 126).
132. On the widening inequality of wealth between whites and nonwhites between 1983 and 1990, see Wolff (1995).
133. To paraphrase Durkheim (1965).
134. The college-educated population continues to show a high degree of similarity in its cultural practices and attitudes over a wide range of areas. See Collins (1979) and Davis (1982). Eleven percent of blacks had a college degree in 1990, compared to 22 percent of whites (United States Bureau of Census 1990b, pp. 151–154).

3. Assessing "People Above" and "People Below"

1. These are referred to by workers as "people above," "the upper half," "professionals," "managers," "businessmen," "the rich," "the powerful," "the elite," "the upper class," "the upper middle class" and, in some cases, "the middle class." I analyze how workers assess members of these variously labeled groups instead of focusing on their assessment of members of specific classes. This is a reasonable strategy because, as shown by Burke (1995), Americans have been reluctant to use the language of class in classifying social groups. As a consequence, this language has been particularly unstable and contested throughout American history. Note that the workers sometimes compare themselves with fine-grained categories of "people above" (distinguishing between elites, the wealthy, and white upper management) while at other times broad categories are lumped together, as if workers blurred distinctions because they see them from afar.
2. This chapter contributes to the literature on class images, building on the work of Ossowski (1963) and others. Following Hiller (1975), I also focus on evaluation of the behaviors and values of other classes, particularity on a dimension of superiority/inferiority.
3. I follow Nam and Terrie (1982) in dissociating subjective prestige (worth) from status. These authors use prestige to refer to the subjective evaluation of worth, and status to refer to social position. On these various dimensions of ranking, see Ollivier (1998).
4. For instance, Chinoy (1955) shows that in the fifties American workers continued to believe in the American dream even without tasting its promises; his respondents did not talk of exploitation and had little autonomy from middle class culture. Similarly, Coleman and Rainwater (1978, p. 220) use quantitative data to argue that workers and middle class people use economic standards to assess status. While some of the discrepancies between my conclusions and those of other studies might be explained by time lags and differences in the socioeconomic status of interviewees, they are nevertheless worth exploring. In a different vein, Sennett and Cobb (1972) discuss how upwardly mobile workers feel indignity if their success is based on education and white-collar work. They simultaneously do not recognize the legitimacy of intellectual work yet feel embarrassed because of their lack of comfort with the world of intellect and culture.

5. Lane (1962, chapter 4) argues that belief in the American dream leads members of lower social classes to devalue their own class members and to view their class identity as a source of discomfort. Also, see the critique of the literature on subjective class association by Vanneman and Cannon (1987).

6. Rubin (1994, pp. 48 and 55).

7. For instance, Willis (1977).

8. The quantitative comparison of white and black workers excludes Euro-American white-collar workers because my sample could not include black white-collar workers. I focus on blue collars only to ensure that my comparisons are significant. However, I quote white-collar workers in the narrative sections of the data analysis. Interviews reveal that Euro-American white-collar workers identify more with the middle class than do Euro-American blue-collar workers. They also attach more legitimacy to education, have a more positive view of power, attribute fewer moral flaws to the upper half, and are less likely to believe that they have a better quality of life than the upper half. In order to determine whether an interviewee identified with the middle class, I compared his position and attitudes toward (1) the attributes of the upper half (income as a criterion of success, power, education, ambition); (2) the moral character of the upper half; and (3) the quality of life and the advantages of the upper half in contrast to those of the working class. Interviewees are classified as "mixed," "middle class identified," or "critical of the upper half" based on the distribution of their positions on twelve items included in these three categories.

9. Kluegel and Smith (1981, p. 7). However, college graduates espouse this view more strongly than others: a 1980 survey found that among white men 63 percent of those without a high school degree believed in the equality of opportunity compared to 72 percent of high school graduates and 84 percent of college graduates (p. 67). Also, 60 percent of those without a high school degree and 64 percent of high school graduates explain the wealth of the rich by the fact that they work hard, as compared to 78 percent of college graduates (p. 96). In fact, Kluegel and Smith compare low, middle, and high status groups based on levels of education and income. I only refer to educational differences because the 1979 income categories used in this survey cannot be easily translated into my class categories. Furthermore, their comparison pertains to white men, white women, and blacks. Here and elsewhere, when presenting results from this study, I only refer to data for white men and blacks because we are not given separate figures for black men and black women (p. 68).

10. Lamont (1992, pp. 65–71) discusses the main conceptions of money in the American upper middle class.

11. Ibid., pp. 74–75.

12. Note, however, that if one considers only comments made explicitly against "people above" and not against their attributes, such as money, power, or ambition, fewer workers can be considered to draw boundaries toward the middle class. Only 37 percent of white blue-collar workers and 27 percent of lower white-collar workers make explicitly negative comments toward people above.

13. Prestige, money, and power are positional goods, resources that are distributed on a zero-sum basis—that is, they exist in finite number and take their value relationally.

14. Kluegel and Smith (1986, p. 97).
15. For instance, Hyman (1966). Willis (1977) points to the adoption of alternative definitions of success by working class youth. Although he does not fully spell out what the alternative conceptions of success would be, we can make inferences from the qualities these "lads" value: practical knowledge as opposed to theoretical knowledge, masculinity, toughness of physical work, ingenuity, and nonconformism in general.
16. According to Della Fave (1974), such an alternative egalitarian logic would develop when workers (a) have a feeling of deprivation; (b) attribute blame to the system; (c) believe social justice requires equality; (d) believe human nature will permit equality; and (e) believe that such a change is possible. This approach is too driven by the Marxist model of working class consciousness and does not pay sufficient attention to the worldview of workers. On these points, see the critique of the literature offered by Katznelson (1986).
17. For instance, see Reinarman (1987, p. 57).
18. This almost exclusive focus on structural and individual explanations of inequality has had a powerful impact on the social-psychological literature on social justice and related issues. For instance, Gurin, Miller, and Gurin (1980) suggest that American working class identifiers have no class consciousness because they do not adopt structural explanations of inequality or buy into the American dream that explains failure by personal characteristics.
19. In Lamont (1992, p. 247, note 12), I indicate that only 15 percent of the New York professionals and managers interviewed expressed indifference or opposition to socioeconomic criteria of definition of worth (p. 251). Seventy percent of these workers scored high on the socioeconomic scale (i.e., they equated people's worth with attributes such as money, power, and occupational prestige).
20. Kerckhoff (1972, p. 55). In contrast, lower class parents tend to emphasize security more than opportunity and achievement.
21. Lamont (1992, p. 252, note 65) found that 66 percent of the New York managers and professionals who score high on the moral score also score high on the socioeconomic scale.
22. Kluegel and Smith (1986, pp. 91–92).
23. Lamont (1992, p. 75). Note also that upper middle class people are more concerned than workers with getting involved in exclusive groups as a means to signal their status.
24. Ollivier (forthcoming).
25. Guppy (1984).
26. Wegener (1992). Also, Jackman (1994) finds that the "frequency and size of distinctions that are drawn between classes increase incrementally as one moves from adjacent classes to classes that are further apart . . . The two highest social classes . . . are most likely to be described categorically" (pp. 331–332).
27. See, for instance, Ollivier (2000); Brint (1996); Lamont (1992); Young and Willmott (1956).
28. This contrasts with a 1980 survey, which shows that blacks with and without a high school degree are roughly as likely as their white counterparts to explain

wealth by the dishonesty of the rich (roughly 40 percent of them do). Fewer black than white men explain wealth by the fact that the rich work hard: 52 percent of blacks without a high school degree believe this, as compared to 44 percent of black high school graduates. For white men, these figures are, respectively, 60 and 64 percent (Kluegel and Smith 1986, p. 96). However, studies have also found that middle class blacks put a greater emphasis on education and achievement than do whites (Willie 1985, p. 275, and Hale 1982, p. 48).

29. Note that Jackman and Jackman (1983, p. 218) find that blacks are less likely than whites to define themselves as belonging to the middle class.

30. If one considers only comments made explicitly against people above, and not against their attributes such as money, power, or ambition, 31 percent of black blue-collar workers can be considered anti-middle class, compared to 37 percent of their white counterparts and 27 percent of the lower white-collar workers.

31. Building on Robert K. Merton, Turner (1974, p. 233) defines liminality as a betwixt-and-between state of outsiderhood "referring to the condition of being either permanently or by ascription set outside the structural arrangement of a given social system."

32. These folk theories of success can be compared with those elaborated by upwardly mobile college-educated young black men, as described by Young (1999).

33. On this point, see Hochschild (1995a, p. 85), who shows that poor blacks care more about achieving material success than do well-off blacks.

34. Hochschild (1995a, p. 73) presents survey data that show that affluent blacks are much more concerned with racial discrimination than are poor blacks. Again, she does not report on workers' attitudes.

35. For instance, a 1989 poll revealed that respectively 69 percent of blacks and 46 percent of whites used discrimination to explain why blacks have worse jobs than whites. Also, 75 percent of blacks and only 43 percent of whites agreed that "blacks are not achieving equality as fast as they could because many whites don't want them to get ahead" (Sigelman and Welch 1991, p. 91). See also Kluegel and Smith (1986, pp. 67 and 289). These authors show that discrimination is the explanation of the racial gap that is favored by blacks, whereas whites favor dispositional explanations that blame the character of the victim over situational ones that point to discrimination (p. 93).

36. Anderson (1990, p. 61) notes that blacks are particularly critical toward upwardly mobile blacks who do not "give back" to the community.

37. See the literature cited by Vanneman and Cannon (1987, p. 236). In particular, Geschwender (1977) provides an analysis of the place given to exploitation in the ideology of a radical auto industry union.

38. Fifty percent of workers and 46 percent of professionals responding to the 1984 General Social Survey agreed that "if someone has a high social or economic position, that indicates the person has special abilities or great accomplishments."

39. Scott (1990) and Willis (1977).

40. For a recent critique of the large literature on resistance, dignity, and empowerment among workers, see Rubin (1996). The literature on working class resistance

has tended to focus on the development of alternative codes of honor and the rejection of mainstream norms of success (Willis 1977). Davies (1995) provides a very convincing critique of Willis, showing that this author overimposed a resistance-focused theoretical framework on the lives of the British youth he studied.

41. Along these lines, in his ethnographic study of San Francisco longshoremen, Wellman (1995) suggested that instead of focusing on the exceptional character of American labor and on traditional forms of empowerment and resistance, we should examine how workers maneuver to increase their autonomy at work, to genuinely adopt a positive self-identity, and to diffuse respect for their selfhood (p. 78). In her study of black domestic workers, Rollins (1985) also shows that black domestics reject devaluation by maintaining cultural orientations that contradict those of their employers. For instance, they measure people's worth by the quality of their relationships and community standing (pp. 212–213). I also aim to move ongoing discussions in this direction.

42. We cannot discount that our findings could be accounted for as an artifact of the research: African Americans who are most identified with middle class values might be more likely to agree to be interviewed for a study conducted by a white academic. However, others might agree to be interviewed to display racial pride. The impact of such selection bias on our results cannot be readily assessed herein.

43. hooks (1997).

44. I am interested in workers' explanations of why these categories are stigmatized. This contrasts with Mohr's (1994) analysis of the moral order of early twentieth-century New York welfare recipient categories, which focuses on moral distinctions embedded in organizational practices.

45. Between 1989 and 1993, five of the most widely read daily newspapers, *the New York Times*, the *Washington Post*, the *Chicago Sun-Times*, the *Los Angeles Times*, and the *Philadelphia Inquirer*, increased by at least one-third the number of stories on these issues over the previous five-year period (Wilson 1996, p. 415). Note that professionals and managers were interviewed in 1987 and 1988.

46. Katz (1989) also argues that for centuries Americans have distinguished between the "deserving" and the "undeserving" poor on the basis of attitude: while the former attempts to remain self-sufficient, the latter is lazy, shiftless, drunken, and/or not self-reliant.

47. Similarly, Lomax-Cook (1979) finds that willingness to provide state support to various categories of recipients is highly correlated with the extent to which recipients are viewed as responsible for their plight. She found that American adults are less likely to want to help poor adults than any other segment of the needy population, including children and the handicapped; they blame the adults for their own fates.

48. Note that individualist explanations of poverty are the most prominent explanations used by Americans (Kluegel and Smith 1986, p. 31).

49. As many workers (88 percent) as professionals (87 percent) who responded to the 1984 General Social Survey agreed that "America is an open society. What one achieves in life no longer depends on one's family background, but on the abili-

ties one has and the education one acquires." Also, 60 percent of workers and 63 percent of professionals agreed that "all in all, [they] think social differences in this country are justified" (my analysis).

50. In surveys, workers are more likely than professionals to believe that "in the United States, there are still great differences between social levels, and what one can achieve in life depends mainly on one's family background." Forty-two percent of workers who responded to the 1984 General Social Survey shared this view compared with 31 percent of professionals and managers (my analysis).

51. Kluegel and Smith (1986, p. 290) explain the paradox between individuals' faith in the American dream and their critical stance toward the importance of social background in achieving. These individuals see the dysfunction of the American dream as exceptional instead of endemic.

52. Cook and Curtin (1987).

53. Gans (1995, chapter 1).

54. Katz, cited by Gans (1995, p. 14). Gans also argues that negative feelings toward welfare recipients are articulated primarily around the view that recipients constitute a threat to safety, cultural standards, economic position, and moral norms and values (p. 76).

55. Patterson (1981, p. vii).

56. Conservatives often condemned the alleged behavioral deficiencies of the poor (concerning their work ethic, respect for law and order, and family values). Recently many liberals have also come to accept this perspective (Silver 1993, p. 345).

57. The conservative approach to welfare reform embodied in the "Contract with America" and the Personal Responsibility Act of 1996" has three aspects: (1) a work-focused approach that forces welfare clients to take jobs while making training and child care available; (2) a transitional support approach based on the creation of empowerment zones, vouchers, and other subsidies; and (3) a behavioral approach aimed at changing the behavior of welfare recipients—for instance, encouraging AFDC recipients to have fewer children out of wedlock (Noble 1997, p. 127).

58. DiMaggio, Evans, and Bryson (1996, figure 6, p. 712).

59. In fact, the value of AFDC benefits declined by 45 percent from 1970 to 1993 (Wacquant 1997, p. 25). In the words of political scientist David Noble, who provides a sophisticated analysis of welfare retrenchment over the last 30 years, the decline in social spending "started earlier in the United States and has lasted longer, and social spending growth rates have tended to slow more dramatically than elsewhere" (1997, pp. 9–10).

60. The conditions that lead to welfare retrenchment are often the opposite of those associated with welfare state growth, such as the strength of a social democratic labor movement or "socialist rule," the political influence of leftist parties, the overall level of economic development, and the impact of state structures. For a review of this literature that moves beyond single-factor explanations, see Skocpol and Amenta (1986) and Uusitalo (1984).

61. Edsall and Edsall (1991, p. 22).

62. Figure cited by Wacquant (1997, p. 25).

63. United States Bureau of Census of the Population (1995, table 744, p. 480). In 1992, blacks represented 12.4 percent of the American population.
64. Figure cited by Gilens (1996, p. 517). This author also cites another survey where 85 percent of the respondents believed that blacks make up half of the poor in this country.
65. For instance, support for race-neutral policy items, such as social security, is only 13 percent higher among blacks than whites. For policies aimed at equalizing wealth, the racial differential is 19 percent higher for blacks. In contrast, support for implicitly racial policy items shows a much wider race differential; this is the case for policies that help the poor (+24 for blacks) and for welfare in particular (+23 for blacks). Race differentials are even larger for policies that explicitly help blacks (+39 for blacks) (Bobo and Smith 1994, p. 388). For an assessment of the literature on racial differences in attitudes toward race-related policy issues, see Schuman et al. (1997, chapters 6 and 7) and Kinder and Sanders (1996, pp. 190–191).
66. Gilens (1995, p. 1006).
67. See note 63.
68. This content analysis focuses on three major newsmagazines (*Newsweek, Time,* and *U.S. News and World Report*) published between 1988 and 1992 and on weeknight news shows on ABC, NBC, and CBS (Gilens 1996, p. 527). On the importance of racial framing by the media, see Gamson and Lasch (1983).
69. This is the argument developed by Edsall and Edsall (1991, p. 22). This conflation of moral, class, and racial boundaries is also mentioned in Halle (1984, p. 248).
70. This argument is made by Quadagno (1994, p. 196). See also Noble (1997, p. 114).
71. An excellent analysis of the political forces and structural causes that led the Democratic Party to abandon the poor is presented by Page (1996).
72. For instance, Handler and Hasenfeld (1991).
73. But see Perin (1988).
74. On this issue, see Wuthnow (1987, p. 122).
75. Page (1996).
76. Link and colleagues (1995) looked at 36 national and state polls conducted between 1978 and 1992. These show that a majority of Americans are willing to help the homeless, and that some are willing to pay more taxes to do so (Gans 1995, p. 175). Moreover, 65 percent of respondents to a 1987 national survey believe that not enough money is spent on assistance to the poor (Bobo and Smith 1994, p. 372). Finally, in the mid-1980s, 47.7 percent of individuals responding to a national survey believed that the government should provide a decent standard of living for the unemployed, while 45 percent opposed government provision of a decent standard of living (Smith 1987, p. 416). For data on change over time, see Page and Shapiro (1992, chapter 4).
77. For a review of the evidence, see Shapiro, Patterson, Russell, and Young (1987).
78. Shapiro and Young (1989, p. 69).
79. These negative attitudes concern whether or not the homeless are perceived as a threat (Link et al. 1995, cited by Gans 1995, p. 89). Kluegel and Smith (1981, p. 31) also suggest that there is a weak correlation between most socio-demographic factors and beliefs about the poor. However, some studies show that family income

(a measure of self-interest) is a good predictor of opposition to welfare (Gilens 1995).

80. Results tabulated from the General Social Survey.

81. Ansel (1997).

82. On the association between structural explanations of poverty and exposure to the poor, see G. Wilson (1996).

83. Katz (1989, p. 3).

84. Trattner (1994, p. 4).

85. Similarly, in an ethnography of a black community located in Corona (Queens), Gregory (1998) found that homeowners try to protect their community and quality of life from poor blacks.

86. G. Wilson (1996) shows that blacks live in more economically segregated neighborhoods than whites.

87. Along these lines, it has been argued that more so than whites, blacks self-identify as middle class based on their ability to uphold mainstream values and behaviors such as maintaining a stable family, being active in community and church affairs, and striving to "get ahead." For a materialist critique of this view, see Vanneman and Cannon (1987, pp. 228–230).

88. Iyengar (1987); see also Bobo and Smith (1994, pp. 383–384). Note, however, that individualist explanations for the black/white economic gaps are most favored by less educated, older, and more politically conservative respondents (Kluegel 1990, p. 523). Similar results concerning the impact of education level on individualist explanations of poverty are presented by Wilson (1991).

89. For a review of the literature showing that blacks are less opposed to welfare than whites, in part because blacks have a more structural view of the causes of poverty, see Kluegel and Smith (1981, p. 41).

90. Lomax-Cook (1979, pp. 106–109). Similarly, Sigelman and Welch (1991) show that blacks are in general more supportive of increased welfare spending and government action (p. 143). Also, Bobo and Smith (1994) draw on national surveys on race and social policy support to show that the black/white percentage differential for support of policies helping the poor and supporting welfare is 24 percent, with 31 percent of whites and 55 percent of blacks supporting such policies (p. 388). In fact, support for governmental spending on social programs is higher among both low- and high-income blacks. In contrast, high-income whites are much less supportive of it than low-income whites (Gilliam and Whitby 1989, p. 96).

91. Jackman and Jackman (1983, p. 48).

92. This is suggested by the fact that wealth accumulation is much lower for blacks than for whites at all socioeconomic levels (Oliver and Shapiro 1997). In 1988, wealth accumulation for whites was $96,000, but it was only $72,000 for blacks (p. 100).

93. Similarly, Newman and Ellis (1999) show how fast-food restaurant workers in Harlem have to struggle to maintain their identity as workers in the face of pressures imposed on them by the unemployed.

94. Pattillo-McCoy (1999) provides an interesting description of the fragility of this boundary in a Chicago black lower middle class neighborhood, and of how it af-

fects child-raising as deviant role models are readily available to children. See also Duneier (1992).

95. Respectively 70 percent and 37 percent of the New York professionals and managers I interviewed ranked high on the socioeconomic and moral scales (Lamont 1992, pp. 260–261). Thirty-four percent of the New Yorkers who ranked high on the socioeconomic scale also ranked high on the moral scale, with 37 percent being indifferent or hostile to moral criteria of evaluation. The correlation between high moral and socioeconomic scores was found to be significant and negative.

96. Also, Jackman (1994, pp. 236–237) suggests that morality plays an important role in justifying inequality in the American context. She is primarily concerned with the traits used by dominant groups to strengthen their position rather than those used to reverse hierarchies. She suggests that to better understand the moral bases of unequal relationships, we need to document both the traits that are popularly selected as salient comparison points between groups and the ways in which these traits are used to delimit the place of each group in society. However, she works with survey data not suitable to documenting nuances in patterns of salience. I view the present study as a direct contribution to her objectives.

97. This differs from the image of the British working class offered by Lockwood (1966). Based on the type of industrial and community milieu inhabited by workers, he contrasted (1) proletarians who posit a dichotomous "us" versus "them" model based on power; (2) deferential workers who posit a prestige hierarchy and are subordinated to management; and (3) privatized workers functioning with a money model who are interested in maximizing their own earning capacity. The picture that emerges from my data is more nuanced—resistance is somewhat detached from traditional models of opposition between bourgeois and radical workers and is found among various groups.

98. Jackman (1994, p. 103) analyzes the results of a 1975 national probability survey that shows weaker negative working class feelings toward the upper half than my findings suggest. In her survey, (1) 29 percent of the working class and 21 percent of the middle class have negative feelings toward the upper class; (2) 33 percent of the working class and 34 percent of the middle class have positive feelings toward the upper class; (3) 41 percent of the working class and 44 percent of the middle class have positive feelings toward the upper middle class. Jackman also shows that "Americans commonly believe that both intelligence and selfishness are found increasingly with ascending social class" (p. 334).

99. However, lower figures are obtained if one considers only pejorative comments, exclusive of their criticisms of middle class attributes and values such as power and ambition. On this topic, see note 12.

100. An earlier study reached similar conclusions, showing that as compared to members of other classes, members of lower classes express the most own-class preference and draw the strongest affective boundaries against higher classes (Jackman and Jackman 1983, pp. 47–51). More specifically, they found that "there is no evidence of a 'deference-achievement' syndrome in people's class feelings. There is no support for the view that, in a society that stresses an ideology of equal oppor-

tunity, class bonds will be strongest among higher classes (the 'successful') and weakest among lower classes (the 'failures'). On the contrary, there is an inverse relationship between class and strength of class bonds, such that lower classes express the most own-class preference. In addition, far from expressing a preference for higher classes, it is in relation to higher classes that people draw sharper affective boundaries" (p. 51). Halle's (1984) findings are also compatible with mine as he presents a contradictory picture of working class attitudes toward the upper half. His ethnography of workers living in Elizabeth, New Jersey, suggests that members of this group identify with the middle class in their private lives and in their realms of consumption, but they identify with the working class at their workplaces.

101. See Chapter 1, note 122.
102. Lipset (1979) and Tocqueville ([1835] 1969).

II. The United States Compared

1. Alexander (1992, p. 291).
2. Specifying this group as white could be viewed as an American bias because skin color is less salient in descriptions of groups in France than in the United States. Furthermore, in the French context, it is taken for granted that the term "French workers" designates white workers. The term "immigrés" is customarily used to designate most nonwhite workers, independently of the length of their stay in France and/or their French nationality. The use of such labels is, of course, reflective of the boundaries that are analyzed herein. The French media debate that followed the attack by Le Bras (1998) of Tribalat's (1995) use of the term *"français de souche"* (French of origin) is indicative of the cultural sensitivity and complexity of labeling groups by their race or roots in the context of French republican culture (to be discussed in Chapter 5).
3. Lemaine and Ben Brika (1997) analyzed how a representative sample of the French population (N = 1,000) defines out-groups residing in France. Responses uniformly point to North Africans, whether they are described in terms of their non-European status (as was the case for 62 percent of respondents), nationality (55 percent), religion (52 percent), or "race" (39 percent). Kastoryano (1996) also shows how Islam has been framed by the state and by politicians and others as the most foreign body in French society. On this topic, see also Guiraudon (2000, chapter 5).
4. See Scott (1997).
5. Lacorne, Rupnik, and Toinet (1990) and Saguy (2000) examine dimensions of French expressions of moral superiority to the United States.
6. For instance, Schnapper (1991). On balkanization, see the position of Alain Touraine in the report of the 1988 Commission de la Nationalité (cited by House 1996). Hollifield (1994; 1997) and Kastoryano (1996) provide other examples of the ways in which the United States is used as an antimodel by French scholars.

7. In Lamont (1995), I used the concept of national boundary work to refer to the process by which one national group defines its identity through an oppositional process. On this topic, see also Borneman (1992).

4. Workers Compared

1. Organization for Economic Cooperation and Development (1992, table 12, p. 11).
2. Organization for Economic Cooperation and Development (1997, p. 261).
3. Organization for Economic Cooperation and Development (1995, table 21, p. A24). This difference in unemployment rate is explained by a larger number of unskilled male workers in France (Lefranc 1997).
4. Organization for Economic Cooperation and Development (1992, table 2.5, p. 38).
5. Visser (1992, table 1). On the impact of industrial politics on union density, see Western (1995). According to Chapman, Kesselman, and Schain (1996, p. 13), "the problems of low membership density, weak organization, rivalry, and dependence on the state have been exacerbated during the present period."
6. Unions play a role in overseeing France's health care, family allowance, and labor tribunal system. For a comparison of unions in the two countries, see Adam and Reynaud (1978, chapter 1).
7. This mobilization capacity is due to the fact that French unions have "retained far more legitimacy in public opinion than other [European] union movements" (Chapman, Kesselman, and Schain 1996, p. 13). A decline in union density is not indicative of a decline in left orientation among French workers (Segrestin 1984, p. 200).
8. For data on the United States, see Introduction, note 2. French data for the 1970–1984 period show stability in income distribution (Atkinson, Rainwater, and Smeeding (1995, p. 66). From 1980 to 1988, of all the European Community countries except the Netherlands, France had the narrowest consumption gap between households in the top and bottom quartiles. This implies not so much stability in income distribution but a tendency toward more egalitarian distribution (European Community 1995, p. 203).
9. In 1989, the top quintile of the population controlled 69 percent of the total of gross assets in France as compared to 75 percent in the United States, while the assets of the lowest three quintiles were roughly comparable (Wolff 1995, table 5-1, p. 25). Income inequality is greater in the United States than in most other industrialized economies (O'Higgins, Schmaus, and Stephenson 1989).
10. Katz, Loveman, and Blanchflower (1993, p. 3). In the United States, insufficient growth in the supply of college-educated workers explains a substantial portion of the increase in educational wage differential (p. 20).
11. See Mann (1973, chapter 4).
12. The median household income of the French interviewees is 190,000 francs a year or 16,000 francs per month. This translates into $28,000 a year based on the 1993 conversion rate of 5.66 francs to the dollar. The mean household income figure for French households for that year (before taxation) was 170,228 francs (Institut national de la statistique et des études économiques (INSEE) 1998, table C.03-2,

p. 172). This same source indicates that the "available income before taxation),"
including social benefits, was 226,000 francs (no information is provided whether
this figure represents the mean or median (table C.03-1, p. 172).

13. For instance, in 1979 the households of employed manual workers saw their primary
income increased 42.7 percent by social benefits. For professionals and managers,
this increase was 11.9 percent (cited by Ambler 1991, p. 13). It should be noted that the
population of the French communes where I conducted interviews have an annual
income average slightly below the national income average, while such is not the
case for the populations of the American towns where I conducted interviews (see
Introduction, notes 43 and 44). This suggests that in fact the French respondents are
located lower in the national income distribution than is the case for their American
counterpart. For details on the annual average income of the population of the
French communes where I conducted interviews, see Appendix B, note 38.

14. Whereas in the mid-eighties, French individuals located in the fourth income
decile category had 22 percent of the total disposable income per adult, their
American counterparts had 18 percent. The proportions for those located in the
third decile were 15 percent in France and 11 percent in the United States. For
those located in the fifth decile, these figures were, respectively, 30 percent and
26 percent (Atkinson, Rainwater, and Smeeding (1995, p. 44). Moreover, in 1991 the
hourly compensation of production workers in manufacturing was 4 percent
higher in France than in the United States (Freeman 1994, pp. 9–11).

15. Ninety-five percent of the French workers belong to a two-income family as compared to 84 percent of the American workers. In 1990, 69 percent of American
women aged 15 to 64 were active in the labor force, compared to 57 percent of
French women (Noll and Langlois 1994, p. 94).

16. On France, see Goux and Maurin (1998). On the United States, see Arum and
Hout (1998). Children from families headed by an industrial worker represented
only 13 percent of the French college population in the 1980s. In 1989, only 36 percent of all French high school students took the state secondary examination that
leads to higher education (the *baccalauréat*). See Ambler (1991, p. 18). In 1985,
30 percent of high school students went on to college (p. 24). In contrast, 58 percent of all recent American high school graduates aged 16 to 24 were enrolled in college that year. See United States Bureau of the Census of the Population (1998, p. 118).

17. Schwartz (1990); Beaud (1995).

18. Among blue-collar workers, 13 were born in Paris and 15 in the provinces (information unavailable in two cases). Among white-collar workers, 6 were born in Paris
and 8 in the provinces (information unavailable in one case).

19. For an illustration of this anonymity, see Haegel's (1998) study of a public housing
project in La Courneuve where I also conducted interviews.

20. Thirteen percent of all French workers used to belong to a union but did not at
the time of the interview.

21. While in the 1944–1978 period this party received on average 23.4 percent of the
vote, in the 1979–88 period it received only 12.4 percent (Piven 1992, p. 10).

22. Twelve define themselves as supporters of the left, eight as supporters of the Socialist Party, and five as supporters of the Communist Party (for a total of 25 left-

leaning respondents among 45). Ten define themselves as supporters of right-wing or center parties, and three are supporters of the far-right National Front (although more interviewees are sympathetic to this party's political platform concerning immigrants). Finally, three define themselves as apolitical, and information is missing in four cases.

23. INSEE (1992, table 20). This compares to 7.9 percent in the United States—by 1997, the U.S. figure had climbed to 10.7 percent (United States Bureau of the Census 1998, p. 55).

24. Between 1850 and 1940, France was the only European country with a net immigration rate (Schnapper 1991, p. 64).

25. Hollifield (1997, p. 29).

26. Feldblum (1993, pp. 53-54). In 1990 European immigrants made up 40 percent of the 3,607,590 foreigners living in France, while Africans made up 46 percent of foreigners and 6.4 percent of the French population. Thirty-four percent of these Africans originated in Algeria, Tunisia, and Morocco, with only 5 percent coming from the sub-Saharan francophone countries (INSEE 1993a, table R-6, p. 16). This last figure is increasing very rapidly: in 1975 sub-Saharan Africans made up only 2 percent of foreigners residing in France. In recent years this group has been at the center of controversies surrounding forced repatriation that have attracted considerable attention from the media. As such, it has played a particularly important symbolic role in French debates concerning racism. See in particular the extensive media coverage of the hunger strike of 300 illegal immigrants who had taken refuge in the St. Bernard Church in Paris during the summer of 1996.

27. This figure is based on data compiled from census information on the percentage of the population born in the Maghreb (INSEE 1992, table 20). In 1978 the French government passed a law forbidding the collection of information on the racial and ethnic composition of its population. Consequently, we can only produce a rough estimate of the size of the Muslim population in France based on census information on nationality and place of birth. Leveau and de Wenden (1988) estimated that the French population includes 2.5 to 3 million Muslims and that 1.5 million of them are Franco-Maghrebis (including 1 million Franco-Algerians). For their part, beurs (or second-generation children of North African immigrants) represent 40 percent of Muslims residing in France. Together, Franco-Maghrebis and beurs represent less than 4.4 percent of the French population.

28. They mostly come from former French colonies in sub-Saharan Africa (for instance, Cameroon, Guinea, Haute-Volta, the Ivory Coast, Mali, Mauritania, and Senegal).

29. These citizens are mostly from the islands of Martinique, Guadeloupe, and Réunion, which are part of the French "Dom-Toms" (or the "Départements d'outre-mer" and "Territoires d'outre-mer"). This figure includes immigrants from black Africa (as opposed to those coming from North Africa, who are almost entirely Caucasians), who in 1990 numbered only 433,338 inhabitants (INSEE 1992, table 20). It also includes less then 340,000 blacks who were born in French departments in the Caribbean and the Indian Ocean and migrated to "metropolitan" (or mainland) France by 1990 (INSEE 1993a, p. 11).

30. Noiriel (1986, p. 133).
31. For details, see Weil (1991).
32. Note that some identified themselves as Kabyles or Berbers, that is, as members of non-Arab (but Muslim) ethnic groups residing in these countries.
33. In this respect they are representative of the immigrant population at large. Eighty percent of foreigners have resided in France for more than ten years (Dubet 1989, p. 13).
34. Seven have left their wives in their country of origin and eleven intend to return.
35. All North Africans born in Algeria before 1962 are French. The proportion of North African immigrants who choose to be naturalized has been increasing in recent years.
36. Beurs are excluded from the study because of their age—most are too young to be used in the sample—and because many of them have French citizenship.
37. This is based on the 1993 conversion rate of 5.66 francs to the dollar.
38. INSEE (1994, p. 55). The professional high school degrees are the CAP ("Certificat d'aptitudes professionelles"), the BEP (Brevet d'études professionelles"), and the BEPC ("Brevet d'études de premier degré"). In 1992, 41 percent of Algerian and 31 percent of Moroccan immigrant men had never attended school (Tribalat 1995, p. 23).
39. Feldblum (1993, p. 52).
40. See Ménanteau (1994) for a discussion of the HLM and of the suburbs in which they are located.
41. Cited by Taguieff (1989a, p. 221). France's right-wing parties, the Rassemblement pour la République (RPR) and the Union pour la démocratie française (UDF), have shared some of these views at times. For instance, in the 1986 elections these two parties called "for stronger measures to encourage immigrants to return to their home countries and a reduction of payments of social benefits to resident immigrants" (Schain 1987, p. 242).
42. These propositions, which are described as "racist" by the researchers who conducted the survey, are "There are too many Arabs in France"; "Too many come here to take advantage of welfare benefits"; "We do not need to fight against racism"; and "Immigrants are too different to be able to integrate into French society." Belgium ranked first, with 55 percent of the respondents supporting propositions defined by the researchers as racist ("How Racist Is France?" *The Economist,* July 18, 1998, p. 44).
43. Jackson et al. (1992, pp. 252–253). With respect to the question of having a relative marry a foreigner of similar background, the French rate of objection (44.4 percent) is again higher than any other country's except for West Germany, where 58.6 percent of respondents would object to a relative marrying a Turk (pp. 252–253).
44. Cayrol (1996, p. 20).
45. Schain (1997) shows that among 23 French towns that were dominated by the Communists from 1947 until the early 1980s, the National Front has attracted an electorate well above the national average. For an analysis of the conditions that led to the rise of this party, see Kitschelt (1998).

46. Martin (1994, p. 29). Schain (1997, table 3) also shows that in 1984–1985, 11 percent of blue-collar and 12 percent of white-collar workers voted for the National Front. By 1995, these figures had grown to 25 and 16 percent, respectively.

47. Mayer (1991, p. 68). For details, see Boy and Mayer (1990).

48. A ranking of the overall importance that workers attribute to the moral dimension in their evaluations of worth put Americans somewhat above the French. Sixty percent of American white-collar workers rank high or very high on the moral dimension as compared to 40 percent of their French counterparts. Among blue-collar workers, 67 percent of Americans rank high or very high as opposed to 47 percent of the French.

49. On this topic, see also Touraine, Wieviorka, and Dubet (1978, p. 78). Note also that, respectively, 35 percent of the French and 49 percent of Americans said that they value being hardworking.

50. Perrot (1986). On antiwork attitudes in the French upper middle class, see Lamont (1992, pp. 43–44).

51. Also, 66 percent of the French men I talked to chose "responsible" as one of five qualities that they most value, compared to 72 percent of American workers.

52. Lamont (1992, chapter 2, especially pp. 48–52).

53. Bourdieu (1984, pp. 38–34, 381–382) notes the importance that workers attach to frankness. However, he does not relate it to a wider appreciation for personal integrity.

54. Noiriel (1986, pp. 196 and 207) argues that this heroism has traditionally been part of working class culture and was particularly strong during World War II, in particular among militants of the Communist Party engaged in the resistance against the Nazis.

55. Lamont (1992, p. 30).

56. On the place of alcohol in the micro-politics of a French blue-collar shop floor, see Pialoux (1992).

57. Lamont (1992, chapter 2, especially p. 54).

58. On this topic, see Michelat and Simon (1977). These authors write "there exists a correlation between a low level of religious integration and sharing the systems of representation and attitudes associated with voting for the left, and particularly for the Communist Party" (p. 461). They show that people who belong to the working class are less likely to identify with Catholicism and are more likely to vote for the left (p. 462). In in-depth interviews, nonreligious workers put considerable emphasis on solidarity, class opposition, and claims for justice (p. 464).

59. Forty-four percent of the French interviewees declared themselves atheist or agnostic, while 48 percent declared themselves Catholic. Forty percent of the declared Catholics are nonpracticing. Information is missing for the remaining 8 percent. Some of the French respondents are vehemently antireligion. In contrast, only one American worker said he disliked religion, and none described themselves as atheist or agnostic. These differences correspond to patterns revealed by surveys showing a higher level of religiosity in the United States than in France. For instance, Chadwick et al. (1994) report on a 1990 survey that showed that 95 percent of the American respondents believed in God, compared to only

57 percent of the French respondents. Among Catholics, 11 percent of the French reported attending Mass, compared to 46 percent of the American Catholics.
60. Dirn (1998, pp. 359–364).
61. See Lamont (1992, chapter 4, and particularly p. 117) on French and American attitudes toward cultural laissez-faire.
62. Sewell, Jr. (1980). For a more contemporary treatment, see Gallie (1983). For a critique of Sewell's work that explores the origins of republican socialism, see Moss (1993).

5. Racism Compared

1. For details on public housing laws and how they affect North Africans, see Blanc (1991).
2. Eric finds this upsetting because family allowances are adjusted to the number of children that an individual has.
3. See the special issue on racism published by *Le Nouvel Observateur*, October 17–23, 1996.
4. See Schain (1987) and Taguieff (1989b).
5. Wieviorka (1992) studies individuals engaged in an intervention that might lessen racist tensions in the area where they live. His analysis privileges the most racist or antiracist actors. In contrast, I am interested in tapping a more diverse range of positions by randomly sampling respondents. Similarly, Bataille (1997) interviews workers and union representatives who have had to confront issues of discrimination. Like Wieviorka (1992) and Beaud and Pialoux (1998), he is more concerned with the specifics of experiences of racism in concrete situations than with the rhetoric of racism per se.
6. Downward mobility and threat to class perpetuation are among the factors often used to account for working class racism (see Wieviorka 1992 and Beaud and Pialoux 1998). Unlike the present study, which does not discuss how the characteristics of place of residence affect racism, de Rudder et al. (1990) compare seven sites that vary in terms of type of urban/suburban location, length of history of immigrant implantation, and composition of the immigrant population. They find that individuals who live in areas whose residents are less than 1 percent foreign are more likely to declare themselves racists than those who live in areas whose inhabitants are more than 10 percent foreign. For a multidimensional explanation of the determinants of racism, see also Gaxie et al. (1997).
7. As in Chapter 2, racist statements are defined as statements supporting the view that ethnic or racial groups are unequal. These figures must be interpreted with caution because of the small size of our samples and because French racists, as compared to American racists, might have been more hesitant to be interviewed for our study for various reasons. These include (1) a context of crisis around issues of racism and immigration in France and (2) a greater suspicion by French workers toward intellectuals and academics, who are generally presumed to be left-leaning. In contrast, American workers might have vaguer views concerning

the political leanings of academics, especially given the lower polarization of the American political spectrum as compared to that of the French.

8. While some social scientists have noted the prevalence of cultural arguments over biological arguments in the French rhetoric of racism (for instance, Balibar and Wallerstein 1991 and Silverman 1992), this has yet to be established by a detailed and empirically grounded analysis of the range of types of arguments used in French vocabularies of exclusion.

9. Gillette and Sayad (1984, p. 210).

10. For an in-depth discussion of the role of work and the workplace in shaping how workers express racism, see Bataille (1997).

11. The unemployment rate of the French-born male children of Muslim immigrants hovers between 40 and 50 percent, depending on the nationality (Hargreaves 1995, p. 63). Almost 20 percent of the foreign population was unemployed in 1990, up from 4.6 percent in 1975 (Hollifield 1994, p. 160).

12. Horne (1977, p. 54).

13. Cohen (1985, p. 306).

14. Figures cited by Body-Gendrot (1998, p. 3). Parallel figures for the United States are ambiguous. For instance, while 44 percent of respondents to a 1994 Harris poll agreed that "A lot of immigrants start new businesses which helps the U.S. economy to grow," 51 percent disagreed, and 4 percent were not sure. Also, 66 percent of respondents agreed that "New immigrants joining the labor force drive down wages"; 31 percent disagreed and 3 percent said "don't know" (Lapinski et al. 1997, p. 369).

15. These include housing, health care, family allowances, unemployment insurance, and subsistence income. While for much of the twentieth century, France was behind most European nations in terms of the social benefits it gives to its population, by 1980 it "stood only behind Denmark, the Netherlands, and Sweden in the size of its social security expenditure as a percentage of GDP. Indeed, France led all nations in Europe in the proportion of public expenditures allocated to social security programs" (Chapman 1995, p. 297). It has been shown that benefits are distributed evenly across all quintiles of the population with no redistributive effect (p. 299). Moreover, means-testing is kept at a minimum for most programs.

16. The main increases occurred under the presidencies of Charles de Gaulle and Valéry Giscard d'Estaing. See Cameron (1991, p. 84). See also Jobert and Théret (1994, p. 65).

17. On the connection between sense of group positioning and racism, see Bobo and Hutchings (1996).

18. Rosanvallon (1990).

19. On this point, see also Beaud and Pialoux (1998). On the challenges to class reproduction that workers meet, see in particular the data presented by Lipietz (1996, p. 112).

20. Body-Gendrot (1998, p. 11).

21. For a similar argument, see Castel (1995) and Wieviorka (1992).

22. Cayrol (1996, p. 20).

23. Haegel (1998).

24. Wieviorka (1992, p. 31). On associations, see also Kastoryano (1996). Islam is the second most common and the fastest growing religion in France. While in 1970 there were only a few mosques and organizations related to Islam, in 1985 there were over 1,000, in addition to 600 Islamic organizations (Képel 1987). Moreover, there are now 2,400 immigrant associations that receive state subsidies from the French Social Action Funds (Body-Gendrot 1992, p. 84). Ethnic businesses are also increasingly visible in mixed neighborhoods as is the organization of religious life, due to a growing number of praying rooms in factories and public housing buildings, ritual butchering warehouses, and Koranic schools.

25. Perrineau (1997, p. 158) argued that overwhelmed by the social, ideological, and political changes of the last few decades, National Front voters are much more likely to feel dispossessed: 86 percent of them, versus 45 percent of the general electorate, believe that in France "on ne se sent plus chez soi comme avant" ("we don't feel at home anymore").

26. Ibid., pp. 101–112. National Front voters are also more likely to derive their sense of personal identity from affiliation with the French nation: 31 percent (versus 18 percent of the general electorate) believe that French nationality is the attribute that best defines them personally (p. 159).

27. Balibar (1991, p. 24) discusses this theme of cultural incompatibility. Concerning differentialist racism, he writes: "The context of contemporary Arabophobia [involves] an image of Islam as a 'conception of the world' which is incompatible with Europeanness."

28. Over the last decades, anthropological and sociological analyses of the transformation of working class culture in France have multiplied, and they often focus on the general themes of nostalgia and the transformation of working class culture in the context of deindustrialization. See Touraine, Wieviorka, and Dubet (1978); Verret (1988); Pinçon (1987, chapter 5); Dubet (1987); Schwartz (1990); and Térrail (1990). Authors are particularly concerned with the transformation of the relationship between the public and the private and with the decline of solidarity within the family and within larger networks of sociability.

29. Factors that account for the differences in the decolonization process in Algeria include the greater significance of Algeria in the French economy, the presence in Algeria of a larger number of French colonizers/farmers (making up 12 percent of the Algerian population) resisting the decolonization process, the longer duration of French rule in that country, and the fact that Algerian decolonization happened at the end of the decolonization period (Smith 1975, p. 113). For a detailed analysis of the decolonization process in North Africa and elsewhere, see Kahler (1984).

30. Donadey (1996, p. 218).

31. Tournier and Robert (1991).

32. Safran (1991, p. 223). This point is also made by Balibar (1991, p. 19).

33. More specifically, according to SOFRES (Société française de recherche, d'études, et de sondages) polls, whereas only 23 percent of the French surveyed in 1985 thought that religion was an obstacle to Muslims' cohabitation with the French, this figure increased to 57 percent in 1989 (Feldblum 1993, p. 66). Also, whereas

58 percent thought Muslim customs were an obstacle to cohabitation in 1989, only 49 percent thought so in 1985. Data on the acceptance of people coming from countries south of the Mediterranean show that the percentage of French people who do not accept such immigrants rises between 1991 and 1993 (to 37 percent), and that this percentage is higher than those found in other countries of the European Community (Melich 1995).

34. See note 9.

35. Social scientists such as Schnapper (1991, pp. 142–143) find here the explanation for the difficulties North Africans experience in assimilating.

36. For instance, Tribalat (1995) found that only 11 percent of her Algerian respondents had attended religious services at least five times in the last 12 months, compared to 34 percent of the Mandingo African respondents. When it came to practicing a religion, 48 percent of the Algerians reported practicing no religion, compared to 36 percent of Moroccan respondents, 31 percent of Turks, and 18 percent of the Mandingo.

37. On France's historic Catholic identity, see Beaune (1985) and Birnbaum (1998).

38. Chadwick et al. (1994) report that even though only 11 percent of Catholics claim to attend Mass, and only slightly over half of French marriages are performed by clergy, 80 percent of the French population considers itself Catholic.

39. Indicative of this are the public debates on the historical Catholic figures of Clovis and Joan of Arc that filled the media in 1996 and that were used by the National Front and other conservative forces to reaffirm France's Catholic roots.

40. Césari (1997) provides an excellent overview of the images of Islam prevailing in Europe over several centuries. Of course, there were also competing hegemonic claims pitting various European nations and denominations against one another, including Catholic France against Protestant England. For an interesting analysis of the anti-British rhetoric developed by the French during the period of North American colonization, see Bell (1998); this rhetoric resembles that used to disparage North Africans.

41. House (1996, p. 224).

42. The Catholic national identity of France is contested in part because the Church has historically been a reactionary force: Catholics were allied with the monarchy and opposed the republic until after World War II (Gaffney 1991, p. 28).

43. Joppke (1998, p. 37). Muhammad (1995, pp. 166–169) discusses the composition of American Muslim communities in America and their differences and similarities.

44. Képel (1987).

45. Kastoryano (1996, p. 74).

46. Ibid., p. 39. Bonnafous (1991) provides results from a content analysis of the treatment of immigrants in ten newspapers and news magazines between 1974 and 1984. She finds that while articles published at the beginning of this period tended to focus on the problems encountered by immigrants as workers, articles published later in this period focused on their integration into French civil society and the challenges they present to the French social contract.

47. For an analysis of the racist components of the National Fronts political platform, see Schain (1997).

48. On this point, see Feldblum (1998). See also Morokvasic and Rudolph (1996).
49. Tribalat (1995) discusses various indicators of assimilation for North African and European immigrants, drawing on a recent and unique survey conducted by the Institut national de démographie (INED). The data she presents indicate that the cultural barriers separating North African immigrants from the French are not very different from those separating European immigrants from the French (see pp. 216–219 for a summary). For instance, the proportion of men who have a good command of the French language is 72 percent among sub-Saharian immigrants, 62 percent among Spaniards, 61 percent among Algerians, and 59 percent among Moroccans (p. 39).
50. Nielsen (1992, p. 22). Also, only 13 percent of the children read the Koran regularly as against 45 percent of the parents. Only about 10 percent of adult men attended the Friday service. Note, however that, while in a 1989 survey, 30 percent of the beurs questioned were in favor of wearing head-scarves at school, in 1993 14 percent declared that they participated in, or approved, of Muslim separatism (Leveau 1997, pp. 149, 153).
51. Noiriel (1996, chapter 1).
52. Duchesne (1997) provides a fascinating description of this organic model of citizenship, as it is understood by ordinary French citizens. Drawing on in-depth interviews conducted in 1989, the author documents a view of citizenship based on inheritance, history, the French geographical space, and the family. Central are an emotional attachment to what is distinctively French and a sense of responsibility for maintaining the French quality of life.
53. Norindr (1996, p. 241).
54. For Freeman (1979, p. 32), this view was based on "a firm commitment to the universality of the French culture and language and to its infinite adaptability to circumstances." On this topic, see also Mauco (1977, pp. 203–214), Conklin (1998), and Lebovics (1999).
55. On the French and British colonial experiences, see Smith (1975).
56. Fredrickson (1997, p. 105).
57. Associationism meant that colonial policies could be flexible, varying from place to place in order to be most effective in different locales. It envisioned economic development resulting from partnership between natives and colonials, and suggested that the framework of native institutions was to be altered only slightly, if at all. It also discarded the notion of a "mission civilisatrice" based on principles of "fraternité, égalité, liberté." See Betts (1961).
58. Nicolet (1992). These republican principles, including the symbolically crucial notion of secular education, have gained a sacred status since the Third Republic. At the end of the nineteenth century, republicans defeated the royalists, who had been fighting a counterrevolution with the support of the Catholic Church since 1789, contesting in particular the principle of the separation of church and state. On the changing content of French republicanism, see Gaffney (1991).
59. For a comparison of the relationship between the state and the common interest in France and the United States, see Rangeon (1986). On French political culture and the general historical role of the French state, see Rosanvallon (1990).

60. "As long as the reason of man continues fallible, and he is at liberty to exercise it, different opinions will be formed . . . The diversity in the faculties of men from which the rights of property originate, is not less an insuperable obstacle to a uniformity of interests. *The protection of these faculties is the first object of Government. From the protection of different and unequal faculties of acquiring property, the possession of different degrees and kinds of property immediately results*" (my emphasis). Excerpt from Madison ([1787] 1987, p. 151). I thank David Abraham for bringing this passage to my attention.

61. On the impact of pluralism on American society as compared to French society, see Lacorne (1997); Kastoryano (1996); Thévenot and Lamont (2000); and Moody and Thévenot (2000).

62. Fassin (1999). On this issue, see also Favell (1997b, p. 183). Republicanism presumes that the assimilation of minority groups is a requirement for the reproduction of the polity and for the defense of majority interests (Noiriel 1992, chapter 3). Brubaker (1992) proposes that this assimilationist approach constitutes the distinctively French cultural idiom of nationhood that characterizes French political culture.

63. Safran (1991).

64. For a comparison of the place given to pluralism in the idealized French and American models, see Schnapper (1991, p. 93).

65. Body-Gendrot (1992, p. 83).

66. This law was based on the understanding that such information would eventually lead to quotas and social balkanization and would represent a danger to individual liberty. In fact, the prohibition against counting the population based on race goes back to 1848, when slavery was abolished in the French West Indies (personal communication with Emmanuelle Saada). The collaboration of the Vichy government with the Nazis feeds into concerns for the protection of citizens' privacy from the state. One of the unintended consequences of this law, however, is that it is difficult to establish access discrimination in the absence of ethnic statistics. See Bleitch (1998, p. 18) and Lieberman (1998).

67. A law against discrimination in employment, housing, and provision of services and prohibiting incitement to racial hatred was passed in 1972 but is rarely enforced. The country was relatively slow to pass it (in contrast to other Western nations) because French decision makers believed that all citizens were equally protected by French law, which de facto embodies republican principles (Freeman 1979, p. 156). Simultaneously, in order to give it more bite, this law was included under criminal law, with the result that relatively few cases are brought to justice because criminal standards of proof are difficult to establish. Indeed, while in 1991 British civil procedures led to 1,471 cases of employment-related discrimination, in France only four cases were brought to justice (cited by Bleitch 1998, p. 4). Bataille (1997, p. 7) offers similar statistics. In general, the law is used less to fight access discrimination in housing or employment, as is the case in the United States, than to fight hate speech (Hein 1993b, pp. 104–105).

68. Noiriel (1996). See also Weber (1976).

69. Schnapper (1991) provides an ideal-typical description of this model and describes it as existing de facto in contemporary France.

70. Pro-republican intellectuals include Dominique Schnapper, Patrick Weil, Régis Debray, Emmanuel Todd, and Pierre-André Taguieff. Intellectuals who take more nuanced and/or pro-multicultural positions include Michel Wieviorka, Pierre Birnbaum, and Sophie Body-Gendrot. While outside France, scholars such as James Hollifield (1994) argue that the republican model survives recent changes, others such as Maxim Silverman (1992) argue that it is seriously threatened by them. For an analysis of the role of French academics in the production of various images of national identity, see Lorcerie (1994).

71. Because their inability to assimilate threatens the right of the French to protect their own way of life and cultural uniqueness, the National Front argues that Muslims should not be allowed to stay in France. As the economic crisis worsened in the 1980s, the Socialists, along with the Communists, also quietly began advocating stricter measures promoted by the right (Schain 1987, p. 242; see also Lochak 1993). Some of these themes are shared with France's right-wing parties, the Rassemblement pour la République (RPR) and the Union pour la démocratie française (UDF). For instance, in the 1986 elections these two parties called "for stronger measures to encourage immigrants to return to their home countries and a reduction of payments of social benefits to resident immigrants" (Schain 1987, p. 242).

72. French republicanism posits that access to nationality and citizenship entails a will to participate in the social contract. This voluntaristic element justifies encouraging second-generation immigrants to express their desire to become part of the country before they officially enter the polity. While some view this law as attacking the republican principle of *jus soli,* others support it as essential to improving the integration of second-generation immigrants in the polity. This understanding of republican citizenship was reaffirmed by the commissions that led to the reform of the Nationality Code in 1996. It was also reinforced by neo-republican intellectuals who have considerable access to the media, and has been supported by defenders of republican ideals on both the left and the right. For an excellent discussion of this debate, see Feldblum (1999).

73. Feldblum (1999). See also Vichniac (1991).

74. This point is made by Noiriel (1996, preface).

75. On this topic, see Noiriel (1986, p. 135). He notes: "It is striking that in the country of Human Rights, if so much was given to the citizen, it is at the detriment of those who stayed outside the nation. Between the two wars, not only do immigrants have no political rights, but they also cannot participate in electing union representatives, even in industries where they represent the vast majority of workers."

76. On the transition from an unsettled to a settled North African immigration after 1974, see Weil (1991).

77. According to Noiriel (1986), the history of immigration to France is marked by only three periods of acute xenophobia in modern times: that directed at Belgian workers in the 1880s, at Jews during the Dreyfus affair (1894–1906), and at North Africans today.

78. Noiriel (1984) describes how during the first half of the twentieth century, Italian and Polish workers were integrated into the French working class largely through their involvement in the French Communist Party. France has a long history of anti-Semitism that was particularly salient during the Dreyfus affair and under the Vichy government. Jews are now viewed as well integrated, and few of them consider themselves the victims of anti-Semitism (Donadey 1996, p. 220). This relative absence of anti-Semitism leads Wieviorka (1992, p. 181) to conclude that French workers do not have a fully elaborated racist ideology, and that in fact they are mere populists expressing sporadic bursts of resentment due to downward mobility.

79. Surveys show that in France "74 percent of Asian immigrants want to become citizens, [as opposed to] only 41 percent of black Africans, 30 percent of Iberians and 16 percent of North Africans" (Hein 1993a, p. 8). Asian immigrants are small in number and highly educated.

80. On this topic, see Zolberg and Woon (1999).

81. Outside France, a few social scientists have come to understand French republicanism as a form of nationalist patriotism promoting a rooted, bounded, and idealized view of the historical political culture of the nation (see in particular Favell 1998, p. 6; Favell 1997b, p. 185; Feldblum 1999; Lloyd and Waters 1991, pp. 49–50; and Fredrickson 1998, pp. 20–21). They concur that in its very substance the culture of republicanism marks strong boundaries between those who share it and those who do not (see also Silverman 1992, p. 33). Unlike these authors, I aim at explaining the weakness of boundaries against blacks in conjunction with the strength of anti-immigrant boundaries. This connection between the boundaries drawn toward blacks and immigrants often escapes some French social scientists involved in these debates, who, along with politicians, sometimes espouse the very republican views that appear to be readily appropriated by the workers I interviewed. Such is the case of the otherwise truly admirable Noiriel (1996). In particular, see his treatment of racism on p. 260, indicating that racism is downplayed de facto in French society because of republican legal principles.

82. Wacquant (1993a) concludes: "If there is a dominant antagonism that runs through the Red belt *cité* and stamps the collective consciousness of its habitat, it is not, contrary to widespread media representations, one that opposes immigrants (especially 'Arabs') and autochthonous French families but the cleavage dividing youth *(les jeunes)*, natives and foreign lumped together, from all other social categories" (p. 376). While not sharing Wacquant's conclusions on the importance of racism in French society, I agree with his conclusion that "racial" tensions "observed in the *banlieues* over the past decade are expressive of the social crisis brought about by persistent un(der)employment and by the spatial conjugation of educational exclusion, housing blight and poverty in areas where immigrant and native working class families compete over diminishing collective resources" (p. 387). Note that his study draws on extensive participant observation conducted in Chicago public housing projects and on an analysis of secondary sources on French banlieues.

83. More Americans did not discuss racial inequality during the interview: this was the case for 20 percent of the American white-collar workers and 30 percent of the American blue-collar workers, compared to 6 percent and 26 percent of their French counterparts, respectively.

84. When presented with a list of traits and qualities and asked which they view most negatively, a quarter of American white-collar workers chose "racist" in contrast to half of the French white-collar workers. Among blue-collar workers, these percentages were a little more than a third in the United States and two-thirds in France.

85. This last group was also found to be younger (half are less than 25 years of age). The number of individuals who uphold antiracist positions has increased in the last few years: while in 1990 only 19 percent of respondents to another national survey said that there are not too many Arabs in France, in 1997 the percentage had climbed to 35 percent (Cayrol 1998, p. 14). This suggests a polarization between racists and nonracists, as support for the National Front also increases.

86. Lambert (1993, p. 241).

87. Cohen (1980).

88. For instance, a carpenter states that "Portuguese people are hard workers and they're honest. But black people are lazy, and they can be very nasty, aggressive. They do it from behind."

89. Other authors reach similar conclusions that race is downplayed in France's patterns of exclusion without necessarily substantiating them with specific data. For instance, in an anecdotal mode, see Todd (1994). Rex (1979, p. 100) suggests that skin color has not traditionally been a strong social marker in France in part because it is not a reliable indicator of colonial status. Moreover, Hein (1993a, p. 64) writes that "language, religion and former colonial status are more important than race." In a different vein, Silverman (1992) notes that since the 1970s France has turned toward a more racialized view of immigration. He equates "racialization" with biological or cultural "essentialization." While acknowledging the importance of naturalization processes, I believe that it is more useful to examine the full range of arguments used in national rhetorics of racism: biological arguments are disappearing, and cultural arguments take so many forms that too much is missed by focusing on the culture/biology opposition only.

90. Gillette and Sayad (1984, p. 210). These authors write that the "relationships that immigrants have with French society are not class relations or relations between segments of a same class (between an immigrant proletariat and a working class): they are caste relationships that tend to look like those that existed between the colonized and the colonizers."

91. Lemaine and Ben Brika (1994, p. 212) find that 85 percent of a nationally representative sample believe that North Africans are physically different from the French. However, a number of North Africans share with the French southern Mediterranean features (Braudel 1986, p. 192). Although Arabs are considered Caucasians, whiteness is epitomized by European features (Dyer 1997, p. 13).

92. See also Freeman (1979, p. 133).

93. Weil (1996, p. 11).

94. Lemaine and Ben Brika (1997). As early as 1966 a national survey revealed that ten negative attributes were viewed as applying primarily to Algerians by 71 percent of the respondents, while only 22 percent believed that these attributes applied primarily to black Africans, and 7 percent believed that they applied primarily to the Portuguese (cited by Kastoryano 1996, p. 74). Similar trends appeared in a 1973–1974 survey (see Girard, Charbit, and Lamy 1974, p. 1028; see also Mauco 1977).

95. Cited by Horowitz (1992, p. 19).

96. Mayer (1987, p. 893). Note that former colonies are among the groups receiving high and low ratings.

97. Many natives from the Dom-Toms are not assimilated to French society and live in a marginal position. Furthermore, the Portuguese, Spaniards, Algerians, and Moroccans all include groups of well-integrated and less-integrated immigrants (de Rudder et al. 1990, pp. 119–122).

98. Tribalat (1995, p. 21) finds that 40 percent of the black Africans she surveyed were from Muslim countries, and 14 percent were from exclusively Christian or animist areas. Nearly half of the black African immigrants are from regions that are heterogeneous in religion.

99. See Chapter 4, notes 26 and 27.

100. Delerm (1964, pp. 522–523) estimated that the black African population in France in 1964 was composed of 10,000 to 12,000 students; 4,000 to 5,000 former students who stayed; 5,000 interns ("stagiaires au titre de la coopération"); and 40,000 to 50,000 workers, of whom 28,000 inhabited the Parisian metropolitan area.

101. Bergues (1973, pp. 73–74) discusses a 1965 survey that revealed favorable views held by the French about black Africans. She wrote: "they are considered pleasant, polite, hardworking, quite childish, but of good disposition . . . Good relations are generally established between black Africans and French workers or other Europeans. Only the relations with the North African groups appear difficult" (p. 74).

102. Tribalat (1995, p. 42).

103. Barou (1996).

104. Meertens and Pettigrew (1997, p. 67). The other groups that engage in subtle prejudice are younger respondents and left-wingers.

105. Taguieff (1988) has criticized the antiracism of French social scientists, intellectuals, politicians, and activists for borrowing the differentialist language of the far right. He argues that in the name of cultural relativism and multiculturalism (the right of immigrants to be different), these groups have fed into the National Front's claim that Muslims cannot be assimilated. He advocates a return to universalistic arguments in line with French republicanism. For a critique, see Grignon (1991).

106. In contrast to liberalism, republicanism promotes solidarity as opposed to individualism by negating social and natural differences in the name of equal dignity, nondifferentiation of roles, and the sharing of universal capacities. Taylor (1992) provides a particularly cogent description of this difference.

107. When asked to choose from a list of traits five qualities that they find particularly important in others, a third of the French workers chose "egalitarian" in contrast to less than a fifth of their American counterparts. Paradoxically, none of the

American antiracists defended egalitarianism as a general principle, although it is a founding principle of American liberal republicanism. Smith (1997) points out that the American liberal democratic tradition, as described in de Tocqueville ([1835] 1969), stresses the absence of one type of ascriptive hierarchy in American society–that based on monarchical and aristocratic lineage. As a result, the United States appears egalitarian in comparison with Europe. However, Smith argues that American political culture is also shaped by other political traditions that have remained a mainstay of American society until recently, such as racism, nativism, and patriarchy that justify ascriptive hierarchies based on race and gender. Smith neglects the place given to class differences in this egalitarian worldview, as if they were taken to be natural.

108. Lamont (1992, chapter 2).

109. The distinctive Catholic doctrine of the "communion of saints" and the "communion of sin" brings forth a special obligation to the poor as members of the community who are marginalized. By uplifting the poor, Catholics uplift themselves and their own community.

110. The complex relationship between French unions and immigrants is described in Mouriaux and Wihtol de Wenden (1987).

111. On this movement, see Dréano (1992, p. 68). Associations such as the MRAP, the LDH, and SOS-racisme played a crucial role in defining and passing antidiscrimination laws and in bringing cases of racism to court or to the public prosecutor's attention (Bleitch 1998, p. 4).

112. Haegel (2000) notes that such work-based arguments are more often used toward older workers than younger ones who are viewed as lazy.

113. Many had been discriminated against when looking for an apartment, and most had been given the most difficult and degrading tasks at work while being more closely supervised than their French coworkers. Some had been fired in favor of Southern European immigrants, while others had faced customers who refused to be served by an Arab. One had a declared National Front supporter as a union representative and another recalled that his longtime employer did not know his name the day he fired him. On the systematic discrimination that North African immigrants encounter in the French workplace, see Bataille (1997, p. 61).

114. Gillette and Sayad (1984, p. 39).

115. These qualities rest on the view that middle positions are preferable in a range of areas. Sociologists have written about the cardinal virtues of Islam. For instance, Ahmed (1992) mentions the importance of *adl* and *ahsan* (balance and compassion) in Islam and indicates that this religion is often described as the middle way–the bridge between different systems (p. 48). See also Ahmed (1987).

116. Being questioned by a white Canadian is likely to make race, nation, country of origin, or religion particularly salient categories to respondents in the context of the interview.

117. Berque (1979, p. 23).

118. Orientalist scholars such as Von Grunebaum (1962, pp. 55–63) have argued that the prophetic tradition is incompatible with cultural relativism: because the truth

given by the Koran is taken for granted, Muslims refuse to regard human beings as arbiters of the value of things, and relativism is literally unthinkable.

119. When describing differences with the French, a roofer, a hotel janitor, and a controller who works in the automobile industry mentioned that they are not familiar with French people because they would have to go to the bistros to know them, which they do not want to do. Here they stress a religious difference between the French and the Muslims by focusing on alcohol consumption, emphasizing an aspect of French identity that is not necessarily salient to the French.

120. Chatterjee (1994, p. 237).

121. Gillette and Sayad (1984, p. 84).

122. Kastoryano (1986, p. 19).

123. This applies to the sacred law but also to trade and crafts, literacy, and understanding human relationships (Rosen 1984, p. 47).

124. Nielsen (1992).

125. Képel (1987).

126. Mouriaux and Wihtol de Wenden (1987).

127. Rosen (1984, p. 28).

128. At the same time, Islam is likely to limit the immigrants' claims concerning equality. In particular, Muslim specialists have argued that the concept of equality between all human beings has traditionally not been a point of reference within this culture. This may explain why interviewees often appear to be more concerned with establishing equivalence and similarity than equality. Muslim theologians have argued that the Sharia—the Islamic law based on the Koran and the Sunnah— is not egalitarian in that it does not recognize the formal equality of all citizens. Most important, it subordinates women to men through the marriage laws. It also attributes to non-Muslims a status of second-class guests within Muslim society— non-Muslims are excluded from a number of public offices and are required to pay a special tax. According to An-Na'im (1987, p. 21), in the Koranic text and the Sunnah, dating from the period when he lived in Mecca, "the Prophet preached equality and individual responsibility between men and women without distinction on grounds of race, sex, and social origin." He changed this message in response to socioeconomic and political realities when he was forced to migrate to Medina following dissent and external attacks. The historical Islamic law known to Muslims today is based on texts from this second period, which are less universalistic than those of the first period. On this point, see Bilgram (1995). Von Grunebaum (1962, p. 66) suggests that despite the nonegalitarianism of this latter period, Islam recognizes the fundamental equality of all believers qua believers.

129. Herzberg (1996).

130. Portes and Rumbaut (1990).

131. Fuchs (1990).

132. This is the case for 25 percent of France's residents, compared with 13 percent of British residents—the European country with the second highest number of individuals falling into this category. See Jaffre (1998, p. 15).

133. Hollifield (1997).

134. Other types of evidence are absent from both the rhetoric of racism and anti-racism deployed in both countries: most respondents view the sources of racism in its victim and not in the characteristics of its perpetrator.
135. Dobbin (1994a).
136. As suggested by Esping-Anderson (1990).
137. Wieviorka (1996, p. 9).
138. Aufderheide (1991); Berman (1992); Kouchner (1989).
139. Hence, Fischer et al. (1996) show that American welfare and redistributive policy choices are less oriented toward social solidarity than the welfare programs of a number of European countries.
140. While research comparing blatant and subtle prejudice in France and the United States is not available, Pettigrew et al. (1998) document the relevance of the distinction between subtle and blatant prejudice in descriptions of European racism. Also, Meertens and Pettigrew (1997) provide evidence that blatant prejudice is more common in France than in the Netherlands, Great Britain, and West Germany.
141. For instance, on November 2, 1991, Bruno Megret, one of the top leaders of the National Front, defended the racial purity of the French and condemned the extinction of human races through interbreeding (Biffaud 1991).

6. Class Boundaries Compared

1. This is also the case for French professionals and managers, as compared to their American counterparts.
2. In 1975, 24 percent of French workers were unionized. This figure had fallen to 10 percent by 1992 (Upham 1993, p. G-20). In the United States in 1994, only 15 percent of the active labor force in the public- and private-sector workforces were union members (Bureau of National Affairs, 1996, p. 9). In 1975, this figure was 29 percent (United States Bureau of Census of the Population 1988, table 666, p. 401).
3. See Wieviorka (1992). See also Mouriaux (1991).
4. Hamilton (1967); Gallie (1983); and Chapman (1991).
5. Lamont (1992, p. 47).
6. See Bourdieu (1984). Overall, my findings are more in line with the view that working class culture is relatively autonomous from the culture of the upper middle class. In the French context, this position is represented by Grignon and Passeron (1989). See also Hoggart ([1957] 1992).
7. Lamont (1992, chapter 4).
8. On the centrality of antielitism and populism in American political culture, see Lipset (1979, p. 220).
9. On this topic, see Bourdieu and Passeron (1990).
10. We will remember that in the United States in 1985, 58 percent of all recent high school graduates aged 16 to 24 were enrolled in college, whereas in France this percentage was 36 percent in 1989. See Chapter 4, note 16.
11. In some cases, mobility is de facto blocked because the government put a limit on the number of times that one can repeat exams.

12. See, for instance, Castel (1995). For more extensive references, see Chapter 5, note 28.

13. Between 1976 and 1983, the percentage of the population that identified itself as working class declined from 27 to 22 percent. Noiriel (1986, p. 260).

14. This delay was caused in part by the many peasants who owned small parcels of land and were able to remain self-sufficient and avoid urban exile. This slowed the urban demand for manufactured goods in particular, and meant that French workers gained access to mass consumption later than American workers did. This process is described in Noiriel (1986, p. 61).

15. In the words of political scientist Jenson (1991, p. 86), "Whereas elsewhere in Europe, the social relations of Fordism [increased workers' consumption] were stabilized in the postwar years, in France, the consensus remained fragile and underdeveloped until well in the Fifth Republic. The Fordism that existed in France until the mid-1960s was characterized by contested state intervention and by authoritarian and conflictual wage relations."

16. Jenson (1991, p. 93).

17. On this topic, see Crozier (1964).

18. An electronic chipmaker in his thirties compares his present boss, who is his age, "with the type of bosses we had before. They were self-taught and were more authoritarian than the younger ones, but they were listened to." In sharp contrast with American workers, a French storage worker legitimizes this traditional authoritarian culture by arguing that bosses should not compliment their subordinates on work well done because the workers could then decide to slack off.

19. A technician says, "I think that bosses should take a psychology course to learn how to manage people. There has not been any progress in industrial relations since my grandfather's days. My boss should explain things well at first, but he says nothing and does not allow errors. We have to work very hard and he is always on top of us. My coworkers become more nervous, more nasty. The bosses really need to be reeducated."

20. For instance, an electrician explains that managers "want to create more communication between higher and lower levels, but it is one-way communication that they want. It means that we have to tell them everything, and they choose what they are going to tell us. They have all the information that they need and we have more pressure."

21. This is noted by Donzelot (1984, p. 173): "Instead of opposing the rights of workers with those of owners, the state calculates the relative risks and benefits of both parties. To the division between capitalists and workers, it substitutes an approach that aims at compensating everyone for the prejudices they have experienced while collaborating."

22. For a comparison of the lasting revolutionary tradition among the French and Italian working class, as compared to their milder British and American counterparts, see Mann (1973, especially chapter 4). Kesselman (1984, p. 2) observes that in the early eighties, France still exhibited more conflictual class relations than did most advanced societies. He concludes: "This confrontational approach appears to reflect the strength and militancy of the French labor movement . . . The

French working class has not paid the characteristic cost [for increasing their standard of living]: integration within dominant institutions and the renunciation of radical goals." There is a large literature that aims at explaining working class radicalism in France. Explanations have focused on the role of organizations such as the French Communist Party and the Confédération générale du travail (Hamilton 1967; Kriegel 1970), the impact of employers' intransigence and state intervention on industry (Chapman 1991), and the impact of the use of massive demonstrations and strikes as political weapons (Shorter and Tilly 1974). For a comparison of working class formation in France and the United States, see Zolberg (1986).

23. Ambler (1991, p. 9) describes this radical position as central to the French working class movement: "Unlike the British labor movement, in which Marxism never played an important role, French labor already before the turn of the century was divided between radicals, like Jules Guesde, who opposed all measures that might extend the life of capitalism, and reformers like Jean Jaurès, who believed that real improvements in the life of workers could be achieved without revolution. This, of course, is the schism that has weakened the political influence of the Left throughout most of French Republican history."

24. Noiriel (1986, p. 64).

25. In the words of Noiriel (1986, pp. 75–76), "The fact that working class neighborhoods had been left to their own devices since the Revolution contributes greatly to reinforcing a collective identity and tradition of struggle among those who live there for several generations. We have talked about the importance of the struggle of the *sans-culottes* on the urban riots of the XIX century . . . If workers see in their bosses irreducible enemies, it is because they have not forgotten the revolts and repressions of 1831, 1834, 1848." On this topic, see the important work of Sewell (1980) on the role of collective memory in sustaining French revolutionary culture.

26. Noiriel (1986, p. 99).

27. While the Socialist-led National Assembly has abandoned policies aimed at redistributing income, it still promotes solidarity with the poor. In the words of Jenson (1991, p. 107), "a discourse of solidarity is compatible with a two-tier labor force (as long as the worst effects of marginal work are eliminated) . . . and with a generally more fragmented society."

28. Others believe that dishonest manipulations, instead of hard work and merit, are generally behind profit-making. For instance, Lucien Maroix, the radar technician, explains: "My firm makes money on nothing–they speculate. Some people become rich because they had a wonderful idea, but this happens very rarely."

29. George Desjardins refused to be promoted to fire chief because "people could tell me 'You are above now. You have to change your personality.' I don't think that I could. . . . I would not like to hurt people. I know the director of a bank. He wants to be very friendly but can't because people don't like it." Gaston Roger, the pastry maker, had recently been promoted to supervisor. He also noted that he is expected to "behave as if you are not supposed to have feelings or need contact with people. Managers are supposed to be more distant, which creates diffi-

cult relationship with workers. We are supposed to say 'vous' to workers but I prefer to say 'tu.' They would like me to change, but I won't. They have no choice about it."

30. For a discussion of the literature on this topic, see Jenson (1991, pp. 48–51).

31. On the importance that workers attach to being natural and unpretentious (as opposed to the behavior of members of the dominant class), see Bourdieu (1984, pp. 376, 381–382).

32. For instance, a carpenter explains that manners are not important to him: "It is for the petit bourgeois to be well educated. You say to people that they are badly educated just because they grew up in a working class family. But the worker, he is who he is, and the bourgeois is different. It means nothing."

33. On this theme, see Perrot (1986, p. 97).

34. Thirteen percent of American white-collar workers, 17 percent of American blue-collar workers, and 7 percent of African-American blue-collar workers made such negative comments, in contrast to none of the French white-collar workers and 3.3 percent of the French blue-collar workers.

35. Noiriel (1986, p. 106).

36. Ibid., p. 185.

37. On this topic, see Pialoux (1995, pp. 30–31).

38. Western (1995).

39. Phillips (1970).

40. Weakliem and Heath (1999). These authors suggest that in the United States, nonvoters are more heavily working class than are Democratic voters. In fact, in class terms, nonvoters are about as far from the Democrats as the Democrats are from Republicans.

41. For a review of the comparative literature on poverty in France and the United States, see Silver (1993, pp. 338–342).

42. Smeeding et al. (1990); Freeman (1994); Weir (1995). In France, the state and unions have maintained wages and employment contracts at the price of a relatively high unemployment rate (Lane 1989).

43. Wacquant (1993b). The conditions in these French housing projects have been deteriorating steadily over the last 20 years. This situation is due to administrative decentralization and budget cuts, the decline in income of the lower segments of the working class, an increase in home ownership among the higher segments, and an increase in the size of the immigrant population residing in these public housing projects.

44. Entman (1992).

45. Respectively, 68 percent of French white-collar workers and 53 percent of French blue-collar workers did not mention the poor in the interview or expressed indifference toward them. Among white American workers, it was the case for, respectively, 20 percent of the white-collar workers and 23 percent of the blue-collar workers. Finally, 65 percent of the African-American workers shared this stance.

46. For a rapid overview of the interpretation of poverty and assistance in political thought, see Mazel (1996).

47. On the use of the United States as an antimodel, see Procacci (1993, p. 319).

48. Procacci (1993, pp. 16–17). The most influential recent study on the relationship between poverty and work in France is undoubtedly Castel (1995).

49. On the French Communist Party's understanding of poverty, see Paugam (1993, pp. 34–37).

50. Silver (1994, p. 14).

51. Silver (1996).

52. Chapman (1995, p. 301).

53. This argument is made by Esping-Anderson (1990) and Skocpol (1990).

54. Donzelot (1984, p. 137).

55. Hourriez and Lebris (1997, pp. 48–49).

56. An excellent analysis of the changing meaning of the term "exclus" from the mid-seventies until the nineties is provided by Didier (1996, p. 14). He argues that social scientists moved from defining exclusion in terms of inadaptation to defining it in terms of legal exclusion and cultural isolation. This latter meaning, which implies that the system is falling into disarray, became the meaning privileged by governmental agencies. In the last few years, the INSEE came to define it in terms of exclusion from the job market. Silver (1998) also provides a useful analysis of the term "exclusion," which highlights the multidimensional nature of social disadvantage.

57. It should also be noted that this term "excluded" has no racial connotation—whereas in the United States, talk of exclusion often points implicitly toward the discrimination and segregation that African Americans experience. This point is made by Silver (1996).

58. For an exhaustive overview of these policies, see Silver (1998). Paugam (1993, p. 17) focuses his attention on the RMI (Revenue minimum d'insertion), a response by French society to the question of poverty, which is perceived as revealing a weakening of social cohesion.

59. Mazel (1996, p. 63). For a comparative perspective, see Baldwin (1993). For a comparison of pensions, private health care, poor relief, and other social benefits programs in France, Canada, and the United States, see Esping-Anderson (1990, pp. 70–71).

60. Note, however, that the universalist principle of equality is sometimes challenged from the right, notably in the 1994 report *La France de l'An 2000* prepared by former prime minister Alain Minc. While critiquing "l'exclusion à l'Américaine," this report proposes to replace the republican principle of equality with that of equity, according to which the needs of citizens would be taken into consideration in the allocation of social benefits. Opposition to this report in the name of universalism was vehement. For a nuanced critique of the concept of equity, see Burgi-Golub (1996).

61. Burgi-Golub (1996, p. 318).

62. Mazel (1996, p. 145).

63. Shapiro and Young (1989, p. 69).

64. See Coughlin (1980).

65. For instance, an association for the defense of the unemployed has orchestrated the occupation of government offices, which received considerable media attention.

66. Gaffney (1991, p. 29).
67. See Katznelson (1986, p. 25). See also Sewell (1980).
68. In the words of Ross and Jenson (1994, p. 174), "The Cult of entrepreneurial inge-
    nuity, the centrality of the firm, and the dynamism of profits increasingly dis-
    placed an older vocabulary of redistribution, social equity, and justice. The task of
    France's mixed economy was now to streamline, rationalize, and high-technologize
    itself for the battle with the Americans, Germans, and Japanese. Nationalized
    firms, once envisaged as agencies of social justice and collective control, were
    rededicated as lean and mean multinationals. Socialists began to defend the
    decision-making and allocative rationality of the market with a new enthusiasm."
69. Jobert and Théret (1994, p. 55).
70. Segrestin (1990, pp. 101–102).

Conclusion

1. This comparative sociology of boundaries contributes to the rich literature on
   ethnic boundaries (Barth 1969, Shanahan and Olzak 1999, Verdery 1994), class
   boundaries (Parkin 1979, Wright and Cho 1992), and national boundaries (Borneman
   1992, Herzfeld 1996).
2. Inkeles (1979); Crozier (1964). For a critique, see Lamont (1992, chapter 5).
3. On cultural structures and institutionalized cultural repertoires, see Sewell (1992);
   Jepperson (1991); and Dobbin (1994b).
4. For a discussion of the changing character of republicanism, see Nicolet (1992).
5. For a critique of the growing influence of neoliberalism in France, see Bourdieu
   (1998).
6. For a description of such mechanisms applied to institutional change, see Thelen
   (1999).
7. See Calhoun (1994, pp. 9–36), who offers an excellent comparison of identity theory in sociology, poststructuralism, postmodernism, feminism, and literary criticism.
8. Drawing on Rorty's antifoundational pragmatism and on Derrida's understanding
   of signification as unstable and shifting, postmodern cultural studies are concerned with the fixity/fluidity of dimensions of identity and the extent to which
   they presume foundational artifice that allows dominant groups to make universal
   statements (Lash 1990, p. 14).
9. For an illustration, see also Stinchcombe (1995).
10. Pakulski and Waters (1996). For a critique of the postmodern stance on this issue,
    see Wright (1996). For an overview and very useful contribution to the debate, see
    Grusky and Sorensen (1998).
11. This confirms the findings of Halle (1984, p. 219).
12. On group identification and social categorization, see Jenkins (1996). Molnar and
    Lamont (2000) apply this framework to the study of African-American racial iden-
    tity.
13. Other factors include the sectarianism of the left, the absence of a labor party, the
    strength of democracy, the capacity of the Democratic Party to absorb protest, the

weak association between the bourgeoisie and the state, the great availability of educational opportunity, the weakness of class consciousness due to the early availability of universal suffrage, the expansion of American economic imperialism, and the development of a large proletarian aristocracy. See Aronowitz (1973); Lipset (1977); and Heffer and Rovert (1988).

14. Rodgers (1998); Shenhav (1999). For discussions pertaining specifically to labor, see Wilentz (1984a) and Cronin (1993). See also Katznelson (1986) and Zolberg (1986).

15. The literature aims at explaining the weaknesses of labor movements, socialist parties, and workers' solidarity (particularly between skilled and unskilled workers) in the United States. Explanations have centered on the incorporation of workers as citizens through consumption and nationalism. See, for instance, Cohen (1990) and Gerstle (1989). Others have focused on the impact of ethnic and racial diversity on working class solidarity (for instance, Katznelson 1981). Lipset (1996) reviews the many ways in which American society differs from other advanced industrial societies, focusing on cultural as well as institutional differences. He argues that American exceptionalism refers mainly to the religious system of the country and to its unique class structure, meaning "the emphasis on egalitarian social relations, the absence of a demand that those lower in the social order give overt deference to their betters and the stress on meritocracy, on equal opportunity for all to rise economically and socially" (p. 53).

16. Wilson and Musick (1997, p. 708) find that higher-status people are less likely to value informal helping than workers.

17. Women's subordinate position in the sexual divisions of labor leads them to value morally grounded conceptions of community (Hartsock 1983). Women consistently rate themselves and are rated by men as more emphatic and altruistic than men (Greeno and Maccoby, 1993, p. 195). For a critique of this literature inspired by the work of Carol Gilligan, see Mansbridge (1993). Note that an analysis of the 1993 General Social Survey also showed that women value different aspects of morality than men: they are less likely to draw boundaries against homosexuality and stress the importance of marriage, but score higher than men on the importance of children and the importance of God (Lamont et al. 1996 p. 44).

18. Along these lines, Bobo (1991, p. 80) finds that those who tend to emphasize social responsibility over individualism in surveys are likely to be individuals with low-status characteristics, namely, blacks and low-income and poorly educated whites.

19. For a review of social-psychological approaches to the self and identity, see Gecas and Burke (1995). Hazel Markus is moving the field of social psychology toward more attention to the impact of culture on conception of self-worth. For a popular summary of her work, see O'Toole (1998).

20. In particular, Bourdieu (1984) and Grignon and Passeron (1989).

21. See Frank (1999). See also Butsch (1991) and Butsch and Glennon (1983).

22. In a study of intragenerational career mobility of men in Austria, France, and the United States, Max Haller et al. (1985) compared their respondents' first job with their job at the time of inquiry, using representative mass data from each of the three nations. They found that the total percentage of mobile men was comparable for France and the United States. Studies also show more wealth inequality

across classes in the United States than in most advanced industrial societies (Tyree, Semyonov, and Hodge 1979). On wealth inequality across classes in the United States as compared to other industrial societies, see Wolff (1995).

23. This perspective differs from that of Hochschild (1995a), who expresses concerns about people's disaffection from the American dream and about this disaffection spreading to blacks. Her study, which does not consider workers, compares how middle class and poor Americans relate to the central tenets of the American dream.
24. Kohn (1987, p. 722).
25. Porter and Washington (1989).
26. Katznelson (1986); Sewell (1980).
27. For instance, see Silver and Zwerling (1992).
28. Lamont (1992, chapter 7).
29. To mention only a few: Barber (1995) on tribalism and cosmopolitanism; Nussbaum (1996) and Nussbaum et al. (1994) on patriotism and cosmopolitanism; and Walzer (1997) on particularism and universalism.

Appendix A

1. For a discussion of these issues in the context of the study of immigration, see Green (1994).
2. Gerstle (1999).
3. Myrdal (1944); Jordan (1968); see also Edsall and Edsall (1991).
4. Logan et al. (1996) show that the "average suburban non-Hispanic white lives in a tract that is 90.5 percent non-Hispanic white. Comparable figures are 84.6 percent for Asians, 65 percent for Hispanics and only 42.4 percent for non-Hispanic blacks," providing additional evidence of the extent of residential segregation (p. 446). Logan and Alba (1996) also show that residential segregation is lower in the New York and New Jersey suburbs than it is nationally. The percentage of blacks marrying outside of their ethnic/racial group is much lower than that of other groups. For instance, in California in 1980 this rate was only 10 percent for men and 3 percent for women (figures cited by Lacorne 1997, p. 294). According to Schuman et al. (1997), "by 1983, the approval of integrated marriage had reached only the same level that approval of integrated transportation had reached in the early 1940s [40 percent]" (p. 195).
5. Gans (1999). For a similar argument concerning the New York metropolitan area, see Mollenkopf (1986).
6. For a discussion of the impact of the L.A. riots on representations of the demographic composition of the American population, see Park (1998); Omi and Winant (1993); and Davis (1993).
7. Demographers project that by the year 2050 people of color will represent just under half of the American population (Murdock 1995, pp. 193–197). However, Frey (1998) finds only 21 "melting-pot" metropolitan areas in the country, defining them as "areas where the percentage of non-Hispanic whites is lower than its share of the national population (73 percent) [and where there are] at least two minority groups with greater than their national representations—11 percent for Hispanics,

12 percent for non-Hispanic blacks, and 5 percent for Asians and American Indians/Inuits. Of 3,142 counties in 1996, only 745 show white populations below the national white percentage, and well over half (1,711) are at least 90 percent white."

8. California is a possible exception, with twice as many immigrants as the other high-immigration states. Between 1967 and 1990, the percentage of whites in California declined from 90 to 69 percent (57 percent for non-Hispanic whites). These percentages moved from 11 to 26 percent for Hispanics (nonwhite only), and from 2 to 9 percent for Asians, with the black population remaining stable. In 1990, the figures for the country as a whole were 75 percent for whites, 9 percent for Hispanics, 3 percent for Asians, and 12 percent for blacks (figures cited by Foucrier 1996, p. 150). This suggests that California's multiracialism is truly exceptional.

9. For an analysis of occupational concentration in the New York suburbs, see Harris (1991). In 1985, 25 percent of blacks and 50 percent of whites lived in suburban areas (Jaynes and Williams 1989, p. 89).

10. For details, see Barou (1980). In 1990, 38 percent of foreigners living in France resided in the Île-de-France region. They represented 12.8 percent of the population of this region and 6.4 percent of the total French population (INSEE 1993a, table R-7, p. 18).

11. The selection of the French *communes* was done in consultation with Nicole Tabard, a specialist on the socio-demographic profile of the Paris suburbs from the Institut national de la statistique et des études économiques.

12. In three cases, we had to pay respondents $15 because of difficulties in finding qualified respondents. Many of the North Africans were contacted directly by phone after we discovered that most are illiterate and could not read the letters of introduction. In 1990, 71 percent of Algerians and Moroccans and 64 percent of Tunisians living in France had no degree (INSEE 1994, p. 55).

13. Fifty-four percent of the individuals contacted in the United States were deceased, ill, or unreachable (after three attempts). Also, 26 percent refused to be interviewed. A large number of these individuals did not qualify for the study and as such are not included in our response rate. Twenty percent of those contacted (N = 412) were willing to be interviewed. Of these, 21 percent satisfied our criteria (N = 88). Note that this relatively low response rate does not affect the validity of the study because I did not aim to create a representative sample by using random sampling; my objective was to tap a wider spectrum of worldviews than those surveyed in site-specific studies. However, the difficulty in finding interviewees may indicate that those who accepted have characteristics distinctive from the rest of the population—namely, higher education for blacks and higher income for whites (see Introduction, notes 43 and 48). These attributes might provide interviewees with a sense of social legitimacy often characteristic of individuals who agree to participate in sociological research. Exhaustive information concerning response rates in France is not available. However, the partial information available led me to believe that it is comparable to the United States.

14. On the limitations of working class community studies at a time when the existence of bounded communities as geographical and cultural entities is being threatened, see Critcher (1980, pp. 23–24).

15. French respondents had to have at least a "certificat d'aptitudes professionelles" (CAP) (the lowest trade certificate) or a "brevet d'études de premier degré" (BEPC). American respondents had to have at least a high school or general equivalence degree (GED).

16. It should be noted that a few North African respondents did not meet the criteria concerning length of residence or employment. However, they were included in the sample because they said they met these criteria when first contacted.

17. The comparison does not include individuals with associate degrees. Focusing only on individuals with a four-year college degree or no college degree provides the most relevant information about the differences between people with high and low market power. Note that by 1974, only half of the students enrolled in post-secondary education were in four-year institutions, while the other half were in community colleges (Hout 1996).

18. Interviewees who are professionals and managers are between 30 and 60 years of age. A wider age range was selected for workers because fewer of them were willing to be interviewed.

19. On categorization as a basic social process, see DiMaggio (1997); Lakoff (1987); and Zerubavel (1997). Cognitive psychologists tend to focus on issues such as whether individuals best embody the characteristics of a category. In contrast, sociologists focus on the criteria of classification, including cultural and moral principles.

20. Sanders (1995) shows that black respondents are more likely to provide more conservative responses to a white interviewer on a range of questions, including items pertaining to race relations. Sanders suggests that matching the race of interviewer and respondent provides no guarantee that racial attribution will not shape survey responses—it simply shapes them differently. See also Davis (1997).

21. In Lamont (1992, chapter 1), I discuss these matters.

22. On this topic, see Fantasia (1988).

23. Miles and Huberman (1984).

Appendix B

1. Commission on the Future of Work-Management Relations, U.S. Departments of Labor and Commerce (1994, p. 22).

2. Harrison and Bluestone (1981).

3. The percentage of nonagricultural employees in service industries increased from 59 to 77 percent of the labor force while the percentage of nonagricultural employees in manufacturing dropped from 34 to 17 percent (Commission on the Future of Work-Management Relations, U.S. Departments of Labor and Commerce 1994, p. 6).

4. However, by surveying trends in the United States since 1900, Romo and Halle (1991, p. 4) find that the number of blue-collar workers was highest in 1989. "Blue-collar" occupations include "precision production, craft and repair" and "operat[ion], fabricat[ion] and [nonagricultural] labor." Indeed, blue-collar workers constituted 27.1 percent of the labor force in 1989, compared with 24.2 percent lower white-collar

workers (clerical, secretarial, and sales). Again, individuals working in managerial and professional occupations included 23 percent of the active population in 1992 (United States Bureau of Census of the Population 1993, table 644, p. 405).

5. Commission on the Future of Work-Management Relations, U.S. Departments of Labor and Commerce (1994, p. 15).

6. Between 1983 and 1992, the part-time workforce increased from 17,314,000 to 19,545,000. During the same period, union membership of part-time workers declined from 8.4 to 7.2 percent (United States Bureau of Census of the Population 1993, table 689, p. 436). The 1995 elections at the AFL-CIO brought to power a team committed to increasing the level of unionization of low-paid service, part-time, female, and immigrant workers (Schurman 1995).

7. Other social scientists have emphasized how deteriorating conditions have reshaped the cultural outlook of various groups in recent years. For instance, Newman (1993) discusses the construction of generational identity in a time of economic downturn. Similarly, Duneier (1992) stresses how "honest" and "genuine" interpersonal relations can triumph over a surrounding moral vacuum. Rieder (1985) emphasizes how economic, moral, and national threats have led to declining racial tolerance and liberalism in two ethnic groups. Finally, Rubin (1994) explains how a sense of economic despair translates into increased racial antagonism among American workers.

8. Rubin (1994, p. 32).

9. Krueger (1997).

10. Schwartz and Zukin (1988, p. 298).

11. Ross and Jenson (1994).

12. Sassen (1991).

13. Ibid., p. 200.

14. Ibid., p. 244.

15. As such, it is second only to Connecticut and has a per capita average income of $28,038 (New Jersey Department of Labor, Division of Labor Market and Demographic Research 1995, p. 4).

16. In 1991, 103 businesses relocated to New Jersey, 75 of which had moved from New York and Pennsylvania (Southwell 1994). Other factors favoring business relocation to New Jersey include urban enterprise zones, relaxed environmental standards, loan programs, and efforts to promote international trade.

17. By 1991, the service sector employed 65 percent of New Jersey workers and the goods-producing sector employed 20 percent (Southwell 1994, p. 51). Between 1976 and 1994, the indicator of the goods-producing sector decreased from 852.8 to 633.7; the service-producing sector indicator increased from 1420 to 2348 as did the public sector indicator, from 80 to 568.

18. New Jersey Department of Labor, Division of Labor Market and Demographic Research (1995, p. 3).

19. Ibid., p. 19.

20. Ibid., p. 3. This reflects the steady erosion of the manufacturing sector and the permanent displacement of workers in need of retraining. Hence, even though the

recession has ended, the situation of workers has not necessarily improved substantially.

21. Beckouche (1994a, p. 101).
22. Ibid., p. 103.
23. Ibid., p. 105.
24. Soulignac (1993, p. 190).
25. Beckouche (1994b, p. 166).
26. In 1990, managers represented 20 percent of the Ile-de-France workforce but only 8 percent of the national workforce (Sassen 1994, p. 152).
27. Beckouche (1994b).
28. American upper middle class interviewees in the 1992 study were chosen from the following towns in New Jersey: Madison, Metuchen, New Providence, River Edge, South Plainfield, and Summit. On Long Island, I interviewed residents of Merrick, Massapequa, and Rockville Center Village. French upper middle class workers were chosen from Argenteuil, Neilly-sur-Seine, Saint-Cloud, Reuil-Malmaison, Sèvres, Saint-Germain-en-Laye, Versailles, and Vincennes.
29. United States Bureau of the Census (1993, table 6, p. 6).
30. Ibid.
31. Computed from United States Bureau of the Census (1992).
32. Southwell (1994, pp. 57–58). Forty-five percent have a high school degree as their highest degree.
33. Ibid.
34. United States Bureau of the Census (1993, table 8, p. 11).
35. United States Department of Commerce, Bureau of the Census (1995).
36. The degree of residential racial segregation prevailing in each of these towns varies. However, the 1980 index of black-white segregation of the Newark metropolitan area, in which several of these towns are located, was very close to the national index of 77. This index was 80 in 1990, up from 73 from 1970 (Jaynes and Williams 1989, p. 78). Whites and blacks often come into contact with one another, offsetting residential segregation.
37. Noiriel (1986, p. 146) notes that this is a period of profound uprooting for French workers: "In twenty years, the population of the Seine department increases by 35 percent . . . Between 1921 and 1926, the population of Bobigny increases by 13.8 percent every year . . . 55 percent of the population who resided there in 1930 was born in the province compared to only 20 percent who were born in Paris."
38. INSEE (1993b).
39. Forty percent of the population of these "cités" is less than 20 years old, compared to 27 percent for the entire Île-de-France region (Soulignac 1993).

References

Adam, Gérard, and Jean-Daniel Reynaud. 1978. *Conflits du travail et changement social.* Paris: Presses Universitaires de France.

Ahmed, Akbar. 1987. *Discovering Islam: Making Sense of Muslim History and Society.* London: Routledge.

———. 1992. *Postmodernism and Islam: Predicament and Promise.* London: Routledge.

Akbar, Na'im. 1994. "The Evolution of Human Psychology for African-Americans." In *Black Psychology,* edited by Reginald J. Jones, pp. 99–123. Berkeley: Cobb and Henry.

Alexander, Jeffrey. 1992. "Citizens and Enemies as Symbolic Classification: On the Polarizing Discourse of Civil Society." In *Cultivating Differences: Symbolic Boundaries and the Making of Inequality,* edited by Michèle Lamont and Marcel Fournier, pp. 289–301. Chicago: University of Chicago Press.

Ambler, John S. 1991. "Ideas, Interests, and the French Welfare State." In *The French Welfare State: Surviving Social and Ideological Change,* edited by John S. Ambler, pp. 1–32. New York: New York University Press.

Ammerman, Nancy. 1987. *Bible Believers: Fundamentalists in the Modern World.* New Brunswick: Rutgers University Press.

Anderson, Benedict. 1991. *Imagined Communities: Reflections on the Origin and Spread of Nationalism,* revised and extended ed. London: Verso.

Anderson, Elijah. 1978. *A Place at the Corner.* Chicago: University of Chicago Press.

———. 1990. *Streetwise: Race, Class and Change in an Urban Community.* Chicago: University of Chicago Press.

An-Na'im, Abdullahi Ahmed. 1987. "Translator's Introduction." In *The Second Message of Islam,* by Mahmoud Mohamed Taha, pp. 1–30. New York: Syracuse University Press.

Ansel, Dana. 1997. "Poor Chances: The Working Poor Speak about Poverty and Opportunity." Unpublished dissertation, Department of Politics, Princeton University.

Anti-Defamation League of B'Nai B'rith. 1993. "Highlights from an Anti-Defamation League Survey on Racial Attitudes in America." New York: Unpublished report.

Appelbaum, Eileen, and Rosemary Batt. 1994. *The New American Workplace: Transforming Work Systems in the United States.* Ithaca, N.Y.: ILR Press.

Aptheker, Herbert. 1992. *Anti-Racism in U.S. History: The First Two Hundred Years.* New York: Greenwood.

Aronowitz, Stanley. 1973. *False Promises: The Shaping of American Working Class Consciousness.* New York: McGraw Hill.

Arum, Richard, and Michael Hout. 1998. "The Early Returns: The Transition from School to Work in the United States." In *From School to Work: A Comparative Study of Educational Qualifications and Occupational Destinations,* edited by Yossi Shavit and Walter Muller, pp. 471–510. Oxford: Clarendon Press.

Atkinson, Anthony B., Lee Rainwater, and Timothy M. Smeeding. 1995. *Income Distribution in OECD Countries. Evidence from the Luxemburg Income Study.* Paris: Organization for Economic Co-Operation and Development.

Aufderheide, Patricia. 1991. *Beyond P.C.: Toward a Politics of Understanding.* Saint Paul, Minn.: Graywolf Press.

Bach, Robert L. 1993. *Changing Relations: Newcomers and Established Residents in U.S. Communities.* New York: Ford Foundation.

Baer, Hans E. 1984. *The Black Spiritual Movement: A Religious Response to Racism.* Knoxville: University of Tennessee Press.

Baer, Hans E., and Merrill Singer, eds. 1992. *African-American Religion in the Twentieth Century: Varieties of Protest and Accommodation.* Knoxville: University of Tennessee Press.

Baldwin, Peter. 1993. *The Politics of Social Solidarity: Class Bases of the European Welfare State.* New York: Cambridge University Press.

Balibar, Etienne. 1991. "Is There a 'Neo-Racism'?" In *Race, Nation, and Class: Ambiguous Identities,* edited by Etienne Balibar and Immanuel Wallerstein, pp. 17–28. London: Verso.

Balibar, Etienne, and Immanuel Wallerstein. 1991. *Race, Nation, and Class: Ambiguous Identities.* London: Verso.

Bane, Mary Jo, and David Wellwood. 1994. *Welfare Realities: From Rhetoric to Reform.* Cambridge: Harvard University Press.

Banton, Michael. 1983. *Racial and Ethnic Competition.* Cambridge: Cambridge University Press.

Barbara, Augustin. 1994. "Mixed Marriages: Some Key Questions." *International Migration* 32(4): 571–586.

Barber, Benjamin. 1995. *Jihad vs. McWorld.* New York: Ballantine.

Barker, Martin. 1981. *The New Racism.* London: Junction Books.

Barou, Jacques. 1980. "Immigration et enjeux urbains." *Pluriel* 2:3–20.

———. 1996. "Les immigrations africaines." In *Un siècle d'immigration en France: 1945 à nos jours. Du chantier à la citoyenneté?* edited by David Assouline and Mehdi Lallaoui, pp. 31–46. Paris: Diffusion Syros.

Barth, Fredrik. 1969. "Introduction." In *Ethnic Groups and Boundaries: The Social Organization of Culture Difference,* edited by Fredrik Barth, pp. 9–38. London: George Allen and Unwin.

Bataille, Philippe. 1997. *Le racisme au travail.* Paris: La Découverte.

Baumgartner, P. M. 1988. *The Moral Order of a Suburb.* London: Oxford University Press.

Beaud, Stéphane. 1994. "L'école et le quartier: Des parents ouvriers désorientés." *Critiques sociales* 5–6: 13–46.

———. 1995. *L'usine, l'école, et le quartier.* Paris: Unpublished dissertation, Ecole des hautes études en sciences sociales.

Beaud, Stéphane, and Michel Pialoux. 1998. "Notes de recherche sur les relations entre français et immigrés à l'usine et dans le quartier." *Genèses* 30: 101–121.

Beaune, Colette. 1985. *Naissance de la nation France.* Paris: Gallimard.

Beck, Ulrich. 1992. *Risk Society: Toward a New Modernity.* Beverly Hills: Sage.

Beckouche, Pierre. 1994a. "Comprendre l'espace parisien: Fausses questions et vrais enjeux." *Le Débat* 80: 97–110.

——. 1994b. "Une économie qui change de base?" *Le Débat* 80: 165–168.

Beisel, Nicola. 1997. *Imperiled Innocents: Anthony Comstock and Family Reproduction in Victorian America.* Princeton, N.J.: Princeton University Press.

Bell, David A. 1998. "Jumonville's Death: Nation and Race in Eighteenth Century France." In *Raison universelle et culture nationale au siècle des Lumières,* edited by Stéphane Pujol and David A. Bell, pp. 227–251. Paris: Honoré Champion.

Bellah, Robert N. 1992. *The Broken Covenant: American Civil Religion in Time of Trial.* Chicago: University of Chicago Press.

Bellah, Robert, Richard Madsen, William W. Sullivan, Ann Swidler, and Steven Tipton. 1985. *Habits of the Heart: Individualism and Commitment in American Life.* Berkeley: University of California Press.

Bénatouil, Thomas. 1999. "A Tale of Two Sociologies: The Critical and the Pragmatic Stance in Contemporary French Sociology." *European Journal of Social Theory* 2(3): 379–396.

Bennett, William J. 1993. *The Book of Virtues: A Treasury of Great Moral Stories.* New York: Simon and Schuster.

Bergues, Hélène. 1973. "L'immigration de travailleurs noirs en France et particulièrement dans la région parisienne." *Population* 28(1): 59–79.

Berman, Paul, ed. 1992. *Debating P.C.: The Controversy over Political Correctness on College Campuses.* New York: Dell.

Berque, Jacques. 1979. Preface to *Le Coran* (translated from Arabic by Jean Grosjean). Paris: Philippe Lebaud.

Betts, Raymond F. 1961. *Assimilation and Association in French Colonial Theory, 1890–1914.* New York: Columbia University Press.

Biffaud, Olivier. 1991. "Ecologie raciale." *Le Monde,* November 5, p. 8.

Bilgram, Akell. 1995. "What Is a Muslim Fundamental Commitment and Cultural Identity?" In *Identities,* edited by Kwame Anthony Appiah and Henry Louis Gates, Jr., pp. 198–219. Chicago: University of Chicago Press.

Binder, Frederick M., and David M. Reimers. 1995. *All the Nations under Heaven: An Ethnic and Racial History of New York City.* New York: Columbia University Press.

Birnbaum, Pierre. 1998. *La France imaginée: Déclin des rêves unitaires?* Paris: Fayard.

Blackwell, James. 1975. *The Black Community: Diversity and Unity.* New York: Harper and Row.

Blanc, Maurice. 1991. "Urban Housing Segregation of North African 'Immigrants' in France." In *Urban Housing Segregation of Minorities in Western Europe and the United States,* edited by Elizabeth D. Huttman, Wim Blauw, and Juliet Saltman, pp. 145–154. Durham, N.C.: Duke University Press.

Blau, Judith. 1989. *The Shape of Culture: A Study of Contemporary Cultural Patterns in the United States.* Cambridge: Cambridge University Press.

Blee, Kathleen M., and Ann R. Tickamyer. 1995. "Racial Differences in Men's Attitudes about Women's Gender Roles." *Journal of Marriage and the Family* 57: 21–30.

Bleitch, Erik. 1998. "Problem-Solving Politics: Ideas and Race Policies in Britain and France, 1945–1998." Paper presented at the annual meeting of the American Political Science Association, Boston, September.

Blumer, Herbert. 1958. "Race Prejudice as a Sense of Group Position." *Pacific Sociological Review* 1: 3–7.

Bobo, Lawrence. 1991. "Social Responsibility, Individualism, and Redistributive Policies." *Sociological Forum* 6(1): 71–92.

Bobo, Lawrence, and Vincent L. Hutchings. 1996. "Perceptions of Racial Group Competition: Extending Blumer's Theory of Group Position to a Multiracial Social Context." *American Sociological Review* 61(6): 951–972.

Bobo, Lawrence, and James R. Kluegel. 1993. "Opposition to Race-Targeting: Self-Interest, Stratification Ideology, or Racial Attitudes?" *American Sociological Review* 58: 443–464.

Bobo, Lawrence, and Ryan A. Smith. 1994. "Antipoverty Policy, Affirmative Action, and Racial Attitudes." In *Confronting Poverty: Prescriptions for Change,* edited by Sheldon H. Danziger, Gary D. Sandefur, and Daniel H. Weinberg, pp. 365–395. New York: Russell Sage Foundation.

——. 1998. "From Jim Crow Racism to Laissez-Faire Racism: An Essay on the Transformation of Racial Attitudes in America." In *Beyond Pluralism: Essays on the Conceptions of Groups and Group Identities in America,* edited by Wendy F. Katkin, Ned Landsman, and Andrea Tyree, pp 182–220. Urbana, Ill.: University of Illinois Press.

Bobo, Lawrence, and Camille L. Zubrinski. 1996. "Attitudes on Residential Integration: Perceived Status Differences, Mere In-Group Preference, or Racial Prejudice?" *Social Forces* 74(3): 883–909.

Body-Gendrot, Sophie. 1992. "Migration and the Racialization of the Postmodern City in France." In *Racism, the City and the State,* edited by Malcolm Cross and Michael Keith, pp. 77–92. London: Routledge.

——. 1998. "The Treatment of Ethnic Challenges in Western Democracies: Confronted to Globalization." Paper presented to the Department of Sociology, Princeton University, October.

Boltanski, Luc, and Laurent Thévenot. 1991. *De la justification: Les économies de la grandeur.* Paris: Gallimard.

Bonnafous, Simone. 1991. *L'immigration prise aux mots.* Paris: Editions Kimé.

Borneman, John. 1992. *Belonging in the Two Berlins: Kin, State, Nation.* Cambridge: Cambridge University Press.

Bourdieu, Pierre. 1984. *Distinction: A Social Critique of the Judgment of Taste.* Cambridge, Mass.: Harvard University Press.

——. 1998. *Acts of Resistance: Against the Tyranny of the Market.* New York: The New Press.

Bourdieu, Pierre, and Jean-Claude Passeron. 1990. *Reproduction in Education, Society, and Culture.* Translated by Richard Nice. Newbury Park, Calif.: Sage Publications.

Boy, Daniel, and Nonna Mayer, eds. 1990. *L'électeur français en questions.* Paris: Presses de la Fondation nationale des sciences politiques.

Braudel, Fernand. 1986. *L'identité de la France: Les hommes et les choses.* Paris: Arthaud-Flammarion.

Braverman, Harry. 1974. *Labor and Monopoly Capital: The Degradation of Work in the Twentieth Century.* New York: Monthly Review.

Brewer, Marilynn B. 1986. "The Role of Ethnocentrism in Intergroup Conflict." In *Psychology of Intergroup Relations,* edited by Stephen Worchel and William G. Austin, pp. 88–102. Chicago: Nelson-Hall Publishers.

Brief, Arthur P., and Walter R. Nord. 1990. *Meanings of Occupational Work: A Collection of Essays.* Lexington, Mass.: D. C. Heath and Co.

Brint, Steven. 1985. "The Political Attitudes of Professionals." *Annual Review of Sociology* 11: 389–414.

——. 1996. "The Status of the Status Group Concept." Paper presented at the annual meeting of the American Sociological Association, New York.

Brubaker, Rogers. 1992. *Citizenship and Nationhood in France and Germany.* Cambridge: Harvard University Press.

Bryson, Bethany. 1996. "'Anything but Heavy Metal': Symbolic Exclusion and Musical Dislikes." *American Sociological Review* 61(5): 884–899.

Bureau of National Affairs. 1996. *Union Membership and Earnings Data Book.* Washington, D.C.: Bureau of National Affairs.

Burgi-Golub, Noelle. 1996. "Egalité, équité: Les catégories idéologiques des politiques sociales." *Politix* 34: 47–76.

Burke, Martin J. 1995. *The Conundrum of Class: Public Discourse on the Social Order in America.* Chicago: University of Chicago Press.

Burke, Peter. 1980. "The Self: Measurement Requirements from an Interactionist Perspective." *Social Psychology Quarterly* 43: 8–29.

Butsch, Richard. 1991. "Class and Gender in Four Decades of TV Families: *'Plus ça change.'*" Unpublished manuscript, Rider College, Lawrenceville, New Jersey.

Butsch, Richard, and Lynda M. Glennon. 1983. "Social Class: Frequency Trends in Domestic Situation Comedy, 1946–1978." *Journal of Broadcasting* 17(1): 77–81.

Calhoun, Craig. 1994. "Social Theory and the Politics of Identity." In *Social Theory and the Politics of Identity,* edited by Craig Calhoun, pp. 9–36. New York: Basil Blackwell.

Callon, Michel. 1986. "Some Elements of a Sociology of Translation: Domestication of the Scallops and Fishermen of St. Brieuc Bay." In *Power, Action and Belief: A New Sociology of Knowledge,* edited by John Law, pp. 196–229. Keele: Keele Sociological Review Monograph.

Cameron, David R. 1991. "Continuity and Change in French Social Policy: The Welfare State under Gaullism, Liberalism, and Socialism." In *The French Welfare State: Surviving Social and Ideological Change,* edited by John S. Ambler, pp. 58–93. New York: New York University Press.

Carson, Emmet. 1989. "The Evolution of Black Philanthropy." In *Philanthropic Giving,* edited by R. Maga, pp. 92–102. New York: Oxford University Press.

Castel, Robert. 1995. *Les métamorphoses de la question sociale: Une chronique du salariat.* Paris: Fayard.

Cauthen, Nancy K., and James M. Jasper. 1994. "Culture, Politics, and Moral Panics." *Sociological Forum* 9(3): 495–503.

Cayrol, Roland. 1996. "Les français vus par eux-mêmes: Nous racistes?" *Le Nouvel Observateur,* October 17–23, p. 20.

——. 1998. "La société française reste taraudée par le racisme." *Le Monde,* July 2, p. 14.

REFERENCES

Césari, Jocelyne. 1997. *Faut-il avoir peur de l'Islam?* Paris: Presses de Sciences Po.
Chadwick, Bruce A., Madeleine Gauthier, Louis Hourmant, and Barbara Wörndl. 1994. "Trends in Religion and Secularization." In *Convergence or Divergence? Comparing Recent Social Trends in Industrial Societies,* edited by Simon Langlois with Theodore Caplow, Henri Mendras, and Wolfgang Glatzer, pp. 173–214. Frankfurt: Campus Verlag.
Chapman, Herrick. 1991. *State Capitalism and Working Class Radicalism in the French Aircraft Industry.* Berkeley: University of California Press.
——. 1995. "French Democracy and the Welfare State." In *The Social Construction of Democracy, 1870–1990,* edited by George Reid Andrews and Herrick Chapman, pp. 291–314. New York: New York University Press.
Chapman, Herrick, Mark Kesselman, and Martin Schain. 1996. "Introduction: The Exceptional Trajectory of the French Labor Movement." *French Politics and Society* 14(4): 1–13.
Chatterjee, Partha. 1994. *The Nation and Its Fragments: Colonial and Postcolonial Histories.* Princeton, N.J.: Princeton University Press.
Chinoy, Eli. 1955. *Automobile Worker and the American Dream.* Boston: Beacon Press.
Clark, Terry N., and Seymour M. Lipset. 1991. "Are Social Classes Dying?" *International Sociology* 6(4): 397–410.
Cochran, John K. 1991. "The Influence of Religion on Attitudes toward Non-Marital Sexuality: A Preliminary Assessment of Reference Group Theory." *Journal for the Scientific Study of Religion* 30(1): 45–62.
Cohen, Elie. 1996. *La tentation hexagonale: La souveraineté et l'épreuve de la mondialisation.* Paris: Fayard.
Cohen, Lizabeth. 1990. *Making a New Deal.* Cambridge: Cambridge University Press.
Cohen, Stanley. 1972. *Folk Devils and Moral Panics.* London: MacGibbon and Kee.
Cohen, William B. 1980. *The French Encounter with Africans: White Responses to Blacks, 1530–1880.* Bloomington: Indiana University Press.
——. 1985. "French Racism and Its African Impact." In *Double Impact,* edited by G. Wesley Johnson, pp. 305–317. Westport, Conn,: Greenwood Press.
Coleman, Richard P., and Lee Rainwater. 1978. *Social Standing in America.* New York: Basic.
Collins, Randall. 1979. *The Credential Society.* New York: Academic Press.
Commission on the Future of Work-Management Relations, U.S. Departments of Labor and Commerce. 1994. *Dunlop Commission Report.* Washington, D.C.: Government Printing Office.
Condit, Celeste Michelle, and John Louis Lucaites. 1993. *Crafting Equality: America's Anglo-African Word.* Chicago: University of Chicago Press.
Conklin, Alice L. 1998. *A Mission to Civilize: The Republican Idea of Empire in France and West Africa, 1895–1930.* Stanford: Stanford University Press.
Connell, Robert W. 1995. *Masculinities.* Berkeley: University of California Press.
Cook, Thomas, and Thomas Curtin. 1987. "The Mainstream and the Underclass: Why Are the Differences So Salient and the Similarities So Unobtrusive?" In *Social*

Comparisons, Social Justice, and Relative Deprivation, edited by John Masters and William Smith, pp. 217–64. Hillsdale, N.J.: Lawrence Erlbaum.

Cornelius, Wayne A. 1982. *America in the Era of Limits: Nativist Reactions to the "New" Immigration.* Research Report Series, no. 3. La Jolla: Center for U.S.-Mexican Studies, University of California, San Diego.

Cornfield, Daniel B. 1989. "Union Decline and the Political Demands of Organized Labor." *Work and Occupation* 16(3): 292–322.

Corse, Sarah. 1997. *Nationalism and Literature: The Politics of Culture in Canada and the United States.* Cambridge: Cambridge University Press.

Coughlin, Richard M. 1980. *Ideology, Public Opinion, and Welfare Policy.* Berkeley, Calif.: Institute of International Studies.

Crane, Diana. 1991. *The Production of Culture: The Media and the Urban Arts.* Beverly Hills: Sage Publications.

Critcher, Chas. 1980. "Sociology, Cultural Studies, and the Postwar Working Class." In *Working Class Culture: Studies in History and Theory,* edited by John Clarke, Chas Critcher, and Richard Johnson, pp. 13–40. New York: St. Martin's Press.

Crocker, Jennifer, and Brenda Major. 1989. "Social Stigma and Self-Esteem: The Self-Protective Properties of Stigma." *Psychological Review* 96(4): 608–630.

Cronin, James E. 1993. "Neither Exceptional nor Peculiar: Toward the Comparative Study of Labor in Advanced Society." *International Review of Social History* 38: 59–75.

Crozier, Michel. 1964. *The Bureaucratic Phenomenon.* Chicago: University of Chicago Press.

Curtis, Richard, and Elliot Jackson. 1977. *Inequality and American Communities.* New York: Academic Press.

Davies, Scott. 1995. "Leaps of Faith: Shifting Currents in Critical Sociology of Education." *American Journal of Sociology* 100(5): 1448–1478.

Davis, Darren W. 1997. "Nonrandom Measurement Error and Race of Interviewer Effects among African-Americans." *Public Opinion Quarterly* 61: 183–207.

Davis, James. 1982. "Achievement Variables and Class Cultures: Family, Schooling, Jobs and Forty-Nine Dependent Variables in the Cumulative GSS." *American Sociological Review* 47: 569–586.

Davis, Mike. 1986. *Prisoners of the American Dream: Politics and Economics in the History of the U.S. Working Class.* London: Verso.

———. 1993. "Uprising and Repression in L.A.: An Interview with Mike Davis by the Covert Action Information Bulletin," In *Reading Rodney King/Reading Urban Uprising,* edited by Robert Gooding-Williams, pp. 142–154. New York: Routledge.

Dawson, Michael C. 1994. *Behind the Mule: Race and Class in African-American Politics.* Princeton, N.J.: Princeton University Press.

DeCecco, John, ed. 1984. *Homophobia: An Overview.* New York: Hawthorn Press.

Delerm, Robert. 1964. "La population noire en France." *Population,* 19(3): 515–528.

Della Fave, L. Richard. 1974. "On the Structure of Egalitarianism." *Social Problems* 22(2): 199–213.

Descombes, Vincent. 1998. "Il y a plusieurs morales et plusieurs éthiques." *Magazine Littéraire* 361: 40–41.

Devine, Flora. 1992. *Affluent Workers Revisited: Privatism and the Working Class.* Edinburgh: Edinburgh University Press.

Didier, Emmanuel. 1996. "De l''Exclusion' à l'exclusion." *Politix* 34: 5–28.

DiMaggio, Paul. 1997. "Culture and Cognition." *Annual Review of Sociology* 24: 263–287.

DiMaggio, Paul, and Bethany Bryson. 1995. "Americans' Attitudes towards Cultural Diversity and Cultural Authority: Culture Wars, Social Closure, or Multiple Dimensions." General Social Survey Topical Report no. 27. Chicago: National Opinion Research Center.

DiMaggio, Paul, John Evans, and Bethany Bryson. 1996. "Have Americans' Social Attitudes Become More Polarized?" *American Journal of Sociology* 102(3): 690–755.

Dirn, Louis. 1998. *La société française en tendances, 1975–1995.* Paris: Presses Universitaires de France.

DiTomaso, Nancy. 2000. "Why Anti-Discrimination Policies Are Not Enough: The Legacies and Consequences of Affirmative Inclusion for Whites." Paper presented at the meeting of the American Sociological Association, Washington, D.C., August 12–16.

Dobbin, Frank. 1994a. *Forging Industrial Policy: France, Britain, and the United States in the Railway Age.* Cambridge: Cambridge University Press.

——. 1994b. "Cultural Models of Organization: The Social Construction of Rational Organizing Principles." In *Sociology of Culture: Emerging Theoretical Perspectives,* edited by Diana Crane, pp. 117–141. Oxford: Basil Blackwell.

Donadey, Anne. 1996. "*Une Certaine Idée de la France*': The Algerian Syndrome and Struggles over 'French' Identity." In *Identity Papers: Contested Nationhood in Twentieth-Century France,* edited by Steven Ungar and Tom Conley, pp. 215–232. Minneapolis: University of Minnesota Press.

Donzelot, Jacques. 1984. *L'invention du social: Essai sur le déclin des passions politiques.* Paris: Fayard.

Douglas, Mary. 1966. *Purity and Danger: An Analysis of Concepts of Pollution and Taboo.* London: Routledge & Kegan Paul.

Dovidio, John F. and Samuel L. Gaertner. 1998. "On the Nature of Contemporary Prejudice: The Causes, Consequences, and Challenges of Aversive Racism." In *Confronting Racism: The Problem and the Response,* edited by Jennifer L. Eberhardt and Susan T. Fiske, pp. 1–32. Newbury Park, Calif.: Sage Publications.

Drake, St. Clair, and Horace Cayton. 1962. *Black Metropolis: A Study of Negro Life in a Northern City,* rev. and enl. ed. New York: Harper and Row.

Dréano, Bernard. 1992. "Racism and Anti-Racism in France: The Beurs and the Republic." *New Politics* 3–4(12): 61–70.

Dubet, François. 1987. *La galère: Jeunes en survie.* Paris: Fayard.

——. 1989. *L'immigration, qu'en savons-nous? Un bilan des connaissances.* Paris: La Documentation Française.

Du Bois, W. E. B. 1935. *Black Reconstruction in America: An Essay toward a History of the Part Which Black Folk Played in the Attempt to Reconstruct Democracy in America, 1860–1880.* New York: Harcourt Brace.

Duchesne, Sophie. 1997. *Citoyenneté à la française.* Paris: Presses de Science Po.

Dudley, Kathryn Marie. 1994. *The End of the Line: Lost Jobs, New Lives in Postindustrial America.* Chicago: University of Chicago Press.

Duneier, Mitchell. 1992. *Slim's Table: Race, Respectability, and Masculinity.* Chicago: University of Chicago Press.

Durkheim, Emile. 1965. *The Elementary Forms of Religious Life.* New York: The Free Press.

Dyer, Richard. 1997. *White.* London: Routledge.

Edsall, Thomas, and Mary Edsall. 1991. *Chain Reaction: The Impact of Race, Rights and Taxes on American Politics.* New York: W. W. Norton.

Ehrenreich, Barbara. 1989. *Fear of Falling: The Inner Life of the Middle Class.* New York: Pantheon Books.

Ellwood, David T. 1988. *Poor Support: Poverty in the American Family.* New York: Basic Books.

Entman, Robert. 1992. "Blacks in the News: Television, Modern Racism, and Cultural Change." *Journalism Quarterly* 69(2): 341–361.

Epstein, Cynthia Fuchs. 1992. "Tinkerbells and Pinups: The Construction and Reconstruction of Gender Boundaries at Work." In *Cultivating Differences: Symbolic Boundaries and the Making of Inequality,* edited by Michèle Lamont and Marcel Fournier, pp. 232–256. Chicago: University of Chicago Press.

Erikson, Robert, and John H. Goldthorpe. 1992. *The Constant Flux: Class Mobility in Industrial Society.* Oxford: Oxford University Press.

Espenshade, Thomas J., ed. 1997. *Keys to Successful Immigration: Implications of the New Jersey Experience.* Washington, D.C.: The Urban Institute Press.

Espenshade, Thomas J., and Maryann Belanger. 1998. "Immigration and Public Opinion." In *Crossings: Mexican Immigration in Interdisciplinary Perspectives,* edited by Marcelo Suarez-Orozco, pp. 363–403. Cambridge: Harvard University Press.

Espenshade, Thomas J., and Charles A. Calhoun. 1994. "An Analysis of Public Opinion toward Undocumented Immigration." *Population Research and Policy Review* 12: 189–224.

Esping-Anderson, Gosta. 1990. *The Three Worlds of Welfare Capitalism.* Cambridge: Polity Press.

——, ed. 1993. *Changing Classes: Stratification and Mobility in Post-Industrial Societies.* Beverly Hills: Sage Publications.

Espiritu, Yen Le. 2000. "'We Don't Sleep Around Like White Girls Do': Family, Culture, and Gender in Filipina American Lives." *Signs* 26(2).

Essed, Philomena. 1991. *Understanding Everyday Racism: An Interdisciplinary Theory.* Beverly Hills: Sage Publications.

European Community. 1995. *Social Portrait of Europe.* Luxembourg: Office for Official Publications of the European Communities.

Ewick, Patricia, and Susan Silbey. 1998. *The Common Place of Law.* Chicago: University of Chicago Press.

Fantasia, Rick. 1988. *Cultures of Solidarity: Consciousness, Action and Contemporary American Workers.* Berkeley: University of California Press.

Farley, Ronald, and Walter R. Allen. 1987. *The Color Line and the Quality of Life in America.* New York: Russell Sage Foundation.

Fassin, Eric. 1997. "Discours sur l'inégalité des races. *The Bell Curve:* polémique savante, rhétorique raciale, et politique publique." *Hérodote* 85: 34–61.

——. 1999. "'Good to Think': The American Reference in French Discourses on Immigration and Ethnicity." In *Multicultural Questions,* edited by Christian Joppke and Steven Lukes, pp. 224–241. London: Oxford University Press.

Favell, Adrian. 1997a. *Philosophies of Integration: Immigration and the Idea of Citizenship in France and Britain.* London: MacMillan.

——. 1997b. "Citizenship and Immigration: Pathologies of a Progressive Philosophie." *New Community* 23(2): 173–195.

——. 1998. "A Politics That Is Shared, Bounded and Rooted? Rediscovering Civic Political Culture in Western Europe." *Theory and Society* 27: 209–236.

Feagin, Joe R., and Hernan Vera. 1995. *White Racism: The Basics.* New York: Routledge.

Feldblum, Miriam. 1993. "Paradoxes of Ethnic Politics: The Case of Franco-Maghrebis in France." *Ethnic and Racial Studies* 16(1): 52–74.

——. 1998. "Citizenship Strategies and Policies in Europe." Paper presented at the Interdisciplinary Seminar in European Studies, Princeton University, February.

——. 1999. *Reconstructing Citizenship: The Politics of Nationality Reform and Immigration in Contemporary France.* New York: State University of New York Press.

Fernandez-Kelly, Patricia, and Sara Curran. 2000. "Nicaraguan: Voices Lost, Voices Found." In *Ethnicities: Coming of Age in Immigrant America,* edited by Ruben Rumbaut and Alejandro Portes. New York and Berkeley: The Russell Sage Foundation and the University of California Press.

Ferree, Myra Marx. 1987. "Family and Job for Working Class Women: Gender and Class Systems Seen from Below." In *Families and Work,* edited by Naomi Gerstel and Harriet Engel Gross, pp. 289–301. Philadelphia: Temple University Press.

Fine, Michelle, and Lois Weis. 1998. *The Unknown City: Lives of Poor and Working-Class Adults.* Boston: Beacon Press.

Fink, Leon. 1994. *In Search of the Working Class: Essays in American Labor History and Political Culture.* Urbana and Chicago: University of Illinois Press.

Fischer, Claude S., Michael Hout, Martin Sanchez Jankowski, Samuel R. Lucas, Ann Swidler, and Kim Voss. 1996. *Inequality by Design: Cracking the Bell Curve Myth.* Princeton, N.J.: Princeton University Press.

Fix, Michael, and Jeffrey S. Passel with Maria E. Enchautegui and Wendy Zimmerman. 1994. *Immigration and Immigrants: Setting the Record Straight.* Washington, D.C.: The Urban Institute.

Fordham, Signithia. 1996. *Blacked Out: Dilemmas of Race, Identity, and Success at Capital High.* Chicago: University of Chicago Press.

Fordham, Signithia, and John Ogbu. 1986. "Black Students' School Success: Coping with the Burden of 'Acting White.'" *Urban Review* 18(3): 176–206.

Foucrier, Annick. 1996. "Immigration et tensions raciales aux Etats-Unis: la Californie, un laboratoire." In *Amérique sans frontière: Les Etats-Unis dans l'espace nord-Américain,* edited by Catherine Collomp and Mario Menendez, pp. 151–176. Paris: Presses Universitaires de Vincennes.

Frank, Robert H. 1999. *Luxury Fever: Why Money Fails to Satisfy in an Era of Excess.* New York: Free Press.

Frankenberg, Ruth. 1993. *The Social Construction of Whiteness: White Women, Race Matters.* Minneapolis: University of Minnesota Press.

Franklin, Clyde W. II. 1992. "'Hey, Home–Yo, Bro': Friendship among Black Men." In *Men's Friendships,* edited by Peter M. Nardl, pp. 201–214. Newbury Park, Calif.: Sage Publications.

Fredrickson, George. 1997. "Race and Empire in Liberal Thought: The Legacy of Tocqueville." In *The Comparative Imagination: On the History of Racism, Nationalism, and Social Movements,* edited by George Fredrickson, pp. 98–116. Berkeley: University of California Press.

——. 1998. "America's Diversity in Comparative Perspective." *Journal of American History* 85(3): 859–875.

Freeman, Gary. 1979. *Immigrant Labor and Racial Conflict in Industrial Societies: The French and British Experience 1945–75.* Princeton, N.J.: Princeton University Press.

——. 1995. "Modes of Immigration Politics in Liberal Democratic States." *International Migration Review* 29(4): 881–902.

Freeman, Richard B. 1994. "How Labor Fares in Advanced Economies." In *Working under Different Rules,* edited by Richard B. Freeman, pp. 1–28. New York: Russell Sage Foundation.

——. 1996. "Toward an Apartheid Economy." *Harvard Business Review* (September–October): 114–121.

Frey, William H. 1998. "The Diversity Myth." *American Demographics* (June) (http://www.demographics.com/publications/ad/98_ad/980626.htm)

Fuchs, Lawrence. 1990. *The American Kaleidoscope: Race, Ethnicity and the Civic Culture.* Middletown, Conn.: Wesleyan University Press.

Gaffney, John. 1991. "French Political Culture and Republicanism." In *Political Culture in France and Germany,* edited by John Gaffney and Eva Kolinsky, pp. 13–34. London: Routledge.

Gaines, Kevin K. 1996. *Uplifting the Race: Black Leadership, Politics, and Culture in the Twentieth Century.* Chapel Hill, N.C.: University of North Carolina Press.

Gallagher, Sally. 1994. "Doing Their Share: Comparing Patterns of Help Given by Older and Younger Adults." *Journal of Marriage and the Family* 56: 567–578.

Gallie, Duncan. 1983. *Social Inequality and Class Radicalism in France and Britain.* Cambridge: Cambridge University Press.

Gamson, William A. 1992. *Talking Politics.* Cambridge: Cambridge University Press.

Gamson, William A., and Kathryn Lasch. 1983. "The Political Culture of Social Welfare Policy." In *Evaluating the Welfare State: Social and Political Perspectives,* edited by Shimon E. Spiro and Ephraim Yuchtman-Yaar, pp. 397–415. New York: Academic Press.

Gans, Herbert J. 1962. *The Urban Villagers: Group and Class in the Life of Italian-Americans.* New York: Free Press.

——. 1979. "Symbolic Ethnicity: The Future of Ethnic Groups and Cultures in America." *Ethnic and Racial Studies* 2: 1–20.

——. 1991. *Middle American Individualism: Political Participation and Liberal Democracy.* Oxford: Oxford University Press.

——. 1995. *The War against the Poor: The Underclass and Antipoverty Policy.* New York: Basic Books.

——. 1999. "The Possibility of a New Racial Hierarchy in the 21st Century United States." In *The Cultural Territories of Race: Black and White Boundaries,* edited by Michèle Lamont, pp. 371–390. Chicago and New York: University of Chicago Press and Russell Sage Foundation.

Gates, Henry Louis. 1994. *Colored People: A Memoir.* New York: Alfred A. Knopf.

Gaxie, Daniel, Loic Blondiaux, Yves Déloye, Brigitte Gaiti, and Marine de Lassalle. 1997. "Rapport final de l'enquête sur les attitudes à l'égard de l'immigration et de la présence étrangère en France." Centre de recherches politiques de la Sorbonne, Département de science politique, Université de Paris 1.

Gecas, Viktor. 1979. "The Influence of Social Class on Socialization." In *Contemporary Theories about the Family,* vol. 1, edited by Wesley R. Furr, Reubin Hill, F. Ivan Nye, and Ira L. Reiss, pp. 365–404. New York: Free Press.

Gecas, Viktor, and Peter J. Burke. 1995. "Self and Identity." In *Sociological Perspectives on Social Psychology,* edited by Karen S. Cook, Gary Alan Fine, and James S. House, pp. 41–67. Boston: Allyn and Bacon.

Geertz, Clifford. 1973. *The Interpretation of Culture.* New York: Basic Books.

Gerson, Kathleen. 1993. *No Man's Land: Men's Changing Commitments to Family and Work.* New York: Basic Books.

Gerstle, Gary. 1989. *Working Class Americanism: The Politics of Labor in a Textile City, 1914–1960.* Cambridge: Cambridge University Press.

——. 1997. "Liberty, Coercion, and the Making of Americans." *Journal of American History* 84(2): 524–558.

——. 1999. "Theodore Roosevelt and the Contraditory Character of American Nationalism." *Journal of American History* 86(3): 1280–1307.

——. Forthcoming. *Civic Nation, Racial Nation: America during Its Twentieth Century.* Princeton: Princeton University Press.

Geschwender, James A. 1977. *Class, Race, and Worker Insurgency: The League of Revolutionary Black Workers.* Cambridge: Cambridge University Press.

Gieryn, Thomas F. 1983. "Boundary Work and the Demarcation of Science from Non-Science: Strains and Interests in Professional Ideologies of Scientists." *American Sociological Review* 48: 781–795.

——. 1999. *Cultural Boundaries of Science: Credibility on the Line.* Chicago: University of Chicago Press.

Gilens, Martin. 1995. "Racial Attitudes and Opposition to Welfare." *The Journal of Politics* 57(4): 994–1014.

——. 1996. "Race and Poverty in America: Public Misperceptions and the American News Media." *Public Opinion Quarterly* 60: 515–541.

Gillette, Alain, and Abdelmalek Sayad. 1984. *L'immigration algérienne en France.* Paris: Editions Ententes.

Gilliam, Franklin D., Jr., and Kenny J. Whitby. 1989. "Race, Class, and Attitudes toward Social Welfare Spending: An Ethclass Interpretation." *Social Science Quarterly* 70(1): 88–100.

Gilman, Sander L. 1985. "Black Sexuality and Modern Consciousness." In *Difference and Pathology: Stereotypes of Sexuality, Race, and Madness,* edited by Sander L. Gilman, pp. 109–130. Ithaca: Cornell University Press.

Girard, Alain, Yves Charbit, and Marie-Laurence Lamy. 1974. "Attitudes des français à l'égard de l'immigration étrangère: Nouvelle enquête d'opinion." *Population* 29(6): 1015–1069.

Glazer, Nathan. 1996. "Multiculturalism and American Exceptionalism." Paper presented at the Conference on Multiculturalism, Minorities, and Citizenship, European University Institute, Florence.

Glazer, Nathan, and Daniel Patrick Moynihan. 1963. *Beyond the Melting Pot: The Negroes, Puerto Ricans, Jews, Italians and Irish of New York City.* Cambridge: MIT Press.

Goldberg, David. 1993. *Racist Culture: Philosophy and the Politics of Meaning.* New York: Blackwell.

Goldthorpe, John H., David Lockwood, Frank Bechhofer, and Jennifer Platt. 1969. *The Affluent Worker in the Class Structure.* Cambridge: Cambridge University Press.

Gottschalk, Peter, and Timothy Smeeding. 1995. "Cross-National Comparisons of Levels and Trends in Inequality." Working Paper no. 226, Luxembourg Income Study. Syracuse, N.Y.: Maxwell School of Citizenship and Public Affairs, July.

Gould, Roger V. 1993. *Insurgent Identities: Class, Community, and Protest in Paris from 1848 to the Commune.* Chicago: University of Chicago Press.

Goux, Dominique, and Eric Maurin. 1998. "From Education to First Job: The French Case." In *From School to Work: A Comparative Study of Educational Qualifications and Occupational Destinations,* edited by Yossi Shavit and Walter Muller, pp. 103–142. Oxford: Clarendon Press.

Green, Nancy L. 1994. "The Comparative Method and Poststructural Structuralism—New Perspectives for Migration Studies." *Journal of American Ethnic History* 13(4): 3–22.

Greenberg, Stanley B. 1995. *Middle Class Dreams: The Politics of the New American Majority.* New York: Times Books.

Greeno, Catherine G., and Eleanor E. Maccoby. 1993. "How Different Is the 'Different Voice'?" In *An Ethic of Care,* edited by Mary Jeanne Larrabee, pp. 193–199. New York: Routledge.

Gregory, Steven. 1998. *Black Corona: Race and the Politics of Place in an Urban Community.* Princeton, N.J.: Princeton University Press.

Grignon, Claude. 1991. "Racisme et racisme de classe, bis." *Critique Sociales* 2: 3–12.

Grignon, Claude, and Jean-Claude Passeron. 1989. *Le savant et le populaire: Misérabilisme et populisme en sociologie et en littérature.* Paris: Gallimard-Le Seuil.

Griswold, Wendy. 1981. "American Character and the American Novel." *American Journal of Sociology* 86: 740–765.

Grusky, David B. V., and Jesper B. Sorensen. 1998. "Can Class Analysis Be Salvaged?" *American Journal of Sociology* 103(5): 1187–1234.

Guillaumin, Colette. 1972. *L'idéologie raciste: Genèse et langage actuel.* Paris/La Haye: Mouton.

Guiraudon, Virginie. 2000. *Les politiques d'immigration en Europe.* Paris: Editions L'Harmattan.

Guppy, Neil. 1984. "Dissensus or Consensus: A Cross-National Comparison of Occupational Prestige Scales." *Canadian Journal of Sociology* 9:69–83.

Gupta, Akhil, and James Ferguson. 1997. "Beyond 'Culture': Space, Identity, and the Politics of Difference." In *Culture, Power, Place: Explorations in Cultural Anthropol-*

ogy, edited by Akhil Gupta and James Ferguson, pp. 33–51. Durham and London: Duke University Press.

Gurin, Patricia, Arthur H. Miller, and Gerald Gurin. 1980. "Stratum Identification and Consciousness." *Social Psychology Quarterly* 43: 30–47.

Gusfield, Joseph. 1963. *Symbolic Crusade.* Urbana: University of Illinois Press.

———. 1975. *Communities: A Critical Response.* New York: Harper and Row.

Haegel, Florence. 1998. "Nous/entre nous/chez nous: Que pourrait-on dire du 'lien' dans une cité de banlieue." Paper presented at the conference on "Dérives et mutations du lien-passages" organized by l'Association rencontres anthropologie et recherche sur les processus de socialisation, Paris, January 15.

———. 2000. "Xenophobic Expression in a Suburban Paris Housing Project." *Patterns of Prejudice* 34(1): 29–38.

Haghighi, Bahram, and Jon Sorensen. 1996. "America's Fear of Crime." In *Americans View Crime and Justice: A National Public Opinion Survey,* edited by Timothy J. Flanagan and Dennis R. Longmire, pp. 16–92. Thousand Oaks, Calif.: Sage Publications.

Hale, Janice E. 1982. *Black Children: Their Roots, Culture, and Learning Style.* Provo, Utah: Brigham Young University Press.

Hall, John R. 1991. "The Capital(s) of Cultures: A Nonholistic Approach to Status Situations, Class, Gender, and Ethnicity." In *Cultivating Differences: Symbolic Boundaries and the Making of Inequality,* edited by Michèle Lamont and Marcel Fournier, pp. 257–288. Chicago: University of Chicago Press.

Halle, David. 1984. *America's Working Man: Work, Home and Politics among Blue-Collar Property Owners.* Chicago: University of Chicago Press.

———. 1987. "Marriage and Family Life of Blue-Collar Men." In *Families and Work,* edited by Naomi Gerstel and Harriet Engel Gross, pp. 316–337. Philadelphia: Temple University Press.

Haller, Max, Wolfgang Konig, Peter Krause, and Karin Hurz. 1985. "Patterns of Career Mobility and Structural Positions in Advanced Capitalist Societies: A Comparison of Men in Austria, France, and the United States." *American Sociological Review* 50(5): 579–603.

Hamilton, David, and Tina Trolier. 1986. "Stereotypes and Stereotyping: An Overview of the Cognitive Approach." In *Prejudice, Discrimination, and Racism,* edited by John F. Dovidio and Samuel L. Gaertner, pp. 127–164. New York: Academic Press.

Hamilton, Richard F. 1967. *Affluence and the French Worker in the Fourth Republic.* Princeton, N.J.: Princeton University Press.

———. 1972. *Class and Politics in the United States.* New York: Wiley.

Handler, Joel F., and Yeheskel Hasenfeld. 1991. *The Moral Construction of Poverty: Welfare Reform in America.* Newbury Park, Calif.: Sage Publications.

Hannerz, Ulf. 1968. "The Rhetoric of Soul: Identification in Negro Society." *Race* 9(4): 453–465.

———. 1969. *Soulside: Inquiries into Ghetto Culture and Community.* New York: Columbia University Press.

Harding, Vincent. 1981. *There Is a River: The Black Struggle for Freedom in America.* New York: Harcourt Brace Jovanovich.

Hargreaves, Alec G. 1995. *Immigration, 'Race' and Ethnicity in Contemporary France.* London: Routledge.

Harris, Fredrick C. 1998. "'I Shall Never Forget It': Collective Memory, Micromobilization and Black Political Activism in the 1960s." Unpublished paper, Department of Political Science, University of Rochester.

Harris, Richard. 1991. "The Geography of Employment and Residence in New York since 1950." In *Dual City: Restructuring New York,* edited by John Mollenkopf and Manuel Castels, pp. 129–152. New York: Russell Sage.

Harrison, Bennett, and Barry Bluestone. 1981. *The Great U-Turn: Corporate Restructuring and the Polarizing of America.* New York: Basic.

Hartsock, Nancy. 1983. *Money, Sex, and Power: Toward a Feminist Historical Materialism.* New York: Longman.

Harwood, Edwin. 1986. "American Public Opinion and U.S. Immigration Policy." In "Immigration and American Public Policy," *Annals of the American Academy of Political and Social Science,* vol. 487, edited by Rita J. Simon, pp. 201–212. Beverly Hills: Sage Publications.

Heath, Anthony, Roger Jowell, John Curtice, Geoff Evans, Julia Field, and Sharon Witherspoon. 1991. *Understanding Political Change: The British Voter, 1964–1987.* Oxford: Pergamon Press.

Heffer, Jean, and Jeanine Rovert. 1988. *Why Is There No Socialism in the United States?* Paris: Editions de l'École des hautes études en sciences sociales.

Hein, Jeremy. 1993a. *States and International Migrants: The Incorporation of Indochinese Refugees in the United States and France.* Boulder, Colo.: Westview.

——. 1993b. "Rights, Resources, and Membership: Civil Rights Models in France and the United States." *Annals of the American Academy of Political and Social Science* 530: 97–108.

Herrnstein, Richard J., and Charles Murray. 1994. *The Bell Curve: Intelligence and Class Structure in American Life.* New York: Free Press.

Herzberg, Nathaniel. 1996. "Des chercheurs traquent les 'discriminations ethniques' dans le monde du travail." *Le Monde,* March 12, p. 11.

Herzfeld, Michael. 1996. *Cultural Intimacy: Social Poetics in the Nation-State.* New York: Routledge.

Higginbotham, Evelyn Brooks. 1993. *Righteous Discontent: The Women's Movement in the Black Baptist Church, 1880–1920.* Cambridge: Harvard University Press.

Higham, John. 1955. *Strangers in the Land: Patterns of American Nativism, 1860–1925.* New Brunswick, N.J.: Rutgers University Press.

Hiller, Peter. 1975. "The Nature and Social Location of Everyday Conceptions of Class." *Sociology* 9(1): 1–28.

Hilton, Michael E., and Walter B. Clark. 1991. "Changes in American Drinking Patterns and Problems, 1967–1984." In *Alcohol in America: Drinking Practices and Problems,* edited by Walter B. Clark and Michael E. Hilton, pp. 105–138. Albany: State University of New York Press.

Hobsbawm, Eric. 1981. "The Forward March of Labor Halted?" In *The Forward March of Labor Halted?*, edited by Michael Jacques and Francis Mulhern, pp. 1–75. Verso: London.

Hochschild, Jennifer L. 1981. *What's Fair?: American Beliefs about Distributive Justice.* Cambridge, Mass.: Harvard University Press.

———. 1995a. *Facing Up to the American Dream: Race, Class, and the Soul of the Nation.* Princeton: Princeton University Press.

———. 1995b. "American Racial Paradoxes." *The Polling Report* 11(23): 1–7.

Hochschild, Jennifer, and Rogers Reuel. 2000. "Race Relations in a Diversifying Nation." In *New Directions: African Americans in a Diversifying Nation,* edited by James Jackson. Washington, D.C.: National Planning Association.

Hodson, Randy. 1991. "The Active Worker: Compliance and Autonomy at the Workplace." *Journal of Contemporary Ethnography* 20(1): 47–78.

———. 1996. "Dignity in the Workplace under Participative Management: Alienation and Freedom Revisited." *American Sociological Review* 61: 719–738.

Hodson, Randy, and Teresa A. Sullivan. 1990. *The Social Organization of Work.* Belmont, Calif.: Wadsworth Publishing Co.

Hoggart, Richard. [1957] 1992. *The Uses of Literacy.* New Brunswick, N.J.: Transaction Publishers.

Hollifield, James F. 1994. "Immigration and Republicanism in France: The Hidden Consensus." In *Controlling Immigration: A Global Perspective,* edited by Wayne A. Cornelius, Philip L. Martin, and James F. Hollifield, pp. 143–175. Stanford: Stanford University Press.

———. 1997. "Immigration and Integration in Western Europe: A Comparative Analysis." In *Immigration into Western Societies: Problems and Policies,* edited by Emek M. Uçarer and Donald J. Puchala, pp. 28–69. London: Pinter.

———. 1999. "Ideas, Institutions, and Civil Society: On the Limits of Immigration Control in France." In *Mechanisms of Immigration Control,* edited by Greta Brochmann and Tomas Hammar, pp. 59–95. Oxford, England: Berg.

Hollifield, James F., and David L. Martin. 1996. "Strange Bedfellows? Immigration and Class Voting on Prop 187 in California." Paper presented at the meeting of the American Political Science Association, San Francisco, August 29–September 1.

Hood, Jane C. 1986. "The Provider Role: Its Meaning and Measurement." *Journal of Marriage and the Family* 14: 349–359.

hooks, bell. 1997. "Representing Whiteness in the Black Imagination." In *Displacing Whiteness: Essays in Social and Cultural Criticism,* edited by Ruth Frankenburg, pp. 165–179. Durham: Duke University Press.

Horne, Alistair. 1977. *A Savage War of Peace: Algeria 1954–1962.* New York: Viking Press.

Horowitz, Donald L. 1985. *Ethnic Groups in Conflict.* Berkeley: University of California Press.

———. 1992. "Immigration and Group Relations in France and the United States." In *Immigrants in Two Democracies: French and American Experience,* pp. 3–35. New York: New York University Press.

Hourriez, Jean-Michel, and Bernard Lebris. 1997. "L'approche monétaire de la pauvreté: Méthodologie et résultats." *Economie et statistique* 8–9–10, no. 308–310: 35–64.

House, Jim. 1996. "Muslim Communities in France." In *Muslim Communities in the New Europe,* edited by Gerd Nonneman, Tim Niblock, and Bogdan Szajkowski, pp. 219–239. Berkshire: Ithaca Press.

Hout, Michael. 1996. "Politics of Mobility." In *Generating Social Stratification: Toward a New Research Agenda,* edited by Alan Kerckhoff, pp. 301–316. Denver: Westview.

Hout, Michael, Clem Brooks, and Jeff Manza. 1995. "The Democratic Class Struggle in the United States, 1948–1992." *American Sociological Review* 60: 805–828.

"How Racist Is France?" 1998. *The Economist,* July 18, p. 44.

Hunter, James Davison. 1987. *Evangelicalism: The Coming Generation.* Chicago: University of Chicago Press.

——. 1991. *Culture War: The Struggle to Define America.* New York: Basic Books.

——. 1994. *Before the Shooting Begins: Searching for Democracy in America's Culture War.* New York: Free Press.

Hunter, James Davison, and Carl Bowman. 1996a. *The State of Disunion, 1996: Survey of American Political Culture.* Vol. 1, *Summary Report.* Ivy, Va.: In Medias Res Educational Foundation.

——. 1996b. *The State of Disunion, 1996: Survey of American Political Culture. Executive Summary.* Ivy, Va.: In Medias Res Educational Foundation.

Hyman, Herbert. 1966. "The Value Systems of Different Classes." In *Class, Status and Power,* 2d ed., edited by Reinhard Bendix and Seymour Martin Lipset, pp. 488–499. New York: Free Press.

Inkeles, Alex. 1979. "Continuity and Change in the American National Character." In *The Third Century: America as a Post-Industrial Society,* edited by Seymour Martin Lipset, pp. 390–453. Stanford: Stanford University Press.

Institut national de la statistique et des études économiques (INSEE). 1992. *Recensement de la population de 1990. Nationalités. Résultats du sondage au vingtième. Démographie et Sociétés no. 19/ INSEE Résultats no. 197.* Paris: Institut national de la statistique et des études économiques.

——. 1993a. *Recensement de la population de 1990. Les populations des DOM-TOM, nées et originaires, résidant en France.* Paris: La Documentation Française.

——. 1993b. *Revenus nets moyens par commune en Île-de-France, 1993.* Paris: Institut national de la statistique et des études économiques.

——. 1994. *Contours et caractères: Les étrangers en France. Portrait social.* Paris: Institut national de la statistique et des études économiques.

——. 1998. *Annuaire statistique de la France.* Paris: Institut national de la statistique et des études économiques.

Iyengar, Shanto. 1987. "Television News and Citizens' Explanations of National Issues." *American Political Science Review* 81: 815–832.

——. 1990. "Framing Responsibility for Political Issues: The Case of Poverty." *Political Behavior* 12: 19–40.

Jackall, Robert. 1988. *Moral Mazes: The World of Corporate Managers.* New York: Oxford University Press.

Jackman, Mary R. 1994. *The Velvet Glove: Paternalism and Conflict in Gender, Class, and Race Relations.* Berkeley: University of California Press.

Jackman, Mary R., and Robert W. Jackman. 1983. *Class Awareness in the United States.* Berkeley: University of California Press.

Jackson, James, with Daria Kirby, Lisa Barnes, and Linda Shepard. 1992. "Racisme institutionnel et ignorance pluraliste: une comparaison transnationale." In *Racisme et modernité,* edited by Michel Wieviorka, pp. 244–263. Paris: La Découverte.

Jaffre, Jérome. 1998. "La France est-elle le mouton noir de l'Europe?" *Le Monde,* July 2, p. 15.

Jasper, James M. 2000. *Restless Nation: Starting Over in America.* Chicago: University of Chicago Press.

Jaynes, Gerald, and Robin M. Williams. 1989. *A Common Destiny: Blacks in American Society.* Washington, D.C.: Academic Press.

Jencks, Christopher. 1994. *The Homeless.* Cambridge, Mass.: Harvard University Press.

——. 1996. "Comments on 'Rationalizing School Spending.'" In *Individuals and Social Responsibility: Child Care, Education, Medical Care, and Long-term Care in America,* edited by Victor Fuchs, pp. 91–105. Chicago: University of Chicago Press.

Jenkins, Richard. 1996. *Social Identity.* London: Routledge.

Jenson, Jane. 1991. "The French Left: A Tale of Three Beginnings." In *Searching for the New France,* edited by James F. Hollifield and George Ross, pp. 85–112. New York: Routledge.

Jepperson, Ronald. 1991. "Institutions, Institutional Effects, and Institutionalism." In *The New Institutionalism in Organizational Analysis,* edited by Walter W. Powell and Paul J. DiMaggio, pp. 143–163. Chicago: University of Chicago Press.

Jobert, Bruno, and Bruno Théret. 1994. "France: La consécration républicaine du néolibéralisme." In *Le tournant néo-libéral en Europe: Idées et recettes dans les pratiques gouvernementales,* edited by Bruno Jobert, pp. 21–86. Paris: Editions L'Harmattan.

Joppke, Christian. 1998. "Immigration Challenges the Nation-State." In *Challenge to the Nation-State: Immigration in Western Europe and the United States,* edited by Christian Joppke, pp. 5–48. Oxford: Oxford University Press.

Jordan, Winthrop D. 1968. *White over Black: American Attitudes toward the Negro, 1550–1812.* New York: W. W. Norton.

Kahler, Miles. 1984. *Decolonization in Britain and France: The Domestic Consequences of International Relations.* Princeton, N.J.: Princeton University Press.

Kallen, Horace. 1924. *Culture and Democracy in the United States.* New York: Boni and Liveright.

Kalmijn, Matthijs. 1991. "Status Homogamy in the United States." *American Journal of Sociology* 97(2): 496–523.

Kanter, Rosabeth Moss. 1977. *Men and Women of the Corporation.* New York: Basic Books.

Kastoryano, Riva. 1986. *Etre turc en France: Réflexions sur familles et communauté.* Paris: CIEMI/L'Harmattan.

——. 1996. *La France, l'Allemagne et leurs immigrés: Négocier l'identité.* Paris: Armand Colin.

Katz, Lawrence F., Gary W. Loveman, and David G. Blanchflower. 1993. "A Comparison of Changes in the Structure of Wages in Four OECD Countries." Cambridge, Mass.: National Bureau of Economic Research.

Katz, Michael. 1989. *The Undeserving Poor: From the War on Poverty to the War on Welfare.* New York: Pantheon.

Katznelson, Ira. 1981. *City Trenches: Urban Politics and the Patterning of Class in the United States.* Chicago: University of Chicago Press.

——. 1986. "Working Class Formation: Constructing Cases and Comparisons." In *Working Class Formation: Nineteenth-Century Patterns in Western Europe and the United States,* edited by Ira Katznelson and Aristide Zolberg, pp. 3–44. Princeton: Princeton University Press.

Kefalas, Maria. Forthcoming. *The Last Garden: Culture and Place in a White, Working Class Chicago Neighborhood.* Berkeley: University of California Press.

Kelley, Robin D. G. 1994. *Race Rebels: Culture, Politics and the Black Working Class.* New York: Free Press.

Kennedy, David M. 1996. "Can We Still Afford to Be a Nation of Immigrants?" *The Atlantic Monthly* (November), pp. 52–68.

Képel, Gilles. 1987. *Les banlieues de l'Islam: Naissance d'une religion en France.* Paris: Le Seuil.

Kerckhoff, Alan C. 1972. *Socialization and Social Class.* Englewood Cliffs, N.J.: Prentice Hall.

Kesselman, Mark. 1984. "Introduction: The French Workers' Movement at the Crossroads." In *The French Workers' Movement: Economic Crisis and Political Change,* edited by Mark Kesselman with Guy Groux, pp. 1–14. London: George Allen and Unwin.

Kinder, Donald R., and Tali Mendelberg. 1995. "Cracks in American Apartheid: The Political Impact of Prejudice among Desegregated Whites." *Journal of Politics* 57(2): 402–424.

Kinder, Donald R., and Lynn M. Sanders. 1996. *Divided by Color: Racial Politics and Democratic Ideals.* Chicago: University of Chicago Press.

Kinder, Donald R., and David O. Sears. 1981. "Prejudice and Politics: Symbolic Racism versus Racist Threats to the Good Life." *Journal of Personality and Social Psychology* 40(3): 414–431.

Kirschenman, Joleen, and Kathryn M. Neckerman. 1990. "'We'd Love to Hire Them, but . . .': The Meaning of Race for Employers." In *The Urban Underclass,* edited by Christopher Jencks and Paul E. Peterson, pp. 203–233. Washington, D.C.: Brookings Institute.

Kitschelt, Herbert (in collaboration with Anthony J. McGann). 1998. *Radical Right in Western Europe: A Comparative Analysis.* Ann Arbor: University of Michigan Press.

Kluegel, James. 1990. "Trends in Whites' Explanations of the Black-White Gap in Socioeconomic Status, 1977–1989." *American Sociological Review* 55: 512–525.

Kluegel, James R., and Eliot R. Smith. 1981. "Beliefs about Stratification." *Annual Review of Sociology* 7: 29–56.

——. 1986. *Beliefs about Inequality: Americans' View of What Is and What Ought to Be.* New York: A. de Gruyter.

Kochman, Thomas. 1981. *Black and White Styles in Conflict*. Chicago: University of Chicago Press.

Kocka, Jurgen. 1980. *White Collar Workers in America, 1890–1940: A Social-Political History in International Perspective*. Beverly Hills: Sage.

Kohn, Melvin L. 1987. "Cross-National Research as an Analytic Strategy." *American Sociological Review* 52: 713–731.

Kornblum, William. 1974. *Blue-Collar Communities*. Chicago: University of Chicago Press.

Kosmin, Barry A., and Seymour P. Lachman. 1993. *One Nation under God: Religion in Contemporary American Society*. New York: Harmony Books.

Kouchner, Bernard. 1989. *Les nouvelles solidarités: Actes des assises internationales de janvier 1989*. Paris: Presses Universitaires de France.

Kriegel, Annie. 1970. *The French Communists: Profile of a People*. Chicago: University of Chicago Press.

Krueger, Alan B. 1997. "The Truth about Wages." *New York Times*, July 31, p. A23.

Kuisel, Richard. 1993. *Seducing the French: The Dilemma of Americanization*. Berkeley: University of California Press.

Labov, William. 1986. "Language Structure and Social Structure." In *Approaches to Social Theory*, edited by Seigwart Lindenberg, James S. Coleman, and Stefan Nowak, pp. 265–290. New York: Russell Sage Foundation.

——. 1993. "Peut-on combattre l'illétrisme? Aspects socio-linguistiques de l'inégalité des chances." *Actes de la recherche en sciences sociales* 100: 37–50.

Lacorne, Denis. 1997. *La crise de l'identité américaine: Du melting-pot au multiculturalisme*. Paris: Fayard.

Lacorne, Denis, Jacques Rupnik, and Marie-France Toinet. 1990. *The Rise and Fall of Anti-Americanism: A Century of French Perceptions*. Translated by Gerald Turner. London: MacMillan.

Lakoff, George. 1987. *Women, Fire, and Dangerous Things: What Categories Reveal about the Mind*. Chicago: University of Chicago Press.

——. 1996. *Moral Politics: What Conservatives Know That Liberals Don't*. Chicago: University of Chicago Press.

Lambert, Michael C. 1993. "From Citizenship to Negritude: 'Making a Difference' in Elite Ideologies of Colonized Francophone West Africa." *Comparative Study of Society and History* 35(2): 239–262.

Lamont, Michèle. 1992. *Money, Morals, and Manners: The Culture of the French and American Upper-Middle Class*. Chicago: University of Chicago Press.

——. 1995. "National Identity and National Boundary Patterns in France and the United States." *French Historical Studies* 19(2): 349–365.

——. 2000. "The Rhetoric of Racism and Anti-Racism." In *Rethinking Comparative Cultural Sociology: Polities and Repertoires of Evaluation in France and the United States*, edited by Michèle Lamont and Laurent Thévenot. Cambridge: Cambridge University Press; Paris: Presses de la Maison des Sciences de l'Homme.

——, ed. 1999. *The Cultural Territories of Race: Black and White Boundaries*. Chicago and New York: University of Chicago Press and Russell Sage Foundation.

Lamont, Michèle, and Marcel Fournier, eds. 1992. *Cultivating Differences: Symbolic Boundaries and the Making of Inequality*. Chicago: University of Chicago Press.

Lamont, Michèle, Jason Kaufman, and Michael Moody. 2000. "The Best and the Brightest: Definitions of the Ideal Self among Prize-winning Students." *Sociological Forum* 15(2).

Lamont, Michèle, and Annette Lareau. 1988. "Cultural Capital: Allusions, Gaps, and Glissandos in Recent Theoretical Developments." *Sociological Theory* (6)2: 153–168.

Lamont, Michèle, John Schmalzbauer, Maureen Waller, and Daniel Weber. 1996. "Cultural and Moral Boundaries in the United States: Structural Position, Geographic Location, and Lifestyle Explanations." *Poetics* 14: 31–56.

Lamont, Michèle, and Laurent Thévenot. 2000. "Introduction: Toward a Renewed Comparative Cultural Sociology." In *Rethinking Comparative Cultural Sociology: Polities and Repertoires of Evaluation in France and the United States,* edited by Michèle Lamont and Laurent Thévenot. Cambridge: Cambridge University Press; Paris: Presses de la Maison des Sciences de l'Homme.

Landry, Bart. 1987. *The New Black Middle Class.* Berkeley: University of California Press.

Lane, Christel. 1989. "From 'Welfare Capitalism' to 'Market Capitalism': A Comparative Review of Trends toward Employment Flexibility in the Labor Markets of Three Major European Societies." *Sociology* 23(4): 583–610.

Lane, Robert E. 1962. *Political Ideology: Why the American Common Man Believes What He Does.* New York: Free Press of Glencoe.

Lapinski, John S., Pia Peltola, Greg Shaw, and Alan Yang. 1997. "The Polls-Trends: Immigrants and Immigration." *Public Opinion Quarterly* 61: 356–383.

Lareau, Annette. 1998. "Class and Race Differences in Children's Worlds." Paper presented at the Eastern Sociological Society, Philadelphia, March.

Lareau, Annette, and Patricia Berhau. Forthcoming. "Social Class and the Daily Lives of Children: A Study from the United States." *Childhood* 7(2): 155–171.

Lareau, Annette, and Caitlin Howley-Rowe. 1995. "Socialization in an African-American Family." Paper presented at the Eastern Sociological Society, Philadelphia, March.

Lash, Scott. 1984. *The Militant Worker.* Cranbury, N.J.: Associated University Press.

——. 1990. *Sociology of Postmodernism.* London: Routledge.

Latour, Bruno. 1987. *Science in Action: How to Follow Scientists and Engineers through Society.* Cambridge: Harvard University Press.

Latting, Jean Latambu. 1990. "Motivational Differences between White and Black Volunteers." *Nonprofit and Voluntary Section Quarterly* 19: 121–136.

Laumann, Edward O., ed. 1973. *Bonds of Pluralism: The Form and Substance of Urban Social Networks.* New York: John Wiley.

Lebovics, Herman. 1999. "Once and Future Trustees of Western Civilization." In *Mona Lisa's Escort: André Malraux and the Reinvention of French Culture,* pp. 27–49. Ithaca: Cornell University Press.

Le Bras, Hervé. 1998. *Le démon des origines: Démographie et extrême-droite.* Paris: Editions de l'Aube.

Lefranc, Arnaud. 1997. "Quelques éléments de comparaison des taux de chômage français et américain." *Economie et statistique* 301–302(1/2): 61–71.

Lemaine, Gérard, and Jeanne Ben Brika. 1994. "Le rejet de l'autre: Pureté, descendance, valeurs." In *Ethnicisation des rapports sociaux: Racismes, nationalismes, ethnicismes, et culturalismes,* edited by Martine Fournier and Geneviève Vermès, pp. 196–234. Paris: Editions L'Harmattan.

——. 1997. "Rejection. From Attitudes to Intentions to Exclude: Social Distance, Phenotypes, Race, and Culture." *Social Science Information* 36(1): 81–113.

Leveau, Remy. 1997. "The Political Culture of the 'Beurs.'" In *Islam in Europe: The Politics of Religion and Community,* edited by Steven Vertovec and Ceri Peach, pp. 147–155. New York: St. Martin's Press.

Leveau, Remy, and Catherine Wihtol de Wenden. 1988. "La deuxième génération." *Pouvoirs: Revue française d'études constitutionelles et politiques* 47: 61–73.

Lévi-Strauss, Claude. 1973. *L'anthropologie structurale,* vol. II. Paris: Plon.

Levine, Lawrence. 1977. *Black Culture and Black Consciousness: Afro-American Folk Thought from Slavery to Freedom.* New York: Oxford University Press.

Lewis, Earl. 1991. *In Their Own Interests: Race, Class, and Power in Twentieth Century Norfork, Virginia.* Berkeley: University of California Press.

Lieberman, Robert C. 1998. "Race and State in the United States, Great Britain and France: Employment Discrimination Policy in Comparative Perspective." Paper presented at the annual meeting of the American Political Science Association, Boston, September.

Lieberson, Stanley, and Mary C. Waters. 1988. *From Many Strands: Ethnic and Racial Groups in Contemporary America.* New York: Russell Sage Foundation.

Lincoln, C. Eric, and Lawrence H. Mamiya. 1990. *The Black Church in the African American Experience.* Durham: Duke University Press.

Lind, Michael. 1995. *The Next American Nation: The New Nationalism and the Fourth American Revolution.* New York: Free Press.

Link, Bruce G., Sharon Schwartz, Robert Moore, Jo Phelan, Elmer Struening, Ann Stueve, and Mary Ellen Colten. 1995. "Public Knowledge, Attitudes and Beliefs about Homeless People: Evidence for Compassion Fatigue." *American Journal of Community Psychology* 23(4): 533–556.

Lipietz, Alain. 1996. *La société en sablier: Le partage du travail contre la déchirure sociale.* Paris: Editions La Découverte.

Lipset, Seymour Martin. 1976. *Political Man.* London: Heinemann.

——. 1977. "Why No Socialism in the United States?" In *Radicalism in the Contemporary Age,* edited by Swekyn Bialer and Sophia Sluzar, pp. 31–149. Boulder, Colo.: Westview Press.

——. 1979. *The First New Nation: The United States in Historical and Comparative Perspective.* New York: Norton.

——. 1996. *American Exceptionalism: A Double-Edged Sword.* New York: W. W. Norton.

Lloyd, Cathie, and Hazel Waters. 1991. "France: One Culture, One People?" *Race and Class* 32(3): 49–65.

Lochak, Danièle. 1993. "Les socialistes et l'immigration, 1981–1993." In *Les étrangers dans la cité: Expériences européennes,* edited by Oliver Le Cour Grandmaison and Catherine Wihtol de Wenden, pp. 43–63. Paris: La Découverte.

Lockwood, David. 1966. "Sources of Variation in Working Class Images of Society." *Sociological Review* 14(3): 249–268.

Logan, John R., and Richard D. Alba. 1996. "Does Race Matter Less for the Truly Advantaged?: Residential Patterns in the New York Metropolis." Paper presented at the 1996 W. E. B. Du Bois Conference on Conservatism, Affirmative Action, and Other Public Policy Issues. Dayton, Ohio: Wright State University, October 17–19.

Logan, John R., Richard D. Alba, Tom McNulty, and Brian Fisher. 1996. "Making a Place in the Metropolis: Locational Attainment in Cities and Suburbs." *Demography* 33(4): 443–453.

Lomax-Cook, Fay. 1979. *Who Should Be Helped? Public Support for Social Services.* Beverly Hills: Sage.

Lorcerie, Françoise. 1994. "Les sciences sociales au service de l'identité nationale." In *Cartes d'identité: Comment dit-on "nous" en politique?* edited by Denis-Constant Martin, pp. 245–281. Paris: Presses de la Fondation nationale des sciences politiques.

Luker, Kristin. 1984. *Abortion and the Politics of Motherhood.* Berkeley: University of California Press.

——. 1996. *Dubious Conceptions: The Politics of Teenage Pregnancy.* Cambridge: Harvard University Press.

Madison, James. [1787] 1987. "Federalist Paper No. 10." In *The American Constitution: For and Against. The Federalist and Anti-Federalist Papers,* edited by Jack Richon Pole, pp. 150–157. New York: Hill and Wang.

Malson, Michelene Ridley. 1983. "Black Families and Childrearing Support Networks." In *Research in the Interweave of Social Roles: Families and Jobs—A Research Annual,* edited by Helena Z. Lopata and Joseph H. Peck, pp. 131–141. Greenwich, Conn.: Jai Press, Inc.

Mann, Michael. 1973. *Consciousness and Action among the Western Working Class.* London: MacMillan.

Mansbridge, Jane. 1983. *Beyond Adversary Democracy.* Chicago: University of Chicago Press.

——. 1993. "Feminism and Democratic Community." In *Democratic Community: Nomos XXXV,* edited by John W. Chapman and Ian Shapiro, pp. 339–395. New York: New York University Press.

Marsden, Peter V., John Shelton Reed, Michael Kennedy, and Kandi M. Stinson. 1982. "American Regional Cultures and Differences in Leisure Time Activities." *Social Forces* 60: 1023–1049.

Marshall, Thomas H. 1950. *Citizenship and Social Class and Other Essays.* Cambridge: Cambridge University Press.

Martin, Philip. 1994. "The United States: Benign Neglect toward Immigration." In *Controlling Immigration: a Global Perspective,* edited by Wayne A. Cornelius, Philip L. Martin, and James F. Hollifield, pp. 83–99. Stanford: Stanford University Press.

Marx, Anthony. 1998. *Making Race and Nation: A Comparison of the United States, South Africa, and Brazil.* New York: Cambridge University Press.

Massey, Douglas. 1996. "The Age of Extremes: Concentrated Affluence and Poverty in the Twenty-first Century." *Demography* 33(4): 395–412.

Massey, Douglas, and Nancy A. Denton. 1993. *American Apartheid: Segregation and the Making of the Underclass.* Cambridge: Cambridge University Press.

Mauco, Georges. 1977. *Les étrangers en France et le problème du racisme.* Paris: La Pensée Universelle.

Mayer, Nonna. 1987. "De Passy a Barbès: Deux visages du vote Le Pen à Paris." *Revue française de science politique* 37(6): 891–906.

——. 1991. "Racisme et antisémitisme dans l'opinion publique française." In *Face au racisme.* Vol. 2, *Analyses, hypothèses, perspectives,* edited by Pierre-André Taguieff, pp. 64–82. Paris: La Découverte.

——, ed. 1996. *Le vote Le Pen: L'électorat du Front National.* Paris: Notes de la Fondation Saint-Simon.

Mazel, Olivier. 1996. *L'exclusion: Le social à la dérive.* Paris: Le Monde-Editions.

McAdams, Doug. 1988. *Freedom Summer.* New York: Oxford University Press.

McClay, Wilfred M. 1994: *The Masterless: Self and Society in Modern America.* Chapel Hill: University of North Carolina Press.

McClosky, Herbert, and John Zaller. 1984. *The American Ethos: Public Attitudes toward Capitalism and Democracy.* Cambridge: Harvard University Press.

McConahay, John B. 1986. "Modern Racism, Ambivalence, and the Modern Racism Scale." In *Prejudice, Discrimination, and Racism,* edited by Samuel L. Gaertner and John F. Dovidio, pp. 91–126. New York: Academic Press.

McConahay, John B., and Joseph C. Hough, Jr. 1976. "Symbolic Racism." *Journal of Social Issues* 32(2): 23–45.

McPherson, James M. 1975. *The Abolitionist Legacy: From Reconstruction to the NAACP.* Princeton, N.J.: Princeton University Press.

Mead, Lawrence. 1986. *Beyond Entitlement: The Social Obligations of Citizenship.* New York: Free Press.

Meertens, Roel W., and Thomas F. Pettigrew. 1997. "Is Subtle Prejudice Really Prejudice?" *Public Opinion Quarterly* 61: 54–71.

Meier, August, Elliott Rudwick, and Francis L. Broderick. 1971. *Black Protest Thought in the Twentieth Century.* Indianapolis: Bobbs-Merrill Co.

Melich, Anna. 1995. "Comparative European Trend Survey: Data on Attitudes toward Immigrants." Paper presented for the ECPR Joint Sessions—Workshop on "Racist Parties in Europe: a New Political Family," Institut d'études politiques de Bordeaux.

Melucci, Alberto. 1996. *Challenging Codes: Collective Action in the Information Age.* New York: Cambridge University Press.

Memmi, Albert. 1965. *The Colonizer and the Colonized.* Boston: Beacon Press.

Ménanteau, Jean. 1994. *Les banlieues.* Paris: Editions Le Monde.

Mendelberg, Tali. 1997. "Executing Horton: Racial Crime in the 1988 Presidential Campaign." *Public Opinion Quarterly* 61: 134–157.

Menninger, Karl. 1973. *Whatever Became of Sin?* New York: Hawthorn.

Merton, Robert K. 1972. "Insiders and Outsiders. A Chapter in the Sociology of Knowledge." *American Journal of Sociology* 18: 9–47.

Messerschmidt, James. 1993. *Masculinities and Crime: Critique and Reconceptualization of Theory.* Boston: Rowman and Littlefield.

Michelat, Guy, and Michel Simon. 1977. *Classe, religion, et comportement politique.* Paris: Presses des la Fondation nationale de sciences politiques.

Miles, Matthew B., and Michael A. Huberman. 1984. *Qualitative Data Analysis: A Sourcebook of New Methods.* Beverly Hills: Sage.

Miles, Robert. 1989. *Racism.* New York: Routledge.

Milkman, Ruth. 1997. *Farewell to the Factory: Auto Workers in the Late Twentieth Century.* Berkeley: University of California Press.

Mishel, Lawrence, Jared Bernstein, and John Schmitt. 1998. "Finally, Real Wage Gains. Lower Unemployment, Higher Minimum Wage Spur Recent Wage Growth." Washington, D.C.: Economic Policy Institute. Issue Brief # 127, July 17 (http://epinet.org/ib127.htlm).

Mithun, Jacqueline. 1973. "Cooperation and Solidarity as Survival Necessities in Black Urban Communities." *Urban Anthropology* 2(1): 25–34.

Mohr, John. 1994. "Soldiers, Mothers, Tramps, and Others: Discourse Role in the 1907 New York City Charity Directory." *Poetics* 22: 327–357.

Mollenkopf, John. 1986. "New York: The Great Anomaly." *Political Science and Politics* 19(3): 591–597.

Molnar, Virag, and Michèle Lamont. 2000. "Social Categorization and Group Identification: How African Americans Shape Their Collective Identity through Consumption." In *Interdisciplinary Approaches to Demand and Its Role in Innovation,* edited by Kenneth Green, Andrew McMeekin, Mark Tomilson, and Vivien Walsh. Manchester: University of Manchester Press.

Moody, Michael, and Laurent Thévenot. 2000. "Comparing Models of Strategy, Interests, and the Common Good in French and American Environmental Disputes." In *Rethinking Comparative Cultural Sociology: Polities and Repertoires of Evaluation in France and the United States,* edited by Michèle Lamont and Laurent Thévenot. Cambridge: Cambridge University Press; Paris: Presses de la Maison des Sciences de l'Homme.

Morin, Richard. 1995. "A Distorted Image of Minorities. Poll Suggests That What Whites Think They See May Affect Beliefs." *Washington Post,* October 8.

Morokvasic, Mirjana, and Hedwig Rudolph. 1996. "Introduction." In *Migrants: Les nouvelles mobilités en Europe,* edited by Mirjana Morokvasic and Hedwig Rudolph, pp. 9–30. Paris: L'Harmattan.

Moscovici, Serge. 1984. "The Phenomenon of Social Representations." In *Social Representations,* edited by Robert M. Farr and Serge Moscovici, pp. 3–69. Cambridge: Cambridge University Press.

Moss, Bernard H. 1993. "Republican Socialism and the Making of the Working Class in Britain, France, and the United States: A Critique of Thompsonian Culturalism." *Comparative Study in Society and History* 35(2): 390–413.

Mosse, George. 1996. *The Image of Man: The Creation of Modern Masculinity.* London: Oxford University Press.

Mouriaux, René. 1991. "Trade Unions, Unemployment, and Regulation: 1962–1989." In *Searching for the New France,* edited by James F. Hollifield and George Ross, pp. 173–192. New York: Routledge.

Mouriaux, René, and Catherine Wihtol de Wenden. 1987. "Syndicalisme français et Islam." *Revue française de science politique* 37(6): 794–819.

Muhammad, Akbar. 1995. "Muslim Relations in the United States." In *Muslim Minorities in the West,* edited by Syed Z. Abedin and Ziauddin Sardar, pp. 159–177. London: Grey Seal.

Murdock, Steven H. 1995. *An America Challenged: Population Change and the Future of the United States.* Boulder: Westview.

Murray, Charles. 1984. *Losing Ground.* New York: Basic Books.

Myrdal, Gunnar. 1944. *An American Dilemma.* New York: Harper and Row.

Nagel, Joane. 1998. "Masculinity and Nationalism: Gender and Sexuality in the Making of Nations." *Ethnic and Racial Studies* 21(2): 242–269.

Nam, Charles B., and E. Walter Terrie. 1982. "Measurement of Socioeconomic Status from United States Census Data." In *Measures of Socioeconomic Status,* edited by Mary G. Powers, pp. 29–42. Boulder, Colo.: Westview Press.

National Conference of Christians and Jews. 1994. "Taking America's Pulse: The Full Report of the National Conference Survey on Inter-Group Relations." New York: National Conference of Christians and Jews.

Nelkin, Dorothy, and Mark Michales. 1988. "Biological Categories and Border Controls: The Revival of Eugenics in Anti-Immigration Rhetoric." *International Journal of Sociology and Social Policy* 18(5): 33–62.

Nelson, Timothy J. 1997. "The Church and the Street: Race, Class, and Congregation." In *Contemporary American Religion: An Ethnographic Reader,* edited by Penny Edgell Becker and Nancy L. Eiesland, pp. 169–190. London: Altamira Press.

New Jersey Department of Labor, Division of Labor Market and Demographic Research. 1995. *New Jersey Economic Indicators.* Trenton: Department of Labor and Industry.

Newman, Katherine. 1988. *Falling from Grace: The Experience of Downward Mobility in the American Middle Class.* New York: Free Press.

——. 1992. "Culture and Structure in the Truly Disadvantaged." *City and Society* 6: 3–25.

——. 1993. *Declining Fortunes: The Withering of the American Dream.* New York: Basic.

——. 1999. *No Shame in My Game: The Working Poor in the Inner City.* New York: Knopf and the Russell Sage Foundation.

Newman, Katherine, and Catherine Ellis. 1999. "'There Is No Shame in My Game': Status and Stigma among Harlem's Working Poor." In *The Cultural Territories of Race: White and Black Boundaries,* edited by Michèle Lamont, pp. 151–181. New York and Chicago: Russell Sage Foundation and University of Chicago Press.

Nicolet, Claude. 1992. "Le passage à l'universel." In *La République en France: Etat des Lieux,* pp. 122–168. Paris: Le Seuil.

Nielsen, Jorgen S. 1992. *Muslims in Western Europe.* Edinburgh: Edinburgh University Press.

——. 1997. "Muslims in Europe: History Revisited or a Way Forward?" *Islam and Christian-Muslim Relations* 8(2): 135–143.

Nightingale, Carl Husemoller. 1993. *On the Edge: A History of Poor Black Children and Their American Dreams.* New York: Basic Books.

Nisbett, Richard E., and Dov Cohen. 1996. *Culture and Honor: The Psychology of Violence in the South.* Boulder, Colo.: Westview Press.

Noble, David. 1997. *Welfare As We Knew It: A Political History of the American Welfare State.* New York: Oxford University Press.

Noiriel, Gérard. 1984. *Longwy: Immigrés et prolétaires (1880–1989)*. Paris: Presses Universitaires de France.

——. 1986. *Les ouvriers dans la société française, XIXième-XXième siècle*. Paris: Seuil.

——. 1992. *Population, immigration et identité nationale en France, XIXième et XXième siècles*. Paris: Hachette.

——. 1996. *The French Melting Pot: Immigration, Citizenship, and National Identity*. Translated by Geoffrey de Laforcade. Minneapolis: University of Minnesota Press.

Noll, Heinz-Herbert, and Simon Langlois. 1994. "Employment and Labour-Market Change: Toward Two Models of Growth." In *Convergence or Divergence? Comparing Recent Social Trends in Industrial Societies*, edited by Simon Langlois, with Theodore Caplow, Henri Mendras, and Wolfgang Glatzer, pp. 89–114. Montreal: McGill-Queen's University Press.

Norindr, Panivong. 1996. "La Plus Grande France: French Cultural Identity and Nation Building under Mitterand." In *Identity Papers: Contested Nationhood in Twentieth-Century France*, edited by Steven Ungar and Tom Conley, pp. 233–258. Minneapolis: University of Minnesota Press.

Nussbaum, Martha. 1996. *For Love of Country*. Boston: Beacon Press.

Offe, Claus. 1987. "Democracy against the Welfare State? Structural Foundations of Neoconservative Political Opportunities." *Political Theory* 15(4): 501–537.

O'Higgins, Michael, Guenther Schmaus, and Geoffrey Stephenson. 1989. "Income Distribution and Redistribution: A Microdata Analysis for Seven Countries." *Review of Income and Wealth*, series 35, no. 2: 107–132.

Oliver, Melvin L., and Thomas M. Shapiro. 1997. *Black Wealth/White Wealth: A New Perspective on Racial Inequality*. New York: Routledge.

Ollivier, Michele. 2000. "Gradational and Relational Concepts of Status." Paper presented at the annual meeting of the American Sociological Association, Washington, D.C., August.

——. Forthcoming. "Too Much Money off Other People's Backs: Status in Postindustrial Societies or Occupational Prestige Revisited—Again?" *Canadian Journal of Sociology*.

Omi, Michael. 1998. "(E) racism: Emergent Practices of Anti-Racist Organizations." Paper presented at the meeting of the American Sociological Association, San Francisco, August.

Omi, Michael, and Howard Winant. 1986. *Racial Formation in the United States from the 1960s to the 1980s*. New York: Routledge.

——. 1993. "The Los Angeles 'Race Riot' and Contemporary U.S. Politics." In *Reading Rodney King/Reading Urban Uprising*, edited by Robert Gooding-Williams, pp. 97–114. New York: Routledge.

Ong, Aihwa. 1996. "Cultural Citizenship as Subject-Making: Immigrants Negotiate Racial and Cultural Boundaries in the United States." *Current Anthropology* 37(5): 737–762.

Organization for Economic Cooperation and Development. 1992. *Historical Statistics: 1960–1990*. Paris: Organization for Economic Cooperation and Development.

——. 1995. *OECD Economic Outlook*, vol. 57. Paris: Organization for Economic Cooperation and Development.

——. 1997. *Labour Force Statistics 1976–1996*. Paris: Organization for Economic Cooperation and Development.

Ortner, Sherry B. 1984. "Theory in Anthropology since the Sixties." *Comparative Studies in Society and History* 26(1): 126–166.

Ossowski, Stanislaw. 1963. *Class Structure in the Social Consciousness*. New York: Free Press.

Ostrower, Francie. 1995. *Why the Wealthy Give: The Culture of Elite Philanthropy*. Princeton: Princeton University Press.

O'Toole, Kathleen. 1998. "Our Culture, Myself: Middle-Class Americans Seek Individualism, Markus Says." *Stanford Online Report* (http://wws.stanford.edu/dept/news/report/news/february 11/markus.html).

Owen, Carolyn, Howard C. Eisner, and Thomas R. McFaul. 1981. "A Half-Century of Social Distance Research: National Replication of the Bogardus Studies." *Sociology and Social Research* 66(1): 80–98.

Page, Benjamin I. 1996. "Trouble for Workers and the Poor: Economic Globalization and the Reshaping of American Politics." Paper presented at the conference on "The Clinton Years in Perspective," Université de Montréal, October.

Page, Benjamin, and Robert Y. Shapiro. 1992. *The Rational Public: Fifty Years of Trends in Americans' Policy Preferences*. Chicago: University of Chicago Press.

Pakulski, Jan, and Malcolm Waters. 1996. "The Reshaping and Dissolution of Social Class in Advanced Society." *Theory and Society* 25(5): 667–691.

Park, Kyeyoung. 1996. "Use and Abuse of Race and Culture: Black-Korean Tension in America." *American Anthropologist* 98(3): 492–499.

——. 1998. "'No Tension, but . . .': Latino Commentary on Koreans and the South Central Aftermath." Paper presented at the faculty seminar on Race, Culture, and Politics, Princeton University, March.

Parkin, Frank. 1979. *Marxism and Class Theory: A Bourgeois Critique*. London: Tavistock Publications.

Passell, Jeffrey S., and Barry Edmonston. 1992. *Immigration and Race: Recent Trends in Immigration to the United States*. Washington, D.C.: The Urban Institute.

Patterson, James T. 1981. *America's Struggle against Poverty, 1900–1980*. Cambridge, Mass.: Harvard University Press.

Patterson, Orlando. 1977. "The Universal and the Particular in Western Social Thought." In *Ethnic Chauvinism: The Reactionary Impulse*, pp. 197–229. New York: Stein and Dayle.

——. 1997. *The Ordeal of Integration: Progress and Resentment in America's "Racial" Crisis*. New York: Counterpoint.

Pattillo-McCoy, Mary. 1999. *Black Picket Fences: Privilege and Peril among the Black Middle Class*. Chicago: University of Chicago Press.

Paugam, Serge. 1993. *La société française et ses pauvres*. Paris: Presses Universitaires de France.

Perelman, Chaim, and Lucy Olbrechts-Tyteca. 1969. *The New Rhetoric: A Treatise on Argumentation*. Notre Dame, Ind.: University of Notre Dame Press.

Perin, Constance. 1988. *Belonging in America*. Madison: University of Wisconsin Press.

Perrineau, Pascal. 1997. *Le symptôme Le Pen: Radiographie des électeurs du Front National*. Paris: Fayard.

Perrot, Michelle. 1986. "On the Formation of the French Working Class." In *Working Class Formation: Nineteenth-Century Patterns in Western Europe and the United States,* edited by Ira Katznelson and Aristide Zolberg, pp. 71–110. Princeton: Princeton University Press.

Peterson, Richard A., and Roger Kern. 1996. "Changing Highbrow Taste: From Snob to Omnivore." *American Sociological Review* 61: 900–907.

Pettigrew, Thomas. 1989. "Nature of Modern Racism in the U.S." *Revue internationale de psychologie sociale* 2: 291–303.

Pettigrew, Thomas, James S. Jackson, Jeanne Ben Brika, Gérard Lemaine, Roel W. Meertens, Ulrich Wagner, and Andrea Zick. 1998. "Outgroup Prejudice in Western Europe." *European Review of Social Psychology* 8: 241–273.

Phillips, Kevin P. 1970. *The Emerging Republican Majority.* Garden City, N.Y.: Anchor Books.

Pialoux, Michel. 1992. "Alcool et politique dans l'atelier: Une usine de carrosserie dans la décennie 1980." *Genèses* 7: 94–128.

——. 1995. "L'ouvrière et le chef d'équipe ou comment parler du travail?" *Travail et emploi* 62: 4–39.

Pierson, Paul. 1994. *Dismantling the Welfare State? Reagan, Thatcher, and the Politics of Retrenchment.* Cambridge: Cambridge University Press.

Pinçon, Michel. 1987. *Désarrois ouvriers: Familles de métallurgistes dans les mutations industrielles et sociales.* Paris: L'Harmattan.

Piven, Frances Fox. 1992. "The Decline of Labor Parties: An Overview." In *Labor Parties in Industrial Societies,* edited by Frances Fox Piven, pp. 1–19. New York: Oxford University Press.

Pleck, Joseph H., and Linda Lang. 1978. *Men's Family Role: Its Nature and Consequence.* Wellesley, Mass.: Center for Research on Women, Wellesley College.

Policar, Alain. 1991. "Racisme et antiracisme: Perspectives théoriques récentes." *Raison présente* no. 100: 39–52.

Porter, Judith R., and Robert E. Washington. 1989. "Development in Research on Black Identity and Self-Esteem: 1979–1988." *Revue internationale de psychologie sociale* 2(3): 341–353.

Portes, Alejandro. 1994. "The Informal Economy and Its Paradoxes." In *Handbook of Economic Sociology,* edited by N. J. Smelser and R. Swedberg, pp. 426–449. Princeton: Princeton University Press.

——, ed. 1995. *The Economic Sociology of Immigration.* New York: Russell Sage Foundation.

Portes, Alejandro, and Ruben G. Rumbaut. 1990. *Immigrant America: A Portrait.* Berkeley: University of California Press.

Portes, Alejandro, and Julia Sensenbrenner. 1993. "Embeddedness and Immigration: Notes on the Social Determinants of Economic Action." *American Journal of Sociology* 98: 1320–1350.

Portes, Alejandro, and Alex Stepick. 1993. *City on the Edge: The Transformation of Miami.* California: University of California Press.

Praeger, Jeffrey. 1987. "American Political Culture and the Shifting Meaning of Race." *Ethnic and Racial Studies* 10(1): 62–81.

Procacci, Giovanna. 1993. *Gouverner la misère: La question sociale en France, 1978–1848.* Paris: Seuil.

Quadagno, Jill. 1994. *The Color of Welfare: How Racism Undermined the War on Poverty.* New York: Oxford University Press.

Quillian, Lincoln. 1995. "Prejudice as a Response to Perceived Group Threat: Population Composition and Anti-Immigrant and Racial Prejudice in Europe." *American Sociological Review* 60: 586–611.

Rainwater, Lee. 1970. *Behind Ghetto Walls.* New York: Aldine.

Rangeon, François. 1986. *L'idéologie de l'intérêt général.* Paris: Economica.

Rasmussen, David, ed. 1990. *Universalism vs. Communitarianism: Contemporary Debates in Ethics.* Cambridge, Mass.: MIT Press.

Reed, Adolf. 1991. "The Underclass Myth." *The Progressive Magazine* (August), pp. 18–20.

Reed, John Shelton. 1983. *Southerners: The Social Psychology of Sectionalism.* Chapel Hill: University of North Carolina Press.

Reinarman, Craig. 1987. *American States of Mind: Political Beliefs and Behavior among Private and Public Workers.* New Haven: Yale University Press.

Rex, John. 1979. *Race Relations in Sociological Theory.* New York: Routledge.

Rieder, Jonathan. 1985. *Canarsie: The Jews and Italians of Brooklyn against Liberalism.* Cambridge: Harvard University Press.

Robinson, Ira E., Wilfrid C. Bailey, and John M. Smith, Jr. 1985. "Self-Perception of the Husband/Father in the Intact Lower Class Black Family." *Phylon* 66(2): 136–147.

Rodgers, Daniel T. 1974. *The Work Ethic in Industrial America, 1850–1920.* Chicago: University of Chicago Press.

———. 1998. "Exceptionalism." In *Imagined Histories: American Historians and the Past,* edited by Anthony Mohlo and Gordon S. Wood, pp. 21–40. Princeton: Princeton University Press.

Roediger, David. 1991. *The Wages of Whiteness: Race and the Making of the American Working Class.* London: Verso.

———. 1998. *Black on White: Black Writers on What It Means to Be White.* New York: Schocken Books.

Rokeach, Milton. 1973. *The Nature of Human Values.* New York: Free Press.

Rollins, Judith. 1985. *Between Women: Domestics and Their Employers.* Philadelphia: Temple University Press.

Romo, Frank, and David Halle. 1991. "The Blue-Collar Working Class: Structural Discontinuity." New York: Working Papers Series, Russell Sage Foundation.

Roof, Wade Clark, and William McKinney. 1987. *American Mainline Religion: Its Changing Shape and Future.* New Brunswick: Rutgers University Press.

Rosanvallon, Pierre. 1990. *L'Etat en France de 1789 à nos jours.* Paris: Seuil.

Rose, Sonya. 1992. *Limited Livelihoods: Gender and Class in Nineteenth Century England.* Berkeley: University of California Press.

Rosen, Lawrence. 1984. *Bargaining for Reality: The Construction of Social Relations in a Muslim Community.* Chicago: University of Chicago Press.

Ross, George, and Jane Jenson. 1994. "France: Triumph and Tragedy." In *Mapping the West European Left,* edited by Perry Anderson and Patrick Camiller, pp. 158–188. London: Verso.

Rubin, Jeffrey W. 1996. "Defining Resistance: Contested Interpretations of Everyday Acts." *Studies in Law, Politics, and Society* 15: 237–260.

Rubin, Lillian B. 1976. *Worlds of Pain: Life in the Working Class Family.* New York: Basic Books.

———. 1994. *Families on the Faultline: America's Working Class Speaks about the Family, the Economy, Race, and Ethnicity.* New York: Harper Collins.

Rudder, Veronique de, Isabelle Taboatta Leonetti, and François Vourc'h. 1990. *Strategies d'insertion, representations, et attitudes.* Paris: Institut de recherches sur les sociétiés contemporaines, Unite de recherches migrations et société, Centre national de recherche scientifique.

Ruggles, Steven, and Matthew Sobek et al. 1997. *Integrated Public Use of Microdata Series: Version 2.0.* Minneapolis: Historical Census Projects, University of Minnesota.

Safran, William. 1991. "State, Nation, National Identity, and Citizenship: France as a Test Case." *International Political Science Review* 12(3): 219–238.

Saguy, Abigail Cope. 2000. "Sexual Harassment in France and the United States: Activists and Public Figures Defend Their Positions." In *Rethinking Comparative Cultural Sociology: Polities and Repertoires of Evaluation in France and the United States,* edited by Michèle Lamont and Laurent Thévenot. Cambridge: Cambridge University Press; Presses de la Maison des Sciences de l'Homme.

Sahlins, Peter D. 1997. *Assimilation American Style.* New York: Basic Books.

Sandel, Michael J. 1996. *Democracy's Discontent: America in Search of a Public Philosophy.* Cambridge: Harvard University Press.

Sanders, Lynn M. 1995. "What Is Whiteness? Race-of-Interviewer Effects When All the Interviewers Are Black." Paper presented at the American Politics Workshop, University of Chicago, January 4.

Sassen, Saskia. 1991. *The Global City: New York, London, and Tokyo.* Princeton: Princeton University Press.

———. 1994. "La ville globale: Elements pour une lecture de Paris." *Le débat* 80: 146–164.

Sayad, Abdelmalek. 1991. "Qu'est-ce qu'un immigré?" In *L'immigration ou les paradoxes de l'altérité,* pp. 49–70. Bruxelles: De Boeck.

Schain, Martin. 1987. "The National Front in France and the Construction of Political Legitimacy." *West European Politics* 10(2): 229–252.

———. 1997. "The National Front and the Politicization of Immigration in France: Implications for the Extreme Right in Western Europe." Paper presented at the Conference on Citizenship, Immigration, and Xenophobia in Europe: Comparative Perspectives. Berlin: Wissenschaftszentrum.

Schnapper, Dominique. 1991. *La France de l'intégration: Sociologie de la nation en 1990.* Paris: Gallimard.

———. 1998. *La relation à l'autre: Au coeur de la pensée sociologique.* Paris: Gallimard.

Schneider, Dorothée. 2000. "Symbolic Citizenship, Nationalism and the Distant State: The United States Congress in the 1996 Debate on Immigration Reform." *Citizenship Studies* 4(2).

Schudson, Michael. 1989. "How Culture Works: Perspectives from Media Studies on the Efficacy of Symbols." *Theory and Society* 18: 153–180.

Schuman, Howard, Charlotte Steeh, Lawrence Bobo, and Maria Krysan. 1997. *Racial Attitudes in America: Trends and Interpretation,* rev. ed. Cambridge: Harvard University Press.

Schurman, Susan J. 1995. "AFL-CIO Election Is a Sign More Changes Are on the Way." *The Record,* November 12, p. 7.

Schwartz, Michael, and Sharon Zukin. 1988. "Deindustrialization in the United States and France: Structural Convergence, Institutional Contrast." *Political Power and Social Theory* 7: 293–320.

Schwartz, Olivier. 1990. *Le monde privé des ouvriers: Hommes et femmes du Nord.* Paris: Presses Universitaires de France.

Scott, James C. 1985. *Weapons of the Weak.* New Haven: Yale University Press.

——. 1990. *Domination and the Arts of Resistance: Hidden Transcripts.* New Haven: Yale University Press.

Scott, Joan W. 1997. "'La Querelle des Femmes' in the Late Twentieth Century." *New Left Review* 226: 3–19.

Sears, David O., Colette Van Laar, Mary Carillo, and Rick Kosterman. 1997. "Is It Really Racism? The Origins of White Americans' Opposition to Race-Targeted Policies." *Public Opinion Quarterly* 61: 16–53.

Segrestin, Denis. 1984. "Collective Action and Union Behavior." In *The French Workers' Movement: Economic Crisis and Political Change,* edited by Mark Kesselman with Guy Groux, pp. 199–209. London: George Allen and Unwin.

——. 1990. "Recent Changes in France." In *European Industrial Relations: The Challenge of Flexibility,* edited by Guido Bablioni and Colin Crouch, pp. 97–126. Newbury Park, Calif.: Sage Publications.

Sennett, Richard, and Jonathan Cobb. 1972. *The Hidden Injuries of Class.* New York: Vintage.

Sewell, William H., Jr. 1980. *Work and Revolution in France: The Language of Labor from the Old Regime to 1848.* Cambridge: Cambridge University Press.

——. 1992. "A Theory of Structure: Duality, Agency, and Transformation." *American Journal of Sociology* 98(10): 1–29.

Shanahan, Suzanne, and Susan Olzak. 1999. "The Effect of Immigrant Diversity and Ethnic Competition on Collective Conflict in Urban America: An Assessment of Two Moments of Mass Migration, 1869–1924 and 1965–1993." *Journal of American Ethnic History* 18(3): 40–64.

Shapiro, Robert Y., Kelly D. Patterson, Judith Russell, and John T. Young. 1987. "The Polls: Public Assistance." *Public Opinion Quarterly* 51: 120–130.

Shapiro, Robert Y., and John T. Young. 1989. "Public Opinion and the Welfare State: The United States in Comparative Perspective." *Political Science Quarterly* 104: 59–89.

Shenhav, Yehouda. 1999. *Manufacturing Rationality: The Engineering Foundations of the Managerial Revolution.* Oxford: Oxford University Press.

Shklar, Judith N. 1991. *American Citizenship: The Quest for Inclusion.* Cambridge, Mass.: Harvard University Press.

Shorter, Edward, and Charles Tilly. 1974. *Strikes in France, 1830–1968.* Cambridge, Mass.: Harvard University Press.

Sidanius, James. 1993. "The Psychology of Group Conflict and the Dynamics of Oppression: A Social Dominance Perspective." In *Explorations in Political Psychology,* edited by Shanto Iyengar and William McGuire, pp. 183–219. Durham: Duke University Press.

Sidanius, James, Seymour Feshbach, Shana Levin, and Felicia Pratto. 1997. "The Interface between Ethnic and Racial Attachment: Ethnic Pluralism or Ethnic Dominance?" *Public Opinion Quarterly* 61: 102–133.

Sigelman, Lee, James W. Shockey, and Carol K. Sigelman. 1993. "Ethnic Stereotyping: A Black/White Comparison." In *Prejudice, Politics, and the American Dilemma,* edited by Paul M. Sniderman, Philip E. Tetlock, and Edward G. Carmines, pp. 104–126. Stanford: Stanford University Press.

Sigelman, Lee, and Steven A. Tuch. 1997. "Metastereotypes: Blacks' Perceptions of Whites' Stereotypes of Blacks." *Public Opinion Quarterly* 61: 87–101.

Sigelman, Lee, and Susan Welch. 1991. *Black Americans' Views of Racial Inequality: A Dream Deferred.* Cambridge: Cambridge University Press.

Silver, Hilary. 1993. "National Conceptions of the New Urban Poverty: Social Structural Change in Britain, France, and the United States." *International Journal of Urban and Regional Research* 17(3): 336–354.

——. 1994. "Social Exclusion and Social Solidarity: Three Paradigms: A Discussion Paper." Geneva: International Institute for Labor Studies, International Labor Organization.

——. 1996. "Culture, Politics, and National Discourses of the New Urban Poverty?" In *Urban Poverty and the Underclass: A Reader,* edited by Enzo Mingione, pp. 105–139. London: Blackwell.

——. 1998. "Policies to Reinforce Social Cohesion in Europe." In *Social Exclusion: An ILO Perspective,* edited by Arjan de Haan and Jose Burle Figueiredo, pp. 38–73. Geneva: International Institute for Labor Studies, International Labor Organization.

Silver, Hilary, and Craig Zwerling. 1992. "Race and Job Dismissals in a Federal Bureaucracy." *American Sociological Review* 57 (October): 651–660.

Silverman, Maxim. 1992. *Deconstructing the Nation: Immigration, Racism and Citizenship in Modern France.* New York: Routledge.

Simmel, Georg. 1978. *The Philosophy of Money.* Boston: Routledge and Kegan Paul.

Simons, Herbert W. 1990. "The Rhetoric of Inquiry as an Intellectual Movement." In *The Rhetorical Turn: Invention and Persuasion in the Conduct of Inquiry,* edited by Herbert W. Simons, pp. 1–34. Chicago: University of Chicago Press.

Skocpol, Theda. 1990. "Sustainable Social Policy: Fighting Poverty without Poverty Programs." *The American Prospect* 1(2): 58–70.

——. 1995. *Protecting Soldiers and Mothers: The Political Origins of Social Policy in the United States.* Cambridge, Mass.: Harvard University Press.

Skocpol, Theda, and Edwin Amenta. 1986. "States and Social Policies." *Annual Review of Sociology* 12: 131–157.

Skolnick, Jerome. 1998. "The Color of the Law." *The American Prospect* (July-August), pp. 90–96.

Skrentny, John David. 1996. *The Ironies of Affirmative Action: Politics, Culture, and Justice in America.* Chicago: University of Chicago Press.

Smeeding, Timothy, Lee Rainwater, Martin Rein, Richard Hauser, and Gaston Schaber. 1990. "Income Poverty in Seven Countries." In *Poverty, Inequality, and Income Distribution in Comparative Perspective: The Luxembourg Income Study,* edited by Timothy Smeeding, Michael O'Higgins, and Lee Rainwater, pp. 57–76. Washington: Urban Institute.

Smith, David Horton. 1984. "Determinants of Voluntary Association Participation and Volunteering: A Literature Review." *Nonprofit and Voluntary Sector Quarterly* 23: 243–263.

Smith, Robert C., and Richard Seltzer. 1992. *Race, Class, and Culture: A Study in Afro-American Mass Opinion.* New York: State University of New York Press.

Smith, Rogers M. 1997. *Civic Ideals: Conflicting Visions of Citizenship in U.S. History.* New Haven: Yale University Press.

Smith, Tom W. 1987. "The Welfare State in Cross-National Perspective." *Public Opinion Quarterly* 51: 404–421.

——. 1990. *Ethnic Images.* GSS Topical Report no. 19. Chicago: National Opinion Research Center, University of Chicago.

Smith, Tony. 1975. "The French Colonial Consensus and People's War, 1946–1958." In *The End of the European Empire: Decolonization after World War II,* edited by Tony Smith, pp. 103–122. Lexington, Mass.: D. C. Heath and Co.

Sniderman, Paul M., with Michael Gray Hagen. 1985. *Race and Inequality: A Study in American Values.* Chatham, N.J.: Chatham House Publishers.

Sniderman, Paul M., and Thomas Piazza. 1993. *The Scar of Race.* Cambridge: Harvard University Press.

Sombart, Werner. 1976. *Why Is There No Socialism in the United States?* Translated by Patricia M. Hocking and C. T. Husbands. White Plains, N.Y.: International Arts and Sciences Press.

Somers, Margaret R. 1994. "The Narrative Constitution of Identity: A Relational and Network Approach." *Theory and Society* 23: 605–649.

Somers, Margaret R., and Gloria D. Gibson. 1994. "Reclaiming the Epistemological 'Other': Narrative and the Social Constitution of Identity." In *Social Theory and the Politics of Identity,* edited by Craig Calhoon, pp. 37–99. Cambridge, Mass.: Blackwell Publishers.

Soulignac, Françoise. 1993. *La banlieue française: Cent cinquante ans de transformations.* Paris: La Documentation Française.

Southwell, Alexander H. 1994. "The Changing Nature of New Jersey's Economy." In *A Stone's Throw from Ellis Island: Economic Implications of Immigration to New Jersey,* edited by Thomas J. Espenshade, pp. 45–111. Lanham, Md.: University Press of America.

Stacey, Judith. 1996. *In the Name of the Family: Rethinking Family Values in the Postmodern Age.* Boston: Beacon Press.

Stack, Carol. 1974. *All Our Kin: Strategies for Survival in a Black Community.* New York: Harper and Row.

Stangor, Charles, and James E. Lange. 1994. "Mental Representations of Social Groups: Advances in Understanding Stereotypes and Stereotyping." *Advances in Experimental Social Psychology* 26: 357–416.

Staples, Robert. 1974. "The Black Family Revisited: A Review and a Preview." *Journal of Social and Behavioral Sciences* 20: 65–78.

Stinchcombe, Arthur. 1995. *Sugar Island Slavery in the Age of Enlightenment: The Political Economy of the Carribean World.* Princeton: Princeton University Press.

Stoler, Ann Laura. 1991. "Carnal Knowledge and Imperial Power: Gender, Race, and Morality in Colonial Asia." In *Gender at the Crossroads of Knowlege: Feminist Anthropology in the Postmodern Era,* edited by Micaela di Leonardo, pp. 51–101. Berkeley: University of California Press.

Stuckey, Sterling. 1987. *Slave Culture: Nationalist Theory and the Foundations of Black America.* New York: Oxford University Press.

Sumner, William Graham. 1906. *Folkways.* New York: Ginn.

Swartz, Thomas R., and Kathleen Maas Weigert. 1995. *America's Working Poor.* Notre Dame, Ind.: University of Notre Dame Press.

Swidler, Ann. 1986. "Culture in Action: Symbols and Strategies." *American Sociological Review* 51: 273–286.

Taguieff, Pierre-André. 1988. *La force du préjugé: Essai sur le racisme et ses doubles.* Paris: La Découverte.

——. 1989a. "Un programme 'révolutionnaire.'" In *Le Front National à découvert,* edited by Nonna Mayer and Pascal Perrineau, pp. 195–227. Paris: La Découverte.

——. 1989b. "La métaphysique de Jean-Marie Le Pen." In *Le Front National à découvert,* edited by Nonna Mayer and Pascal Perrineau, pp. 173–194. Paris: La Découverte.

——. 1991. "Les métamorphoses idéologiques du racisme et la crise de l'anti-racisme." In *Face au racisme.* Vol. 2, *Analyses, hypothèses, perspectives,* edited by Pierre-André Taguieff, pp. 13–63. Paris: La Découverte.

Tajfel, Henri, and John C. Turner. 1985. "The Social Identity Theory of Intergroup Behavior." In *Psychology of Intergroup Relations,* edited by Stephen Worchel and William G. Austin, pp. 7–24. Chicago: Nelson-Hall.

Taylor, Charles. 1992. "The Politics of Recognition." In *Multiculturalism: Examining the Politics of Recognition,* edited by Charles Taylor and Amy Gutmann, pp. 25–74. Princeton: Princeton University Press.

Taylor, Robert Joseph. 1990. "Need for Support and Family Involvement among Black Americans." *Journal of Marriage and the Family* 52: 84–90.

Teixeira, Ruy A., and Joel Rogers. 1996. *Volatile Voters: Declining Living Standards and Non-College-Educated Whites.* Washington, D.C.: Economic Policy Institute.

Térrail, Jean Pierre. 1990. *Destins ouvriers—la fin d'une classe?* Paris: Presses Universitaires de France.

Thelen, Kathleen. 1999. "Historical Institutionalism in Comparative Politics." *Annual Review of Political Science* 2: 369–404.

Thévenot, Laurent, and Michèle Lamont. 2000. "Exploring the French and the American Polity." In *Rethinking Comparative Cultural Sociology: Repertoires of Evaluation in France and the United States,* edited by Michèle Lamont and Laurent Thévenot. Cambridge: Cambridge University Press; Paris: Presses de la Maison des Sciences de l'Homme.

Thompson, Edward P. 1966. *The Making of the English Working Class.* New York: Vintage Books.

Thompson, J. Phillip III. 1998. "Universalism and Deconcentration: Why Race Still Matters in Poverty and Economic Development." *Politics and Society* 26(2): 181–219.

Tilly, Charles. 1994. "Citizenship, Identity, and Social History." Working Paper Series, Center for Studies of Social Change, New School for Social Research, New York.

——. 1995. "Social Movements and (All Sorts of) Other Political Interactions—Local, National, and International—Including Identities: Several Divagations from a Common Path, Beginning with British Struggles over Catholic Emancipation, 1780–1829, and Ending with Contemporary Nationalism." Working Paper Series, Center for Studies of Social Change, New School for Social Research, New York.

——. 1997. *Durable Inequality.* Cambridge: Harvard University Press.

Tocqueville, Alexis de. [1835] 1969. *Democracy in America.* Garden City, N.Y.: Anchor Books.

Todd, Emmanuel. 1994. *Le destin des immigrés: Assimilation et ségrégation dans les démocraties occidentales.* Paris: Seuil.

Touraine, Alain, Michel Wieviorka, and Francois Dubet. 1978. *The Workers' Movement.* Translated by Ian Patterson. Cambridge and Paris: Cambridge University Press and Editions de la Maison des Sciences de l'Homme.

Tournier, Pierre, and Philippe Robert. 1991. *Etrangers et délinquances: Les chiffres du débat.* Paris: L'Harmattan.

Trattner, Walter I. 1994. *From Poor Law to Welfare State: A History of Social Welfare in America,* 5th ed. New York: Free Press.

Tribalat, Michèle. 1995. *Faire France: Une enquête sur les immigrés et leurs enfants.* Paris: La Découverte.

Turner, John C., Penelope J. Oakes, S. Alexander Haslam, and Craig McGarty. 1994. "Self and Collective: Cognition and Social Context." *Personality and Social Psychology Bulletin* 20(5): 454–463.

Turner, Victor. 1974. *Dramas, Fields, and Metaphors: Symbolic Action in Human Society.* Ithaca, N.Y.: Cornell University Press.

Tyree, Andrea, Moshe Semyonov, and Robert W. Hodge. 1979. "Gaps and Glissandos: Inequality, Economic Development, and Social Mobility in 24 Countries." *American Sociological Review* 44(3): 410–424.

United States Bureau of Census of the Population. 1988. *Statistical Abstracts of the United States 1988,* 108th ed. Washington, D.C.: U.S. Government Printing Office.

——. 1990a. *Selected Ethnic Characteristics for New Jersey: 1990.* Washington, D.C.: Bureau of the Census.

——. 1990b. *Statistical Abstracts of the United States 1990,* 110th ed. Washington, D.C.: U.S. Government Printing Office.

——. 1992. *Statistical Abstracts of the United States 1992,* 112th ed. Washington, D.C.: U.S. Government Printing Office.

——. 1993. *Statistical Abstracts of the United States 1993,* 113th ed. Washington, D.C.: U.S. Government Printing Office.

——. 1995. *Statistical Abstracts of the United States 1995,* 115th ed. Washington, D.C.: U.S. Government Printing Office.

——. 1996. *Statistical Abstract of the United States: 1996,* 116th ed. Washington, D.C.: U.S. Government Printing Office.

——. 1998. *Statistical Abstract of the United States: 1998,* 118th ed. Washington, D.C.: U.S. Government Printing Office.

United States Bureau of the Census. 1992. *Ethnic Profiles for States.* Washington, D.C.: Bureau of the Census.

——. 1993. *1990 Census of Population: The Foreign-Born Population in the United States.* Washington, D.C.: United States Department of Commerce, Economics and Statistics Administration, Bureau of the Census.

United States Department of Commerce, Bureau of the Census. 1995. *County and City Data Book 1994.* Washington, D.C.: Bureau of the Census.

United States Department of Labor, Bureau of Labor Statistics. 1989. *Handbook of Labor Statistics,* Bulletin 2340. Washington, D.C.: Bureau of Labor Statistics.

Upham, Martin, ed. 1993. *Trade Unions and Employers' Organizations of the World.* London: Longman Group Ltd.

Uusitalo, Hanny. 1984. "Comparative Research on the Determinants of the Welfare State: The State of the Art." *European Journal of Political Research* 12: 403–422.

Van Deburg, William L. 1992. *New Day in Babylon: The Black Power Movement and American Culture, 1965–1975.* Chicago: University of Chicago Press.

Van Dijk, Teun A. 1993. *Elite Discourse and Racism.* New York: Sage.

Van Maanen, John, and Stephen R. Barley. 1984. "Occupational Communities: Culture and Control in Organizations." *Research in Organizational Behavior* 6: 287–365.

Vanneman, Reeve, and Lynn Weber Cannon. 1987. *The American Perception of Class.* Philadelphia: Temple University Press.

Verdery, Katherine. 1994. "Ethnicity, Nationalism, and State-Making: Ethnic Groups and Boundaries, Past and Future." In *The Anthropology of Ethnicity: Beyond Ethnic Groups and Boundaries,* edited by Hans Vermeulen and Cora Govers, pp. 33–58. Amsterdam: Het Spinhuis Publishers.

Verret, Michel. [1988] 1996. *La culture ouvrière.* Paris: L'Harmattan.

Verter, Bradford. 1994. "Aiming the Canon: A Preliminary Investigation into the Determinants of Public Opinion in the Curriculum Debate." Paper presented at the meeting of the American Sociological Association, Los Angeles.

Vichniac, Judith E. 1991. "French Socialists and *Droit à la différence:* A Changing Dynamic." *French Politics and Society* 9(1): 40–56.

Visser, Joelle. 1992. "Union Organization: Why Countries Differ." In *9th World Congress Proceedings,* by the International Industrial Relations Association, pp. 158–179. Geneva: International Industrial Relations Association.

Von Grunebaum, Gustave E. 1962. *Modern Islam: The Search for Cultural Identity.* New York: Vintage.

Wacquant, Loic. 1993a. "Urban Outcasts: Stigma and Division in the Black American Ghetto and the French Urban Periphery." *International Journal of Urban and Regional Research* 17(3): 366–383.

——. 1993b. "The Comparative Structure and Experience of Urban Exclusion: 'Race,' Class, and Space in Chicago and Paris." In *Poverty, Inequality, and the Future of Social*

Policy: Western States in the New World Order, edited by Katherine McFate, Roger Lawson, and William Julius Wilson, pp. 543–583. New York: Russell Sage Foundation.

——. 1997. "Les pauvres en pâture: La nouvelle conception de la misère en Amérique." *Hérodote* 85: 21–33.

Waldinger, Roger. 1996. *Still the Promised City? African-Americans and New Immigrants in Postindustrial New York.* Cambridge, Mass.: Harvard University Press.

Walzer, Michael. 1983. *Spheres of Justice: A Defense of Pluralism and Equality.* Blackwell: Oxford.

——. 1992. *What It Means to Be an American.* New York: Marsilio.

——. 1997. *On Toleration.* New Haven, Conn.: Yale University Press.

Warner, W. Lloyd, J. O. Low, Paul S. Lunt, and Leo Srole. 1969. *Yankee City.* New Haven: Yale University Press.

Warner, W. Lloyd, and Paul S. Lunt. 1942. *The Status System of a Modern Community.* New Haven: Yale University Press.

Waters, Mary. 1990. *Ethnic Options: Choosing Identities in America.* Berkeley: University of California Press.

Watts, Jerry. 1997. "'The Personal Responsibility and Work Opportunity Reconciliation Act of 1996,' by the Congress of the United States." *Contemporary Sociology* 26(4): 409–412.

Weakliem, David, and Anthony Heath. 1999. "The Secret Life of Class Voting: Britain, France, and the United States, 1935–92." In The *End of Class Politics?* edited by Geoff Evans, pp. 97–136. New York: Oxford University Press.

Weber, Eugen. 1976. *Peasants into Frenchmen: The Modernization of Rural France, 1870–1914.* Stanford: Stanford University Press.

Weber, Max. 1958. *The Protestant Ethic and the Spirit of Capitalism.* New York: Scribner.

——. 1978. *Economy and Society,* vol. 1. Berkeley: University of California Press.

Wegener, Bernd. 1992. "Concepts and Measurements of Prestige." *Annual Review of Sociology* 18: 253–280.

Weil, Claude. 1996. "Racisme: comment ils jugent la France." *Le Nouvel Observateur,* October 17–23, pp. 10–18.

Weil, Patrick. 1991. *La France et ses étrangers: L'aventure d'une politique d'immigration.* Paris: Calman Levy.

Weir, Margaret. 1995. "The Politics of Racial Isolation in Europe and America." In *Classifying by Race,* edited by Paul E. Peterson, pp. 217–242. Princeton: Princeton University Press.

Wellman, David. 1993. *Portraits of White Racism,* 2nd ed. New York: Cambridge University Press.

——. 1995. *The Union Makes Us Strong: Radical Unionism on the San Francisco Waterfront.* Cambridge: Cambridge University Press.

Western, Bruce. 1995. "A Comparative Study of Working Class Disorganization: Union Decline in 18 Advanced Capitalist Countries." *American Sociological Review* 60(2): 179–201.

Wetherell, Margaret, and Jonathan Potter. 1992. *Mapping the Language of Racism: Discourse and the Legitimation of Exploitation.* New York: Harvester Wheatsheaf.

Wieviorka, Michel. 1992. *La France raciste*. Paris: Points.

——. 1996. "Cultural Differences and Democracy: United States and France." Paper presented at the Conference on Multiculturalism, Minorities, and Citizenship, European University Institute, Florence.

Wilentz, Sean. 1984a. "Against Exceptionalism: Class Consciousness and the American Labour Movement 1790–1920." *International Labor and Working Class History* 16: 1–24.

——. 1984b. *Chants Democratic: New York City and the Rise of the American Working Class, 1790–1850*. New York: Oxford University Press.

Wilkinson, Rupert. 1988. *The Pursuit of American Character*. New York: Harper and Row.

Williams, Allan M. 1995. *The European Community: The Contradictions of Integration*. New York: Blackwell.

Williams, Brett. 1988. *Upscaling Downtown: Stalled Gentrification in Washington D.C.* Ithaca, N.Y.: Cornell University Press.

Williams, Bruce B. 1987. *Black Workers in an Industrial Suburb: The Struggle against Discrimination*. New Brunswick, N.J.: Rutgers University Press.

Williams, Raymond. 1980. "Base and Superstructure in Marxist Cultural Theory." In *Problems in Materialism and Culture: Selected Essays*, pp. 31–49. London: Verso.

Willie, Charles V. 1985. *Black and White Families: A Study in Complementarity*. Bayside, N.Y.: General Hall.

Willis, Paul. 1977. *Learning to Labour: How Working Class Kids Get Working Class Jobs*. New York: Columbia University Press.

Wilmore, Gayraud. 1983. *Black Religion and Black Radicalism: An Interpretation of the Religious History of Afro-American People*. Maryknoll, N.Y.: Orbis Books.

Wilson, George. 1991. "Low-SES Whites' Beliefs about the Causes of Poverty." Paper presented at the meeting of the North Central Sociological Association.

——. 1996. "Toward a Revised Framework for Examining Beliefs about the Causes of Poverty." *Sociological Quarterly* 37(3): 413–429.

Wilson, John, and Marc Musick. 1997. "Who Cares? Toward an Integrated Theory of Volunteer Work." *American Sociological Review* 62: 694–713.

Wilson, William J. 1978. *The Declining Significance of Race: Blacks and Changing American Institutions*. Chicago: University of Chicago Press.

——. 1996. *When Work Disappears: The World of the New Urban Poor*. New York: Alfred A. Knopf.

Wolfe, Alan. 1997. *One Nation After All: What Middle Class Americans Really Think about God, Country, Family, Poverty, Racism, Welfare, Homosexuality, Immigration, the Left, the Right, and Each Other*. New York: Viking.

Wolff, Edward N. 1995. *Top Heavy: A Study of the Increasing Inequality of Wealth in America*. New York: Twentieth Century Fund Press.

Wood, Michael, and Michael Hughes. 1984. "The Moral Basis of Moral Reform: Status Discontent vs. Culture and Socialization as Explanations of Anti-Pornography Social Movement Adherence." *American Sociological Review* 19: 86–99.

Wright, Erik Olin. 1996. "The Continuing Relevance of Class Analysis Comments." *Theory and Society* 25: 693–716.

Wright, Erik Olin, and Donmoon Cho. 1992. "The Relative Permeability of Class Boundaries to Cross-Class Friendships: A Comparative Study of the United States, Canada, Sweden, and Norway." *American Sociological Review* 57(1): 85–102.

Wuthnow, Robert. 1987. *Meaning and Moral Order: Explorations in Cultural Analysis.* Berkeley: University of California Press.

——. 1991. *Acts of Compassion: Caring for Others and Helping Ourselves.* Princeton: Princeton University Press.

——. 1994. *God and Mammon in America.* New York: Free Press.

——. 1996. *Poor Richard's Principle: Recovering the American Dream through the Moral Dimension of Work, Business, and Money.* Princeton: Princeton University Press.

Young, Alford, Jr. 1999. "Navigating Race: Getting Ahead in the Lives of 'Rags to Riches' Young Black Men." In *The Cultural Territories of Race: Black and White Boundaries,* edited by Michèle Lamont, pp. 30–62. Chicago and New York: University of Chicago Press and Russell Sage Foundation.

Young, Michael, and Peter Willmott. 1956. "Social Grading by Manual Workers." *British Journal of Sociology* 7(4):337–345.

——. 1974. *The Symmetrical Family.* New York: Pantheon.

Zerubavel, Eviatar. 1997. *Social Mindscapes: An Invitation to Cognitive Sociology.* Cambridge: Harvard University Press.

Zolberg, Aristide R. 1986. "How Many Exceptionalisms?" In *Working Class Formation: Nineteenth Century Patterns in Europe and the United States,* edited by Ira Katznelson and Aristide R. Zolberg, pp. 397–456. Princeton: Princeton University Press.

——. 1992. "Reforming the Back Door: Perspective historique sur la réforme de la politique Américaine d'immigration." In *Logiques d'états et immigrations,* edited by Jacqueline Costa-Lascoux et Patrick Weil, pp. 221–250. Paris: Editions Kimé.

Zolberg, Aristide R., and Long Litt Woon. 1999. "Why Islam Is like Spanish: Cultural Incorporation in Europe and the United States." *Politics and Society* 27(1): 5–38.

Index

Sorel, Roland, 164, 167, 237
SOS-racisme, 197, 330n111
Stack, Harvey, 121–122
stereotypes, 297n36, 300n69
straightforwardness, 36–37
success, alternative definitions of, 112–116,
   128, 147, 230–233, 242, 307n15; criteria
   of, 100–101

Taguieff, Pierre-André, 326n70, 329n105
Taylor, Billy, 24, 69, 113, 137–138
Taylor, Charles, 329n106
Taylor, Joe, 46
Terrie, E. Walter, 305n3
Thévenot, Laurent, 294n7
Thompson, J. Phillip, 49
Todd, Emmanuel, 326n70
Tribalat, Michèle, 184, 273n34, 323n36,
   324n49, 329n98
Trump, Donald, 100
Turner, Dick, 36, 89
Turner, Victor, 308n31

unemployment, 278n59
Union pour la démocratie française,
   318n41, 326n71
universalism, 69, 74, 87, 249, 294n4,
   297n37, 302n85, 336n60
upward mobility, 228

Van Deburg, William, 81
Van Dijk, Teun, 294n10
violence, 64–65, 180–181
volunteering, 290n106
Von Grunebaum, Gustave, 330n118
vulgarity, 287n82

Wacquant, Loic, 327n82
Wallace, George, 72
warmth, 206–207
Warner, W. Lloyd, 271n17
Washington, Bill, 46, 121, 144, 146
Washington, Booker T., 77
Weakliem, David, 335n40

Weil, Patrick, 326n70
Welch, Susan, 291n115, 312n90
welfare, 132, 135–136, 140, 274nn38,41,
   303n114, 310nn54,57,59,60, 312n90,
   332n139
Wellman, David, 295n17, 297n33, 309n41
Wetherell, Margaret, 294n10, 295n13
whites: and antiracism, 68–71, 72–73; on
   black morality, 63–68; on black work
   ethic, 60–63; compared with blacks, 11,
   21; on immigrants, 90–93; and people
   below, 131–132; racism of, 71–72; and
   social status, 102–112; view of blacks,
   3–4, 60–73
Wieviorka, Michel, 320n5, 326n70,
   327n78
Williams, Robin, 301n72
Williams, Tim, 24, 62, 103, 106–107,
   111–112, 134, 139, 141
Willis, Paul, 307n15, 309n40
Willmott, Peter, 272n17
Wolfe, Alan, 280n7, 296n22
women, 34, 287n82
Woolworth, Dick, 40, 91
Woon, Long Litt, 90
work ethic, 54, 60–63, 95, 129, 161–162,
   172–174, 198–199, 202–203, 281n14. *See
   also* responsibility
worldview: of American workers, 8–9;
   individualistic, 79; and morality, 51; role
   of politics in, 5
worth, defining of, 9, 22–23
Wright, Larry, 126, 289n98
Wrong, Richard, 103, 108, 109, 113, 141
Wuthnow, Robert, 290n103

Young, Dennis, 26, 99, 108, 109, 111, 132,
   139, 141
Young, Michael, 272n17
youth, 189, 307n15

Zaller, John, 304n125
Zolberg, Aristide, 90